M000308558

EDWARD R. ROYBAL

The
MEXICAN
American
STRUGGLE
for **POLITICAL**
EMPOWERMENT

EDWARD R. ROYBAL

The
**MEXICAN
AMERICAN
STRUGGLE**
for **POLITICAL
EMPOWERMENT**

DR. FRANK JAVIER GARCIA BERUMEN

Bilingual Educational Services, Inc.
Los Angeles, California

Bilingual Educational Services, Inc., Los Angeles 90007

© 2015 Edward Roybal, Bilingual Educational Services, Inc., and California State University, Los Angeles

All rights reserved. Published 2015
Printed in the United States

ISBN 978-0-86624-010-9

*To Julie Mendoza, whose extraordinary courage, dignity, and grace
in her daunting adversities have inspired me and many others.
I dedicate this book to you with respect,
solidarity, and everlasting love.*

In Memoriam

I WOULD LIKE TO HONOR THE MEMORY OF THE FOLLOWING PERSONS, who directly or indirectly helped in this project, mentored me about Chicano history, or guided me with their friendship and wisdom:

Adolfo "Rudy" Vargas (October 18, 1942–June 4, 2009), co-founder of the Educational Opportunity Program (EOP) at California State University, Los Angeles, filmmaker, activist for social change.

Mario Vasquez (November 25, 1946–July 10, 2009), attorney and civil rights activist.

Jeanne Saenz Gonzalez (June 4, 1955–May 16, 2008), who transcribed the majority of the interviews for this book and was a dedicated supporter of this project.

Gene Buckman (died September 23, 1986), activist for social change.

Rudy "Dudie" Rendon (October 5, 1953–February 6, 2000), activist for social change, educator, and friend.

Contents

Acknowledgments

I WISH TO THANK AND ACKNOWLEDGE THE FOLLOWING PERSONS:

Congressman Edward R. Roybal, for selecting me to write his autobiography and for his interviews, all of which occurred after he had suffered a stroke. Despite his physical limitations and constraints, he bore his difficulties with grace and dignity and never complained.

His children, Congresswoman Lucille Roybal-Allard, Lillian Roybal Rose, and Ed Roybal Jr., for their interviews and for sharing family information that provided an invaluable portrait of their dad as a private person.

Irma Núñez, niece of Mr. Roybal (through his wife, Lucille Beserra), and her husband, Juan Gonzalez, for their several interviews and vast amount of anecdotes, memories, and information. Also, thanks to Irma for facilitating the Roybal family member interviews and for her unswerving support of this project for many years.

The surviving siblings of Mr. Roybal, Elsie Roybal and Louis Roybal, for sharing their rich and invaluable memories and reminiscences of the Roybal family in New Mexico and California, their beloved parents and late siblings, and their brother Edward R. Roybal.

Evelyn Verdugo, niece of Mr. Roybal, for her several interviews. As the Roybal family historian and keeper of family history, she contributed her vast knowledge and history of the Roybals and Tafoyas (Mr. Roybal's mother's family) of New Mexico and California.

David N. Sigler, Special Collections Assistant and his staff at California State University, Los Angeles (CSULA), for their gracious and generous assistance in my research into more than a hundred boxes of information in the Edward R. Roybal Papers and other collections.

The staff at the UCLA Chicano Studies Research Center Edward R. Roybal Collection.

The staff at the Widener Library and other libraries at Harvard University, where I reviewed the Congressional Record, tons of newspaper clippings, and virtually every book ever published on the Mexican American experience in the United States, U.S. history, and the U.S. Congress.

The following scholars, who undertook research on the political campaigns of Edward R. Roybal years ago: Katherine Underwood, Kenneth C. Burt, Beatrice W. Griffith, Richard A. Donovan, and Maria Linda Apodaca, among others.

The following newspapers: the *California Eagle*, the *Eastside Sun*, the *Northeast Bulletin News*, owned by the Koevner Family, which provided a rich, precious, and valuable history of the daily living of Mexican Americans and other communities in East Los Angeles; the *Daily News*, the *Los Angeles Times*, *Newsweek*, *Time* magazine, the *Washington Post*, the *Miami Herald*, the *Congressional Record*, the *New York Times*, the *Boston Globe*, *La Opinion*, the *San Francisco Chronicle*, the *Fresno Bee*, and the defunct *Los Angeles Herald-Examiner*.

The following persons provided invaluable information and perspectives through their gracious interviews: Jorge Lambrinos, former chief of staff to Mr. Roybal and director of the Edward R. Roybal Gerontology Center; Henry Lozano, former chief of staff to Mr. Roybal; Antonia Hernandez, director of the Mexican American Legal Defense Fund (MALDEF); Dolores Huerta, co-founder of the United Farm Workers union (UFW); Congressman Esteban Torres; Jaime Regalado, political scientist and director of the Pat Brown Institute at CSULA; Richard Santillan, professor emeritus of ethnic and women's studies at Cal Poly Pomona; and Rose Marie Sanchez, a former resident of Chavez Ravine.

Last but not least, I wish to thank David Sandoval, who was the key person in convincing CSULA to produce the Edward R. Roybal biography. He served as liaison among CSULA, Jeff Penichet (publisher), and the Roybal family for years and provided material, political, and logistical support for this project. Thanks must also go to Aliza Zepeda-Madrid and Jeanne Saenz Gonzalez, who did the interview transcripts and provided much invaluable technical and material support for the project for years.

Many other persons I wished to interview for the book were inaccessible, chose not to be interviewed, were infirm with age or illness, or had passed away (e.g., Bert Corona, Anthony Quinn, Henry B. Gonzalez) while I was in the process of establishing their respective interviews. In reality, not every individual one wishes to interview for a book will necessarily be available for many reasons, and one always ends up with a fraction of the input for which one wishes; such is the process of research.

This book was researched, written, and completed without the benefit of any foundation monies, grants, or stipends. Neither was there a staff, assistants, or committee to provide additional support. Instead, there were many well-meaning people who contributed by their interviews, feedback, and support on a purely voluntary basis. The book has come to fruition in the old fashioned barrio way, with corazón and ganas.

Finally, I wish to thank the indulgence of my family, friends, and loved ones, who put up with my monastic existence, highs and lows, impatience, and out-of-the-ordinary temperament for many years as I deprived them of the customary time, attention, support, and love that one gives to all those whom one cares for and loves.

Foreword

FRANK GARCIA BERUMEN HAS WRITTEN AN EXTRAORDINARY BOOK ON the life and times of Edward R. Roybal, one of the greatest Mexican American leaders of the twentieth century. This book is a major contribution to American literature regarding the untold history of the Mexican American people in the United States, especially the generation represented by Roybal that experienced firsthand the Great Depression, World War II, and the postwar civil rights movement.

The entire life of Congressman Roybal is a life that parallels the most significant historical events in the past 100 years. Dr. Berumen has brilliantly chronicled the preeminent life of Congressman Roybal alongside these remarkable historical events. His ability to link together the personal and professional lives of Congressman Roybal and to join them with Chicano history is exceptional in scope in this outstanding book.

Berumen walks us through, with great clarity, the eight decades of the congressman's life. New Mexico had only been granted statehood a few years prior to Edward R. Roybal's birth there. The generations-long political postponement of New Mexico statehood can be traced to the Mexican American War of 1846. Thus, the shadow of Roybal's lifespan reached back to the original Mexican settlers of the Southwest and into the first years of the twenty-first century.

In the first part of the book, Dr. Berumen richly documents Congressman Roybal's early childhood and details the important role of his loving family. With historic precision, Dr. Berumen shares with us how the young Roybal's firm commitment to social change was clearly shaped early on by his close family networks and his community.

The first half of the book also covers the involvement and experiences of a young Roybal as he confronts and tries to make political sense of historical events that would overshadow most of his middle years: the Great Depression, the Repatriation Program, the contributions of Mexican American men and women during World War II and Korea, the Sleepy Lagoon and Zoot Suit Riots, the post–World War II civil rights movement and organizations including the GI Forum and the Community Service Organization (CSO). All of these events and others would eventually place the World War II veteran on the political stage as he would run and win a seat on the Los Angeles City Council in 1949.

Regarding the 1949 campaign, Dr. Berumen shares with us a wealth of information about this monumental milestone that placed the first Mexican American on the Los Angeles City Council in nearly seventy years. Berumen's unique insider perspective is in large part the result of personal interviews with the congressman and many of those who labored tirelessly in breaking down racial barriers so many years ago.

As we later learn in the book, this groundbreaking election in 1949 set the stage for the gradual increase of Mexican Americans elected and appointed as officials for years to come and extending to this day. Equally important, Congressman Roybal mentored and helped many members of later generations to take their rightful places in the American political landscape.

Congressman Roybal, above all others, was almost solely responsible for elevating Mexican American politics to its highest position after World War II and into the late 1990s. His political fingerprints can be found in almost every significant Mexican American election since the end of World War II. Indeed, many Mexican American elected officials in California today fully understand the powerful significance of both the 1949 city council election and the 1962 congressional election to their own political careers.

In addition to the political events of the book, Dr. Berumen invests considerable space to the family life of Congressman Roybal, including his longtime marriage to Lucille and their special relationship with their three children and four grandchildren. His children have, in many ways, traveled in the same political footsteps as their father, and his wife is often credited with being the quiet yet masterful advisor throughout his political career. We also see the private life of Congressman Roybal as he displays throughout his career all of his wit, intelligence, humanity, cleverness, and unassuming manner toward all he met.

Often, books about great men and women pay token acknowledgment to the family life of their subjects. But Dr. Berumen places family at the center stage of Congressman Roybal's exceptional life, and in this manner he has transformed the academic way we view distinct men and women regarding the special roles of spouses and children.

The second half of the book is an overview of Roybal's election to the United States Congress in 1962 and his unselfish and tireless efforts on behalf of people of color, senior citizens, women, immigrants, children needing bilingual education, the working class, and those often forgotten by politicians once elected. His lifetime work on education, voting rights, health care, AIDS, foreign policy, and other human and civil rights issues has cemented his political legacy in the annals of American political history and the Mexican American community.

The second half of the book is also distinctive in that we view the congressional and political life of Congressman Roybal through his various relationships with the presidents with whom he served: John F. Kennedy, Lyndon B. Johnson, Richard M. Nixon, Gerald Ford, Jimmy Carter, Ronald Reagan, and George H. W. Bush. Dr. Berumen details many of the national issues that confronted the nation while Roybal served in Washington, D.C., from the Vietnam War to the symbolic end of the Cold War with the fall of the Berlin Wall. Congressman Roybal lived through several extraordinary chapters of American history and oftentimes found himself in the vanguard for social change or resisting oppressive measures against the people he so defended all his life.

Congressman Roybal retired after his term expired in 1992. He was seventy-six years old and wished to spend the last part of his life with his family, especially his loving and devoted wife. His entire life to that point had been dedicated to public service, to his country, to his community, and to his family. Yet he still would not completely retire, as he later invested considerable time in the field of gerontology. Thus, even after the prime of his political life, and until his last breath, Congressman Roybal continued to live a life of principle, dignity, and self-respect.

He died in 2005 at the age of eighty-nine. Today, there are only a handful of community leaders still living from the Roybal generation who struggled, sacrificed, and led the colossal fight to make the Declaration of Independence and the United States Constitution a reality for everyone. Congressman Roybal and so many others of his generation were the political pioneers who opened wider the doors of opportunity to millions in later generations. Dr. Berumen, who himself devoted a decade of research on this book, has paid tribute to this remarkable man and his generation by writing a book of this magnitude on one of the giants of our times.

Dr. Richard Santillan
Professor Emeritus
Ethnic and Women's Studies
California Polytechnic University, Pomona

Introduction

I FIRST MET EDWARD R. ROYBAL, THE CONGRESSMAN, IN 1970 WHEN HE came to Second Street School in in Los Angeles for a visit. As an elementary school teacher of English learners, I was very impressed with his commitment to the public school system and also with his support of bilingual education programs for Spanish-speaking children in the community. Who would have known that in 1998 I would meet him again over lunch to discuss the writing of his biography?

David Sandoval, director of the Educational Opportunity Program at Cal State L.A., and a close friend of mine, organized the meeting with Congressman Roybal. Later, David was instrumental in getting the university on board to lend support to the Roybal biography project. The three of us met in the faculty dining room, and I savored my encounter with the man of humble demeanor who was regarded as a giant in the Latino community.

As we discussed the project, Edward Roybal made it evident that he wanted a biographer who had a fighting spirit and who understood the struggles of East Los Angeles well. Also, since he was a boxing enthusiast, Roybal was hoping to have someone who had ring experience as well. Fortunately, I was able to engage Dr. Frank Berumen, who met both of Roybal's criteria and had recent experience writing articles on Latino history.

Through a collaboration of efforts, this book has come to fruition. I want to express my sincere gratitude to David Sandoval for his shepherding of the project and to Frank Berumen for his research and authorship.

I would also like to acknowledge and thank several others for their important roles with this project. Dr. James M. Rosser, then president of Cal State Los Angeles, did not hesitate to make a full commitment to the project, both monetarily and personally. Further, through all the years, he remained steadfast in his belief that Roybal's story was an important one and needed to be shared with future generations. Lillian Roybal Rose, daughter of the congressman, acted on behalf of the family to provide many of the facts and photographs. Dr. Felix Gutierrez reviewed selected chapters and provided valuable feedback. Susan Herman provided excellent editing services with an eye for enhancing accessibility for the readers. And Ellen Frisbie Smith provided active support with this project.

It is my hope that this book will serve to showcase Edward Roybal's accomplishments as a leader in the political struggles of his time and to inspire us all to work for the betterment of our communities. It is also my intention to publish biographies of other Latino political leaders.

Jeffrey Jorge Penichet
Publisher

Edward Roybal (center) with (from left to right), Adolfo "Rudy" Vargas, book publisher Jeff Penichet, Jesus Trevino, and Carlos Penichet at a political fundraiser.

Prologue

EDWARD R. ROYBAL WAS A MEXICAN AMERICAN POLITICAL PIONEER. He played a defining role in making a new American political tradition. He set in motion a way to voice political demands and conduct electoral politics that allowed many Americans to have their voices heard for the first time. That tradition is still evolving, and its impact is still being felt.

Edward R. Roybal was a Los Angeles city councilman (1949–1962) and a U.S. congressman (1963–1993). He was the first Los Angeles–elected official and the first congressman of Mexican descent since California became a U.S. territory in 1848. In a sense, he played a pivotal political role in the long transition from nonresponsive government to the present time, in which Mexican American and Hispanic representation is increasing. How important this is can best be measured by his constituents' responses. After all, first and foremost, Edward R. Roybal was a public man.

Roybal was part of that generation of civic and political leaders that included Texas Congressman Henry B. Gonzalez, longtime labor and community activist Bert Corona, civic leader Antonio Rios, and GI Forum founder Hector B. Garcia. It's surprising that, to date, no one has written a book linking Edward Roybal's life to his accomplishments and those robust and meaningful times. That political legacy, its context in perspective, helps everyone to better appreciate our contemporary political leaders and their responsibility to improve the lives of people.

Present generations can benefit from knowing the context in which Roybal lived—the formative events that shaped him and those who had an important influence on him and on his peers. Leaving his place of birth, living through the Great Depression, and losing members of his community to the mass deportations known as the Repatriation all had an impact on young Ed Roybal. He was part of that generation during the New Deal whose members entered adulthood while joining fledgling labor unions and were drafted or enlisted during World War II. When he returned from the conflict, he and his peers had a new expectation of normalcy. They wanted the equality and social justice, the unity of purpose they had experienced in the armed forces. Too often commentators have condensed this to a reference about "rising expectations." This generation founded national Mexican American advocacy organizations that are influential to this day or that didn't last as long but whose legacy has endured.

These people were, in the mid-1940s and 1950s, among the first of Mexican descent to run successfully for elective office. In the late 1960s and 1970s, Mr. Roybal's generation was also sometimes to clash with its progeny, the Chicano generation.

I would like to comment about how I came to write this book. Over the years, several individuals had approached Congressman Roybal about writing his biography. Some well-known writers were among them. However, for reasons unknown to me, the biography was never undertaken. I also learned that Hollywood actress-director Ida Lupino borrowed a large number of Roybal's documents to use in penning a screenplay. However, that project, like the others, did not come to fruition. Time passed, and with Congressman Roybal's retirement in 1992, it seemed that a biography was even more urgent than before.

In 1996, I published my first book, entitled *The Chicano/Hispanic Image in American Film*. My longtime friend Irma Núñez, Congressman Roybal's niece, gave her uncle a copy, and she told me later that he liked it. About the same time, David Sandoval at California State University, Los Angeles, and Jeff Penichet of Bilingual Educational Services persuaded the university to support the writing of the congressman's biography. The project soon stalled, and during that time I attended the Harvard Graduate School of Education.

In the summer of 1997, David Sandoval informed me that Congressman Roybal now actively sought a writer for the biography. He was now retired from Congress and serving as the director of the CSULA Edward R. Roybal Institute for Applied Gerontology. Mr. Roybal granted me a fifteen-minute interview as part of his effort to find a biographer. Although I felt honored to be in the running, I had few illusions. In any case, I arrived, accompanied by David Sandoval, and before long I entered Mr. Roybal's office.

Having grown up in the Lincoln Heights and Boyle Heights areas of East Los Angeles, I had, of course, a long and deep awareness of Edward Roybal's importance to this part of the city and to California. His achievements were legendary. He was already in life a man to be remembered in granite. I had, however, never met him.

Soon after I was ushered into Mr. Roybal's office, David Sandoval introduced me to him and then departed. Awards, plaques, commendations, photographs of him with presidents, movie stars, historical figures, and family lined the walls. They documented a lifespan and milestones in the political empowerment of the Mexican American people. Mr. Roybal wore a striking brown coat that he quickly took off. He rolled up his white shirtsleeves, indicating he was ready to go to work. He was in his element: going through and shuffling some papers, checking the phone messages on the desk. Roybal was the dynamic, animated, and genuine person of his reputation. He buzzed his secretary, asking to hold calls for fifteen minutes. He didn't want to be disturbed, he said.

He wanted me to tell him about myself, and I complied, telling him about my parents, growing up in East Los Angeles, experiences in school, fighting as an amateur boxer. I told him about attending Cal State Los Angeles, being part of the student MEChA group,[1] working as a high school teacher, and then attending Harvard. I had been particularly focused on community concerns centering on education, equality, justice, and immigration. Also, I shared that sensation, that feeling, about living in two worlds—toggling between mainstream social expectations, with few Mexican Americans, and the comfort of home. Most of all, I told him about the importance of documenting our history and passing it on as knowledge and a narrative to the next generation. As I talked about all this, he interspersed with his own recollections. He talked about growing up in Boyle Heights during the Depression, attending school and later the University of California, Los Angeles, and that he too had been an amateur boxer. Later he worked with unions, joined the army during World War II, and ran for office at the beginning of the era that we so easily refer to today as the "Mexican American struggle" and the beginning of "political empowerment," but back then those terms had not yet been invented yet. And he talked about living in those two worlds, of being an outsider when things of consequence happened only on the inside. Mainly, he talked about the next generation of Mexican American political leaders.

His reminiscences and his anecdotes were colorful and humorous. He was reflective, unpretentious, and just plain wise. An hour went by; after two, he called his secretary to hold his calls for the rest of the day. More than three hours of conversation had gone by when he looked at his watch. He appeared invigorated by his recollections. Then, in his amicable, soft-spoken way he looked straight at me and said, "I want you to do my biography." I was speechless for a while, and he repeated the words, adding that the university would contact me about the details. His instructions were that he wanted an objective biography but that I would have to look for any documentation he could not provide. After thanking him, I told him I would do my very best and left, not exactly knowing why he chose me. Perhaps he saw the ganas or some raw hunger. I think, however, that he maybe saw something that reminded him of himself, of his younger self, someone who balances between self-assurance and ambivalence to an approaching unknown. Perhaps he saw me calculating how much endurance this undertaking would require, evaluating current resources and which ones the project would need, a strategy of estimating struggle and adjustments. Perhaps he saw the instincts of somebody who had been in the ring and who, in turn, saw in him the heart of a fighter.

A number of delays followed during the next several months, leading me to think that the Roybal biography might have been stillborn and was not going to happen. Finally, I was informed that the project was moving forward.

I had originally intended to conduct a series of extensive interviews with Congressman Roybal. However, by the time the project was approved, Mr. Roybal had suffered a stroke. His condition would curb how available he could be to me, and although he was not mentally impaired, his condition limited his ability to elaborate on his personal recollections.

By this time, Mr. Roybal's wife of more than fifty years, Lucille Beserra Roybal, had herself been very ill and was unavailable for any long or tiring interviews. In this way, the two protagonists who knew more than anyone else were unavailable to share their special knowledge. That invaluable knowledge through oral history was lost to me. How could I tell this story? How would I make the narrative compelling without the protagonists participating? How else to tell the story now? I realized after some soul searching that I had to make some hard adjustments.

I decided to write a political biography that profiles Congressman Roybal's era, one that came to be called the Mexican American generation. Many of the events and conditions that formed those times are unfamiliar to many Americans. Those were, I believe, the compelling events and socioeconomic forces forming the political context which in turn shaped Roybal's way of thinking. Those experiences formed a way of thinking to address the social and political issues that he confronted. The fruits of those political struggles became his legacy.

Finally, no book could ever completely document the entirety of a man's life. In the case of Congressman Roybal's political career, I have not attempted to recite every motion, resolution, bill, or law that he sponsored or co-sponsored. Such a task is more adequately the purpose of an encyclopedia or the *Congressional Record*. Rather, I have sought to document Mr. Roybal's political priorities in legislation, issues, and concerns both as a Los Angeles city councilman and as a U.S. congressman, in the context of the times.

Chapter 1

In the Beginning
(1916–1940)

ARE GREAT MEN BORN THAT WAY, OR IS GREATNESS THRUST UPON THEM? Sometimes both. And, perhaps, greatness comes from an ability to learn from circumstances and respond with skill and split-second timing, like that which a boxer uses to prevail. Edward Ross Roybal's private and public lives were filled with those kinds of events.

He was born at a pivotal moment, at the turn of the twentieth century. Between 1910 and 1920, the Mexican Revolution's convulsions had forced more than 2 million Mexican refugees into the United States. Those who amassed along the border were mainly desperate, dislocated people. They crossed when they could or needed into the United States to rid themselves of the chaos, the violence, and the uncertainty. According to some statistics, Texas and California were the two main destinations of Mexican immigrants during and in the aftermath of the Mexican Revolution.[1]

Coming mostly from agrarian areas, they trickled onto U.S. farms in the southwestern states and crowded into the cities nearest the border. They dramatically increased the Mexican-descent population by supplementing the number of those who had preceded them or who originated as grant holders, landowners, farmers, and stakeholders in the United States. This expansion of the Mexican population at the turn of the century also coincided with economic expansion and industrialization in the southwestern region, often made possible by the railroad, the automobile, telegraph lines, and the telephone. The people of Mexican descent faced a mixed reception—jingoistic nativists strongly opposed their presence; others were simply nonplused, not fully understanding the forces behind the migration. For agribusiness interests, they were heaven-sent.[2]

The sustained influx of large numbers of Mexicans into the Southwest had several effects. It helped rejuvenate a strong Mexican cultural presence in the United States. Although Mexican Americans welcomed that, it would have to take a backseat to their own perceived self-interest. Some Mexican Americans felt they were being forced to compete for jobs, housing, and social services. While these cleavages within the Mexican American community became present during the prosperous 1920s, it was not until the 1930s, with the Great Depression and Great Repatriation, that the issue of ethnic and national identity was severely tested. Before 1910, most Mexican Americans defined themselves as culturally Mexican in comparison with European Americans, but the large influx of Mexican nationals compelled them with reappraise how they defined themselves. Although Mexican Americans at times disparaged Mexican nationals for their presumed provincialism, Mexican nationals in turn labeled Mexican Americans as *pochos*, slang for someone cut from their culture. Nonetheless, the intimate contact among Mexican Americans and Mexican nationals often helped break down barriers and contributed to cooperation.

The Roybals of New Mexico

The Roybal surname first appeared in America when Ignacio de Roybal y Torrado, a twenty-one-year-old soldier, born in Caldas de Reyes, a few miles south of Compostela, in Galicia, Spain, came as part of the Reconquest of New Mexico in 1693. The native peoples of the area had expelled the Spaniards in 1680. In an effort to colonize what is now New Mexico a second time, Don Diego de Vargas was appointed to reconquer the area in 1692 after the native Pueblos had been weakened by wars among themselves. Vargas recruited new soldiers and civilian colonists from Spain and New Spain (that is, the Valley of Mexico and the area around Zacatecas). The viceroy himself had selected sixty-seven Spanish families living in the Valley of Mexico and Mexico City.

After the Reconquest, only a few "gentleman soldiers" stayed on to found families like Roybal, Paez Hurtado, and Fernandez de la Pedrera. Ignacio received land grants in Santa Fe and the San Ildefonso (Jacona) area and served most of his life as high sheriff of the Inquisition. He is thought to have several brothers who came with him or later from Spain. He died in Santa Fe at the age of eighty or more years on July 14, 1756. He had belonged to the Confraternity of La Conquistadora. He and his wife had several children who continued to live in the area.

These initial Spanish settlers and their descendants remained remote and isolated due to the harsh desert geography, lack of roads, and raiding Native Americans. The Spanish mixture with the local native peoples such as Pueblo and Navajo obviously took place over the following centuries. Lillian Roybal Rose noted that the Spanish colonizers had been in New Mexico for hundreds of years, but the "colonization had been so brutal, particularly against the Native Americans, that to have an ounce of Spanish blood could possibly spare you…from harsh discrimination, so this became a pattern of protection. And this is the way it plays out in New Mexico, to say 'somos espanoles,'"[3] even when the speaker in fact has a greater number of Native American than European ancestors.

Edward Ross Roybal was born in Albuquerque, New Mexico, on February 10, 1916, to Baudilio Roybal and Eloisa Tafoya. The Roybals and Tafoyas had roots that went back to Santa Fe's founding in 1609; the families lived on Spanish land grants in Pecos and Albuquerque, New Mexico, respectively. According to Ed Roybal's niece, Evelyn Roybal Verdugo, there exists documented intermarriage (on the Tafoya side) with the Native American Apache tribe in the 1700s.

The surname of Roybal was at times spelled Roibal, an older Spanish spelling. The family in fact had a lineage connecting them to sixteenth-century explorer Álvar Núñez Cabeza de Vaca. Both the Tafoyas and the

Roybals considered themselves Mexicans or Spanish, emphasizing their European roots regardless of their complexion. Native Americans who identified themselves as such were always at risk of being sent to a reservation, harassed, and discriminated against by the dominant European American society.[4]

Baudilio Roybal was born on March 22, 1894, in Pecos, New Mexico, a settlement about twenty-eight miles from Santa Fe, in northern New Mexico. It was a little town with a church in the center, populated by subsistence farmers. He had several siblings. He had a fifth-grade education, which was not unusual for a boy to achieve at that time.[5] As a young man, Baudilio worked as a farmer, as his predecessors had done, but he later moved to Albuquerque with his oldest and married sister, Agripina Roybal Carrillo, because the opportunities were few in Pecos. According to his son Louis Roybal (youngest brother of Edward R. Roybal), Baudilio was about five feet ten inches tall and was light skinned, often mistaken for an Anglo. Louis recalled that he never heard an argument between his father and mother. He never heard a dirty word, neither in English nor in Spanish. Louis remembered his father as a very patient man who never got excited. He "was only happy when she [his wife] was around."[6] Irma Núñez, a niece of Edward R. Roybal, remarked that her uncle was the same with his wife, Lucille: "Now I understand where he got it from."[7]

Edward's mother, Eloisa Tafoya, was born in Albuquerque to a very large family. Even after she was married, her brothers and sisters came often to where she lived. Her father was a carpenter and businessman who was involved in various community organizations. The most prominent of these in Mexican communities since the mid-1800s were the mutual aid societies, or mutualistas. They were organizations formed in the United States by Mexican Americans and Mexican nationals.[8]

Eloisa Tafoya had an eighth-grade education at a time when a girl who completed that many years of Catholic schooling was considered college-ready and sufficiently educated to seek salary or wage work, which many did. According to Ed Roybal's daughter Lucille Roybal-Allard, the

Tafoya family was very politically active in New Mexico. Growing up as he did in Albuquerque with the Tafoyas, Ed was clearly influenced by the community activists in that family. As an illustration of the political climate in which the Tafoya family participated on behalf of their Mexican American community, one month after Edward's birth—on March 8, 1916—Mexican guerrillas under General Francisco "Pancho" Villa attacked the small New Mexico border town and military camp at Columbus. The news flashed by telegraph all over the nation, making headlines throughout the United States, citing no cause or provocation for the attack. Fresh reinforcements arrived by train at Camp Furlong, the military outpost. Led by General "Black Jack" Pershing, who later commanded the Allied forces in World War I, the U.S. Punitive Expedition launched an incursion into Mexico that proved fruitless. The attack aroused wrath against Mexicans in New Mexico and elsewhere.

Ed's youngest sister, Elsie, remembers her grandmother (Manuela Chavez Tafoya) as a short woman, dark, and opinionated. She recalled that "she was very smart, very smart and she was great at math and you couldn't fool her. She was ahead of you."[9] Her own mother (Eloisa Tafoya Roybal) insisted that they do well in school. She often chastised them that if they ever got in trouble in school, she was not going to support them but was going to take the teacher's side. She was strict about cleanliness and kept the house spotless.

Baudilio and Eloisa Tafoya met quite by accident when Baudilio took a job in Albuquerque. He went to work as a mortician with a man who promised to teach him the business. The couple met at a funeral, which as Ed Roybal much later would say, "is a ridiculous place to start a romance."

After their marriage, Baudilio and Eloisa began their family. Edward was their first child, born on February 10, 1916. He was followed by their first daughter, Mercedes (Verdugo), who was born on August 15, 1917, also in Albuquerque (she died on December 2, 1998, in Mission Hills, California). Two children, Baudilio I and Eloisa Roybal I, died in early childhood during the flu epidemic of the 1920s. Baudilio II was born on March 5, 1923, in Los Angeles, California. He died on May 5, 1991, in Los Angeles, California. A third son, Robert, was born in 1925, in Los Angeles, California. He would die on January 3, 1945, in Manus Island, in the Asiatic Pacific Campaign of World War II. Their fourth son, Louis, was born on February 6, 1928, in Pecos, New Mexico, and is living at the time of this writing. The youngest daughter, Elsie (Wilder) was born on September 15, 1930, in Los Angeles, California. Mother Eloisa died on September 3, 1943 following surgery at age forty. Her death certificate states she died of "shock" from blood loss.

While World War I (1914–1919) raged in Europe, the Spanish flu pandemic broke out and claimed 675,000 lives in the United States. Worldwide, it took 50 million lives. All the Roybal children contracted the virus. Edward himself came very near death. Baudilio I and Eloisa I died within days of each other. Baudilio was so shaken by their deaths that he declared he couldn't see any more babies die. Baudilio quit his job as a mortician and became a carpenter. The pandemic moved fast and killed many; medical knowledge was unable to respond in the absence of a cure or vaccine. The Roybal family members who survived attributed their survival to the care and treatment by Dr. Easterde, a noted human- itarian physician who became a hero to the Mexican American families who endured because of the many young lives that he saved. The bilin- gual doctor's efforts made a deep impression on Ed's parents, relatives, and the young Edward, who would attribute to Dr. Easterde his lifelong commitment to providing health care for all.

In her mini-biography of Edward Roybal, Janet Morey recounted an interesting story in his childhood that affected his future life. A jeweler came to the Roybal residence with a watch for his father, Baudilio. The young Ed stood and marveled at the jeweler's clothes, a suit and a tie. He asked his mother Eloisa if he could someday also wear a tie. His mother responded, "That man is wearing a tie because he has an education and became a professional man. If you want to wear a tie all the time, you have to be a professional person, and for that you have to go to school."[10] Thereafter, the young Ed wanted to be a professional and dedicated himself to school. By this time, his father worked for the railroad an average of ten hours a day.

Ed's dream of wearing a tie came true when his father bought him one. He proceeded to always wear it. His young peers teased him, and sometimes it provoked scuffles. Despite these altercations, Ed refused to discard the tie. He recalled many years later, "No one was going to take that tie away from me!"[11]

Ed's father had a lifelong political influence on him. Esteban Torres recalled that when both he and Ed Roybal were in Congress in the 1980s, Ed would tell him a story about his father. Ed said that the first thing he remembered about politics was when his father would come home; it was hard work, so he would come home dusty, and he'd come into the house, and he'd lay down on the floor. On one occasion, Roybal commented, "I was a little kid, so I would lay down next to him, and then my father would take a nap for about ten minutes, but then he would wake up and say, 'I got to go vote, I gotta go vote.' And I would go with him. So, I remember that my father was very serious about voting." Torres added that even in Congress, Ed Roybal recollected that very basic obligation of being a citizen.[12]

In 1922, the Roybal family was compelled to move to Los Angeles after a railroad strike[13] and growing opposition to Mexican immigration in New Mexico and Arizona.[14] Eloisa Tafoya Roybal apparently had two sisters in Los Angeles, "Lala" Candelaria Barela and Virgilia Tafoya, who were both established and working. However, the Roybal family then moved back to New Mexico due to the inability to find employment in Los Angeles. Baudillo loved his father dearly and had always wanted to go back to the farm.[15]

The lingering effects of the national economic downturn of 1922 and 1923 created much labor unrest in New Mexico. Baudillo Roybal was deeply involved in the union movement. Evelyn Roybal Verdugo stated that he "was a great union man." As a consequence of being a union man, he was often the last hired and the first one fired. The family's finances inevitably suffered. The family finally came back to Los Angeles for good at the end of 1928.

The Roybal Family Moves to California

Edward was six years old when the family moved from Albuquerque to East Los Angeles and Boyle Heights the first time. Edward's youngest brother, Louis, had been born in Pecos some six months before the family's second move to Los Angeles. Baudilio's parents stayed in Pecos, but his siblings would come and visit him and his family in Los Angeles. Louis remembers his dad's brother Anthony visiting them frequently. Another of his dad's brothers, Manuel, would visit them often during the World War II years. According to Lucille Roybal-Allard, Baudilio Roybal worked as a carpenter when he came to Los Angeles. Simon Tafoya, Baudilio's father-in-law, trained Baudilio for the trade.

East Los Angeles had developed in the aftermath the of 1849 Gold Rush, which brought a large influx of European Americans.[16] Boyle Heights—bordered by Indiana Street on the east, Marengo Street on the north, the Los Angeles River on the west, and Olympic Boulevard on the south—became an incorporated area appendage of East Los Angeles.[17] This area, the heart of the future 9th City Council District, was the Roybal family's new home.[18]

While Mexicans and Russian Jews, for example, worked together in factories, attended the same neighborhood schools, and perhaps worked together on some political campaigns, there was little sustaining or encouraging closeness at the social level.[19] The competition for jobs did not lead to combativeness between adults, in general.[20] Adolescent rivalries were more frequent and, not unexpectedly, combative.

Ed attended Soto Street School and then Euclid Avenue School. Compared to the schools in Albuquerque, Los Angeles schools were not very exacting. "The schools were not better at all," Roybal would later recall. He found the Catholic nuns better teachers and their skill at instruction "a lot better than the teaching here. Whatever teachers we had in Albuquerque were stricter, and you learned or else. While here, that was not the case at all."[21]

Education for Mexican American children in California was increasingly segregated and unequal.[22] In East Los Angeles, among the fourteen primary schools located in the area around 1926, three had an estimated 80 percent Spanish-surnamed enrollment and three more had at least 60 percent Spanish-surnamed enrollment.[23] Children, by policy, were not allowed to speak Spanish in grammar school and in junior high school. "We didn't understand why," Roybal admitted. The policy simply prohibited the Spanish language on school grounds. "And if we did [speak Spanish], you're punished." Punishment, in grammar school, meant standing in front of the class facing the wall in a corner, singled out in a way so that your schoolmates could see you. The idea was to embarrass the individual and impose shame on him or her. Roybal said, "That was embarrassing because kids would make fun of you and everything else." Another punishment was to deny children their half-pint bottle of milk during recess. He remembered, "That was the hardest punishment of all. But no matter what punishment it was, it was hard to understand why we couldn't do things, speak Spanish, for example, and hard to understand why anyone would have the right to punish us as they did." Those measures began to take their toll. "So we started to think to ourselves that being Mexican must be a curse."[24] Roybal remembered one time when a teacher said, "'I want all the American children to stand on this side of the room and the rest of the kids on this other side of the room.'" Of course, the children of Mexican descent went to the American side. They were Americans, albeit of Mexican ancestry. "'No, no, no you get over here,' the teacher ordered. 'Stand on the Mexican side.'"[25] The social distinctions—a cruel socialization—were creating inequalities and even physical damage. Congressman Esteban Torres, who attended Los

Angeles public schools beginning in 1936, spoke of enduring similar discriminatory practices in public places and public schools. He recalled many years later, "If you're a Mexican and can't come in here, or if we spoke Spanish in the classroom or the playground, we were punished. And that taught me a lesson because I learned to stand up for myself, and to first be proud of who you are and don't let anybody put you down."

Despite these traumatic experiences, Roybal persevered in school academics, as well as sports. For Ed Roybal, coming from a small town, it was evident, "I was not really welcome." To belong meant defending territory and himself. "You belonged if you got into a few fights and you were able to survive, which I happened to have done."[26]

Ed's youngest siblings, Elsie and Louis, appear to have had less-discriminatory school experiences. They attributed this to the fact that Ed and other older siblings had gone earlier to the same schools. Ed had a reputation as a good student, a polite young man, a leader, who challenged discriminatory practices at the school.

The Roybal family built their own house at 2729 East Fifth Street in Boyle Heights in 1930. In 1937, when Baudilio lost his job, they rented the house to tenants to make payments and moved in with relatives at 722 South Mott. Baudilio worked as a cabinetmaker and carpenter during this time. Both Elsie and Louis recalled that the block they lived on was populated by Mexican, Jewish, Anglo, and (until removed in 1941) Japanese families. They also remembered Russians and Armenians in the immediate vicinity.

Ed attended Hollenbeck Junior High School, where he played baseball. He then attended Roosevelt High School, where he ran the 440-yard dash and added boxing to his sports repertoire. Young Edward became a good boxer as a consequence of the neighborhood street scraps. He liked the competition in the ring and sparred often. Soon, he began to consider whether to become a professional boxer. "The worst part of it is that I used to like to fight. I was happiest when I was fighting someone," he said, "which was bad." Eventually, his father set him straight. "My dad advised me not to continue boxing because I just didn't have the killer instinct [for it]. He said, 'If you don't have a killer instinct in this business, forget it because you're going no place.' And I took his advice."[27]

Although Spanish was banned in the elementary and junior high school hallways, it was considered worthy of academic study in high school. Ed was chairman of the Spanish Club at Roosevelt High School in 1932. His classmate Lucille Beserra was also a club member. He saw a lot of her, noting that she "helped do all the work for me, arranging the food and things of that kind. That's how we originally met. She was bright. She still is."[28]

Elsie and Louis Roybal remembered their older brother as being very active in school clubs. Evelyn Roybal Verdugo recalled, "I had my mom's yearbook from Roosevelt, and it shows group pictures of the clubs on campus. It had Eddie in the Spanish Club and there was also a leadership club. He was [also] in track…It was in 1933 they had this great earthquake in Long Beach. He was running that day at Jefferson High School, and the school collapsed. They were taking showers, and he said everyone was running out there with no clothes!"[29]

The Roybal family appear to have had a pleasant home life and community life. Elsie and Louis remembered walking with their siblings to school. The family would have a Fourth of July picnic at Hollenbeck Park (in Boyle Heights), and the siblings would set off firecrackers. They remembered the whole family getting together at the Evergreen Playground around a bonfire. They would cook the potatoes they'd grown in the backyard, and everyone would join in. Elsie recalled, "And summertime, we went to the beach. Eddie would drive and we had five flats going, none coming and all the family would get there some way or another. So it was all family."[30]

Elsie Roybal Wilder also remembered creating some mischief for her brother Ed when she was three or four years old. "Every morning, I would get a match and put it in the tire of Eddie's car and let the air out of all four tires. So every morning he'd be so angry, and he'd be with that pump, pumping them up and wondering what was wrong, and in the evening he'd come to check to see if there was a hole in them. He couldn't find any, but he'd check them out and the next morning the same thing. I didn't know I was doing anything wrong. I really didn't—I just thought it was great. I loved the hiss."[31] Ed eventually caught her and was going to spank her, but his mother yelled at him, "¡No le pegues!"

Most other memories were very pleasant for Elsie. She recalled, "He [Ed] played the guitar and he sang beautifully. He had a good voice. I remember that when he was going with Lucille and he was eighteen, nineteen, or older, on Fridays or Saturdays many times he would come and serenade my mother,"[32] to practice. At one time, the adolescent Ed appeared to have seriously leaned toward becoming a singer. Elsie recalled that her brother would often go to the Strand Theatre to sing and play his guitar during the amateur hour. Family gatherings at times would consist of "just spending the evenings singing on the porch" and "a lot of joking." The other great pastime of Ed Roybal in his late adolescence was dancing.

Ed's repertoire consisted of traditional Mexican songs, Mexican Revolution corridos, and New Mexico folk songs. One of his favorite groups was a well-known trio, Las Hermanas Padilla. Ed's mother had at one time sung in the church choir in Albuquerque, and people would come from the villages for the mass especially to hear her sing. She had "a beautiful voice and apparently there was a couple from the East there and they tried to arrange for her father's permission to take her back to New York to train and my grandfather wouldn't allow it. But they [the Tafoyas] all sang. The whole family…And some played guitar so they'd all get together. I don't care what gathering we had, it ended up singing."[33] In the isolated agricultural communities of northern New Mexico, cultural traditions such as music and storytelling flourished long before radio, movies, and television.

The young Ed Roybal was also known for his great sense of humor and the telling of jokes. His niece Evelyn Roybal Verdugo commented,

"I think that's something that a lot of people didn't know about that side of his personality." She recalled years later at fundraising dances and events, "He would introduce his wife, his children, his father, and his siblings, and when he introduced my mother, Mercy Verdugo, he would say, this is my older sister, and she would get so upset because she was not older—she was actually a year younger. And she would complain to him, and he'd say, 'Well, I have two sisters; you're the older of the two!' It was a running thing."[34]

The Roybal family had close relationships with their relatives and neighbors. Louis Roybal remembered, "My mother would go see her mother every night. She'd finish dinner, wash dishes, and my father and mother would go down to Mott Street every night until their parents passed away. And that's where we would have these [social and political] discussions; sometimes it was kind of passionate. They would have their opinions, contrary, and they wouldn't agree to everything, and it was fascinating to watch, and I used to wonder why we didn't go out and play. Well, there was a better show in the house. This is where all the fun was!"[35]

The Roybals were especially close to the Morales family right across the street. Both Delia and Armando Morales grew up with the Roybal children. Armando supported Ed politically, but the two also developed a lifelong personal friendship. Armando became a well-known psychologist at UCLA and in 1972 authored an important book entitled *Ando Sangrando* (*I Am Bleeding*) about LAPD-Chicano community relations in the 1960s.

Another young man Ed Roybal knew in his adolescence who was to become famous was Anthony Quinn. They played baseball together. Lucille Roybal-Allard recalled, "My dad knew him as an adult, and I remember he got a card saying, 'Hey, Ed, let's get together and talk about old times,' and it said, 'Tony Q.' I remember asking my father, 'Who is Tony Q?' And he said, 'Oh, that's Anthony Quinn.' Anthony Quinn grew up in Maravilla, I think, and my dad grew up Boyle Heights. Somehow they ran across each other. I don't think they were best friends. I don't think it was until they became successful that they…acknowledged to each other that they were from East L.A. and remembered each other."[36] Lillian recalled that Ed had a picture of him and Quinn when they used to play baseball as kids. Many years later, the Academy Award–winning actor became a strong supporter of Ed Roybal when he was elected to the Los Angeles City Council and the U.S. Congress.

The Pachuco Phenomenon

Even as early as 1929, a generational distinction was already detectable, a disconnect between the immigrating and migrating generation and their sons and daughters, the Mexican youth of the second generation. Young people began to feel contempt for farm work and disdain for the lives and sweat-and-grime work origins of their parents. Meanwhile, the embarrassing marginality and the sense of alienation that gripped their parents and the adult world exacerbated the disconnect between first and second generations. Those hardworking people who sacrificed so much failed to secure a place in the social scheme of their adopted country. [37]

Some in the second generation adopted a style, set of behaviors, and mindset that they termed *pachuco*. Pachucos spoke a hybrid Spanish-English street slang that came to be known as *caló*, and they often imprinted themselves with tattoos. They were known to wear, on occasion, inventive and distinct zoot suits, characterized by long jackets and padded shoulders, pegged pant legs, wide-brimmed pancake hats, thick-soled shoes, and long watch chains. They sported ducktail haircuts. They were hip, listened to cool sounds, and were daring and partook in yesca or marijuana.[38]

Pachuco style caught on in many urban cities and towns throughout the Southwest, but nowhere was it elaborated with such resonance as in East Los Angeles during the late 1930s. Mexican youth—some truly wanting to lose themselves in an alternative lifestyle, others needing a style just to be cool—adapted their social behaviors within age-graded, male clans called *palomillas* that identified strongly through group loyalty, territoriality, and neighborhood. Willing or not, youth in virtually all major Mexican barrios were impacted by these groups. By the 1930s, some of palomillas developed into formal gangs, with defined territories and names, street nicknames, and an oppositional stance toward the larger society's mores. They were known for settling disputes with their fists, clubs, and—on rare occasions—knives.[39] Only some 6 percent of Mexican American youth experienced the pachuco life at this extreme, however.

Although many of his peers certainly went through that adolescent male experience, the young Ed was able to bypass it in large degree due to the cohesiveness of his parents and strong family unity. In addition, his success in school and sports nurtured in him a sense of belonging and of achieving something significant. The fact that he worked early in his adolescence contributed an early maturity and a sense of responsibility as well.

The pachuco experience nonetheless made him realize that many Mexican American youth were susceptible to this lifestyle because of the cultural and economic stresses that their families underwent, especially immigrant families. His later compassionate concern for Mexican youth, especially the more marginalized gang youth, had its origins in his own experience growing up in Boyle Heights. He also became aware that the increasing presence of gangs tended to further aggravate the poor relations between the Mexican community and the Los Angeles Police Department. Both Elsie Roybal Wilder and Louis Roybal remembered the police-community relations as "really tough." They remembered being stopped by the police "for no reason."[40]

Pachucos had a marked presence in Boyle Heights. Ed Roybal remembered them by their representation of "independence" and defiance: "That's the way they were going to dress whether society liked it or not."[41] Later, they came to signify to the majority society a subculture with nothing to contribute, an image deserving of nothing other than eradication.

The Great Depression, FDR, and Mexican Repatriation

Ed Roybal was thirteen years old when the prosperous Roaring Twenties came to a screeching halt on Black Tuesday, October 29, 1929.

Through junior high and high school, the young Ed Roybal experienced the nation's economic collapse and mounting unemployment (officially estimated to be one-third of the workforce, but unofficially much higher). Between 1929 and 1932, some 400,000 farms were lost through foreclosure, forcing many families into poverty as tenant farmers.

During those years, a drought brought havoc to the Great Plains. Both the drought and the wind worsened the ecosystem. Little grass remained to hold the soil in place. Wind storms scattered the topsoil hundreds of miles. This became known as the Dust Bowl. The hardest hit areas were Oklahoma, Kansas, Texas, Colorado, and parts of Arizona. Thousands of farmers and sharecroppers packed up their belongings and families and left their lands and headed west. They became known as Okies, a term initially referred to people from Oklahoma but which came to be used negatively for all migrants.

The State of California recruited more migrant agricultural workers but became overwhelmed by some 7,000 Okies per month, far more than the state could use. During several months in 1936, the Los Angeles Police Department sent 136 deputies to the state line to turn back migrants who had no visible means of support. In turn, bordering states such as Nevada and Arizona urged Okies only to move through and not stay.[42]

Ed was in high school when Democrat Franklin Delano Roosevelt was elected president in 1932, bringing hope to many. However, times were hard on everyone, especially the poor and minorities. An ugly xenophobia against Mexicans arose, which portrayed them as responsible for taking jobs from "Americans." That belief led to restrictive and punitive policies referred to as repatriation, to put a positive light on the practices of deporting individuals and breaking up split-nationality families.

Possibly 500,000 to 600,000 Mexicans and their U.S.-born children departed from the United States from 1929 to 1939. Most of those people were living in Texas and California. U.S.-born children, who made up 60–75 percent of the total, had little choice in the matter.[43] Little distinction was made between income-earning and non-income-earning spouses when one of the adults was of Mexican nationality. Immigration authorities manipulated the process to drive Mexicans out of entire sections of cities and rural areas. Mexicans were harassed and pressured to repatriate when relief was distributed by the welfare system. After the El Monte berry strike of 1933 was settled, for example, the County Charities Department investigated the predominantly Mexican workforce to determine who would soon be out of work. An undercover agent, charged with ridding the country of potential troublemakers and non-citizen welfare relief recipients, was placed among the workers to persuade them to return to Mexico.[44] Although Ed was too young to participate in the efforts of the Mexican community to survive and fight against the repatriation, he witnessed the mistreatment of Mexicans.

Esteban Torres, who would later become a U.S. congressman, recalled that his father was repatriated, and he never saw him again. He commented that "the repatriation of Mexicans, both citizens and immigrants, caused great havoc for our community and to families, mine included. For a long time we kind of wandered around the landscape of Arizona, my mother, my grandfather, and I, moving from town to town, my mother trying to find work." Torres commented that "Mexicans who didn't question the power of the government and the mandate and went along, and they said, 'Well, we got to go, they don't want us here, let's go.'"

At this time of great stress and crisis, even the institution the Mexican community venerated, the Catholic Church, was complicit in repatriation. Torres recalled that his future father-in-law and mother-in-law went to their Catholic parish to seek some counseling on the repatriation and found church leaders there processing Mexicans for repatriation. "[Someone gave my father-in-law an envelope], and he opened it and looked inside, and there in it were one-way tickets to Mexico by train, and he was sort of shocked that he was being recruited to going back to Mexico without really any consultation." He threw away the envelope in a waste basket and went back to his house. Torres added that his future father-in-law was bitter for years. "He changed religions, as a matter of fact, he was so upset."[45]

Louis Roybal remembered that the Roybals had been very active Republicans in New Mexico. They remained Republicans until the Depression changed that. Elsie Roybal Wilder recalled that her brother Ed's political heroes growing up were Franklin Roosevelt, Benito Juarez, and U.S. Senator Dennis Chavez (who was related to the Roybals). Ed remembered community efforts by mutual aid societies to help displaced families, and spoke of that and the Great Depression as forces that affected his political choices ever after. The Great Depression became for him "an experience that one can talk about, but everyone that listens to you doesn't believe it. No one believes that we could be that poor during the Depression. No one believes that there were families that didn't have anything to eat. I don't want to ever have to live through a Depression again, and I hope that we never have a Depression in this country because that's the worst thing one could possibly live through. Or that we could be so dumb to let the nation go as it did. But it did, and that's why Franklin D. Roosevelt was a hero for everyone. That's where the Democrats get the reputation that they look after the poor and the Republicans look after the wealthy."[46]

Ed's mother-in-law (Prudenciana Moreno Beserra) was an especially strong supporter of FDR. Lucille Roybal-Allard remembered standing on the corner of Whittier and Soto with her grandmother, handing out FDR leaflets for his last election in 1944. Lillian Roybal Rose commented that her grandmother "had an altar with Jesus Christ and FDR" on it.

Louis Roybal recalled the Great Depression's impact on his family vividly, even though he was then only a child, particularly the tough period when his father lost his job and the family had to rent out their home. When things got better, the family was able to move back into their Fifth Street home, but for a time early in the Depression, his parents received help from the Catholic welfare organization because there was no Social Security.

Elsie Roybal Wilder remembered the soup kitchens and the hobos and the Okies wandering the streets. "They'd offer to do some work, and my mother would always give them food. The house was on Mott Street, which was way on top of a hill and they would go to our door rather than to go to the house across the street, [which was on level ground]. And they would climb up all those steps to the little house and ask my mother, and she always would give them something. She'd make sandwiches and have them [ready]. She always wondered if there was some kind of sign that they put in front that let people know that hey, here's where you could eat. I heard later that they did do that, and they had some kind of a signal. They knew who the generous people were. It was hard to climb up the stairs, and they were rickety. There was forty stairs."

Within the family as well, people looked out for each other. Elsie recalled that her uncles would arrive from Albuquerque, and everyone would help each other. "If one got a job somewhere, then they'd tell the others and then sometimes they would work at the same place. They would share enough to keep everybody else going. I remember my uncle Lito came from New Mexico to stay with us on Mott Street, and I heard the story that he was riding the rail. He had no money, and there was another man from Oklahoma and he had nothing and he had nobody to go to. My uncle had his family. He had thirty-five cents in his pocket and he gave it to the man from Oklahoma because he figured this guy had nothing. But they helped each other."[47]

Searching for a Place to Belong and a Mexican Identity

In 1934, at eighteen years of age, Ed completed his secondary education. Throughout his schooling, Ed Roybal had been a conscientious student—dedicated and excellent, by all accounts. By now he had learned that fighting an adversary, as a boy in the streets with his fists, was one thing. Inside a ring, it was something else. And it was entirely distinct from the fights that would follow—the ones that involved neither fists, nor gloves, nor ring. Instead, he would climb into a tougher arena. These were the fights not for himself but for others. In these other fights he was preparing for, winning looked less like a championship bout and more like an inconclusive sparring round. In the fights that would come, what was at stake was whether some would be worse or better off. And for this he did have the heart.

Ed pointed to his parents' precepts to explain his motivations. "My father taught all of us how to survive and how to be careful with ourselves. But you always deal with the truth. Because half truths don't count. And no truth at all, that's even worse. So he, as well as my mother—between the two of them, I think—we grew up understanding that the best way to deal with life is to deal with it in a fair, honest way. And I think that in itself is a good legacy to have from parents."[48] Ed's father appears to have been a very frank man, but also fair and firm. They were traits that young Ed would make part of his own character.

Ed's mother also had a strong influence on him. Louis Roybal noted, "[Ed] and my mother were very close and used to talk. She was always advising him and he would confide in her just about everything, even about health, and [she] was very influential in guiding him."[49]

By 1935, the repatriation had drastically altered the composition of the Mexican population, especially in Los Angeles. The city lost about one-third of its Mexican residents, which included much of its low-level white-collar workers.[50] The trauma stemming from the repatriation and the Great Depression made all Mexicans and Americans of Mexican descent realize that equal protection under the law, though a democratic ideal embedded in the Constitution, was often violated when it came to them. For all practical purposes, Mexicans had to choose between cultural loyalties. The antidote to that abuse was that they must organize politically to defend their civil liberties. They also became aware that civil rights and job protection were only a stone's throw away from each other. The way to secure both civil rights and job rights was by joining a labor union to have collective bargaining. This was the turning point for people of Mexican descent, and a harsh realization.

While Mexico and Mexican culture (given the proximity and history of the Southwest) struck an emotional chord within them, people shifted from having a Mexico-based to a U.S.-based ethos. What that meant, as a practical reality, remained to be defined. And not everyone chose the same avenue. Some people chose to assimilate by denying their children and themselves the Spanish language and their notions of Mexican culture. Others went further by developing a sense of shame or even inferiority about their Mexican culture and history, their own origins. However, for the majority of Mexican Americans, the shift was toward integration. A national focus was shaping where people's sense of identity was less tied up in the towns and villages in Mexico, or even in the Southwest, but was becoming that of a regional people, who had in common a former language, a past history, and a United States future. This was needed for economic stability. In this evolution, they were moving from being Mexicans to becoming Mexican Americans.

The Depression provoked this tectonic change as a reaction to the increasing discrimination against Mexicans. In the face of an economic downturn, those who were economically and politically weak were dispensable, resulting in the massive Mexican deportations. For those who remained, there was blatant discrimination. Roybal recalled that "Mexicans could only expect to go [into the swimming pools] once a week. The rest of the week [we] were not permitted. In Los Angeles, there was only one side of the [movie] theater where you could sit…you grew to reluctantly comply."[51] That was not to say anyone liked it. But the norms for how to resist had not yet been developed.

Both Elsie Roybal Wilder and Louis Roybal, the youngest of the Roybal children, did not remember their immediate family being endangered by the Great Repatriation, perhaps because they were too young.[52] Another reason may be the fact that the Roybals and Tafoyas were from New Mexico. In New Mexico, Mexicans or Hispanos (as most nuevomexicanos called themselves) remained the majority population well into the twentieth century. Mexican or Hispano politicos traditionally were able to deliver the nuevomexicano vote in exchange for political favors and pork barrel from European American elites.

The Civilian Conservation Corps Experience

The Civilian Conservation Corps (the CCC) was a New Deal program fondly remembered for the positive effects that it had. The CCC was founded in March 1933, at the height of the Depression, to get people back to work. Its purpose was to promote environmental conservation and to develop good character through disciplined and vigorous outdoor work. It was close to the heart of President Franklin D. Roosevelt and addressed two of his vital concerns, universal service for youth and conservation. He believed that this civilian "tree army" would relieve the rural unemployment and keep the youth "off the city street corners."[53]

Ed Roybal found work with the CCC and, in turn, he helped out his hard-pressed family. He applied for his position with the Bureau of County Welfare in Los Angeles on October 12, 1934. His Individual Record shows that he was eighteen years of age, lived at 722 S. Mott St. in Boyle Heights and listed his mother, Eloisa Roybal, as his nearest relative. His height was measured at five feet and eight inches, his weight as 134 pounds. The rest of his description lists brown eyes, black hair, dark complexion, perfect 20/20 vision in both eyes, and overall good physical condition. He indicated his position as student (but a high school graduate) and that he had been unemployed since June 1934. He documented that he had been a member of the Boy Scouts, Troop 182, in Los Angeles. He was formally enrolled in the CCC on October 12, 1934. His position was that of member laborer and he was paid $30.00 per month. He was a member of Company 1959 and stationed at Camp Buckeye, in Three Rivers, California.[54]

He cherished that job opportunity for the rest of his life, saying, "The CCC, as it was called, was the best [thing] that ever happened to this country. They would put hundreds of young men—and not so young—to work. There were married men that would support their family or help their families with twenty-five dollars a month that we sent home." Ed went to live and work in a CCC camp called Camp Buckeye, in Three Rivers, California, one of 148 CCC camps in the state. The camps provided room and board. This made it possible for many to save their earnings. Roybal noted, "I would send twenty-five dollars myself. My mother would save it for me, and she would give me the twenty-five dollars [back] most of the time. But she saved some [of it for me]. But for others that was their survival [money]. That's all they had. We built roads in the national forests and we built firebreaks and [finished] things that were just left undone. We also learned to build bridges and how to read blueprints. So, it did the young men a lot of good, I think. It did the nation much good."[55] Elsie Roybal Wilder and Louis Roybal both remembered several of their uncles also working for some of the New Deal programs that were enacted under President Franklin Roosevelt. Ed's brother-in-law Leo also worked in the CCC camps.

Many years later, Ed's daughter Lillian Roybal Rose recalled the lifelong importance of CCC experience to her father. She remembered her father talking about that experience all the time and that everyone was hopeless at that time and that they were saved by the CCC. She recalled, "It also instilled a sense of pride in him and the people that were in the CCC camps because they were making a contribution. I remember when we would go up to the Sierra Nevada and my dad would point out that he had worked on this particular road, and he said it with a lot of pride. They were earning money, they were making a contribution to the community and they felt good about the experience."[56]

Ed was formally discharged from the Civilian Conservation Corps on May 5, 1934. His Certificate of Discharge listed the camp commander's estimate of his membership as "excellent." The CCC was more than important to Ed Roybal. It was formative, even character building. And for the rest of his life he would remain a fervent New Dealer, with a faith in the ability of government to intervene and do well during an economic or catastrophic downturn. He was impressed by the efficiency and effectiveness of the federal government when there was a political will. It must have stirred in the young Ed the feelings that government could be an effective means to transform society for the better.

Growing Up and the Cultural Influences of Los Angeles

Roybal's parents were his role models for steadfastness during those difficult times. However, like any child of that period, he was always looking for new role models to motivate and inspire his young mind and heart. In sports, he greatly admired Jack Dempsey, who was the heavyweight boxing champion during the 1920s; he also liked the Argentine heavyweight contender Luis Angel Firpo,[57] and later Joe Louis.[58] He would have a friendship with Joe Louis in the 1950s. From motion pictures, he idolized cowboy star Tom Mix and especially Ramon Novarro, the first Mexican Hollywood film star.

One day in the mid-1930s, young Ed Roybal met his film idol Ramon Novarro. Novarro went to Boyle Heights to see a friend, a neighbor of the Roybals, who wrote for the newspaper *Heraldo de Mexico*, a Texas newspaper with wide distribution in Southern California. A very good-looking man with a pleasant manner, Novarro was a rags-to-fame legend. In addition to having a distinguished acting career that took him to superstardom in the film industry of the 1920s and 1930s, Novarro was very supportive of the Mexican community and its youth. [59] "We thought he was great and greatly admired him," said Roybal.[60] The matinee idol was introduced around to the neighborhood kids, and that was how Ed got to meet him. In the years that followed, they became friendly. "We did get to the point where he would acknowledge me and I would acknowledge him" in public gatherings.

Ramon Novarro's film stardom ushered in a Mexican cultural renaissance, originating in Los Angeles but spreading out into the entire Southwest, that continued into the 1940s. Besides Novarro and Dolores Del Rio,[61] several other Mexican film stars—Lupe Velez,[62] Gilbert Roland,[63] Jose Mojica,[64] and Lupita Tovar[65]—were favorites in leading roles.

American cinema promoted and nurtured the American Dream to the entire world. It professed the ideals of democracy, equality, and that anyone who worked hard and diligently could accomplish anything in the United States of America. Most often than not, the films of the

1920s, 1930s, and 1940s were escapist in nature, a cheap and accessible venue for the masses to escape the cares and woes of everyday life in the Great Depression, World War I, and later World War II. Films seldom dealt with the great issues of the day or flaws in the nation such as prejudice, segregation, and racism. Nevertheless, for Mexicans and Mexican Americans, the power of the motion picture medium was significant. Film replicated the ideal American values and lifestyle and impacted the social mores and fashions of the day. The impressive number of important Mexican and Latino film stars was the cause of great pride in the Mexican community. Mexican and Latino film stars exemplified talent, hard work, and the fact that the barriers of race and class could be overcome. The community had also a special affinity for Mexican and Latino stars in the 1930s due to the fact that many, like Ramon Novarro and Dolores Del Rio, actively helped repatriated Mexicans. Films were also a prestigious and lucrative source of employment for Mexicans and Latinos, especially in the decade when more than 100 Spanish-language films were made in Hollywood and New York. Mexican and Latino film stars were ambassadors of the American Dream come true to fellow Mexicans and Latinos.

For the young Ed Roybal, cinema appears to have been a powerful stimulus for his sense of adventure in childhood and adolescence and a representation of the American dream for him as young adult. Unlike actors in the Black community, who were generally segregated in all-Black films, Mexican and Latino actors were portrayed as fully integrated in American cinema (contrary to real life). Mexican and Latino film stars were major stars, known throughout the world, and played every type of role, although stereotypes coexisted along with the positive portrayals. They were both heroes and villains, heroines and cantineras. The Roybal family were avid filmgoers. The young Ed Roybal, who was eleven years old in 1927 and twenty-four in 1940, must have sat through countless films, like other Mexicans transfixed by the adventure, romance, and drama but perhaps also by the growing realization that all was possible and reachable in this nation. He saw many of his own people having reached their own dreams. It must have stirred his dreams to be hopeful, as well as confident.

Mexican immigrants were huge movie patrons who supported a Latino entertainment renaissance, mainly far out of the sight of the majority of other Angelenos.[66] The Mexican community alone also supported five theater houses between 1918 and the 1930s: Teatro Mexico, Teatro Capitol, Teatro Zendejas (later Novel), Teatro Principal, and Teatro Hidalgo.[67] These theaters featured vaudeville, melodramas, comedies, and motion pictures. The cultural production of Mexican and Mexican Americans in film, music, and theater infused the Mexican community with diversion and sometimes inspiration during difficult times.

Movie fans filled the theaters. The newsreel brought to life images of the personalities and the events of the day. Daily news from far-flung places found its way into the pages of *La Opinion*, which began operations in 1926. It soon became the most widely read Spanish-language newspaper in the United States. Radio became increasingly popular in the late 1920s. By the early 1930s, Pedro J. Gonzalez was the first Mexican to have a regularly scheduled Spanish-language radio program. Mexican families were devoted radio listeners, especially when Spanish-language music began to make the sound waves. This was a time when musicians from Mexico flocked to Los Angeles and established local traditions, entered the movie industry with the talkies, and became a significant segment of a Mexican cultural renaissance.

The second-generation Mexican youth in particular were caught up in the dance craze of the 1930s. They went to the dance clubs in droves. More often than not, the dance fever did not go over well with Mexican immigrant families. Although closely chaperoned in community centers and school clubs, teens' conduct when unchaperoned in dance clubs was often offensive to older Mexicans. However, peer pressure was almost impossible for the children to overcome.[68] Most club musicians and clientele were Mexican; the music preferred included that by such artists as

Agustin Lara, Tito Guizar, Jose Mojica, and Lucha Reyes. It also included Latin American music styles such as the bolero, rumba, and danzon, as well as U.S.-inspired music styles such as jazz, boogie woogie, and swing.

Mexicans and the Catholic Church in the 1920s and 1930s

The Mexican communities of Los Angeles in the 1920s and 1930s were predominantly Catholic, at least nominally so. The most important Catholic church for Mexicans was Nuestra Señora la Reina de Los Angeles, which was located in La Placita, across from Olvera Street, the oldest part of the city. Nonetheless, other denominations were always trying to find ways to entice the Mexican churchgoers. In fact, the Plaza Methodist-Episcopal Church opened its doors near to Olvera Street. Each local Catholic church was the cornerstone of each barrio. Priests and nuns presided over religious festivities—baptisms, weddings, funerals, first communions, confirmations. The blessing of the local priest was necessary for any important community or individual endeavor.

Unlike other newcomers, Mexicans did not have a large number of clergy who immigrated with them. They were often served by clergy of other ethnicities, most often Irish. The Catholic Church was slow to respond to the large influx of Mexicans in the twentieth century. In 1918, Bishop Cantwell finally secured the money for "Americanization work" among the immigrant population. One cleric in particular, Father Robert E. Lucey, a native Angeleno and later Archbishop of San Antonio, quickly distinguished and endeared himself to the Mexican population with his concern for social justice and the poor.[69] He was later appointed assistant pastor at Immaculate Heart of Mary to head the Bureau of Catholic Charities. In 1920, the bureau reported that that 32 percent of the people they served were Mexican, 7 percent Italian, 4 percent Irish, and 34 percent American (or other European Americans).[70]

The Roybal family belonged to the Catholic faith, and it played a central role in the social evolution of Ed Roybal. Baudilio and Eloisa Roybal were married by the church, baptized their children, and buried relatives and friends in accordance with church doctrine and family tradition. The young Ed Roybal and his siblings were likewise brought up in the Catholic faith and passed through all the church sacraments on their way to adulthood. It was in one of these rituals or social activities that Ed met Father Robert E. Lucey, with whom he would keep a lifelong friendship. The young man was impressed by Lucey's commitment to social activism for the poor and social justice.

Lucille Roybal-Allard remembered her father as being a religious man. She commented, "He was very Catholic, but not blindly so. I would say that he was a progressive, liberal Catholic, in today's terms. I mean, my dad took up issues such as on pro choice. I am assuming he believed in birth control. He never talked to us against it."[71]

Elsie Roybal Wilder, Ed's sister, commented, "We went to church every Sunday; we never missed. We'd go to catechism. We had fish on Friday, regardless of the reason, we followed the rules. [My mother] was very Catholic…She was very devoted to the Virgin Mary. She'd go in, and maybe she'd ask God for something and in return she would go and wash all the pews in the church or something, like that."[72] The Roybal parish was Nuestra Señora de la Virgen de Talpa, located on Fourth Street in Boyle Heights.

The decades of the 1920s and 1930s were the formative years for young Ed Roybal. At the age of four, he lost two of his siblings to the Spanish flu pandemic, but the family had survived. He learned that life comes with some losses, in order to make us value and appreciate both continuity and gains. He had seen doctors perform humanitarian work and understood what that meant to people's health and to the community's well-being. He was six years old when his family moved from Albuquerque to Los Angeles in the early 1920s. In New Mexico, Mexicans were the majority population, but in California, a submerged minority. Nonetheless, Los Angeles as a city had the largest Mexican population in the nation. In his new, mixed community of Boyle Heights, his cultural identity underwent an evolution. His parents' liberalism made him tolerant, open minded, and respectful of cultural differences. He was thirteen years old when the Great Depression began. As with all others who lived during these difficult times, the experience was a transforming one for Ed.

It appears his father was able to sustain employment, though at times precariously. Young Ed took numerous odd jobs to contribute to his struggling family. The economic catastrophe taught him a strong-willed sense of responsibly, obligation, and perhaps a little frugality. He witnessed the Great Repatriation of Mexican nationals and Mexican Americans and came to understand the fragile sense of citizenship and civil liberties of Mexicans in the United States.

He was seventeen years of age in 1933, when Franklin D. Roosevelt was elected president and reminded the hard-pressed nation that "the only thing we have to fear is fear itself." His service in the Civilian Conservation Corps let him witness how young recruits did public works that made a difference. The CCC's organization, coordination, and plans for the public good inspired him to serve. He discovered how people were amazingly cooperative and willing to apply themselves to a common good. This was not what many others assumed, but it was what he witnessed. He had already seen how school policy—enforced segmentations and social hierarchies formed inefficient distinctions and prejudices and how that held people back from reaching their capacities.

More important, his personal moral character was shaped from an ethic, which had been instilled at home, that valued loyalty and making an effort. He had a strong ethical sense and a moral map made up of concentric loyalties: to family and to community. His work in the CCC reinforced what he learned at home: that everyone was better off when people were helped up when they were down. And he was developing a sense that somehow all this was connected to politics and government.

The most important influence in the life of Ed Roybal appears to have been his parents. Their love and support, sense of faith and hope, positive cultural identity, work ethic, and frankness instilled in the young Ed Roybal self-confidence, resourcefulness, ethnic self-esteem, and a pragmatic view of life. He was influenced strongly as well from growing up in Boyle Heights. In school and social activities, he learned to work and socialize with people of different cultures. In the boxing rings and playgrounds of the neighborhood, he learned the fundamentals of discipline, how to adjust, and the importance of tenacity and heart. He learned how to be street smart in the tough working-class environment of his neighborhood, which included union organizers and political activists, pachucos and zoot suiters, hard-pressed workers and laid-back roving mariachis. He learned to navigate his two worlds, his Mexican cultural world and the outer White world.

Elsie Roybal Wilder remembered hearing the stories about what may have been her brother Ed's first conscious political act. Ed and his cousins would go play and swim every week. However, Mexicans could only go swimming on Wednesday, the day before the swimming pool was cleaned. Ed was about fourteen years of age when he and his cousins determined to stop the discriminatory practice. Ed made a presentation before the Los Angeles City Council about it. According to Elsie, the Los Angeles City Council changed the policy, allowing Mexicans to swim any day. She commented, "That's how I learned to swim."[73]

The genesis of his political consciousness began during these formative years and in the tumultuous personal and national events that transpired. His parents' liberalism gave him a moral compass, his neighborhood provided him with avenues for personal inquiry, and the events in the outer world gave him a powerful reinforcement of certain truths.

Chapter 2

Being and Becoming
Mexican American
(1941–1946)

WHEN HE ENROLLED AT THE UNIVERSITY OF CALIFORNIA, LOS ANGELES (UCLA), Extension, Ed Roybal became the first of his family to attend university. He began a course of study toward a bachelor's degree in business administration. Mexicans and Mexican Americans were virtually absent from university campuses during the 1930s. Ed later remembered, "I really had no student life," in those years, "because I was working all the time and I was attending classes during the afternoons, sometimes in the mornings, sometimes at night." He did not see himself as a conventional student who could enjoy the perquisites of a collegian. "So I was not actually a student as one describes a student."

Ed Roybal caught a ride each day from the milkman who made deliveries in East Los Angeles and to the Roybal household. The young milkman lived in Westwood, in the direction of the university, and gave Ed a ride in the morning. During this period, Roybal worked afternoons and between classes. He worked at several cleaners, doing delivery and hand press, and other places that would give him work whenever they needed his help and he needed the money. He longed, however, for a life as a full-time student. "I wish I could have gone to school all day long but had I done that I would not have done the things I was finally able to do."[1] He was caught in the realization that he was a working-class university student. He was hungry for knowledge and loved the intellectual inquiry, but he did not have the luxury to be a full-time college student, especially during the Depression. However, the fact that he had to work and sacrifice for his education made his education more precious. He was forced to drop out of college soon after enrollment due to his work commitments and was never able to finish his studies at the UCLA Extension. Ed took classes sporadically between September 22, 1947, and January 31, 1952. His later commitment to education as an elected official could be traced to this valuable experience.

By juggling schedules, Ed developed a sense of handling mixed agendas, the contradictions of needing to be at one place filling one role and then at another filling another. While it made life more complex and even difficult, not to mention making him stand out from others, he saw it as a mixed blessing. Roybal was conscious that he was the only Mexican American student in his accounting classes and remembered seeing only one other student on campus who shared his ethnicity, a young woman named Theodora. Bert Corona, a contemporary and friend of Ed Roybal, remembered that he was only one of four Mexican Americans in UCLA during the mid-1930s. Life for Mexican American university students was not easy. Corona remembered, "Racism certainly existed at USC, although, with so few minority students, it was not very visible… [T]he teachers, once they knew that you were Mexican, were either patronizing or hostile. I did not have a single inspirational professor during my time at USC."[2]

Around 1937, while an undergraduate student at UCLA, Ed wrote a term paper that would impact the rest of his life. The paper focused on organizing low-income barrios for political action. The plan was based on an organization for community service, one that would produce votes in neighborhoods with promises of "service to come."[3] Ed had apparently carried the idea for a long time beneath his mild-mannered exterior. In the process of riding along with the milkman, working through college, and attending class, all with a serious demeanor that at times bordered on dour, he had refined his idea of the community service organization over and over again until it sparkled. Ed left off his studies at UCLA to work and contribute to his family, but a short time later he was accepted at and attended Southwestern University, where he studied law. It was not until some ten years later when he entered politics that Ed returned to the term paper.

Within Ed's family, party identification and affiliations were changing with the times. He remembered that his maternal grandfather was a Republican. His mother became a Democrat to cancel out her father's vote, saying, "Those Republicans are not for us." Then came Franklin D. Roosevelt and the presidential campaign of 1933. His grandfather switched parties and became a Democrat, after which time father and daughter were able again to return to discussing politics. Reflecting on his political background, Roybal said, "I like to think that [having a party affiliation and seeing the importance of party politics] was a legacy that I got from both my parents."[4]

The Resurgence of the Mexican Presence in Los Angeles

In the mid-1930s, the Mexican presence in Los Angeles was growing again, after the first traumatic round of repatriation came to an end. Mexican residents predominated in the barrios. There was a barrio called Sonoratown near to the railroad depot, where Chinatown is located today. A smaller barrio was located above Angel's Flight (a rail car that transported people up from Broadway to Hill Street in downtown Los Angeles), which was bordered by Grand, Flower, Olive, and Figueroa Streets. Today the area is known as Belmont. Mexican families lived in broken-down old homes.

Compton began as an all-White retreat from Watts, but by the mid-1930s, Mexicans were already moving in. Wherever there were industries, colonias had sprung up for the Mexican laborers. Colonias were growing around Bethlehem Steel and U.S. Steel plants in Torrance, Bell, Gardena, and Maywood. Farther south toward the ocean, by

Long Beach and Torrance, there were barrios next to the oil refineries in Harbor City and Lomitas. Little capillas, or shrines, dotted the neighborhoods, most often as memorials to workers killed in accidents on the job or elsewhere.

Toward downtown Los Angeles, there were Mexican pockets all along Main Street in what was called Dogtown and Santa Rita. By the intersection of Main, North Broadway, and Mission, a colonia blossomed directly under the bridge. Along the Red Car line, an electric train run by the Pacific Electric, traveling east from downtown Los Angeles through the San Gabriel Valley to San Bernardino were the colonias of Alhambra, San Gabriel, Temple City, El Monte, Ontario, Colton, Pomona, Ramona, and La Verne.

However, the greatest concentration of Mexican population was in the growing barrios of East Los Angeles and Belvedere, east of the Los Angeles River. A part of East L.A. called the Flats was situated on the opposite side of the river from the meatpacking plants operated by Swift, Wilson, Cudahy, and Armour. The smell was terrible, as they poured the leftover meat into the river itself. Many of the Mexican workers who worked in the plants lived on Mission Street, around the San Antonio Winery, in Lincoln Heights. Farther down from the Flats was Boyle Heights. By then, the increasing numbers of Mexicans were replacing the Jews, who were themselves moving west to the West Adams area. Between Lincoln Heights and Boyle Heights was City Terrace, occupied by Mexicans and Jews.

Finding the Perfect Mate

Roybal, with an athletic build, stood about five feet ten and a half, and had a handsome face and overall energetic disposition. He was entering young manhood in the mid-1930s. He was studious and hardworking and supported his family; Ed never swayed into a party crowd or the enticing nightlife of the big band era that seduced many young men. However, he evidently had a great talent and passion for dancing. During those carefree days of late adolescence and young adulthood, he often attended dances and must have been a conspicuous favorite dance partner of many a young lady. But he had already found his ideal mate.

Love blossomed between Ed and Lucille Beserra, his high school class-mate. Louis Roybal remembered that his brother began dating her around 1936–1937, and they courted for a long time before they got married. Elsie Roybal Wilder recalled that the family lived on Mott Street when he first met Lucille. "She was beautiful; she was friendly, kind, sweet, funny, a good sense of humor. I mean, it was like having a movie star in the house." During their post-high school years, Lucille would come to the Roybal house and study with Ed in the kitchen. His parents liked her.[5]

Ed and Lucille appear to have had a rocky start. When they first met, he was the president of the Spanish Club at Roosevelt High School. Lucille didn't like him at first because he put her to work, always calling on her to organize events, knowing that she would follow through. She thought he was too bossy. She must not have complained too much about Ed to others, because Louis Roybal recalled his future sister-in-law Lucille as "very gracious. Always friendly, she was a wonderful person, and we loved her from the moment we saw her." Elsie Roybal Wilder described her as "always a lady."[6]

Lucille Marguerite Beserra was born on January 5, 1917, in Los Angeles, California. She graduated from Roosevelt High School in 1935 and continued her education for two years at a business college. Her parents were Prudenciana Moreno Beserra (ca. 1879–1954) and Alberto Manuel Beserra (ca. 1880–1959).[7] Lucille had three siblings: Leo Alfonso Beserra (February 20, 1914–December 13, 1996); Hortencia Virginia Beserra Núñez (June 23, 1915–April 10, 1988); and Albert Beserra Jr. (July 1, 1921–January 2001).

Lucille's family had lived in California since before California was part of the United States. Her great-great grandfather, General Mariano Guadalupe Vallejo, was a prominent leader in the Mexican-American War, known for fighting in the Euro-American "Bear Flag" Revolt. After the war, he was elected U.S. senator from California. Representing another branch of Lucille's family, Juan Lopez had come with Father Junipero Serra when he founded the missions. The granddaughter of Juan Lopez, Juana Lopez, had a daughter with General Vallejo, Prudenciana Vallejo Lopez de Moreno.[8] The original Moreno was Mathew Brown, an Englishman, who changed his name to Matias Moreno upon marrying into the family; his granddaughter was the daughter of Vallejo and Lopez.[9]

Lucille's sister, Hortencia Beserra Núñez, and her husband, Eddie, grew up in Boyle Heights. Lucille and Hortencia's home was in El Hoyo, under the Fourth Street Bridge. Hortencia was called Tencha and Lucille was called Auntie Luchi. Irma Núñez recalled, "The fact that his [Ed Roybal's] children are so close to my brothers and sisters and me is because we grew up together—and they did live with us for awhile—[so] that we're brothers and sisters even though we're cousins. My mom and dad were like their second mom and dad."[10]

In mid-1940, an incident happened that Ed Roybal would never forget and that he would often recall to others. He and Lucille had gone out to have dinner, when several Los Angeles policemen approached them. "This is something that I will never forget. And I will never forget because this was the evening I asked my wife to marry me... The policeman lined us up, about fourteen couples, and made us put our hands over our heads. And they went through our pockets. Then, they asked us to show credentials. I handed [over] my wallet. After I gave it to a policeman, and he looked at it. This policeman started taking the cards out of my wallet and dropped them on the sidewalk. After he did that, he said, 'Now, you pick them up.' I remember getting on my knees and picking them up. This is something of course that a young man who had just asked his best girl to marry him will not forget."[11]

To the young Ed Roybal, it was a reminder of the tenuous respect Mexicans lived under. He had heard of police misconduct and abuse and had seen it perpetrated firsthand. However, his personal experience with this type of disrespect left a mark on him that he shared with many in his community. It was an issue that he would confront and address again in the future.

However, the incident failed to mar Ed and Lucille's happiness, as they were married on September 27, 1940. Their love for each other never wavered or failed. It flourished and endured until his death and beyond.

The nation was coming out of the Depression, thanks to the enormously popular New Deal economic recovery program, when events that would lead to World War II began to unfold in Europe and Asia. In 1931, the Japanese military seized control of the rich Chinese province of Manchuria. The Japanese perpetrated one of the most hideous crimes of the war in late 1937 in what became known as the Rape of Nanking, where some estimated 300,000 Chinese civilians were slaughtered and some 20,000 women raped. In 1936, Benito Mussolini's fascist regime of Italy invaded the helpless country of Ethiopia. On September 1, 1939, Adolph Hitler's Nazi Germany invaded Poland, formally beginning World War II. The Roybals, like the world at large, were shocked by the very sweep of aggression.

At home, Edward and Lucille prepared to begin their family and a domestic life together. In 1942, Ed began working as a public health educator for the California Tuberculosis Association. The work was important to him, as the loss of his infant siblings in the flu epidemic and the premature death of his mother lingered in his memory. His work for the association inspired his lifelong involvement in health matters.

The War Comes Home

The Roybal family, like other Mexican American families of their generation, had already endured and survived two major catastrophes, the Great Depression and the Repatriation. Ahead of them lay a host of challenges, personal and otherwise, but an indomitable hope, faith, and tenacity guided them. Ed and Lucille were married fifteen months before the Japanese attack on Pearl Harbor. Lucille Eloisa, the first of their three children, was born on June 12, 1941, just six months before the attack.[12]

The war had come to the United States of America. Now the war came to Edward R. Roybal, a married man with a child at home, when in 1942 he was drafted into the U.S. Army.

The Japanese attack on United States naval forces at Pearl Harbor, Hawaii, on December 7, 1941, brought the United States into World War II. Mexicans and Mexican Americans responded patriotically in record numbers and entered the armed services. The grating issues marking the binational relations between Mexico and the United States were set aside for a time and cooperation prevailed after the Mexican republic declared war on the Axis powers, served as a coastal guard and set up defenses, and sent an air expeditionary force to the Pacific. Mexico also served the home front by entering an agreement to provide labor to U.S. farms, which were in desperate need of workers.

Americans of Mexican descent and many Mexican nationals made a tremendous contribution to the war as members of the armed forces. But there were difficulties. Mexicans faced discrimination in the armed forces and at home. While at first Mexican units were segregated, mexicanos were later given the choice to join either an integrated or all-Mexican unit. Segregated units proved unworkable, while integrated ones functioned. Besides, there was the practical consideration that Mexican American servicemen and their relatives might be voting in their home districts and the matter could become an issue of political survival.[13]

Mexican Americans fought in every branch of the armed forces and in every theater of the war, most in infantry units, filling the lower, more dangerous ranks. Mexican American officers were very rare. Between 375,000 and 500,000 Mexican and Mexican American men and women served in the armed forces. While Mexicans made up 5 percent of the Los Angeles population, they made up 10 percent of that city's casualties.[14] All this notwithstanding, Mexican Americans and other Latin Americans served with distinction and received more decorations for valor than any other ethnic group. Mexican Americans alone earned seventeen Congressional Medals of Honor, the nation's highest possible decoration.

However, even as Mexican Americans were fighting and dying for their country, they were denied the very rights they were fighting for. Even highly decorated Mexican war heroes were not safe from the degradation of the discrimination tolerated in its time. For example, the dark-pigmented Sergeant Macario Garcia, a Congressional Medal of Honor recipient from Sugarland, Texas, was not permitted to buy a cup of coffee in a restaurant in Richmond, California. He was chased out by a baseball-wielding Anglo.[15] About 150 towns and cities in Texas alone had public places that had refused to serve Mexican and Mexican American servicemen.[16] Numerous incidents occurred that brought dishonor to civilian life at a time of the nation's mobilization and foreign-war efforts.

For the many hundreds of thousands of Mexican men and women who served, their wartime service had an incalculable impact. War training taught them about complex organizations, the value of training and preparation, how to enter unknown international settings, and how to apply technologies to accomplish difficult missions. Men and women of different nationalities and races worked together for a common cause. They saw the benefits of a more liberal, open society. When they returned home, they had a firm basis for their disquietude, an inability to readapt to situations that had not changed as they themselves had changed.[17]

The large influx of Mexican Americans going into the armed forces severely limited the labor available for agribusiness, the railroads, and some low-wage industries. As a consequence, the governments of the United States and Mexico came to a preliminary agreement in 1942 under the Emergency Labor Program to allow Mexican workers to enter the United States to work in the agricultural fields and railroads. Congress approved the executive measure as Public Law 45, popularly known as the Bracero Program.[18]

Mexican American women, like other Rosie the Riveters on the home front, joined the workforce in record numbers due to the labor shortages, especially after 1943. They worked in aircraft assembly-line factories, as drivers of heavy machinery, and as translators, secretaries, and medical personnel. They filled many gaps in the railroad and meatpacking indus-tries particularly. This work experience helped them acquire new skills; with skills came a new autonomy and independence of spirit. Now that social conventions were changing, a new attitude arose among Mexican women, especially toward community involvement and their own edu-cational aspirations.

The 1940 U.S. Census showed that more than 1.6 million people of Mexican stock were living in the United States.[19] Some historians have ar-gued that the population was undercounted, and that it was actually more than 2.1 million.[20] In California, the Mexican population numbered about 457,900, out of a total state population of 6.9 million. Los Angeles had a Mexican population of 315,000, or nearly 6.9 percent of the state total.[21]

Ed Roybal was drafted to serve in the United States Armed Forces, as were many in his family. His brothers Robert and Benny served in the Navy in the Pacific. Ed had two cousins from New Mexico who were in the Bataan Death March, in the Philippines. Many of Lucille's family also served in the different branches of the U.S. services.

Lillian Roybal Rose, Ed's younger daughter, recalled a pivotal moment of her father's service during World War II. After Ed was drafted, he was sent to boot camp, and then his battalion, which was predominantly made up of Mexican American soldiers from East Los Angeles, assembled at the Los Angeles train station with an order to ship out to the front. The entire Roybal family and other relatives gathered at the train station to see them off. Before the train was to depart, a high-ranking officer appeared, and the soldiers stood at attention. The officer then proceeded to call five people, including Ed, to step out of line. Everyone held his or her breath in anticipation of what was going to happen next.

The intervention of the high-ranking officer was both ironic and anti-climatic. Ed and the four other young men asked to step out of line were sent to Fort MacArthur to serve the next four years in office duties. Ed was assigned to accounting tasks. He had been spared likely death and injury due to his college education and accounting skills.

A year after Ed was drafted into the army, Ed and Lucille Roybal's second child, Lillian, was born, on April 6, 1943. The young couple, now with two children, faced a time of separation, but they considered themselves lucky. Many of the soldiers in his original battalion did not come back from the war. Ed Roybal was traumatized by the death of his former comrades and by the injustices suffered by veterans. Likely these issues both motivated and radicalized him to fight for the Mexican American community and other disfranchised people.

Ed's brother Baudilio (Benny) served in the U.S. Navy in the South Pacific. He operated landing crafts that brought the troops on shore. He would later say that the Japanese kamikazes were the most frightening thing in the war. Ed's other brother Robert was in the Navy Reserve and was called up to also serve in the U.S. Navy. He drowned during a fierce storm in the Admiralty Islands in 1944. He was knocked down by the force of the wind, hit his head, and went over the side. He was awarded the American Area Award, Asiatic Pacific Campaign Award, and a letter of commendation. Robert Roybal was only nineteen years old when he died.

Lucille Roybal's older brother, Leo Beserra, worked for Lockheed and the U.S. Air Force. He did intelligence work in China and earned the rank of colonel. He worked closely with the Flying Tigers, a group of prewar U.S. air pilots who battled the Japanese when they invaded China. Her younger brother, Albert Beserra, saw action in Italy. He and all the other relatives, just like all soldiers during the war, endured many traumatic experiences that haunted them the rest of their lives.

On the home front, Lucille Roybal and her sister, Hortensia Beserra Núñez, worked as bilingual secretaries in war factories. They went through a long period of being self-reliant and independent, doing the work of the men who were fighting at the front. Although they returned to being housewives after the war, they had developed immeasurable resourcefulness and character.

The war changed the lives of the men and women of the Roybal and Beserra families. Elsie Roybal Wilder noted, "The war experience opened them up, and they realized there that they had not seen or known many things about the world beyond. I think it changed their attitudes, and they came back with the desire to bring about social change in this nation."[22] She credited her brother Ed's public service aspirations to his war experience.

Evelyn Roybal Verdugo commented, "I know my dad always said that it took World War II to make him an American, to where he could be able to get a job at Lockheed. My dad said that before the war the lines to apply for a job were filled with people from everywhere back East. He talked with them, and they had no aeronautic experience. My father had taken some classes and you'd have thought he would have been hired, but [he wasn't until after the war]."[23]

The War and Racial Tensions: The Japanese Relocation

A new series of racial tensions gripped the West Coast following the attack on Pearl Harbor. It derived from paranoia and xenophobia that made Japanese and Japanese Americans a suspicious class. In early 1942, the War Department ordered the mass evacuation of all Hawaiians of Japanese extraction. General Delos Emmons, the military commander of Hawaii, resisted, due to the fact that some 37 percent of the population of the islands' population was of Japanese ancestry. In the end, some 1,444 (or 1 percent of the Japanese-ancestry population of Hawaii) were interned. On February 19, 1942, President Roosevelt signed Executive Order 27, which removed all the people of Japanese ancestry from California, as well as parts of Oregon, Arizona, and Washington for reasons of "national security." Eventually, some 110,000 people of Japanese ancestry were rounded up for the ten internment camps described by the press as "relocation centers." They were in reality no different than the Native American reservations or prison camps.

At a community meeting in Boyle Heights, Ed Roybal spoke up. He said the internment orders were a disgrace. One day, he said, this act would be the nation's shame. People booed him. They turned on him, hostile; they felt insulted and thought him unpatriotic. They showed him the way out.[24] Most Japanese Americans in Los Angeles lived in Boyle Heights and were an integral part of that community. The law turned neighbor on neighbor. People commonly took pejorative license and referred to the Japanese as "Japs." However, in the Roybal household, the word was never allowed. The public presumption was that all Japanese American citizens were potential collaborators and spies for the Imperial power. It was in turn possibly a prejudice emerging from the racialist beliefs that people were predisposed toward certain behaviors by nature and genetics. Ideas like that, and their residue, die slowly and still not fully.[25] No specific charges of criminal activity related to the war were filed against any Japanese person in this country, nor any espionage or treason ever uncovered. Nevertheless, they lost their homes, businesses, and health, along with their freedoms of association and movement. Japanese Americans fought in the courts and in Congress for rectification. In 1944, the Supreme Court decided in *Korematsu v. United States* that the evacuation was justified on the basis of "military necessity."[26]

The Sleepy Lagoon Case and the Zoot Suit Riots

Two events in particular exposed anti-Mexican malignancy at a time when many young people from that background were serving, fighting, and even dying abroad, not to mention providing much-needed, back-breaking labor in the agricultural fields and the railroads connecting America's cities and towns.

Sleepy Lagoon was a gravel pit in Los Angeles' outskirts where young Mexican Americans, denied use of city public swimming pools, often went.[27] On the evening of August 1, 1942, some members of the 38th Street gang were jumped by a rival gang at the lagoon. When additional members of the 38th Street gang arrived, the rival gang had left. The 38th Street members then proceeded to crash a party at the nearby Williams Ranch, where a fight ensued. The next day, Jose Diaz, who had been an invited guest, was found murdered.

Newspapers printed lurid tales about the crime. The *Los Angeles Herald-Examiner*, owned by William Randolph Hearst, who had a long history of jingoism and anti-Mexican sentiment, was especially sensationalistic. The Los Angeles Police Department quickly arrested most of the 38th Street gang's members and accused twenty-two of them with criminal conspiracy (a charge resulting when an agreement is made between two or more persons to commit a crime). A special grand jury committee accepted a report, by Lt. Ed Duran Ayres, justifying the gross violation of the defendants' civil rights. The report admitted that discrimination had occurred but concluded that Mexicans were inherently criminal and violent. Ayres further stated that Mexicans were Indians, that Indians were genetically Orientals, and that Orientals had a "disregard for the value of life," making them—if you follow the reasoning—naturally prone to violence.[28] At trial, Judge Charles W. Fricke permitted a number of irregularities, including disallowing the defendants to change clothes or get haircuts during the duration of the proceedings.

While generally agreed that the prosecution was not able to prove its conspiracy theory, the court on January 12, 1943, passed sentences that ranged from assault to first-degree murder, many of which resulted in life imprisonment. The Mexican community reacted by establishing the Sleepy Lagoon Defense Committee in support of the defendants. The noted journalist, lawyer, and, later, author Carey McWilliams chaired it.[29] The government and the media red baited McWilliams and the committee. The California Committee on Un-American Activities charged that the defense group was a communist front organization and that McWilliams was a fellow-traveler because he opposed segregation and supported miscegenation (the genetic mixing of racial groups).[30] However, the support committee gained a lot of sympathy in the Mexican community, and it was bolstered by the active support of Hollywood luminaries like Rita Hayworth (formerly Rita Cansino), Orson Welles, and Anthony Quinn. Finally, on October 4, 1944, the 2nd District Court of Appeals reversed the lower court in a unanimous decision. It specifically charged that Judge Fricke had violated the defendants' constitutional rights and that there was no evidence linking the defendants to the murder of Jose Diaz.[31]

The other wartime incident is referred to as the Zoot Suit Riots. In the aftermath of the Sleepy Lagoon case, tensions remained high. In the spring of 1943, a large number of servicemen on furlough went to the Los Angeles USO Hollywood Canteen, where movie stars socialized with servicemen. The place was a magnet for homesick soldiers. Many of the servicemen were from the South and had ingrained prejudices against Mexicans and African Americans. Many also apparently approached Mexican women as they would a prostitute, given that Hollywood films often portrayed Latinas as women of easy virtue. The servicemen's boisterous, disrespectful, and rude behavior to Mexican women brought them in conflict for social space with some Mexican young people in zoot suits who resented the servicemen's marauding behavior.

Between June 3 and 11, 1943, thousands of U.S. servicemen rioted throughout the downtown area and East Los Angeles. They accosted, beat up, and otherwise assaulted every young Mexican American zoot suiter on the streets, in clubs, and in other public places. Law enforcement stood by idly or ignored the servicemen's depredations and arrested the Mexican youth instead. Newspapers and radio whipped up hysteria. For example, *Los Angeles Daily News* writer Manchester Boddy (at one time considered a liberal) wrote in an editorial on June 9, "The time has come to serve notice that the City of Los Angeles will no longer be terrorized by a relatively small handful of morons parading as zoot-suit hoodlums. To delay action now means to court disaster later on." The riots were an international incident. The Mexican government expressed concern for the safety of people of Mexican descent. Eleanor Roosevelt, the First Lady, commented in her newspaper column that the cause of the riots was due "to the long-standing discrimination against Mexicans in the Southwest."[32] The Zoot Suit Riots took World War II out of the headlines for a while and damaged the United States' credibility as a land of freedom and tolerance. Under growing pressure, both the army and navy declared Los Angeles off limits to servicemen.

The Sleepy Lagoon case and the Zoot Suits Riots traumatized the Mexican community down to the core. It reminded them again that, aside from the patriotic rhetoric, civil rights were not an entitlement as purported, and could not necessarily be earned, either. Even if they were U.S. citizens, it was clear that Mexican Americans were of the second-class kind. Job discrimination was also a precipitating cause of the unrest. An FBI report of January 14, 1944, reported that the Los Angeles Police Department had only twenty-two Mexican American officers out of a total force of 2,547, while the Los Angeles Sheriff's Department had approximately thirty Spanish-surname deputies out of a total of 821.[33]

The social prejudices that had spilled out into the streets and mob violence that ensued demonstrated that an arbitrary justice prevailed and the government designed to protect citizens would cast a blind eye of neglect when it was convenient. The incidents galvanized the Mexican community and brought them some support from the larger community. While those who would make up the Mexican community's future leadership ranks were at war during this period, and not at home, the problems that needed attention were being defined. The task of addressing the Mexican community's social issues, many of which had been simmering for decades, would fall to a large degree to the returning Mexican American GIs, whose expectations for a better life had been elevated by their war experiences.

Chapter 3

Rising Expectations
(1947)

THE PERIOD RIGHT AFTER WORLD WAR II WAS A PECULIAR TIME. THE Sleepy Lagoon case and the Zoot Suit Riots defined a new rip in the American social fabric. Yet, quixotically, there was an attraction and allure to things Latin American and Spanish American. Rita Hayworth (née Cansino)[1] and the Dominican Maria Montez[2] were especially popular pinups with GIs. People moved and swayed to Latin music and gravitated to the Latin personalities they met on the big screen. It seemed that all Americans needed imagery, especially the fiction captured in movies, to give them direction, or hope, or at least a pause through entertainment. It was the working class—the people who most sought acceptance—whose images kindled antipathy. Popular imagery of Latinos thus conveyed mixed messages.

During the war years, the Mexican communities sought escape and entertainment in popular culture.[3] Their favorites included Cuban American Cesar Romero and the fast-rising former Boyle Heights resident Anthony Quinn.[4] Several already established Mexican stars filled the marquees across the nation, most notably Tito Guizar,[5] Arturo de Cordova,[6] and Ricardo Montalban.[7] Movie stars like these carried the message of getting ahead through the roles they played and the glamorous success stories they embodied. The community that Ed Roybal left behind when he was drafted began awakening. Mexican Americans realized that they were not as loved in their country as they had assumed and that they were more appreciated in the countries that they had helped liberate.

Coming Home

World War II finally came to an end with the Japanese surrender on September 2, 1945. Unfortunately, a few months later, a whole new set of hostilities began: the Cold War between the United States and the Soviet Union, with its ideological and socioeconomic struggle, war games and preparations, and the threat of a nuclear holocaust. For a short interval, however, an exhausted and grateful world prayed and celebrated peace. Soldiers and sailors looked homeward with longing. Spouses and children eagerly awaited their arrival. Many of the soldiers were by now fathers, greeting their new babies or their growing children after distance, deprivation, sacrifice, and dread had separated them, sometimes for years. Edward Roybal was discharged in 1945, and he returned to his family in Boyle Heights, happy to be home. He, like other servicemen, had changed over the previous years, owing to the things he experienced and witnessed during the war.

Although Ed Roybal's war service did not include combat, he saw scores of returning GIs in his military base, public places, and everywhere else. Some were maimed or disabled; others suffered from combat fatigue and insomnia, victims of nightmares they had witnessed. Others never returned, buried anonymously in some distant battlefield. The United States had suffered 298,000 war dead; 671,801 military wounded or missing; and 139,709 civilians wounded or missing. All who served lost their innocence. War made them cognizant of the most important things in life: family, children, relatives, and friends. Those who did not serve made a different type of sacrifice. They endured excruciating uncertainty and the loss or permanent disability of loved ones. Ed Roybal saw all this, as well as the fact that the country had been united in more ways than one to win the war. The unity had been inspiring, healing, and reassuring, but once the war was over, everyone would go back to his or her private life once again.

The Rising Expectations of Mexican Americans

While Mexican Americans and other minorities had served their country, they knew deep down that the country must change. Although they had served in both integrated and segregated units and experienced humiliations in the process, they all were preoccupied with the urgency of the war effort. Many swore to change this demeaning status quo but felt they should wait until after the war was won. However, news came of the refusal of restaurants to serve even highly decorated Mexican American war veterans and, even more nauseating, refusal by White city fathers to bury Mexican American servicemen in their hometowns. The Veterans Administration too dragged its feet in providing adequate care for disabled Mexican American veterans. The GI Bill of Rights provided little educational or home buying assistance to them until prodded by the GI Forum. Increasingly, many Mexican American GIs saw the urgency for change; business as usual would not do anymore. If the war had been about making a better world, it must start at home. They had rising expectations that social justice and equality must truly see the light of day.

After the war, Roybal continued his work with the California Tuberculosis Association. He became the Los Angeles County Tuberculosis and Health Association's health education director, remaining at that post until 1949. He easily gravitated to his old vocation of helping to eradicate tuberculosis and provide better health care for everyone. It was not easy for Mexican Americans to get jobs at that time, especially at this high level of responsibility. However, federal law imposed priority treatment for war veterans seeking employment. In addition, Ed Roybal had already had made an impression in his position; moreover, none could deny that his added maturity due to the war experience was an asset.

Ed Roybal's expectations matched those of his contemporaries. "We all expected to come home to be sure that we restart our careers," he said, "whatever they happened to have been." He believed that buying a house or returning to college was an expense that each individual would have to pay for himself. Instead, he found that veterans were to receive a postwar dividend from the government that would relieve the burden on the individual and produce remarkable social progress.

The GI Bill of Rights, when it was passed in 1946, was universally hailed by returning servicemen for helping them attend college and buy homes. For Mexican Americans and African Americans especially it was a unique opportunity. Home ownership and a college education were largely inaccessible to these groups, whose communities suffered from poverty, segregation, and discrimination. For Ed Roybal, the GI Bill also demonstrated how government could encourage people to reach to higher aspirations and serve as a partner in their achievements.

In March 1948, Dr. Hector Garcia,[8] a World War II veteran, founded the GI Forum with the express purpose of developing political empowerment in the Mexican American community and encouraging Mexican war veterans to take advantage of the GI Bill. "He did a tremendous job of convincing young men and women that they should be taking advantage of the GI Bill of Rights, not only for education but also to buy a home and any other benefit coming under the GI Bill," said Roybal. "He was one of the foremost leaders at that particular time in selling the idea to young men and women. Many of them just didn't care but once they started to learn what was in the bill, then they started to care, and I think he awakened a good many of us to the fact that there was something good in the GI Bill of Rights."[9]

Not everyone who was eligible used these benefits, although a majority did, which made a big difference in the stake many now had in their communities and the leadership that emerged.[10] Roybal bought a house under the GI Bill and once more enrolled at UCLA Extension courses that specialized in cost accounting. Ed Roybal continued to take college courses after the war, most likely under the GI Bill.

Readjusting to Civilian Life

Upon his return from the armed forces, Roybal continued his work with the Los Angeles County Tuberculosis and Health Association. There, he arranged the schedule for the mobile unit with an x-ray machine and a technician. He also traveled outside Los Angeles County to various towns throughout the state. He talked to local community leaders, mainly Mexicans, on making the unit available as a free public service. Local leaders were needed to get the word out at key places and to enlist others to help when the time came. He crosscut various communities, seeing similarities and distinctions, real differences and perceived ones. Health matters, he knew, were a common denominator. Another person's well-being may depend on one's own. He went to community groups, churches, and clubs, sampling California's diversity. "The job to me was very, very interesting," he said.[11]

It was also at this job and through the experiences that came his way that he first began to contemplate the possibility of elected public service. "Before that particular time I didn't know I had that type of desire," said Roybal.[12] Through his work, he was gaining an immense understanding about how health, economics, and political conditions intersected. He could see especially the privations and how they affected the Mexican community. "I found them worse than when I left. Everyone was competing with somebody else for a job, for loans, for whatever it was that they needed. There was no real unity in the community. Not only in our community, but unity anywhere."[13]

The year 1947 would prove pivotal. The U.S. Supreme Court handed down their decision in the *Mendez v. Westminster* school segregation case. In early 1945, in Orange County, California, Gonzalo Mendez, a tenant farmer in Westminster, and his wife, Felicitas, a native of Puerto Rico, along with a group of Mexican American World War II veterans, filed a lawsuit in federal court. They sought an injunction against four Orange County school districts (Westminster, Garden Grove, El Modena, and Westminster) to stop the segregation of Mexican children. On April 14, 1947, the 9th Circuit U.S. Court of Appeals in San Francisco ruled that school districts could not make children of Mexican descent go to separate schools. This milestone case laid the foundation for *Brown v. Board of Education* in 1954. Thurgood Marshall (who was later the lead attorney on the *Brown* case) filed one of the amicus curiae briefs. Other organizations filing amicus curiae briefs included the American Jewish Congress, the American Civil Liberties Union (ACLU), and the Japanese American Congress.

The Cold War Comes Home: The McCarthy Era

The nation's political climate was changing. In 1947, the Cold War chilled U.S.-Soviet relations by several degrees. A series of actions, policies, and miscalculations on both sides heightened the possibility of atomic war. The Soviet Union, which had suffered enormous devastation and lost between 20 and 30 million in World War II, felt justified in its claim to Eastern Europe in order to stop another invasion from the West. In turn, Winston Churchill termed this policy the creation of an "Iron Curtain." Incoming United States president Harry S. Truman developed a policy of containment and began the Marshall Plan to rebuild Europe against the communist threat. The Soviet blockade of Berlin in 1949 resulted in the United States founding the North Atlantic Treaty Organization (NATO), a military pact with Western Europe. The fateful year of 1949 brought the triumph of communism under Mao Zedong in China and the explosion of the first atomic bomb in the Soviet Union. That year also brought the founding of the state of Israel and the beginning of its long-term conflict with its Arab neighbors. In 1950, North Korea invaded South Korea, which began the Korean War (1950–1953), and subsequent United States intervention. The world was divided into two camps, the anticommunist West and the communist East, at the brink of atomic annihilation.

At home, fueled by anticommunist hysteria, officials began to root out the "communist elements." In 1947, the Taft-Hartley Act outlawed union shops, crippling the union movement and touching off the slow decline of labor union membership. The same year, the House Un-American Activities Committee (HUAC) held hearings on the perceived communist influences in Hollywood by "fellow-travelers," "premature antifascists," and "the disloyal." The government created fear through its notion of "subversion" and villainized dissent, compelling people to conform to national policy.[14]

Ed Roybal Runs for Los Angeles City Council

Instead of moving forward, it seemed that no substantial progress was at hand. The GI Bill was a huge boost, but it also encouraged those veterans who took advantage of it to move into new homes, leaving behind the old neighborhoods. A new notion was taking hold: suburban living. As he made the rounds with community leaders and began to understand how neighborhoods and communities were structured, Ed Roybal found confirmation for his idea that the way to make a difference was through local politics. The Los Angeles City Council was one body with high potential to make a difference in civic matters. After all, one would think that issues of public health, city streets, water and sewage, and police and emergency protection were less partisan and less ideological than party politics. But up to this point Mexican Americans had been systematically excluded from representation. "Just like all legislative bodies," Roybal said about the city council in 1947, "they just didn't include us and we were left out wherever they possibly could leave us out."[15]

No Mexican American had been elected to the Los Angeles City Council since the late 1800s. The notion was new, but perhaps, Ed reasoned, the conditions in Boyle Heights and other East Los Angeles neighborhoods were attributable to lack of citizen involvement and lack of governmental representation. California's Mexican population had grown from 416,140 in 1940 to 760,453 in 1950. The growth was mostly due to Mexican immigration. Some 60 percent of Mexican immigrants chose California as their destination. Mexicans in California were the most urbanized in the Southwest, at 85.4 percent. Mexicans in the city of Los Angeles made up about 10 percent of the population in the 1950s. Many Mexicans were not citizens, and those who were often did not register to vote. If they voted, it was mostly Democrat. The Democratic Party took for them for granted and gerrymandered their districts to keep liberal incumbents in power. Los Angeles elites did not need a political machine. The city's power brokers were the Chandler family (owners of the *Los Angeles Times*); the real estate, petroleum, and insurance interests; and old-line merchants. They controlled the mayor, the police, and the five county supervisors. As such, they influenced the planning and zoning commissions, which controlled land use in Los Angeles. These elites were headquartered at the California Club. Their circle excluded women, Jews, and minorities.

The Mexican community in Los Angeles was politically powerless. They were denied their fair share of city services and were brutalized by the city police. They endured segregated housing and completed high school at abysmal rates. During the war years, several housing projects were built in East Los Angeles: Aliso Village and Pico Gardens near Downtown Los Angeles, and Ramona Gardens, which was between the Lincoln Heights and Boyle Heights neighborhoods. During the war years, the housing projects had given priority to servicemen, families of servicemen, or those working in the war industries. With the end of the war and the building of newer suburban developments, some of the former tenants moved out. Bert Corona recalled, "Mexicans who had lived in more congested areas wanted to move into the projects. Some families outside the projects had been doubling and even tripling with other families because of a housing shortage and high rents. Housing was particularly critical for the returning Chicano veterans as well as for mexicano workers who were being laid off, especially from war industries. If you didn't have a job, you weren't eligible to live in the projects. For all those reasons, housing was a major issue for the Mexican community in L.A."[16]

Roybal's chances of winning, should he enter a race, were of course slim, but perhaps by running there was a more important point to make—one that would make running worthwhile, even ennobling.

He understood that if change were going to come, it would have to come from the bottom up, from the local level first. Changes in the big picture would come from changes in the little scenarios—what happened in the streets, in the neighborhoods. Popular messages would have the citizenry believe that the real issues were about ideology. But they were not. Most of them were about the necessities of civic life—health, education, police protection, city services, and a semblance of equality. Thanks to his armed forces experience, Ed's new capacities and confidence enabled him to expect better, sooner than had been tolerable before. Life after the war could not mean business as usual. Hopes delayed too long often become hopes deferred indefinitely. Speculation was mounting about whether Ed Roybal would enter the city council race.

Roybal was just thirty years old when some friends and associates tried to persuade him to run for the Eastside seat.[17] Running, and the prospect of winning, had a certain appeal to Roybal. It would give him a platform from which to promote his health programs. Some of his followers reasoned, why not make the race? They also thought that he would be hard pressed to turn down friends who wanted him to enter the contest.[18]

Actually, "I ran [in that first race]," said Roybal, "because the opportunity arose." He had already designed what he called "a five-year plan" that included registering voters. He had no other political plans in mind. The encouragement he received he interpreted as an endorsement by friends and groups urging him to make up his own mind. No one asked him for favors, nor did he offer any.[19]

During the war years, Lucille and the children moved in with her mother. Each day she endured the multiple concerns of her husband's well-being, growing a family, and siblings serving in the armed conflict. She hoped that the aftermath of the war might bring a sense of normalcy.

There were some pressing practical considerations, however. The couple had bought a small cottage in El Sereno, a neighborhood next to Lincoln Heights, not far from Boyle Heights. It was Lucille's "dream house." The very night Lucille was going to tell Ed that the mortgage had been arranged and they had a move-in date, Ed came home to tell her his news. "He didn't look excited," she said. "He told me that there was a group of people who wanted him to run for city council. He told me that if he ran we would have to stay in the district. I started crying." She asked him if that was what he really wanted to do. He said he wanted to try. "I said okay, go ahead and run."[20]

Consequently, Ed and Lucille convinced Baudilio, Ed's father, to move into the house in El Sereno. In exchange, Ed, Lucille, and the children moved in to his Boyle Heights house on Fifth Street, in the 9th Council District. The families agreed that, should Ed lose, they would swap houses again. As it turned out, Ed and Lucille never got to live in the El Sereno house.

Ed Roybal and his city council campaign made costly mistakes. It didn't help that they had entered a race against nine-term incumbent Parley P. Christensen. Christensen was no lightweight politician. Between 1900 and 1904 Christensen served in various capacities as a Republican state officer, including party chairperson. Each year from 1906 to 1912 he unsuccessfully sought the Republican nomination for Congress. Switching to the Utah Progressive Party (which supported Theodore Roosevelt's presidential candidacy), he was elected to the U.S. House of Representatives for one term, 1914–1916. Between 1915 and 1920, he became increasingly involved with several left wing and labor groups in Utah. He helped organize the Utah Labor Party in 1919. He was nominated for the office of United States president by the newly created Farmer-Labor Party, polling 265,000. After the election he traveled to Europe and the Soviet Union, where he met Vladimir I. Lenin. In 1923, he settled in Chicago, where he chaired the Illinois Progressive Party and was their candidate for the U.S. Senate in 1926. In the 1930s, he moved to California and became involved with the End Poverty in California (EPIC) crusade of Upton Sinclair, along with the Utopian Society and other leftist groups in the state. He served in the Los Angeles City Council from 1935 to 1937 and then 1939 to 1949. In 1936, he ran unsuccessfully as a Democratic congressional candidate.[21]

Anthony P. Rios remembered that everything about the Roybal campaign was late. The main reason may have been that they had no money in the campaign treasury, and "a lot of us didn't know each other."[22] Rios would become Roybal's lifelong personal friend and political ally. He was a tireless, dedicated labor and community organizer. Independent of his alliance with Ed Roybal, he was a legendary figure, who began in the 1930s as a farm worker labor organizer and contributed to a multitude of causes over the years.[23] The Roybal home on Fifth Street served as campaign headquarters. Most meetings were held there or at the Rios home.

The Democratic Party didn't endorse Roybal to the city council seat, nor did any newspaper, union, or other organization. *La Opinion*, the largest Spanish-language newspaper in Los Angeles, was sympathetic but claimed impartiality.[24] The campaign undertook very little street canvassing, which was a mistake for a first-time candidate. Also, Roybal erred in assuming that Mexican American voters would support him because of their shared ethnicity.[25] Even if he had calculated that correctly, the 9th District was ethnically diverse. Ed Roybal would have to count on far more support from other places than he was getting.

Roybal lost in his first bid for city council. He had little name recognition and could point to few achievements that convinced voters he was capable of doing good things for the district. He failed to seize and ride on an issue, then tie it to the office and the consequences to the voters if they failed to vote for him.[26] Basically, voter response to Ed Roybal was what might be expected for any idealistic young politician.[27]

Parley Christensen defeated his four challengers in the race, winning reelection with a total of 8,948 votes. His challengers trailed him by wide margins: Julia Sheehan, 3,783; Roybal, 3,350; Filmore Jaffe, 3,101; and Fred Shalmo, 1,235. Coming in third, Roybal got 15 percent of the vote, almost 75 percent of it coming from the Eastside. This, in political calculus, was encouraging.

"What Are You Going to Do Now?"

Still, Roybal was shaken by his loss. Even though it was far from an overwhelming defeat, it was not a near win, either. He had made a significant impression on his many volunteers, however, and on other grassroots organizers. He was heartened when famed community organizer Saul Alinsky[28] sent him a seven-word telegram following the defeat. It said, "What are you going to do next?"[29] Alinsky was a legend in his time. Beginning in the 1930s, he had emerged from the settlement house organizing movement and had trained many progressives, labor unionists, and leaders of left-leaning causes.

Roybal met Alinsky at a social work convention held in San Antonio, Texas, in the early 1940s. The progressive Catholic Archbishop Robert E. Lucy introduced Roybal to Alinsky. Fred Ross, one of Alinsky's associates, had told him that Roybal was already applying some of the organizing principles that they taught. Roybal was suspicious of radical and leftist activities. He asked the bishop, "What about this man? He's quite a leftist." The bishop is said to have smiled and retorted: "Well, he's a leftist, but so am I."[30]

In the 1940s, membership in civil rights and social welfare groups spanned a wide range of ideologies. Some members were socialists or communists. Most joined not for reasons of doctrine, however, but simply to be in solidarity with others. Franklin D. Roosevelt was known as a progressive; Kennedy- and Johnson-era liberals espoused policies that were considered left of center. Still, the term *left* was used loosely then as now, so it's likely that while Roybal considered himself to be on the left, he used the term *leftist* in this context to ask the bishop whether Alinsky was a communist.

Roybal had previously taken Saul Alinsky's forty-hour community organizing training seminars in 1945, 1946, and 1947, in Chicago.[31] However, it was not until Roybal entered electoral politics that he began to make use of the techniques. Many years later, Roybal assigned much importance to the training. "Well, I learned many skills from him," he said.[32] An important friendship between Roybal, Ross, and Alinsky thus began and flourished through the years.

Founding the Community Service Organization (CSO)

After the city council defeat, Anthony Rios, Roybal, and members of the Committee to Elect Edward Roybal engaged in a lot of critical discussion about the errors made, what worked and what didn't, and how mistakes could be avoided or rectified the next time. From this intensive analysis of Ed Roybal's failed city council bid, Antonio Rios, Herman Gallegos, Dolores Huerta, Roybal himself, and others eventually founded the Community Service Organization (CSO) in the fall of 1947. They understood that some ongoing, community-based vehicle was needed to rouse the Mexican residents from their dependency on the Democratic Party. The CSO's early goal was to develop grassroots leadership by encouraging those who were not citizens to become citizens and those who were citizens to register to vote. These efforts, it was thought, would transform political apathy into commitment. What appeared more and more necessary was a venue of empowerment through an organization, which could then be mobilized for electoral politics. Thirteen of Roybal's most intimate associates, both men and women, formed the organization.[33]

The CSO was based in Boyle Heights, but chapters later expanded the group to other areas. The organization was the culmination of a plan that Roybal had envisioned about ten years earlier (around 1937) and sketched out in an undergraduate term paper.

Roybal offered the idea to the Latin American division of the Los Angeles Democrats, but they rejected it. Undaunted, Roybal then took the idea to the Los Angeles Democratic Committee. The Democratic leadership dismissed it as "sheer idealism."[34] After this second rejection, Roybal shelved it.

After Roybal met Alinsky, the germ of the CSO idea received assistance from Industrial Areas Foundation (IAF), via Alinsky's associate Fred Ross. He sent Ross[35] to assist the CSO in the summer of 1947. The IAF had been founded by Saul Alinsky to provide assistance to groups struggling for political empowerment. The IAF provided the CSO with staff, Ross's expertise, and some financing. The technical support was crucial. Roybal, Ross, and the other leaders now set out to recruit members. The CSO's first office was set up on Fourth Street and Mott Avenue, across from Roosevelt High School in East Los Angeles.[36] Bert Corona, a member of the CSO beginning in 1949, recalled, "I joined and helped organize CSO in northern California because I thought it had a good program of defending the rights of the Spanish-speaking, of advocating redress of their grievances, and of seeking to bring them into the mainstream of American life, especially through voting. One thing I didn't like, however, was that one of its stated reasons for organizing was to keep 'reds' from establishing a base in the communities." According to Corona, the "reds" referred to the Communist Party and the Asociación Nacional México-Americana (ANMA).[37] The latter organization had been founded in 1949, in Phoenix, Arizona, in order to protect the rights of Mexican workers.

The CSO organization was structured on a committee system. The Executive Committee included a president, vice president, secretary, treasurer, and chairpersons of the other committees. These included the Youth Welfare Committee, the Social Committee on Fundraising, and the Race Relations Committee, which reached out to other minority communities and often presented workshops on prejudice. The Housing Committee dealt with housing discrimination and segregation.[38] The CSO consciously avoided working with communist organizations.[39] They took up issues that Roybal would later include in his campaign platform for city council. Among the issues that CSO focused on were voter registration (especially for Mexican Americans), education, civil rights, neighborhood improvement, citizenship,[40] and pensions for noncitizens.[41]

CSO meetings were conducted in both Spanish and English and were held every evening. They specifically focused on engaging the residents of the district in problem issues and how they could be resolved. These were like town hall meetings. People identified common problems and planned useful actions, then strategized about how to carry them out. Many Mexican Americans, in this manner, learned a democratic way to take control of issues and contributed to the national drive for equality.[42] CSO's work was carried out by volunteers. Although at the beginning all its officers were men, women were represented in the Executive Committee and later elected officers, filling challenging roles (and defying social expectations in the process).[43] Some of the women who were very active in CSO included Ursula Gutierrez and Dolores Huerta. Bert Corona remembered, "Many women were active in CSO, as officers, organizers, and door-to-door voter registrars. The women, like the men, were from working-class families or lower-middle-class ones."[44]

Bert Corona recalled another early key member of CSO this way: "When CSO started and I was in northern California, word came through that there was a hell of an organizer by the name of César Chávez from a barrio in San Jose called Sal Si Puedes (Get Out if You Can). His fame had preceded him. Those in the Catholic Church, the Quakers, and other religious groups involved with developing leadership and organization in the Chicano communities spoke very highly of this dark, short, very serious, and very committed mexicano."[45]

The CSO approach to civic action had a certain appeal, distinct from the Mexican-American organizations that conducted their meetings exclusively in English and sought membership from a U.S.-born Mexican population. Membership in the CSO grew to about 800 in two years and continued expanding at a rapid pace throughout the 1950s. By 1963, the CSO had thirty-four California chapters with about 10,000 members.[46]

Although its main legacy and reputation is that of a Mexican American organization, the CSO was originally broader than that. The Jewish community's contributions and participation were quite prominent. The majority of Jewish Americans at that time were poor and frequently discriminated against. The progressive elements in Los Angeles reflected the understanding, still not widespread in the broader community, that the time was at hand for someone of Mexican descent to run for council who would represent the interests of the whole community.[47]

Although he had been defeated in his first bid for office, Edward Roybal succeeded in realizing his long-cherished plan for CSO. As this happened, he meanwhile contemplated another run for the 9th District seat.

Chapter 4

Running for Los Angeles City Council
(1948–1951)

THE COMMUNITY SERVICE ORGANIZATION (CSO) WORKED TO BRING both Mexican Americans and Mexican immigrants together. Its organizing efforts differed from most previous Mexican American advocacy groups. Other groups, such as the GI Forum and League of United Latin American Citizens (LULAC), appealed mainly to citizens and the second generation. CSO instead bridged the gap between Mexican immigrants and Mexican Americans by not imposing a citizenship requirement on members; in fact, it encouraged noncitizens (and non-mexicanos) to join.[1]

This departure from how other organizations functioned was especially important in light of the advancing Cold War and McCarthyism. That social atmosphere often cast suspicion on "foreigners" and noncitizens. Mexicans and Mexican Americans were grouped in that class of suspicious people whose ulterior motives were questionable. The prevailing perception was that these so-called foreigners—the term *minority* had yet to be invented—were perpetrators threatening plots, or at least nurturing ideas of such. These people were often stereotyped as prone to violence, criminality, and delinquency.

This Cold War mentality—also later termed a *bunker mentality*—had the unintended consequence of accentuating paranoiac fears about things unfamiliar; localized on again–off again nativism prevailed. Racist acts went mainly undeterred. Fear-based federal legislation, such as the McCarran-Nixon Internal Security Act of 1950, only fanned those sentiments into outrage.[2]

In 1954, the U.S. Immigration and Naturalization Service began a deportation program called Operation Wetback, targeting Mexicans who crossed the border without documentation (mainly for agricultural work). For many, the program brought back the dark memories of the Repatriation roundups, during which many families were displaced, separated, sometimes never to be reunited. To counteract Operation Wetback, Roybal and others advocated that citizenship, voting, and active political involvement offered the best protection against personal calamity. On one occasion while discussing why Mexicans should become citizens, Roybal said, "so that they may feel they are a part, and that they do count in the democracy of America."[3]

Reckoning by attendance at the Friday night meetings, the CSO had 165 active members. These members led and took part in English-language and citizenship classes. And they taught public involvement, to show members how by organizing together, they could obtain street lighting and other city improvements. The organization provided youth services and health screening and also made referrals. People were shown how to redress and advocate at the local and state levels. CSO conducted education drives and offered legal advice. Through committees, members researched issues such as police brutality, discrimination, and education. CSO also initiated litigation to counteract police abuse and housing discrimination. The underlying idea was to build individual capacity by teaching people self-help, and in the process empower them to become proactive.

Many years later, Ed's daughter Lucille commented that the founding of the CSO was one of her father's proudest achievements, "particularly in the beginning of his political career. Because that really was the foundation that gave the Latino political movement in California a beginning."[4] Ed Roybal Jr. stated, "It was the first really sustained Chicano political organization. There was, prior to that, no real organization other than… some merchant associations and disparate political organizations."[5] Some 99 percent of the organization membership was composed of young men and women between the ages of twenty-two and thirty-five.

Voter Registration: The Seed of Political Empowerment

Throughout 1948, Roybal and members of the Elect Roybal Committee meticulously analyzed the mistakes made during the 1947 campaign. They refined and readjusted their political strategy for another run in 1949, and they continued to work on CSO's evolution.

The Industrial Areas Foundation, having provided assistance through a grant to CSO, specifically prohibited the organization direct partisan political involvement. There was some conceptual harmonizing needed, since the very founding of CSO was considered a political act. It had originally posed a civic alternative to political leaders. Antonio Rios and Gilbert Anaya, both Steelworkers Union activists and CSO founders, had even wanted the group to be named the Community Political Organization.[6] Finally, the decision was made to remain faithful to Roybal's thesis to use CSO as a tool for empowerment and to dodge direct partisan involvement.

One effective way to do that was by launching a massive voter registration drive. When they started this initiative, Ed's wife Lucille and one other person were the only Spanish-surnamed deputy voter registrars in the county. To get more registrars, the county registrar had to be convinced that a new kind of effort was necessary. He challenged Roybal and CSO, but finally relented and said, "I'll deputize anyone you send me," according to Roybal. The registrar then added that before he did so, each candidate had to read English and Spanish. For this, the CSO recruited volunteers from its English classes. One hundred and twenty-eight individuals came forward to get trained on how to enroll new voters. But then there was a new obstacle.

These prospective deputy voter registrars could not afford to miss work during the day to get trained. CSO leaders and the Central Labor Council of the American Federation of Labor, known as the AF of L, teamed up to convince the county to offer the volunteers night classes. Finally, that was done. Those who completed the course were sworn in as deputy registrars and began their work enrolling new voters.[7] The voter registration drive began in October 1947 and was in full swing by the time of the 1949 city council elections.

Henry Nava led the registration drive during the 1948–1949 seasons. He was assisted by volunteer union members of Mexican descent. Volunteers from La Placita, Our Lady of Talpa, Our Lady of Lourdes, and St. Mary's Catholic Church participated. The clergy from these churches were also active. Nightly precinct walks were organized and went through the neighborhoods to register residents. These drives roused the Mexican communities from their political lethargy. People responded enthusiastically. By the time of the 1949 election, CSO had registered 17,000 new voters, and about 15,000 of them had Spanish surnames.[8]

Consequently, more people went on the voter rolls and became political participants without making CSO into a political club. This even helped boost CSO's membership and also compelled new voters to develop their own criteria before supporting candidates. Roybal commented, "We realized that Americans of Mexican ancestry would receive representation in public office only with voter registration and organization."[9] In this manner, he was helping to empower the community.

The new deputy registrars were also involved in CSO's committees or other activities. Roybal remembered, "There wasn't a single person who was idle…That kind of coalition had never been built before and we did it in a way that today could be emulated."[10]

Although CSO focused on the Mexican American community, they also reached out to Jewish Americans. They did so through contact with the Jewish Community Relations Committee, headed by Fred Herzberg. According to Kenneth C. Burt, "Developing a working relationship with the Mexican American community would reduce the implicit danger of nationalism and help insure against the targeting of Jews during the next economic crisis."[11] Later, through the participation of Saul Alinsky, the Jewish Community Relations Council contributed funds to the CSO.

The CSO, reaching out to other minority communities, established a Southern California Advisory Committee, which included a cross-section of prominent community members: Rabbi Edgar F. Magnin, Judge Thomas White, Sheriff Eugene W. Biscailuz, Monsignor Thomas O'Dwyer, Democratic National Committeeman James Roosevelt, Church Federation of Los Angeles leader E. C. Farnham, and Hollywood film star Melvyn Douglas.[12] Douglas's wife, Congresswoman Helen Gahagan Douglas[13] (herself a former movie star) would support Roybal's Los Angeles City Council election bid in 1949.

Building a Multiethnic Coalition

Roybal's 1949 bid for the 9th District seat became a textbook example of a grassroots campaign. Roybal selected Roger Johnson, a former journalist, as his campaign manager. Johnson knew many people in both government (he was a personal friend of Eleanor Roosevelt) and the entertainment industry. Johnson took Ed to Stuart Hamilin, a big cowboy recording and radio star at that time. Hamilin, who was from Texas, had his own radio program. Hamilin liked Ed immediately and supported him, so he gave him radio time.[14] Johnson worked without pay. The campaign was mainly underwritten by small amounts from neighborhood people, and part of Johnson's job was to make sure that funds from business interests did not dilute or overshadow monies coming from neighborhood interests.[15]

Ordinary people were moved and transfixed by Roybal's campaign, especially its down-to-earth style and accessibility. It was refreshing and inspiring for Mexicans and other minorities who too often had been taken for granted by faceless politicians and the wealthy or vested interests that bankrolled them. People responded with what they could—nickels, dimes, quarters, or more. Most of the fundraisers consisted of raffles, the prizes donated by local merchants and often consisting of shaving sets, perfumes, and other practical necessities. Dances drew in the younger crowd. At house parties, residents could talk to Roybal over tacos, enchiladas, and tostadas. Although political campaigns were not as expensive then as they are today, it has been estimated that the 1949 Los Angeles City Council campaign cost about $15,000 per candidate, while Roybal's in turn cost a modest $5,500.[16] Perhaps the largest contribution came from the CIO Steelworkers, who also provided human resources and several sound trucks.

One thing that the Committee to Elect Roybal had was volunteers by the hundreds, of every ethnicity, age, and occupation. Roybal's own wife, Lucille, worked tirelessly, inspiring others. According to Roybal himself, she was an equal partner in every aspect of the campaign, intellectually, strategically, and in guarding confidentiality. She recalled later, "There was a time that I couldn't go with him when the kids were real little or sick. You find yourself feeling sort of left out. On the other hand, I did spend a lot of time away from them. There was time that I felt guilt more than anything else."[17]

According to Irma Núñez, Ed Roybal had promised his wife, Lucille, that if he lost the first election for city council he would keep his promise to her to move to their house in El Sereno. However, Lucille told him no. She reminded him that despite losing he had made a good showing. Nunez commented, "[Lucille] says, 'We can't give up now; we're not going to move and you are going to run again because you are going to win the council district in order to help the community.' And so my aunt was in a position to say, forget it, it's too much work, it's not worth it, and we want a better life for our family, let's go to our new house and move on. But she was the one who said, no, the community comes first even before the family. My Aunt Lu had said to me that my uncle had asked her permission to run. He said, 'I'm not going to run unless I have your blessing.' And my aunt said, 'Absolutely, I support your career whatever it is that you want to do. And because you believe in the community and you feel you can make a difference, I support you in whatever way you would need me to support you.'"[18]

Women played a crucial role in Ed Roybal's campaigns from the very beginning. His daughter Lucille Roybal-Allard commented, "I think women were the backbone of Dad's campaigns. Starting with my mother.

I mean, every tardeada that we held as a fundraiser, we'd be making taquitos till five in the morning. The women cleaned, they cooked, they took care of the kids, went door to door. The headquarters were full of women carrying out activities. The men did do work, but women were certainly the backbone in some areas. I think we need to differentiate between those women who were there at that time who were professional women, like Henrietta Villaescusa, versus grassroots women who would come and help with the mailings and organize all of that."[19] Of the women who were very active in her dad's campaigns, especially in the early years, Lucille recalled Henrietta Villaescusa, Patel Fisher, and Marian Graff, among many others.

The 9th District was a mixture of different ethnicities. Roybal downplayed his ethnicity but did not shun it. Thanks to some meticulous research by his staff, he was able to present factual data on the inferior living conditions in comparison to the rest of the city. Roybal confided to Katherine Underwood, "My presentations were more in the nature of a lecture...I had a film presentation, maps, charts showing the health conditions of the people of the 9th District, the income levels, their education and so forth, pointing out the city had been negligent all this time...So I appealed to them, the differences between what they had in the 9th District, and what they had on the West Side. The only thing we wanted was to be the same, no more, no less."[20]

Roybal emphasized his experience as a long-time resident of Boyle Heights and his service of many years to the district, with the x-ray unit and his founding of the CSO. He highlighted the accomplishments of the CSO, noting how the organization had obtained "new traffic signals, sidewalks, and paving for the neighborhood; made juvenile-delinquency studies; helped send children to summer camps; investigated police injustices, school and housing segregation and discrimination; and put on health drives."[21] Roybal printed cards with the message "Give a Young Man a Chance." He included his photo on them so voters could distinguish him from other candidates. His platform included a Fair Employment

Practices Commission, a police civilian review, and an end to housing discrimination. African Americans often would approach him and ask why they should support his candidacy. Roybal would respond by naming issues that affected both Mexican Americans and African Americans. Roybal would tell them, "Our skin is also brown—our battle is the same. Our victory cannot but be a victory for you, too."[22]

The presence of African Americans in Los Angeles dated back to the city's beginning. Mexican settlers sponsored by the Spanish Empire founded Nuestra Senora la Reina de Los Angeles on September 4, 1781. Included in the twenty-two adults were nine Indians, one "half breed," seven "mulattos," and two African Americans. In the first census that was taken in 1790 of the new village, the total population of 141 people included twenty-two of mixed African and European ancestry. After the United States takeover of California in 1848, more African Americans came to Los Angeles. The first U.S. census of Los Angeles County in 1850 documented twelve African Americans and 1,598 Mexicans and Europeans. The African American presence in Los Angeles grew very slowly throughout the 1800s. By 1900, some 34 percent of Los Angeles African Americans owned and lived in their own homes, which far exceeded the homeowning rates of both Mexicans and Japanese. It far exceeded the homeowner rates of African Americans in other cities. During the 1920s, exclusionary policies made it impossible for African Americans, Mexicans, and Japanese Americans to buy homes in European American neighborhoods, thus creating the first African American ghetto. Thousands of African Americans moved to the city of Watts, which was incorporated into the city of Los Angeles. The ghetto consigned them to segregation, poor schooling, low-paying jobs, and poverty.[23]

The Race Is On

In the 1949 election, 9th District Councilman Parley P. Christensen was again Roybal's rival. However, Christensen had been slowly losing his political base, primarily due to missing a significant number of city council votes. Christensen's coalition included communists and others on the left, as well as labor and minorities. However, by 1949, many in his political base were expressing frustration with the aging Christensen.

Roybal's improved political strategy, grassroots style, integrity, accessibility to prospective voters, modest campaign finances, and visible public accomplishments through the CSO broadened his appeal in 1949. Even before the primary election in April, he was able to obtain some significant endorsements such as the National CIO Council, the Steelworkers, and several AFL locals, although the Central Labor Committee of the AFL supported the incumbent Christensen. The Independent Progressive Party supported Roybal's candidacy and attempted to formalize their relationship with the Mexican American community by selecting former assembly candidate and CSO member Jose Chavez as one of five of its local vice presidents. One of two newspapers serving the African American community, the *California Eagle*, also supported Roybal.[24] However, three newspapers that would have been expected to support his candidacy did not. The *Daily News*, the city's lone Democratic newspaper, supported his former challenger from 1947, Julia Sheehan. The *Eastside Sun* of Boyle Heights supported Christensen. *La Opinion* was noncommittal.

Roybal beat two of his challengers in the primary, Daniel Sullivan and Julia Sheehan. Although he won 36.7 percent of the total number of votes, he had to face a runoff election against Christensen in the May general election. Roybal obtained the majority of votes cast in the Eastside, but Christensen won in South Central, Downtown, and the heterogeneous areas west of the Los Angeles River and east of Main Street.

Roybal had made definite inroads into the interethnic community in Boyle Heights, but what concerned him was that he had yet to win over the majority of African American and White voters. This fact compelled Roybal and his staff to reflect on this and to redress by making some adjustments to campaign strategy. One of the Roybal campaign's mistakes was having sent out Mexican American volunteers to canvass

African American communities. This situation was rectified by the time of the general election. African American volunteers campaigned in Black-majority areas of South Central and other places. The idea was to form identity politics. Likewise, Chinese, Jewish, Japanese, and Russian volunteers worked in their own neighborhoods for Roybal.[25] Precinct walking was also dramatically increased for the general election. Volunteers walked the precincts six times a week. An eighty-five-person telephone team followed up. In the final days of the May 30th election, sound trucks went out through neighborhood streets, blaring the campaign message and encouraging people to go vote.

Invigorated by the support it was getting, the campaign won the important endorsements of Assemblyman Gus Hawkins (the first African American elected to California state office), the *Daily News*, and the *California Eagle*. The *Daily News* editorialized that Roybal would "bring dynamic leadership for his underprivileged district."[26] In turn, the *California Eagle* commented that Roybal "was the real voice of the working people, and if elected will be the exponent of a better life for the struggling masses."[27] However, the other African American newspaper, the *Los Angeles Sentinel*, remained noncommittal as it had before, and the most important Spanish-language newspaper, *La Opinion*, which was based in downtown Los Angeles, had empathy but did not express visible support for Roybal.

A few weeks before the general election, a group called the Boyle Heights Committee was formed and announced its support for Roybal. The committee was co-chaired by William (Bill) Phillips, a Brooklyn Avenue business leader, and Jack Y. Berman, a theater-chain operator. The Boyle Heights Committee supported Roybal because of his position on a municipal fair employment practices law, his pledge to work to end housing discrimination, and his support for the construction of a city health center within the district.[28] Because most of the members were Jewish, the committee was seen as a proxy for the Jewish community's support.[29] Among its members was Samuel Goldwyn Jr., son of the legendary motion picture pioneer and producer of the same name.[30]

Unions and Jewish American supporters contributed many volunteers to help deliver voters to the polls. "If the Jewish area had been against us," Antonio Rios said, "it would have been very tough." But fortunately, 50 percent voted for Roybal in the primaries. In the runoff they all did.[31]

Roybal was building a progressive, multiracial coalition based on common needs, ethnic tolerance, and political integrity. The incumbent councilman, Parley Christensen, under mounting threat from the challenge, turned to running a dirty campaign. Christensen's campaign impugned ethnic prejudice and played on anticommunist hysteria by appealing to voters' basest instincts. Christensen campaign workers telephoned White voters with the message "We don't want Mexicans in the city hall, do we? Roybal is a Mexican." But when they called African American voters with English-language surnames, the tactic backfired.[32] Another Christensen ploy was to mail out postcards with Roybal dressed in Mexican charro attire and playing a guitar with the message in Spanish that Roybal was "a Communist in disguise."[33] Roybal's telephone volunteers employed a disciplined nonresponse, avoiding the same political chicanery.

On the very day of the general election in May 1949, volunteers staged an intense get-out-the-vote effort. They made impassioned telephone calls to prospective voters. Telephone volunteers started at 8:00 a.m., calling the list of 10,000 Spanish-speaking voters from a list organized by street, so that callers could determine who had not yet voted early in the day. Those who had not could be tracked down by precinct workers later. Car pools took voters to the polls and sound trucks crisscrossed the 9th District all day with the vote-for-Roybal message.

Making History

Roybal won with 59 percent of the total 35,106 votes cast. About 70 percent (12,684 votes) of the 20,540 votes he received came from the Eastside. Roybal succeeded by making significant inroads into the ethnic communities. He won the majority of the votes from South Central and from the heterogeneous areas as well. Also victorious that day was Los

Angeles Mayor Fletcher Bowron,[34] who was re-elected for another four-year term by defeating City Engineer Lloyd Aldrich. Bowron obtained 101,452 votes to Aldrich's 87,746 votes.

Roybal made history by becoming the first person of Mexican descent to win election to the Los Angeles City Council since 1881. The grassroots campaign strategy and platform had tremendous voter appeal. They de-emphasized Roybal's ethnicity, but in designing the approach, he showed how well he understood the social, political, and material distinctions among the 9th District's residents. He stood out by stressing that he was committed to action and change.[35] Mexican Americans had not been a significant voting bloc, least of all in a multiracial coalition. But Roybal's election set a precedent. "There were efforts made before to get the Mexican community and other groups together to vote as a bloc," Roybal recalled. "It really didn't materialize until the people themselves wanted to do it. Again, the whole thing centers around people. People who wanted to do something for themselves and for their community and we did it."[36]

Ed Roybal's daughter Lucille (Roybal-Allard) was seven years old when her father was elected to the Los Angeles City Council. She recalled, "I remember grown men crying, and I remember being scared about it and asking my mother why people were crying, and my mother said those were tears of happiness and that was the first time that was explained to me, but that was the kind of victory it was. I remember that vividly."[37] Ed's electoral victory had a profound impact on his family. Lucille remembered that on the weekends her father would sit in the living room, play the guitar and sing, and her mother would join him. She recalled, "All that disappeared when he got elected to office. We had lost some of our identity as individuals, and [I] became known as Roybal's daughter. That had a tremendous impact on our lives because everything was attributed not to our ability or our intellect or our own talents, but it was always dismissed in many ways as well, you know, well, that's Roybal's daughter. So, that was the downside, but what it did was I think made each of us more determined to prove ourselves. We worked harder and [fought] harder for our successes."

Ed's children also experienced a world far beyond Boyle Heights. They went places their contemporaries and friends would not dream of going. Lucille commented that when living in the barrio "there are always imaginary boundaries." However, she also experienced what any Mexican faced once leaving the confines of the barrio when attending places like the Hollywood Bowl and the Greek Theatre: "I remember we were sitting there with my parents one time and the people in the back of us were making fun of us, like 'Hey Pancho, I'm in the Hollywood Bowl.'"[38] Despite these and other unpleasant experiences their father always cautioned against the temptation to react in a negative way toward others. Lillian Roybal Rose recalled, "One of the things our father taught us was not to be vindictive. He did not get even with people. There are a lot of politicians who do, but my father never did. He always took the high road."[39]

Both of Ed's daughters felt that their mother, Lucille, was central to his success and that without her, he would not have been as successful politically. She held the family together, supported him, and ran the campaign headquarters.

The Roybal victory was also one for a Latino-Jewish progressive coalition. African Americans at this time were an integral part, but they were not major players. Ed Roybal's victory was made possible by reworking his strategy that had failed in 1947 but also capitalizing on his experience growing up in multiethnic Boyle Heights.

Ed Roybal was dedicated to serving the Asian American community. Lillian Roybal Rose affirmed, "My dad took a primary role in trying to get legislation to provide reparations for Japanese Americans who had been interned in the United States during World War II."[40] Ed Roybal Jr. recalled, "When my parents grew up in Boyle Heights at Roosevelt High School, there was a Japanese Garden. There were Japanese students in school. My mother talked about friends that were Japanese but weren't there anymore. I remember many times just as a kid my father taking me to community events in Little Tokyo."[41] Ed's daughter Lucille added, "The people of Chinatown loved my dad" too.

Roybal's Victory Reverberates

The symbolism of Edward R. Roybal's political leadership was not lost on perceptive politicians. Political scientist Jaime Regalado would say later, "What I think was also unique about Roybal's emergence is that he experienced a lot of discrimination that Latinos faced in East Los Angeles at the hands of the Los Angeles police Department (LAPD) and [in] other portions of the Southwest. And so his candidacy was of a person who had been tinged as a victim of racism, he and his family. He was very, very socially aware and socially conscious of what victimization meant because he had experienced it personally. The hard reality was that Mexican GIs came back to a society that was still as racist as ever and perhaps even more so because of the Cold War. Not only racism, but if you were also progressive, if you also started to demand a certain form of rights you were labeled…as a communist or a socialist politically."[42]

The *Daily News* said Roybal's victory was "the beginning of a valuable bridge building process that would at last incorporate the Mexican American community." Congressman Chet Holifield was so impressed by the importance of Roybal's election that he placed a statement titled "Election of Roybal—Democracy at Work" in the *Congressional Record* and passed out copies to his constituents in East Los Angeles.[43] The 1949 council race was one of those rare moments in U.S. politics when a social movement fundamentally transforms the balance of power through the massive infusion of new votes. The old voting pattern was realigned. "Roybal's victory proved the political maxims that votes count, coalitions matter, and organization make a difference," wrote scholar Kenneth C. Burt.[44]

The *Militant*, the newspaper of the Los Angeles Local of the Socialist Workers Party noted, "The road for Roybal, if he is to keep faith with the movement which is bigger than he and which placed him in office, is to conduct an aggressive, militant struggle against discrimination and poverty, and at the same time to give leadership in the struggle for independent political action of labor and minority groups toward the building of a labor party."[45]

The *Daily News* published an evocative editorial on the Roybal victory, summing up with, "Yes, something new has been added to Los Angeles civic life. The municipal household has a brighter, more up-to-date look. And the local precedents' shattering by Roybal's election indicate democracy is stepping steadily forward on the homefront—that the distance of caste and culture is shrinking to fight the shrunken world."[46]

Even though Ed Roybal wasn't to be sworn into office until July 1st, he got an early start by attending a police conference on delinquency among Mexican American youth in the 9th District. The meeting was held at the Hollenbeck station in the heart of the Eastside. Assistant Police Chief Joe Reed chaired the meeting. The fifteen persons present included representatives of the CSO. Also attending was Msgr. Thomas J. O'Dwyer of the Catholic Social Bureau, Rev. Joe Hill of the Catholic Youth Organization, special officers from the police juvenile gang division, and CYO and CSO social workers who worked with gangs.

There were several tense moments during the meeting. Roybal called for intensive investigation of alleged police brutality, reasoning that it worsened the attitudes of young people. The police in turn claimed that so-called police brutality was simply a matter of forcibly making an arrest when the suspect resists. Roybal noted his objection to the practice, widespread on the Eastside, of stopping cars and "frisking" drivers and passengers. He complained of failure by police to enter a playground to cooperate with social workers in charge. It was decided that police should work more closely with social agencies and churches in identifying gangs for preventive work, that the department should install Spanish-speaking officers to hear complaints, and that police officers working in the area would be trained in the culture and psychology of the community. Despite these positive moves, however, the issue of police misconduct was one that would not go away.

Roybal's First Term as Los Angeles City Councilman

When Edward R. Roybal was sworn into office in June 1949, he was the only person of color on the council and the only one with a progressive outlook. He was sworn in by City Clerk Walter C. Peterson. On that first day, Roybal had a speech in his pocket already prepared when the president of the city council, Harold A. Henry, introduced him. Roybal was introduced as "the Mexican-speaking city councilman representing the Mexican people of his district." At that point, Roybal laid aside what he called "the nice speech" and "gave them a little lesson in history, going back to the fact that the City of Los Angeles as well as other cities throughout the country had Mexicans before people came in the Mayflower. That we were here first before they came here. They didn't like it, but it's true."[47]

However, Roybal was also conciliatory. In his speech, he said that his job was to "represent all the people in my district," an area that was "one of the most cosmopolitan in our city."[48] He stated that he would seek an improved health center, better lighting, and playgrounds for his district. He said he would ask for the abolition of the police Board of Rights in favor of a citizens' committee to try officers accused of misconduct.

The Los Angeles City Council for 1949–1951 was made up of Leland S. Warburton (1st District), Lloyd G. Davies (2nd), J. Win Austin (3rd), Harold A. Henry (4th), George P. Cronk (5th), L. E. Timberlake (6th), Don A. Allen (7th), Kenneth Hahn (8th), Edward R. Roybal (9th), G. Vernon Bennett (10th), Harold Harby[49] (11th), Edward J. Davenport (12th), Ernest E. Debs (13th), John C. Holland (14th), and George H. Moore (15th). At the helm of the city was Mayor Fletcher Bowron. Although his agenda was different from that of other council members, Roybal nevertheless tried to reach out and work with his colleagues on city council. As expected, Council President Harold Henry named Ed Roybal chairperson of the Public Health and Welfare Committee and as a member of the Recreation and Parks Committee. In both assignments he succeeded Kenneth Hahn of the 8th District.

On his tenure as councilman, Roybal commented, "I had a long career in the council. I was there thirteen years. I was the chairman of the Health Committee. I also had other subcommittees, Police and Fire, and committees that I picked myself because of certain things I wanted to do with the police department. I think the other was Parks and Recreation. I wanted to build pools. I wanted to build better playgrounds, improve parks and recreation, and put young men and women to work in CCC camps. I got better police stations that we built. Everything that we did had a reason for it, or a motive behind it."[50]

Roybal's relationship with the media was cordial, but at times frosty. His ethnicity and liberalism was often the subject of scrutiny. Regarding the media, Roybal commented, "Well, I tried to be cooperative but they were not very cooperative with me. Let us just say I was not one of their favorites.... So the relationship was not as it should have been but it wasn't the worst either."[51]

Despite the political constraints—he often didn't have enough council votes to carry a majority—the press in the Mexican and Black communities supported Roybal's issues, but the larger newspapers like the *Los Angeles Times* were more often than not lukewarm. Of course, no media outlet would or could cover every single proposed bill or law sponsored or voted on by Ed Roybal in his 1949–1962 tenure on Los Angeles City Council.

Roybal faced a host of adversities when he was elected. Nevertheless, he remained committed to improving quality of life for the residents of the 9th District. Besides pushing to end housing discrimination and police brutality (which was not even recognized officially), Roybal established a civilian police review, and he supported rent control, as well as improvements to streets, health services, parks, and recreation facilities. He took a courageous but unpopular stand against a communist registration ordinance.

In addition to his role in the city council, Roybal continued to work with Mexican and Latino organizations to expand political empowerment. On July 1949, he was selected to head the organization committee at the first convention of the Latin American Civic and Political Organization. The convention at the Biltmore Hotel in Los Angeles had as its objective to establish a large umbrella organization that would represent all Latin American clubs. Around 300,000 convention delegates attended. Other officers of the organization committee included Henry Nava, vice president, and Edward Maldonado, second vice president.

An Activist Approach

Elected officials are often defined by the issues they identify on the campaign trail and sometimes by the nature of the political and social conditions in their base. Lucille Roybal-Allard commented on her dad's political agenda in the Los Angeles City Council: "I think my dad's agenda in general terms was to improve the quality of life for the people in the 9th District. That was his political agenda and any other pressing issues at that time. Those are the issues that dictated what his focus was at that time. One of the first things Dad did was to provide basic city services: pave streets, put up stop signs, and street ights. The [9th] District had been totally neglected by the city councilmen before him. My dad created an infrastructure that didn't exist before."[52]

From the beginning, Roybal displayed an activist hands-on approach to issues of concern in his district. During late August 1949, the Los Angeles Board of Supervisors ordered the condemnation of property adjoining the juvenile hall, 1369 Henry Street (the area north of Zonal Avenue, between Mission Road and San Pablo Street, in Lincoln Heights). The land was acquired by the county for $3,500,000 for improvement and enlargement of the juvenile hall site. Some 150 families lived in the vicinity and faced eviction. Under Roybal's leadership, the residents met and decided to take immediate legal action. They also agreed that as a last alternative they would ask for more money for the families being evicted. Roybal indicated that an alternative site on Brooklyn Avenue (now César Chávez Avenue) would be preferable for the new juvenile hall and would cause hardship to nobody. On the day of the decision, Roybal led a delegation of affected families at a protest meeting before the Board of Supervisors.[53] The protest ultimately failed; the proposed new site was not accepted. Still, Roybal had tasted political risk and had chosen to continue on.

Roybal's next risk-taking action was to propose to city council an ordinance for fair employment. In August 1949, he made a motion that the city attorney be instructed to draft the measure. He sponsored the measure and stated that its supporters were not "communists or left-wingers" and that it was being made only after careful study of the problem. The measure affected employers of five or more workers, city agencies, employment agencies, and labor organizations, as well as freelance employers doing work under city contract.[54] The *Los Angeles Times* wrote, "The citizen may be curious to know why such an ordinance is being proposed in spite of defeats of similar measures. The answer is that the ordinance is part of a nationwide movement, with the utmost influence being exerted by pressure groups. The drive was not initiated by Communists, but the Communists aware that it contains the seeds of turbulence, are busily pushing it."[55]

The Los Angeles City Council rejected the proposal for fair employment on September 27, 1949, after a continuous six-hour session attended by some 600 people. Voting for the measure were Ed Roybal, Don A. Allen, G. Vernon Bennett, Kenneth Hahn, Harold Harby, and George H. Moore. Voting against the measure were J. Win Austin, George P. Gronk, Ed J. Davenport, Lloyd G. Davies, John C. Holland, L. E. Timberlake, Lee S. Warburton, and Harold A. Henry,[56] the council president. Councilman Ernest E. Debs was absent due to hospitalization for a throat operation but sent word that he would have voted for the measure had he been present. Eight affirmative votes were necessary to keep the measure alive.

The defeat of the measure was felt to have ended, for the present, the efforts of the Council for Equality in Employment to establish a fair-employment bill. A similar proposed state law had been defeated by voters two years before. Ed Roybal, who had led the floor fight for the measure, argued that even opponents of the measure had to admit that discrimination existed in Los Angeles. Speaking in support of the measure, Judge Isaac Pacht, chairman of the Council for Equality in Employment, stated that discrimination in employment was "un-American and immoral, and contrary to fair play and democracy."[57] Opponents of the measure repeatedly charged that the measure was inspired by communists. Their official spokesman was Frank P. Doherty, attorney and former president of the Los Angeles Chamber of Commerce. The African American newspaper the *California Eagle* wrote of the tumultuous council session, "Proponents of the bill presented charts, facts and figures on the workability of the measure in other American cities, while the opponents made an emotional pitch on racial, religious and color lines. The *California Eagle* was charged with having originated the FEP program, and it was further charged that the whole idea had originated in Moscow in 1920. The ugly term n----r and the idea of Los Angeles being a 'white Christian community,' was the strongest argument advanced by the foes of the measure."[58]

Another measure Ed favored was an ordinance that would require all hotels and apartments of three stories or more to enclose all vertical openings (staircases, light walls, etc.) as a fire prevention measure. The council defeated it by an 8–4 ballot during mid-September 1949. Roybal argued that the matter of money should be entirely disregarded and consideration should be given to the number of lives saved, but to no avail.

During a September 1949 council debate on a proposal to rezone a San Fernando Valley tract from suburban to single family residence category, Roybal revealed to the city council that he had once been rejected as a prospective homeowner because of his ethnic background. He had gone to a real estate firm to buy a home, exercising his benefits as an ex-serviceman under the GI Bill of Rights. According to Lucille Roybal-Allard, her dad had passed the required credit rating, apparently because the surname of Roybal was not commonly known as a Spanish surname. She recalled, "He shows up with my mother, and I think we were with him to look at houses, and they saw my dad; they said, 'Gee, we're sorry, we made a mistake,' and they tried to back out. And then my dad handed them his card, [showing] that he was a city councilman, and they went, 'Oh, we're sorry, you know, you're different.' And my dad said, 'I'm not different.' I remember picketing the real estate office [afterward]."[59] Ed Roybal recalled that when he was asked if he was a Mexican, he replied that he was "an American of Mexican descent."[60] Roybal commented, "When I said I was, the man said, 'Sorry, we can't sell to Mexicans, but if you say you are of Spanish or Italian descent we will sell you a house."[61] He went on to state that a recent survey showed only six developers in the county did not discriminate against minorities and that eleven would sell if the prospective purchaser claimed Spanish descent.

The 9th District began to receive some of the first fruits of Ed Roybal's labors in November 1949. This included long overdue surfacing and other major street repairs on more than twenty streets in East Los Angeles.[62] During the same month the long-awaited Bunker Hill Recreation Center broke ground. The building would cost $123,646 and would occupy a near-acre-sized lot at Second and Hope Streets. At the groundbreaking ceremony, Ed Roybal, the councilman for Bunker Hill, was accompanied by George Hjelt, general manager of the city's Recreation and Parks Department. Roybal explained that the center would combine playground facilities for children and gathering space for senior citizens.[63] Through the efforts of Ed Roybal, the City of Los Angeles took over the $250,000 Lou Costello Jr. Foundation for $97,500 plus $5,000 in back taxes. The recreation center located on East Olympic Boulevard in Boyle Heights had been established by comedians Lou Costello and Bud Abbott the previous year. These three community improvements were some of the first of hundreds to come under Ed Roybal's efforts, first as a councilman and later as U.S. Congressman.

During late November 1949, Ed Roybal gave a candid talk about the CSO at a community meeting at the Japanese Institute in West Los Angeles. He commented that CSO had been a vital experiment in grassroots democracy. He stated that the organization had been effective in the area of elections and that it had been able to increase the number of deputy registrars of voters from two to sixty-three in Boyle Heights, resulting in a voter turnout increase from 29 percent of eligible voters to 87 percent in the last municipal election. An additional CSO project was the diphtheria immunization program for preschool and school children, in conjunction with the Health Department, which also conducted x-ray tests for tuberculosis.

Ed Roybal was consistent in fighting racism, both within and outside the city council. During meetings of the CSO in early 1950, he spoke out against local White supremacists who denied home rental to Mexican, Negro, and Nisei GIs. He cited the heroism of Negro units of the 25th Division, the Spanish surnames on the weekly Korean War casualty lists, and the heroism of Hideo Hashimoto (a Japanese American), saying, "How ironical. We send billions of dollars and tens of thousands of men across the seas to protect the spread of communism and at the same time allow destructive forces among us to subject these men to the humiliation and insult of being rejected when purchasing homes because of their names or complexion differ from those other applicants." He encouraged all GIs who had been "Jim Crowed" to report to the offices of the CSO, at 2307 ½ East First Street. He said that the Community Service Organization, the American Civil Liberties Union, and the National Association for the Advancement of Colored People were anxious to tackle any complaints.

In late March 1950, Ed Roybal was named treasurer of the nonprofit Community Medical Center, located at 5503 South Broadway. The center, founded in 1946, had served more than 9,000 patients to date at its various clinics. The fees averaged three dollars per visit. Roybal announced to the press that he and the Community Medical Foundation sponsors would launch a $50,000 campaign on April 1. He indicated that the funds would be used to provide free and partial-pay treatment for patients of the interracial clinic, expand the center's present facilities, and install a low-cost dental clinic and laboratory. Roybal stated, "There are hundreds of men and women in Los Angeles who cannot afford dental or medical care and it is for these medically starved people that we are planning."[64]

On January 10, 1950, the Los Angeles City Council heard an address in Spanish for the first time in seventy years when Councilman Roybal officially welcomed and talked to an elementary school class from the Chavez Ravine area. Afterwards, the Association of American Municipalities asked Roybal to serve as interpreter for visiting Mexican and Latin American officials at an international convention of mayors.[65]

As chairman of the city council's Public Health and Welfare Committee, Roybal moved to speed up a city receiving hospital in the Eastside in January 1950 with the idea to secure ambulance and emergency service for local residents sooner than originally planned.[66]

By mid-year, in July 1950, the city council held hearings on lifting rent ceilings in Los Angeles. This was leftover legislation from World War II to protect against price gauging during housing shortages. For low-income renters, this was a way to get decent housing at a decent price. The U.S. Congress had extended controls until December 31, 1950. Lifting controls was not subject to Governor Earl Warren's discretion under the federal act. A city survey earlier in the year indicated that Los Angeles only had a 2.6 percent rental housing vacancy rate; therefore, according to proponents of the ordinance, the city no longer suffered a shortage to justify continued rent control.

Rent control was controversial and an emotional issue, one with passionate advocates on both sides. The decontrol measure would especially affect the hard-pressed Mexican and African American populations, which had very low home-ownership levels. However, landlords used their political muscle and had their way. At a final showdown, the majority in attendance at the Los Angeles City Council were landlords and their representatives, who cheered wildly when the body voted to end rent control. The final vote was 10–4. The four council members voting against rent decontrol were Roybal, Kenneth Hahn, G. Vernon Bennett, and George Moore.

Another incendiary issue came up, this time in September of the same year. Three communist registration ordinances were up for a vote. These "loyalty oaths" required a person to say that he or she was not a communist. If the person in question refused for whatever reason to sign the oath, that action was taken to mean that he or she was not loyal. Los Angeles—based on nothing but rumor and innuendo—was presumed to be a hotbed of communist sympathizing, disloyal people. Or as council member Edward J. Davenport said, "Los Angeles is the most red-hot city in the United States outside of New York City."[67]

Roybal attempted to withhold his vote, a parliamentary procedure that would have put off consideration of the ordinance to the next council meeting. Roybal had evidently contemplated his stand on this issue very deeply. In an impassioned speech to the council he stated, "Democracy means everything to me. Seven sons of my aunt, Mrs. Anastasia Barela, were killed fighting to preserve democracy in the last war. My two brothers and I also fought for the same cause, and only two of us survived. My brother Robert of the Navy, was killed, and Benjamin and I returned. We contributed to the preservation of democracy and I'm going to continue to fight for it. I don't believe we should give up democracy now; we should fight for more of it. I'm thinking too, of the GIs of minority groups who today protest the fact they are permitted to have all the space between the 38th parallel and Pusan in which to die and yet at home can find no place in which to live because of discrimination against them on the part of private builders…I realize, of course, that what I do here today will count for very little since the great preponderance of opinion in this body differs from mine and the ordinance before us will be passed. I do not propose to shrink from the responsibility of my decision."[68] Without room to put it off any longer, the measure went to a vote. It passed 13–1.

One councilman, Lloyd G. Davies, was absent because of illness. The sole dissenting vote came from Councilman Roybal. Those speaking in favor of the legislation included State Senator Jack B. Tenney; David Levitt, representing the Screen Actor's Guild; Norman Jacoby, co-publisher of antisubversive pamphlets; J. Henry Orme of the American Defense League; Ruth Singer of Gold Star Mothers; and Rola J. Weiser, representing the Los Angeles County Republicans Club.

"The doctrine explicit in this ordinance carried to its logical conclusion," Roybal said, "places every citizen and every organization whose word or act resembles at any time those of the communists, at the mercy of any biased crackpot who may decide to report the matter to the police department as subversive."[69] Taking that stand was like "signing his own death warrant—politically," as he admitted to a *Herald Express* reporter.[70]

When Roybal left the council chambers following the vote, he was on the verge of tears, according to some people present. He was booed by the overflow crowd of 500 people who had jammed the chambers to pressure the outcome and witness the vote count.

Roybal was now facing the consequences of his own creed. He was basing his political decisions on his deeply felt faith: "You do things because they're right, not because they are politically expedient." This would become Roybal's dictum for the rest of his political career. At the city council chamber, Lillian Roybal-Rose recalled, "We were walking, and people [were] screaming at my dad, 'Go back where you came from, dirty Mexican!' and stuff like that, and my father had his hands on our shoulders. My father just leaned over and said, 'You look straight ahead and you keep walking and you don't look at anybody. You just keep walking.' And I remember they spit on us and I had spit running down my face and I was too scared to wipe it off my face."[71]

Ed's decision to fight the communist registration law was a courageous act. Lillian also recalled, "I remember Dad sitting down [saying] that he just wanted us to know that we were going to be hearing some terrible things about him. That he wasn't un-American, that he wasn't a traitor,and he wanted us to understand what he was fighting for and so he explained it to us and we understood the best we could." She remembered being chased home and kids shouting, "Your father is a communist! Your father is a communist!"[72]

Roybal was earning increased respect and support in the district. During early November 1950, he was honored with a testimonial dinner at the popular Los Angeles Breakfast Club in recognition of his courage and leadership. It was attended by hundreds of people, including leaders from labor and the religious, political, and entertainment worlds. Brief addresses were given by Helen Gahagan Douglas, writer Carey McWilliams, Msgr. Thomas J. O'Dwyer, Ernest Debs, Loren Miller, Judge Isaac Pacht, and Leslie Claypool.[73] Helen Gahagan Douglas described Edward R. Roybal as "a man of principles, a man of high morals." The dinner was sponsored by the Community Service Organization. Ed Roybal's busy, energetic, and productive first term was setting the agenda and pointing toward a promising political career. There was much, much more to be done.

Chapter 5

Fighting the Good Fight
(1952–1960)

THE STRUGGLE FOR MEXICAN AMERICAN POLITICAL EMPOWERMENT IN the 1950s was shaped by sociopolitical events playing out in the international arena. The culture of the new decade was strongly influenced by the Cold War—the ideological, economic, and strategic military rivalry between the United States and the Soviet Union.

Powerful forces for both nationalism and social justice were erupting throughout the Third World, as anticolonial movements arose to oppose the decaying British, French, and Portuguese empires. Most countries took sides with one group or another; however, a few adopted nonalignment policies, which became a challenge to hegemony. Both camps intervened when their perceived spheres of influence were in jeopardy. The United States intervened in Iran, Guatemala, Vietnam, and Cuba. The Soviet Union, in turn, intervened in Hungary and Czechoslovakia. In the United States, people of color witnessed with wonder and hope the unraveling of centuries-old empires. They saw people like themselves taking power and beginning to determine their own destiny as they tackled the legacies of colonialism, neocolonialism and their byproducts: racism, illiteracy, ignorance, uncontrolled disease, and unproductive approaches to increasing poverty.

Communism and Color

However, the modern notion of racial/ethnic minorities had not yet been born. That would not happen until the Civil Rights Act of 1965.

People groups were mainly differentiated as Black, White, and Yellow. The Brown people were invented (that is, recognized as a distinct group) later. Their struggle for social justice, equality, and inclusion was constrained by the anticommunist crusade; still, political empowerment after World War II included the exercise of the right to vote and to have some of their own run for political office, the end of gerrymandering, nondiscrimination in employment and housing, and integrated schools. The country enjoyed an unparalleled material prosperity, a prosperity sowed under Presidents Roosevelt and Truman. The financial and economic power of the United States after World War II in relation to the rest of the world was impressive.[1]

However, the appearance of equality of opportunity for access to the American dream was deceptive. In 1954, the U.S. Supreme Court case of *Brown v. Board of Education* finished what *Mendez v. Westminster* had begun in 1947. The court had set a precedent in *Mendez* to diminish de jure segregation; *Brown* made de facto segregation unconstitutional. The decision launched a national civil rights movement. Implementation of integration would prove difficult and divisive and take decades. Meanwhile, de facto segregation continued as a reality throughout the nation for a long time to come.

In 1952, the McCarran-Walter Act was passed over President Truman's veto. Among its provisions was a piece stating that a naturalized citizen's legal status could be revoked and he or she could be deported for political reasons. Senator Pat McCarran of Nevada had argued that the "national origin formula" had to stay in the legislation in order to prevent "in the course of a generation or so" changing the nation's "ethnic and cultural composition."[2] Following this new law, Operation Wetback, a military style campaign, resulted in the deportation of more than one million Mexican nationals and Mexican Americans between 1953 and 1955.

Both Operation Wetback and the McCarran-Walter Act were bitter reminders to Mexicans of the Great Repatriation, the expulsion of the early 1930s. Mexicans born in the United States adopted the identifier *Mexican*

American about this time, mainly to distinguish themselves as distinct from Mexicans. The term *Mexican* was pejorative and usually was taken to mean lower-class, marginalized people. Regardless of their citizenship, this group was vulnerable and was, in the eyes of the law, expendable.

A resurgent Republican Party, after having been out of leadership since 1933, by the late 1940s had begun accusing President Truman of being soft on communism. Prodded by this criticism, Truman established the Federal Employer Loyalty program in March 1947.[3] Later that same year, the House Un-American Activities Committee (HUAC) garnered headlines by beginning an investigation of communist influence in the Hollywood film industry. Hundreds of actors, screenwriters, and others were blacklisted or "gray listed," the latter an ambiguous list of performers deemed suspect and thereby also unemployable.[4]

During 1950, Senator Joseph McCarthy, a Republican from Wisconsin, was looking for a winning issue to get re-elected in 1952. He began to make brazen charges that communists were starting to dominate the federal government and that the Democratic Party, for being soft on communism, was guilty of "twenty years of treason." President Truman, perhaps in part reacting to this criticism, enacted a "containment" policy, leading the anticommunism crusade into the Korean War (1950–1953).

As always, Mexican Americans volunteered and were drafted by the thousands and displayed a high level of heroism under combat. Eight Mexican Americans won the Congressional Medal of Honor, many of them posthumously.[5] Many others were recipients of other medals of valor.

The Status of the Mexican Community

The small and growing Mexican communities—located mainly in the southwestern states, the West Coast and in the Midwest—underwent tremendous changes during the 1950s. People moved from the rural areas to cities. By the end of the decade, 80 percent of the Mexican population was in urban centers.[6] The Mexican population grew to nearly 2.6 million people by 1950 (a jump from nearly 1.9 million in 1940 and

1.4 million in 1930). Still, the official count did not include hundreds of thousands of undocumented immigrants and braceros, who were classified as "temporary workers."

The Mexico-born population declined by 1950. Where in 1930, Mexicans born in Mexico accounted for 44 percent of the total Mexican ancestry population in the United States, in 1940, it was down to 20 percent, and by 1950, it was only 17 percent. Mexicans of both U.S. and Mexican origin dispersed around the country during these three decades (mostly to the Mid-North, Illinois and Michigan). In 1930, only 8 percent of people with Mexican ancestry lived outside the Southwest; in 1940, the number rose to 10 percent, and in 1950, 12 percent did so.[7]

Correspondingly, U.S. agribusiness became increasingly dependent on braceros and other Mexican laborers in the 1950s, specifically due to Public Law 78, which was renewed in 1951. This kind of labor intensive and increasingly mechanized agriculture was only sustainable because of imported Mexican labor. In 1942, the number of braceros entering the United States was 4,203. It increased more than twelve times in 1943 to 52,098. During the war years, the numbers remained high, fluctuated, and then increased significantly again in 1949 to 107,000 and in 1950 up to 192,000. The numbers more than doubled by 1951, to nearly 438,000. In seventeen years, from 1942 to 1959, the number of braceros increased 104 times.[8]

During the 1950s, there was a pronounced differentiation among the Mexican and Mexican American populations. As mentioned before, Mexican nationals were designated as "Mexican," and U.S.-born Mexican-ancestry people were called "Mexican Americans." Some people of Mexican ancestry, especially in New Mexico, referred to themselves as "Hispanos" or "Hispanic." Other peoples with origins in Latin America were called "Latin Americans" or "Latins "during this period. By the 1960s, they were called "Spanish-speaking," sometimes "Spanish-surnamed," and then "Mexican Americans."

Although a middle class was emerging, people of Mexican ancestry in the United States continued to be consigned to extreme poverty, de facto housing and school segregation, minimum educational levels, poor health conditions, and political marginalization. Mexicans were not part of the national consciousness or part of the national political debate. School textbooks reduced Mexican American history to a few paragraphs. Mexican Americans were termed "Spanish" and thus robbed them of their Native American roots. They were not acknowledged as building agriculture, cattle raising, and mining in the Southwest. School textbooks, popular literature, and film continued to portray Mexicans as lazy, backward, and culturally deprived, unable to control their violence and sexuality. Mexican Americans did not inspire any great debates or social crusades among liberals who were otherwise distraught by poverty, racism, and Black exploitation.[9] Mexican ancestry people were, in the words of later commentators, an "invisible minority."

Several venues of political empowerment were available to Mexican Americans despite the array of socioeconomic conditions that affected their lives. One form of political empowerment was the founding of national organizations, beginning with the Alianza Hispano-Americana (AHA) in 1894 in Arizona; the League of United Latin American Citizens (LULAC) in 1929 in Corpus Christi, Texas; and the American GI Forum in 1949 in Texas. They were all active in the struggle for civil rights, education, segregation, and social justice. However, no regional leadership had emerged. The evolution from Mexico-born to U.S.-born leadership shifted concerns from one generation to the next. English became the language of reform, creating a dilemma of identity; citizenship and constitutional rights replaced the notion of Mexicanness and worker's rights.[10] Over time and especially during the 1950s, some of the Mexican community's leaders became assimilationist, conformist, and exclusionary.

Another road to political empowerment for Mexicans was as active members in labor unions. Workers of Mexican ancestry joined unions in large numbers. Unions appeared to be the one institution that offered the best protection of their livelihood. This was especially vital after the Great Repatriation of the early 1930s. However, unions were dealt a setback by the Taft-Hartley Act in 1947. By the 1950s, unions had declined. For example, union membership was 13 percent in 1930, 14 percent in 1935, 27 percent in 1940, and 35 percent in 1945, but stood at 30 percent in 1950 and would drop after that.[11]

Most Mexican and Mexican American leaders that emerged in the postwar period were former servicemen, college educated, native born, middle-class, and possessed a marked assimilationist bent. Moreover, the Catholic Church, the religious institution of most Mexicans, promoted both conformity and intolerance (e.g., Bishop Sheen) against a godless communism. Most soldiers or fervent civilian supporters from the World War II and Korean War mobilizations acquired a national identity and a fierce national loyalty. For many of them, the military had provided an opportunity to be "American," while the wars had given them an arena in which to develop skills, organization, and discipline and become task-oriented team players and enhance their general capacity. Military service also socialized them to the federal government's foreign policy and anticommunist Cold War, but their relationship to local government was another story.[12]

Assimilationism and conformism were facilitated by service in the armed forces. Likewise, the media (especially the phenomenon of television) promoted becoming monolingual in English. As the media created an insatiable appetite for consumer goods, urban employment promoted the ideals of U.S. capitalism. The U.S.-Mexico border symbolized to many the First World versus the Third World. Schools and schooling played a vital part in the assimilation process as well. Ignacio M. Garcia pointed out: "The contrast between their homes and schools worked to create a duality of thought and action among Mexican American students...Many could not deal with these contradictions and lost the necessary desire to overcome linguistic difficulties, bad schooling, and poverty. They subsequently dropped out of school. Others, however, learned to compartmentalize their lives. They were Mexicans at home and Americans in the school."[13] For some Mexicans, the duality of cultural worlds resulted in a sense of inferiority or shame, or even worse, a sense of self-hatred. Some would take an overdose of assimilation for an entire lifetime. All these factors shifted the Mexican American leadership away from the traditional working-class venues of empowerment: mutual aid societies, unions, and other self-help entities.

Political empowerment for the Mexican people also meant electing political leaders who were reformers. The emerging generation of Mexican American political leaders was cognizant of the socioeconomic and political climate that predominated and aware of the limitations imposed. As native-born Americans, they were also interested in full access to American society's benefits from formal legal procedures, the prospect of an open society, and economic stability. These reformers shifted some of the blame for barrio conditions to discrimination, segregation, and Anglo American antipathy.[14] They challenged the long-held belief that Mexicans were inferior by noting their patriotism. Specifically, they noted the high level of Mexican American participation in World War I, World War II, and the Korean War, their roles in the building of the nation, and as productive individuals. Finally, these political leaders amplified the voices of organizational leaders clamoring for justice and equality from the grassroots.[15]

The Beginning of Mexican American National Political Representation

The most important Mexican American politicians in the postwar era were Henry B. Gonzalez[16] of Texas; Joseph Montoya[17] and Dennis Chavez[18] of New Mexico; and Edward R. Roybal of California. These four leaders were the pioneers of Mexican American electoral politics in the twentieth century. Their longevity in elected office reflected their ability to understand their constituents' needs and aspirations and to respond to those social concerns. Montoya and Chavez had an advantage in that Mexicans remained the majority population well into the twentieth century in New Mexico. In turn, Gonzalez (in Texas) and Roybal (in California) had the challenge of organizing and galvanizing a Mexican population that was truly a minority in numbers and in political power. All began their political careers at the local level and eventually became U.S. congressmen or

U.S. senators. Along the way, they helped to educate the nation on the plight of the Mexican community and its long historical presence, one that preceded the United States. They all ran grassroots campaigns and remained close to the pulse of their respective communities.

They led their communities into the end of the twentieth century, at which time new era of mass media politics developed and a new type of elected official was born. This era was based more on sound bites, demagoguery, and the largesse of special interests.

Mexican American political empowerment through elected representation was made difficult in California because of the declining number of Mexican Americans in the state. In part, the Great Repatriation of the 1930s had begun a depopulation that was evident in the 1950s. Edward Roybal's election to the Los Angeles City Council represented a turning point in California Mexican American electoral politics. Roybal's multiethnic coalition succeeded in winning reelection bids in 1951, 1953, 1957, and 1961. He never received less than 67 percent of the vote. Although voter turnouts from the Eastside declined dramatically between 1949 and 1961, in general, Roybal's proportion of support continued to increase after receiving challenges twice, in 1951 and 1961. Even after redistricting in 1956, which expanded the 9th District into South Central-Avalon region (with an 85 percent African American population), he ran unchallenged in the election the following year.

Roybal's 1951 bid for re-election began with a large banquet at the San Kwo Low Restaurant on February 19, 1951, sponsored by the Citizens Committee to Re-Elect Roybal.[19] Its members' ethnic diversity was impressive: Mexican, Japanese, Chinese, Jewish, European Americans, and other ethnicities. It included a wide range of professions and fields: political activists, business, professional organizations, artists, labor unions, and average community citizens. William (Bill) Phillips chaired the event, and the master of ceremonies was Dr. E. I. Robinson, Southern California chair of the National Association for the Advancement of Colored People (NAACP). A snappy song, entitled "Eddie Roybal, Keep It Up," sung to the tune of "Yankee Doodle Dandy" was written by Eli Kovner, the editor and publisher of the *Eastside Sun*:[20]

> Roybal went to city hall, into the council chambers
> Met a sport named Davenport who cried, 'Unwelcome stranger.'
>
> Chorus: Eddie Roybal, keep it up, Eddie Roybal, DANDY!
> Eddie Roybal, keep it up, And with your votes be handy!
>
> Roybal went to city hall, into the council chambers:
> Voted no on decontrol—he knew high rental dangers.
> Chorus (repeat)
>
> Roybal went to city hall, and on that registration—
> Voted no because he knew it would enslave the nation.
> Chorus (repeat)
>
> Roybal fought for FEPC, for equal job improvement.
> A Trojan horse was there in force and sabotaged the movement.
> Chorus (repeat)
>
> Roybal saw his people's health was in a sad condition
> He slew a trillion TB germs and sent them to perdition!
> Chorus (repeat)
>
> The fight for better housing was Old Eddie's choicest hobby
> And that's why he's the sweetheart of the real estate's lobby.
> Chorus (repeat)
>
> Eddie came to old Boyle Heights riding on a trolley,
> Met with his constituents and had a time so jolly.
> Chorus (repeat)

Ed looked down from Bunker Hill, saw woes beyond description.
There was so much he had to do that he had a near conniption.
Chorus (repeat)

Send Eddie back to city hall, into the council chambers;
He'll fight for all his people's rights and keep them out of danger.

Not everyone was happy with Roybal. Richard A. Donovan documented one angry civic leader saying, "If Roybal runs on that unification
of minorities claptrap again, we'll hang him with it. We'll buy ourselves
a Negro, a Mexican, and a Japanese for a thousand bucks each, and
we'll run them all."[21] Despite this and political threats, Roybal had in
the end only one challenger, Irving Rael, a furniture store owner and the
Community Business Men Association's president.

True to the political climate, Rael's campaign tried impugning
Roybal's patriotism and hung a liberal label on him. Rael boasted that
he was for "100 percent Americanism and against any other kind of ism."[22]
His campaign literature red baited Roybal. Articles entitled "Catholics
Told of Red Menace" and "The Communist Press Praised Incumbent"
attempted to galvanize community residents prone to reactionary impulses
and fear.[23] Rael showed no desire to debate Roybal in a public forum. Fred
Ross telephoned and mailed letters inviting him to a CSO nonpartisan
civic forum, but Rael did not respond. The Eastside Democratic Club
invited Rael to debate Roybal as well, but Rael didn't show up. Roybal
went ahead with a speech to the 250-member audience, at the end of
which the executive board endorsed Roybal.[24]

Roybal acquired an impressive list of strong endorsements, including
the United AFL Voters League, the Greater Los Angeles CIO Council, the
Joint Executive Board of the Southern California Steelworkers, the Los
Angeles Amalgamated Clothing Workers of America, the Aeronautical
Industrial Lodge 727 of the International Association of Machinists, and

the International Brotherhood of Firemen and Oilers, Local 152.[25] The *Eastside Sun*, the *Daily News*, and the *New Japanese American News* gave him their endorsements. *La Opinion* was silent. Other endorsements came from the Women's Political Study Club, the Los Angeles Tenants Council, the Eastside Committee to Keep Rent Control, and the Booker T. Washington Unit.

Although he was in a nonpartisan race, Roybal garnered support from both Democratic and Republican parties, including the Eastside Democratic Club, the 44th Assembly District delegation to the Democratic County Committee, and the four state assemblymen whose districts covered portions of the 9th District (Augustus Hawkins, 62nd District; Edward Elliot, 44th District; William Munnel, 51st District; and William Rosenthal, 40th District). They sent letters of recommendation and expressed willingness to provide other support. He also received a letter from the Republican Committee to Re-Elect Roybal endorsing his re-election.

The Los Angeles and Police Protective League praised him with these words: "It has been generally stated that he has been the most pleasing surprise ever sent to the City Council, as he has devoted himself seriously and conscientiously to every task, and it is predicted that he will win this primary race handily but that he has a great political future ahead of him."[26]

Roybal and his re-election committee did an outstanding job in its fundraising, canvassing, getting endorsements, and getting the vote out. A politician's dream organization was in the making. However, the 1951 campaign lacked some of the strong grassroots visibility the campaign of 1949 had enjoyed due in part to the CSO's absence from electoral politics. The CSO had retired from electoral politics following Roybal's 1949 election[27] and thereafter concentrated on small-scale, neighborhood-level community service programs.

Roybal handily won the April 1951 re-election campaign with 70 percent of the total votes to Rael's 23 percent (5,840) of the total. The Eastside was his greatest base of support. Boyle Heights provided 60 percent of the votes (10,726), and 21 percent came from the Downtown area (3,744). The South Central and heterogeneous areas earned him 7 percent and 8 percent, respectively.

The 1951 election, with 25,557 votes cast, had a lower turnout than in 1949 when 30,533 votes were cast. The 1949 race was historic and set precedent, sparking the electors' attention to participate. But, as mentioned before, the difference in the 5,000 votes could be attributed also to the absence of CSO and its voter registration drives. Grassroots political education is more effective when it occurs over successive elections.[28] Still, Roybal's re-election in 1951 proved that his 1949 victory was no fluke and that he had come a long way as a political campaigner.

Dealing with Police Brutality and Harassment

In February 1952, during Roybal's second term, police brutality in the Los Angeles Police Department, a long-simmering issue, came to a head. Roybal told the city council that he had received complaints in the past three months and now had evidence for fifty cases of police brutality against citizens. He said it was "a problem not only in my [Eastside] district but prevalent throughout the city." The situation was spinning out of control, sowing "hatred of the police by youngsters" and putting some police officers at risk of attack when people decided to take matters into their own hands. "Certainly brutality by policemen generates hate and at least, loss of respect for officers."[29] Roybal wanted a meeting with Chief of Police William H. Parker with the "hope it will result in eliminating abuses committed by the police."

Two incidents had ignited the firestorm. One involved Tony Rios. He was chairman of the Community Service Organization, a member of the Democratic County Central Committee, and a leader in CIO labor councils. Rios charged that police officers had beaten and jailed him and Alfred Ulloa on public drunkenness charges. Both men claimed that they were beaten at the Hollenbeck police station, and that Councilman Roybal had intervened and advised them of their rights by phone. Rios and several prospective witnesses had been threatened, Rios alleged.

In the other incident, Dr. Arthur Sierra, a staff pediatrician at Indiana Emergency Hospital in the Belvedere community, near Boyle Heights, charged that a police officer had fired at him at close range as he sped on the Hollywood Freeway as he answered an emergency call.

During March 1952, the Los Angeles County grand jury voted to investigate the police brutality issue. Police Chief William H. Parker gained some public sympathy when he lashed out, saying that "these people who pretend to speak for American justice"—those who charge police brutality—"should practice a little of it themselves."[30] But Roybal was joined in criticizing police methods by Edward W. Mehren, who was chairperson of the County Conference on Community Relations; Milton Senn, chairperson of the Police Relations Committee; and Anthony Rios, chairperson of the CSO. For his part, Mayor Fletcher Bowron promised there would be a genuine investigation.

Both of Ed's daughters remembered that their father was the victim of constant police harassment and intimidation. Lillian Roybal Rose recalled, "The police in unmarked cars would be at the corner, and we were told as kids that if a policeman were to stop us, to talk to us, that we were to run as fast as we could for home. We used to have to talk in code to communicate about anything that was happening in the house. Every time my dad left the house, a police car would follow him as part of intimidation. They'd follow us to school." One night she recalled waking up in the middle of the night and her dad getting a phone call. The caller said that he had been a witness to an act of police brutality and wanted to meet with him. Her mother didn't like Ed going out to see the witness at that time of night and felt it didn't make any sense. Lucille remembered, "They gave him an address in some seedy part of town, and Dad was saying, 'This might be the break we've been waiting for.' The next thing I know is we're being wrapped up and they're taking us to grandma's house…My mother had decided to go with him. She wouldn't let him go alone. So, when they got to where the address was, my dad knocks on the door, and a scantily clad woman, probably a prostitute, opens the door and there's a man with a camera and the problem of course is they didn't think he'd take his wife. And it was a setup. So, from that moment, my father never left the house by himself."[31]

Lillian Roybal Rose remembered that two policemen who were opposed to the harassment of Roybal would moonlight and guard his house. They confided to Ed that people in the Los Angeles Police Department had it in for him, and if they ever caught him, they would set him up. Ed Roybal Jr. commented that a threat was made to his father and mother by phone. Lucille recalled that their house was broken into and ransacked several times when they lived on Cummings Street and also at Evergreen Avenue. Police cars would also cruise by Ed Roybal's house and bombard it with searchlights. According to Ed's children, the police harassment went on for some four to five years. The experience was unnerving to both Ed and Lucille Roybal, but perhaps even more so to their children.

Roybal's re-election bid to the Los Angeles City Council also coincided with an addition to the family. On June 4, 1951, the Roybals welcomed their third child, Edward R. Roybal Jr. He was born at the White Memorial Hospital in Boyle Heights. He would attend Our Lady of Talpa Elementary School until fourth grade and, thereafter, a Catholic military academy in West Los Angeles.

Councilman Roybal: The Los Angeles City Council Years

Roybal's 1951 re-election bid became a model for subsequent re-elections.[32] As happens for incumbents, some grassroots passion atrophies with each campaign, and some of the excitement from the previous campaign disappears. Roybal had no opponents in 1953 and 1957. Given that these two re-elections were foregone conclusions, his campaigns received less media attention than before. Public housing was the most important issue in the 1953 election.

The issue pitted Roybal against the *Los Angeles Times*. Roybal's constituents were vehemently opposed to discrimination and exclusionary policies. Incredibly, the *Los Angeles Times* sought to defeat elected officials supporting the city's housing program. Others had begun red baiting the issue as a sign of "creeping socialism." The newspaper, which never endorsed any of Roybal's re-election bids, in 1953 wrote disparagingly of the 9th District and described it as the home of "many so-called minority groups including a large segment of the Mexican colony, and settlements of Japanese, Chinese, and other strains." The newspaper grudgingly acknowledged Roybal's sincerity and dedication on behalf of his constituents.

Other newspapers made no recommendations for the city council: the *Los Angeles Sentinel*, the *Mirror*, and the *Examiner*. However, the *California Eagle* and the *Daily News* gave Roybal enthusiastic endorsements. Ironically, *La Opinion* did not even mention Roybal in its coverage of the election. Roybal was endorsed by the Greater Los Angeles Chapter of Americans for Democratic Action, The Greater Los Angeles CIO Council, and groups affiliated with the Democratic Party.

Despite the media's limited attention, Roybal was re-elected with a larger percentage than in 1951. He garnered 73 percent (10,228 votes) of the total 29,857 votes. Significantly, the total number of voters abstaining (through roll-off voting) was higher than in the previous elections. Approximately 27 percent (8,071) of the total votes were abstentions, 44 percent of them in South Central.

Then in September 1952, City Councilman Ed J. Davenport[33] made the shocking charge that Councilman Roybal had threatened him with a knife. Later, Davenport changed his tune a bit and said the charge was "more of a quip than [an] accusation...I never intended to make any such charge. As far as I am concerned, the incident is closed."[34] The alleged knife threat occurred at the climax of several tumultuous sessions during which the city council engaged in a prolonged controversy over a $110,000 public housing program that Davenport vehemently opposed. The California Legislative Conference demanded that Davenport apologize to Roybal. Davenport, in turn, charged that the conference was listed with the Department of Justice as a Communist Party front organization. Roybal said in response,

"This is an attempt to link me with a subversive organization and to further degrade the City Council. I am not a Communist, never have been one, and never intend to become one."[35] Roybal had prophetically told the *Eastside Sun* in September 1952, "There are those who would have us believe that to believe that to preserve Democracy and fight Communism, we must sacrifice our Democracy, at least temporarily. I am not one of these. I believe we must push for more rather than less Democracy."[36]

Ironically, Davenport's erratic behavior was cut short by his sudden death on June 24, 1953. On September 1, 1953, the Los Angeles City Council appointed his wife, Harriet, to replace him. This was the first time in the council's history of a councilman being succeeded by a spouse.

Roybal, in this political milieu, was constantly subject to having his character brought into question. It was a price to pay for being farsighted and progressive in a time when McCarthyism was running rampant.

1954: Roybal Runs for Lieutenant Governor of California

In 1954, when Pat Brown decided not to run for California governor, Democratic leaders drafted Richard Graves[37] to run against Goodwin Knight. Knight had ascended to the governorship following Warren's successful appointment to the U.S. Supreme Court. Councilman Roybal, who was already becoming known at the state level, received a nod for lieutenant governor in a grassroots uprising at the Fresno Democratic Nominating Convention. Sharing the Democratic ticket with Roybal was Richard Graves, who was nominated for governor. Graves had been the head of the League of California Cities. He had acted as a consultant, legal advisor, and legislative representative of all the cities of California. Both Roybal and Graves ran on the issues of expanding employment, increasing unemployment benefits, repealing of the Jurisdictional Disputes Act, protecting and strengthening civil liberties, and the right of unions to organize.

Lillian Roybal Rose remembered how her dad was nominated for lieutenant governor, "[My parents] had gone to dinner to get a bite to eat, and someone came in saying, 'Hey, they're yelling your name,' and that my dad didn't know what was going on, and that they walked in and when they saw Dad the place went nuts and the higher ups were furious."[38] She said that one of the key people who helped Ed Roybal's nomination was Glen Anderson, who was a good friend of his and strongly supported him. Lucille Roybal-Allard commented, "As he was walking up when they were drafting him, he was being told, don't you run, don't you accept, and that's the wrong thing to tell my dad. Don't tell my dad don't do something. He ran a totally grassroots campaign statewide and actually he received more votes than Graves. He led the ticket. Goodwin Knight was the one who was elected. But people knew him [Ed Roybal] and remembered him from the reputation he had in the city council and his public health days when he traveled up and down the state. I think they were at the Democratic Convention and my mom told me that everyone was on their feet screaming, 'Roybal, Roybal!' and they [the political leadership] were hammering away and saying, 'Sit down!' and no one would sit down."[39]

Roybal expressed his philosophy in politics this way: "I listen to all sides, including that one presented by lobbyists. Then I make up my mind and do what I think is right."[40] The media made much of the fact that Roybal was a Mexican American running for state office and acknowledged that his political future was bright. It was an opportunity for Roybal to educate the public about the state of the Mexican community and some of their pressing issues. He stated, "I'll be campaigning weekends, when the council's not in session, right down to Election Day. I'm going to make as good a fight as I can...I've got a chance."[41]

The *California Eagle* endorsed Roybal, saying, "Edward R. Roybal, the Democratic nominee for lieutenant governor is so well known that his preference over his rival Harold Powers needs little explanation. As a member of City Council, Roybal has been progressive and alert for the public interest. As a member of a minority, he has an obvious appeal to the Negro voter which is enhanced by that record."[42]

During late November 1954, Ed Roybal began a series of lectures at his former alma mater, UCLA. The first lecture was co-sponsored by the Department of Sociology, Anthropology and Political Science and the Council of Student Unity under the auspices of the Welfare Board. The first lecture was entitled "Mexican-American: A Sleeping Giant." Ralph Richardson, professor of speech, commented, "In this district, Roybal has made democracy real and vital for people who before have not exercised their rights of citizenship." For Ed Roybal, it presented an opportunity to educate another generation and also opened up the possibility that he could in the future return to academia as a professor.

By now, Ed Roybal had inspired a new generation of Mexican Americans, among these, a young factory worker at Chrysler and union organizer in Los Angeles, Esteban Torres. Torres was a precinct worker and distributed leaflets for Roybal for Lt. Governor. He got to meet Roybal at a rally. By that time, Torres was married, and his wife would say, "What are you going to do with your life?" He replied, "Someday I want to get out of the auto plant and work my way up and be like Edward Roybal. I want to be like him." The auto workers union volunteered his house for a coffee clutch during the Roybal for Lt. Governor campaign and Torres organized his neighbors to meet Roybal. Torres commented, "He was really a role model I could follow. I wanted to be like him. So that was my beginnings with Edward Roybal. I was impressed because he was college-educated…I remember [him] as a very conscientious man, very articulate. I was impressed."[43]

At the end, Graves and Roybal were defeated in their bids for governor and lieutenant governor. Graves defeated Goodwin J. Knight in the Democratic primary but was beaten by Knight in the general election.[44] Roybal was defeated by Harold J. Powers.[45] For Roybal, this political defeat, like his defeat for the Los Angeles City Council in 1947, was cause for reflection and reassessment. It would serve him later as a lesson learned in working within his own party for reforms and improvement.

The Struggle to Save Bunker Hill

Politics in Los Angeles continued in spite of the national election. On November 15, 1954, the Los Angeles City Council voted 14–1 to permit the Community Redevelopment Agency (CRA) to buy the property in an area known as Bunker Hill. Under the agency's plan, $33 million in federal money and some $7 million city credit would be used to purchase 136 acres between Hill and First Streets, the Harbor Freeway, and Fourth and Fifth Streets. Then the CRA would demolish 475 structures, which included 382 residential buildings. They would relocate 11,507 people, build streets, install utilities, and make other improvements in order to prepare the area for a new phase of construction. William T. Sesnon Jr., the CRA chairman, stated that the proposed project sought to eradicate Bunker Hill's "slum," which he termed "an eyesore and one of the worst firetraps in the city." He added that the project would increase the present $4,920,180 assessed value and increase it to $35.5 million with a boost of tax revenue of $332,000 to $2,056,000. He said that once the area was cleared it would be sold to the highest bidder at an estimated four dollars per foot, or $19 million, which would then be used to repay the federal loan. The new owners would then develop the area under plans worked out by city agencies for "an integral community." He concluded that the city would get its $7 million investment back by receiving credit for improvements in the area and by the difference between the old and new taxes until the full amount would be paid.

Ed Roybal, the lone dissenter, passionately sought a twenty-four-hour delay to give Bunker Hill tenants and owners an opportunity to be heard. Although Roybal favored redevelopment in Los Angeles, he argued that other slum areas needed it first and that the land values in Bunker Hill would mean apartments would be rented for $100 to $150 per month.

What Mr. Sesnon did not mention was that the Bunker Hill area as it stood was a predominantly low-income area. It was the third time that the Mexican community was bearing the brunt of redevelopment. East Los Angeles had been dismembered from its northeast area by the construction of three freeways (the San Bernardino, the Golden State, and the Santa Ana Freeways). Another predominantly Mexican community at Chavez Ravine was about to be taken over for the proposed construction of housing projects, and now Bunker Hill was being targeted. Roybal argued vehemently, "There are other areas in which people live next to industry and these should be taken care of first. This will dispossess hundreds of families. Other areas have more juvenile delinquency, police and health problems. Many in Bunker Hill won't be eligible for public housing. Those who are eligible will get priority over veterans in other parts of the city. How can rents here be moderate when the redevelopers will have to pay big prices for the land and charge high rents to get their money back and make a profit? There isn't a real estate agency in Los Angeles that wouldn't like to see Bunker Hill cleared so they could buy it and redevelop it."

Sesnon retorted that the city would have control over rent. Roybal repeated that Bunker Hill was not a place to start a redevelopment area. Roybal got some limited support from L. E. Timberlake, who stated that a smaller area should have been selected, like Venice. Rosalind Wiener Wyman demanded some proof that Bunker Hill was the city's worst slum. She stated that "The redevelopers have to get pretty high rents for apartments on Bunker Hill." The enabling council resolution by Ernest E. Debs called for a prompt application, while at the same time Mayor Norris Poulson also urged that this step be addressed.[46]

On April 25, 1955, the Los Angeles City Council, in one of its longest sessions in years, approved the acceptance of a $365,825 grant of federal funds for a Bunker Hill survey. Councilman Roybal voted against it and was joined by Councilman Baker. Councilman Harby was absent. William Sesnon Jr., president of the Community Redevelopment Agency, stated that the contract approval was a formality, and it was obligated to come before the council for final approval of any type of program it would develop. The only control the city council had over the autonomous CRA was to confirm or reject any of the mayor's appointments to its board.

Opponents of the Bunker Hill project continued to depict it as a scheme to build a civic auditorium and to place 20,000 higher-income apartment tenants within walking distance of the downtown area. At the meeting, Councilman Roybal indicated that the 11,500 people who lived in Bunker Hill had an average income of $1,600 per year and that they would be forced to live in slum areas. Roybal said that the average rent at Bunker Hill was $45 per month and this population would be unable to pay the expected higher rents of $80 to $100 that would be charged after the renovation.[47]

In an editorial, the *Citizen News* leveled some hard facts about the Bunker Hill project. "The scheme is clear to everyone, is one solely in the interests of certain downtown business groups. Though it is represented as being a slum-clearance project its chief advocates are those who expect to profit personally from it. Why do so many councilmen, who represent other sections of the city other than downtown, support the scheme? The answer is easy: downtown newspapers are important factors in the election of most of the Councilmen. The downtown interests that will profit include not only some newspapers but also big supporters of downtown newspapers."[48]

1955: Freeways Across East Los Angeles

In early March 1955, the Eastside took another blow from developers. East Los Angeles lost its battle against the proposed Golden State Freeway when the Los Angeles City Council approved an agreement with the State of California. Councilman Roybal was the lone dissenter on the vote. Roybal pointed out that the freeway would cut the Eastside in two, running through Boyle Heights north and south from the Santa Ana Freeway near Seventh Street, then past Hollenbeck Park, parallel to State Street, and then across the Ramona Freeway near General Hospital. The Golden State would then run through Lincoln Heights, the Riverside-Atwater area, and go through Griffith Park in order to join an already built route at the Glendale City line, by Riverside Drive.

Lucille Roybal-Allard recalled the struggle to stop the freeways through East Los Angeles, saying, "My dad fought that. I remember meetings at the house, community meetings, my dad making speeches and the way I understand it what was behind the freeway system were the oil companies. They wanted freeways and my father wanted public transportation and of course with the idea of protecting the environment. He was absolutely right."[49]

Indeed, Roybal worked closely with the California Committee Opposed to Oil Monopoly. He spoke out against Proposition 4, which he said would bypass the state legislature on a key issue, jeopardizing the state's stake in tidelands oil royalties. He further stated that the proposition would create a monopoly, cause unemployment by curtailment of oil production in the state, and not result in conservation.

The struggle against the freeway project had been going on for almost two years, at city hall and in Sacramento. Opposition groups formed immediately after the proposed route was announced in the summer of 1953. In the Eastside, a resident's committee led by Roybal had been organized. Committees from the Eastside and other affected areas presented a petition carrying 15,000 signatures to the city council meeting, but it was ignored.

Among other protestors at the city council meeting was George Hjelte, general manager of the Parks and Recreation Department, who argued that the freeway would take away valuable recreation space in the park. He had proposed an alternate route to the east side of the Los Angeles River bed. Paul C. Harding, the assistant state highway engineer, also countered that both Burbank and Glendale opposed the plan because it would cut through valuable industrial areas. The heirs of Colonel Griffith J. Griffith, who had donated the area to the city with the stipulation that it be used for recreation purposes, threatened to sue the city for recovery of the property if it was used for the freeway. At the end, fourteen members of the Los Angeles City Council had their way, at the expense of the residents of the affected areas. In reality, the route was not the city council's prerogative, since the location of the proposed freeway was solely under the state's jurisdiction. The council could have withheld the agreement as a significant protest against the plan. It could have delayed the project from eighteen months to three years or forced another route.

Advocating for Fair Employment Practices and a Minimum Wage Increase

During May 1955, Ed Roybal, as chairman of the Los Angeles City Council's Committee on Public Health and Welfare, held hearings at city hall for the Fair Employment Practices (FEP) measure he had introduced previously. The hearing was to provide a forum for advocates on both sides of the measure. More than 1,000 people attended. Roybal held the hearings in order to determine whether or not the committee would again recommend passage of the ordinance. Other members of the Public Health and Welfare Committee included Councilman Charles Navarro (of Italian ancestry) and Rosalind Weiner (of Jewish extraction), who was in Washington, D.C., on official business and unable to attend the hearings. Councilman Harold Darby attended to sit in on the hearings and weigh the merits of the FEP measure. Roybal informed the crowd that eight votes were necessary to get the bill out of the council and on Mayor Poulson's desk for his signature. Roybal indicated that he had been assured of seven votes. Present and in support were representatives of labor, churches, women's organizations, and the NAACP. All gave graphic examples of discrimination and segregation. Wesley Brazier, executive secretary of the Urban League, recited a laundry list of instances of discrimination in local business firms as evidence of the need for FEP. Attorney Loren Miller informed the committee that similar ordinances had been passed in thirty-seven other cities and that they had proved effective and workable.[50] Despite all the testimony, the measure was defeated.

In June, Roybal again introduced the Fair Employment Practices ordinance to the Los Angeles City Council. It was defeated again, this time by a one-vote margin. The yes votes came from Roybal, Don Allen, Everett Burkhelter, Ernest E. Debs, Gordon Hahn, John Gibson, and

Rosalind Wyman. The opposition was led by Randolph Van Nostrand, spokesman for the Merchants and Manufacturing Association. Their allies in the city council who voted against the measure were Earle D. Baker, Harold Harby, Harold A. Henry, John C. Holland, Charles Navarro, L. E. Timberlake, Robert Wilkinson, and Harriet Davenport.

Although Ed Roybal was the only ethnic minority member on the Los Angeles City Council, he developed strong friendships with several elected officials. According to Lillian Roybal Rose, "He was very close to Supervisor Hahn. They served in the council together. John Anson Ford is one of the supervisors that my father mentioned in his early, early years. He really liked my dad and encouraged him."[51]

The introduction of the Fair Employment Practices measure irked several human relations agencies, including Milton A. Senn, director of the Anti-Defamation League's Pacific Southwest Region. He accused Roybal of "inexplicable" conduct in trying to have the measure passed at an inopportune and precipitous time. Senn's charges were published in the July issue of *B'nai B'rith Record*, the official lodge publication.

Roybal countered, "We came closer to an FEP ordinance and we did better than in 1949 when this fight was headed by Milton Senn," and went on to say that the effort was made regardless of the fact that "we knew we didn't have the votes." After the measure went down to defeat, Councilman Harold Harby attacked the National Association for the Advancement of Colored People and called it the "National Association for the Agitation of Colored People." In the same floor battle, Councilman Wilkinson admitted that he was half-Jewish, but proceeded to vote against the measure. Roybal denied that his efforts were pressured by the *Los Angeles Tribune*, an African American community newspaper. Roybal stated, "Instead of losing in committee [Public Health and Welfare Committee], we took the chance of urging passage and seeing an additional vote in the council. That's the reason I brought it out and at least made a fight of it."

The same month (June 1955), Ed Roybal announced his support for increasing the minimum wage to $1.25. He stated, "There are bills providing this increase in the national level before the United States Congress and on a statewide level before the California legislature. I respectfully call upon our legislators, both national and state, to vote in favor of this needed legislation, and I urge all people who place a value on the ability of America's working people to meet basic standards for decency and self-respecting lives to add their voices to mine and notify their senators, congressmen, and assemblymen of their feeling…Representing, as I do, a district with a population which does not enjoy the best employment opportunities I have seen too many examples of families forced to struggle along on pitifully inadequate earnings." Roybal's announcement in support of the minimum wage was small beginning step into the realm of national politics.

In early October 1955, Ed Roybal announced his intention to run for John Anson Ford's position on the Los Angeles Board of Supervisors in 1958. Anson had been expected to retire at the end of his term, creating a vacancy in the 3rd Supervisory District.

Roybal's announcement by then was not a surprise, as rumors had been circulating throughout the district for many months. Rumors had also circulated that Councilman Debs might be Roybal's rival for the post. Debs had run unsuccessfully in 1954 for the supervisory position. Roybal countered the possibility that U.S. Congressmen Chet Hollifield was planning to also run for the position. Roybal commented that Hollifield was a friend, and "I wouldn't run against him."[52]

Advocating for Children and Education

In early June 1955, Ed Roybal was the recipient of the Henrietta Szold Award, given by the Los Angeles chapter of Hadassah for "outstanding service to children." It was only the fourth such award given by the group. Hadassah recognized Councilman Roybal for his efforts in fighting juvenile delinquency and his long and dedicated service to scores of social welfare organizations. These groups included the Boy Scouts, the Holy Family Adoption Service, and the Variety Boys Club. Roybal was also credited with beginning the Armando Castro Scholarship Fund at Roosevelt High School. Castro, a student and track star at Roosevelt, had been murdered while trying to stop a fight between two individuals. Film star Robert Ryan presented the award to Roybal.

At another scholarship banquet the same month—the Mexican-American Educational Committee of Sanger—Roybal was the key speaker and talked at length about the status of Mexican American education. He stated that Mexicans had predated the Pilgrims in the East but that Mexicans had become second-class citizens, and that in 1950, only 1.8 percent of college students were Mexican Americans. He termed the Mexican American community "a sleeping giant of a million persons." He called for the Mexican community to unite and leave aside the petty jealousies that destroy organizations. He concluded by praising the organizations with an established purpose and predicted that their scope of activities would grow with the passage of time.

In May of the following year, Roybal had another chance to prove his dedication to children. The City of Los Angeles introduced a plan to put all baby clinics on a cash basis. Roybal criticized the plan as the first step to move to take the City Health Department out of the public health field. Roybal stated that the Welfare Planning Council was considering a way to determine the income of the parents before they used the clinic services. He said, "Only 85 percent of those attending the clinics come from families whose income is enough to allow them to pay for the services." In 1955, 2925 clinic sessions were attended by some 85,000 children. In 1956, the Health Department estimated some 3,103 sessions. Roybal explained that the baby clinics were using an educational approach to health problems. He commented, "They only advise parents on health of babies until they reach 2 years of age. After that, they go to private physicians."[53]

1956: Race and Representation

During February 1956, Ed Roybal immersed himself in national politics once again by supporting the presidential candidacy of Democratic candidate Adlai E. Stevenson. Roybal said, "Stevenson will carry forward to new heights the great liberal traditions of the administrations of Franklin D. Roosevelt and Harry S. Truman."[54] He pledged his "unequivocal support" for the Stevenson candidacy.

In May 1956, Roybal consolidated his standing in the national Democratic Party when he and Assemblyman Augustus F. Hawkins were appointed Get Out the Vote co-chairmen for all of Southern California by Attorney General Edmund G. Brown, the California campaign chairman for Adlai Stevenson. In accepting the appointment, Roybal commented, "I fully appreciate the importance of the task and undertake it gladly. I know that Adlai Stevenson is by far the best-qualified Democratic contender to be our presidential nominee, and every technique at my command will be put to use in getting him the biggest possible vote on June 5."[55] Roybal and Hawkins would supervise a number of diverse projects to maximize the Stevenson vote, including the distribution of campaign literature, phone committees, transportation committees, and house-to-house calls.

Ed Roybal was tenacious in his objective on the issue of integration, both in housing and in city employment. In April 1956, he asked the fire chief and fire commission for a full report on the progress of racial integration in the fire department. He said that he had heard that the integration program was having difficulties and he wanted to know about them.

Roybal's motion was defeated by a 7–6 vote. Those voting with Roybal included Councilmen Allen, Burkhalter, Debs, Hahn, Wyman, and Gibson. Those voting against Roybal's motion were Councilmen Baker, Callicott, Harby, Henry, Holland, and Timberlake. Councilmen Navarro and Wilkinson were absent. The councilmen voting against the motion stated that they welcomed a solution to the issue but that Roybal's proposed report would, "throw this thing wide open again." A committee report noted that many letters had been received by the public regarding integration and that they had been filed.[56]

During May 1956, the Roybal family was grieved to receive the news that Prudenciana Beserra, mother of Ed's wife, Lucille Beserra de Roybal, had died in San Francisco at the age of seventy-five. She had died soon after visiting her son Leo in Sacramento, California. She left in addition to her daughter Lucila, one other son, Alberto Becerra, his wife, Hortencia Núñez, and eleven grandchildren.

Prudenciana Moreno Beserra was born in Baja California, but had spent most of her life in Los Angeles, where she had been very active in Catholic Church organizations. Her family was related to some of the oldest families in California. She was related to Jose Matias Moreno, the secretary to Governor Pío Pico, and General Mariano Guadalupe Vallejo. She had been married to the late Alberto Manuel Beserra and was well-known to many in Los Angeles. Funeral arrangements were held at the Nuestra Señora de Guadalupe Church at 4123 Fisher Street.

By October 1956, the presidential election between incumbent Republican President Dwight D. Eisenhower and Democratic nominee Adlai Stevenson was gearing up and stirring passions on both sides. Ed Roybal accompanied Stevenson on a campaign swing of Southern California, where he received the welcome of large and enthusiastic crowds. Although Roybal had been increasingly pessimistic about Stevenson's chances, he had a different opinion after the candidate's visit. He commented, "If you had asked me two weeks ago I would have said we would lose by about 250,000 votes in Los Angeles County. Today I would say Los Angeles County can go either way. It is going to be a very close race."[57]

Roybal criticized the Democratic Party in California for not appealing to the state's minorities. He said he was "baffled" by the party's oversight in not carrying their message to Latin American, Spanish-speaking peoples, African Americans, and others in the state. He indicated that Senator Kuchel had a task force to campaign among minorities and urged Democratic Party leaders to organize a similar effort at the state level.

He pointed out that he had received more than 400,000 votes among minorities when he had run for lieutenant governor two years before and that a "mere 100,000 minority votes either way might spell victory or defeat for our party in the close election coming up. We can't afford such a loss." He stated that he had raised the issue months before to encourage the party to take organized action but that as of yet nothing had been done. In the previous week, he had held a private meeting with U.S. Representative Clair Engle, who headed the Stevenson-Kefauver ticket in California, and raised the issue once again. He also planned to attend a statewide meeting of 200 leaders of minority groups in the state, and he intended to urge them to take immediate political action.[58]

The Democratic Party continued to be less than forthcoming on its commitment to civil rights. In February, a high-level closed-door session of the new Democratic National Advisory Council attempted to craft a civil rights compromise. The council included the Democratic presidential nominee Adlai Stevenson, Averell Harriman of New York, and Senator Hubert Humphrey. The draft called for Democrats in Congress to live up to the party platform promises, to create bills designed "to eliminate discrimination of all kinds, in relation to the right to vote, to engage in gainful occupation and the other specific discriminations mentioned in the civil rights plank in the platform."

The draft however, was deemed hypocritical and too general by lower-ranked Democratic leaders. Ed Roybal, along with Alan Cranston, president of the California Democratic Council; State Senator Richard Richards of Los Angeles; Albert (Blackie) Lunceford of the Greater Los Angeles CIO Council; and others took up a similar theme, acknowledging that it might mean breaking up with Southern Democrats.

During October, the issue of race and representation stirred another controversy in the Los Angeles City Council. The city council voted to deny African American representation by shifting the 7th Council District from the South Central part of Los Angeles to the city of San Fernando. Bennett Johnson, board member of the local NAACP, charged the city council with "gerrymandering" and stated that his organization was "deeply concerned" about the movement of the 7th District. Former Councilman Don Allen spoke and recommended two more council districts be created to give residents of the south central part of the city representation. Councilman Ernest E. Debs came out in support of Allen's recommendation.

The map approved by the city council also allowed Ed Roybal to keep the downtown area. The 9th District also gained sections of Hahn's district in the southeastern part of the city between Slauson and Vernon Avenues. Roybal urged the creation of two more council districts to give more representation of South Central and the San Fernando Valley. Roybal stated, "I'm surprised at Mr. Hahn. He knows you can't divide the Central District like pieces of pie into three equal parts and come out with the proper number of voters."[59]

Ed Roybal built outside support from the Black community from the beginning. He had empathy for all people who suffered discrimination and injustice. As a Mexican, he was personally well-acquainted with segregation, prejudice, poverty, and exclusion. Ed Roybal Jr. recalled, "One of the stories is when my father was first elected to the city council and they introduced him as the new Mexican councilman here to represent the Mexican community, who 'speaks Mexican.' My father stood up and he said, 'You know, I represent everyone in my district.' I think my father always had the respect of the African American community because it was part of his belief, always do what is right. He didn't care if the issue was in the Black community or in the Chicano community or whatever, my father would fight for whatever it was."[60]

The changes by the council greatly affected the African American representation in Los Angeles. The African American population was essentially dispersed in different districts where they did not have the majority in any of them. The 1st District, represented by Everett G. Burkhelter, included the Sunland, Tujunga, and North Hollywood areas. The district however, gave up part of its territory to form a new district in the Valley, which would be known as the 7th District. The 3rd District, represented by Robert M. Wilkinson, included the San Fernando Valley, Chatsworth, Reseda, Northridge, Woodland Hills, Tarzana, and Encino. The district gave up a large portion to the new 7th district.

The 8th District, represented by Gordon R. Hahn, would continue to represent the southern part of the city in addition to taking up most of the old 7th District. It would also give up some parts to the 9th and 15th Districts. In the 10th District, Charles Navarro would continue to represent the central and southwestern parts of the city but give up a section of Wilshire Boulevard. In the 15th District, John Gibson would continue to represent Wilmington, Wilshire, and the strip connecting the city with the harbor, and would gain some area of the 8th District.

On November 27, 1956, Ed Roybal proposed that the Los Angeles City Council be increased by two members, bringing the total to seventeen. One of these would be designated to the southeast part of the city, where the majority of the African American population resided. He stated, "The various districts which share the Southeast part of the city are all larger than they should be. A new district should be created here and another in the San Fernando Valley because of its continuing growth." He argued that all segments of the population should get council representation and that a southeastern district "would give the Negro community an opportunity to have a representative in the council." Councilman Ernest E. Debs supported Roybal's proposal and stated, "No other major city in the United States with such a large Negro population is without a Negro councilman."[61] Council President John S. Gibson Jr. urged the council to appoint a study committee.

On December 5, Ed Roybal formally made a proposal to the city council for the creation of two more council districts, bringing the total to seventeen. However, some immediately argued that dividing the council along racial lines was not democratic. These opponents also argued that the next logical stage would be the creation of districts for Jewish people, Catholics, Protestants, and so forth. To the surprise of many, George Thomas, an African American civic leader and a candidate for the city council in 1955 against Charles Navarro in the 10th District, argued against Roybal's proposal. He argued that it was not healthy for a representative to depend upon a racial vote.

Roybal responded that that it was "not perfect democracy" to have the council devise a district where an African American could be elected to the council. Nonetheless, he said that it was a necessity for the Black community to have a representative in the council, because it would more quickly achieve the Democratic ideal of government representation regardless of creed or race. He went on to say that the arguments suggesting districts for Catholics, etc., were mere roadblocks to providing representation for a racial minority desperately in need of it.

On November 30, Ed Roybal spoke at the opening of an American Civil Liberties Union (ACLU) chapter in East Los Angeles. Roybal noted the importance of coordinating the work of all those organizations dedicated to the rights and liberties of the Eastside. He cited the discriminatory provisions in the McCarran-Walter Immigration Act as one of the most severe problems facing the Mexican community. Other speakers at the event included Frank Paz, Council of Mexican-American Affairs; J. J. Rodriguez, Community Service Organization (CSO); Eliseo Carrillo, ACLU member; and Raoul Morin, GI Forum. Dr. Ralph Guzman, a college professor, presided as the panel chairman. The speakers focused on police misconduct and discrimination against the Mexican community in employment, education, and housing.[62]

1957: Announcing a Political Coming of Age

By 1957, Roybal had three terms in the Los Angeles City Council. The first two terms were for two years each, and the third and fourth terms were for four years. Having consolidated his multiethnic coalition, the re-election committee once again aligned a broad assortment of people and groups. It included Assemblyman Edward Elliot; Assemblyman Augustus F. Hawkins; Joseph E. Kovmer, editor and publisher of the *Eastside Sun*; Albert T. (Blackie) Lunceford, secretary-treasurer of the Greater Los Angeles CIO Council; J. J. Rodriguez, president of the Los Angeles Community Service Organization; W. J. Basset, secretary of the AFL Central Labor Council; Ignacio Lozano Jr., publisher of *La Opinion*; Eileen Siedman, past president of the Wabash-City Terrace Coordinating Council; Mike Quevedo, Laborers' Union Local 300; Tony Ponce and Mike Otto, the international vice president and Pacific Coast director, respectively, of the International Ladies Garment Workers Union.

Basically, each leader stimulated voter support within his or her organization. What was interesting here is that as a three-term incumbent, Roybal "relied on the strength of elite political support and a top-down rather than a bottom-up electoral strategy."[63] Many of these labor supporters in leadership positions were present five days before the April 3 election at the testimonial dinner (held at Carl's Restaurant) to honor Edward R. Roybal.

Irma Núñez recalled a perpetual state of campaigns, saying, "I just remember all my life our living room being filled with boxes up to the ceiling of campaign literature and we were constantly stuffing envelopes, licking stamps, address labels, and we had a huge assembly line of family members and friends who would be pumping out the campaign literature. My mom also was one of the key people involved in organizing his campaigns. From my perspective, it was the women who were really the hardest workers, working behind the scenes. One of the things I remember about my uncle's campaigns, before it was popular, was always including something that represented culture and the arts. We were always performing at his campaign events. So since I was five or six years old we were always the entertainers for his events, but also the Olivarez family who were an important part of [our] family."[64]

The city's major newspapers continued to be cool to Roybal, but the *Eastside Sun* endorsed him again, as did the *Los Angeles Sentinel* for the first time. The *Los Angeles Times*, the *Mirror*, and the *Examiner* simply reported on the campaign, as did *La Opinion*. The *Los Angeles Herald & Express* backed Roybal's re-election bid, describing Roybal as "perhaps the council's leading liberal" and noting that he "favored rent control, public housing, a fair employment practices ordinance, a Skid Row cleanup and authored a compulsory rabies vaccination law."[65]

As expected, Edward R. Roybal was elected to serve a fourth term. The 1957 voter turnout was bigger than the 1953 election, in which he garnered 23,085 votes, 74 percent of the total. He obtained a majority in all of the district's four areas—Eastside, Downtown, South Central, and heterogeneous areas. Voter turnout in the South Central area, for the first time, exceeded that of the Eastside (41 percent to 40 percent). This happened because the city council's 1956 redistricting extended the 9th District thirty-seven blocks into the South Central area, while there was a decline in Eastside voter turnout.[66]

In late March 1957, the CSO held its convention at the Fresno Hacienda Motel and by then was consolidating a strong working relationship with many other minority organizations, as well as with labor unions. One of the main speakers at the convention was Frank Williams, regional counsel of the National Association for the Advancement of Colored People. He stated, "We compare our state, in population and political and economic influence, with New York, Pennsylvania and New Jersey, but we are far behind. In all of those powerful states, non-discrimination in employment is guaranteed by law. In California there is no such law. In those states, discrimination in public housing is prohibited by law. In this state it is not." He stated that there were more than 5 million minority people in California but they had attained very little politically. He called for joint political action and joint educational campaigns between the NAACP and CSO.

Ed Roybal, the keynote speaker, stated that the Spanish-speaking people of California were coming of age politically. He stated, "The sleeping giant is beginning to awaken and it will not be long before his strength begins to be felt in the state and local elections." He called for increasing support of the CSO's program of citizenship and education by which Mexican Americans could improve their position politically and economically. Among the key speakers in the convention, which went on for several days, was Saul D. Alinsky, executive director of the Industrial Foundation, which continued to sponsor the CSO.[67]

That same month, Ed Roybal socialized with two film stars whom he had idolized when he was a youth. Roybal donated trophies, which were presented to Mexico's basketball team in Mexicali. Actress Inez Pedroza, who had been named queen by the championship team, made the presentation. On hand were film stars Gilbert Roland and Antonio Moreno. Both had begun in silent films as romantic leading men. Roland had gone on to become the first Mexican-origin Cisco Kid in the popular film series and gone on to play more dramatic roles in the 1950s. Moreno had directed the first Mexican sound film (*Santa*) and had settled in as a character actor.

Also in March 1957, Ed Roybal met one of the most revered Mexican presidents, Lázaro Cárdenas. Cárdenas had been president of the Mexican Republic during 1934 to 1940 and had carried out some of the most cherished objectives of the Mexican Revolution (1910–1920). Cárdenas presided over more acres of land distribution than all Mexican presidents before or since. In addition, he nationalized the prized Mexican oil fields in 1938, which had largely been owned by the United States and Great Britain. He compensated both countries, but his gesture of nationalism had won him the endearing love of all Mexicans.

By the time Cárdenas visited Los Angeles in 1957, he was an authentic hero and legend. At the formal reception, Councilmen Ed Roybal and John S. Gibson represented the city of Los Angeles. Also attending were Adolfo Pedro Dominguez, Mexican consul general, and Braulio Maldonado, governor of Baja California. For Roybal, it was an opportunity to meet and talk to one of his political heroes, one he truly admired.

During April 1957, Ed Roybal represented Los Angeles officialdom in the Chamber of Commerce on a fourteen-day tour of western Mexico. The trip was a goodwill and business-building mission headed by Allerton H. Jeffries, chairman of the chamber's Southern California–Northwest Mexico Committee. The U.S. delegation traveled in twenty cars with a rendezvous in Tucson and then headed southward to Nogales, Hermosillo,

Guaymas, Culiacán, Mazatlán, Tepic, Guadalajara, and finally to Mexico City.

In June 1957, Ed Roybal authored a Los Angeles city ordinance that prohibited racial discrimination in the occupancy of redeveloped property. It was passed by unanimous vote by the Los Angeles City Council. Roybal, who had long tried to pass an ordinance that prohibited racism in housing, commented, "This measure establishes a mandatory antidiscrimination rule to ensure equal opportunity for the enjoyment of the benefits of residential and business property redeveloped with the assistance of the city. Beyond that, however, it also provides a model and a guide to encourage more democratic practices in the rental and sale of wholly private housing which is developed without the assistance of public funds." The city ordinance was a sweet victory for Ed Roybal and all minority communities after so many years of disappointments and rising expectations.

In August 1957, the CSO held its tenth anniversary. At the convention banquet, held at the Biltmore Hotel, Ed Roybal was the guest of honor. Ralph Richardson, a member of the Los Angeles Board of Education and professor of political science at UCLA, presented Roybal with a plaque on behalf of CSO. In his acceptance speech, Roybal also mentioned Tetsu Sugi, a Nisei who had made a great contribution to the CSO. Sugi served as the first chapter president of the CSO in the Lincoln Heights area. The event was presided over by CSO president James J. Rodriguez.[68]

The Struggle for Chavez Ravine

One of the most emotional and hardest-fought battles Roybal took up during his tenure in the Los Angeles City Council was that of the struggle to save Chavez Ravine.

The 400 acres known as Chavez Ravine were situated in the middle of Elysian Park, north of Downtown Los Angles. In pre-Spanish times, the area had been a Native American burial site. Later, in the late 1800s, people established the small community which became known as Chavez Ravine. Most of the residents were Mexican. It had the feel of a small rural community, with chickens, dogs, and other pets running free up and down the hillsides. In 1946, a study for the Los Angeles Housing Project designated Chavez Ravine as a "blighted area."

On July 24, 1950, a letter was sent to the residents of Chavez Ravine informing them that a housing project was proposed for the site. Eviction notices were sent out and some residents left or sold their homes. In October 1950, the Los Angeles City Council approved a $100 million budget for building 10,000 housing units to be built in eleven sites. The well-known architects, Robert Alexander and Richard Neutra, considered the area a plum, as only 40 percent of the area was occupied. Neutra designed twenty-four thirteen-story towers and 163 two-story buildings.

During 1951, some opponents of the proposed project attacked it as "creeping socialism." By December 26, 1951, the Los Angeles City Council voted to cancel the city contract for redevelopment by an 8–7 vote. The housing authority then sought the court's legal ruling on whether the contract cancellation was legal. The city council in turn established a referendum for the June 3, 1952, election, to determine what the public thought of the issue, whether to continue or stop the project. In April 1952, the California Supreme Court ruled that the Los Angeles City Council could not void the contract and that the referendum could have no legal effect on said contract. Nonetheless, the council continued with the referendum, in which 600,000 voted at a proportion of three to two against the housing project. California's U.S. senators, Richard M. Nixon and William F. Knowland, backed federal legislation to legalize the contract cancellation. In the meantime, several houses in Chavez Ravine were demolished or set ablaze by the fire department in the training of recruits. Some residents, however, refused to leave, arguing that they were not being paid the market value of their homes. Some stayed on the principle that it was plainly unfair and illegal for the city to condemn their community.

In the midst of rabid anticommunism in the autumn of 1952, the three top administrators of the Los Angeles housing project were red baited and called before the California Senate Un-American Activities Committee. All three pleaded the Fifth Amendment but were fired from their posts. Soon thereafter, the U.S. Supreme Court ruled with the California court's decision that the contract cancellation was illegal. During June 1953, Mayor Norris Poulson vowed to end "federal domination of the city" and then negotiated with the housing authority to abandon the two largest housing projects, including Chavez Ravine. In July of the same year, the U.S. Congress passed legislation permitting the federal government to absorb the difference (loss) between funds spent and the future sale price of Chavez Ravine for other purposes. In August, the Los Angeles housing project sold 170 acres of Chavez Ravine to the City of Los Angeles for some $1.25 million, which was a loss to the federal government of $4 million. Finally, Congress permitted the sale of the land under the condition that the city use the land "for a public purpose only."

During the same time, Walter O'Malley was unable to negotiate for a new stadium site with the City of New York for his Brooklyn Dodgers baseball team. Early in 1957, Mayor Poulson and other Los Angeles city and county officials conferred with O'Malley in order to offer him a baseball stadium site.

In late August 1957, Ed Roybal intervened personally to give one of the last residents of Chavez Ravine a two-week stay on an eviction notice. The family of Manuel Arechiga, seventy, and his sixty-year-old wife and four granddaughters refused to be evicted when Sheriff Sergeant Al Turner and Deputy Gabrielle Johnson arrived. A brief tussle ensued, and police were called to forcefully restrain Arechiga's daughter, Victoria Augustin, but no charges were filed. She expressed what many felt: "The city condemned our property in 1953 for a low-cost housing project, but they offered only $10,500 for it when it has been appraised for $16,000. Now there is not going to be a housing project. The city wants this land to build a ball park for the Brooklyn Dodgers. Well, we are not going to give up our lifelong house and property for that. My sick mother said she would stay right out there on the street if they put us out. We have no place to go."[69]

Roybal stated that the extension would permit arbitration on the city's claim that the Arechiga family owed $400 for rent since the housing authority took over the house four years before. He indicated that the city had attached $10,500 for the housing authority to cover what they had put in escrow for purchase of the triple lot. Roybal said that other families similarly affected were planning a lawsuit challenging the city's authority to condemn private property for a baseball team.

Roybal also criticized the methods of the city to evict residents of Chavez Ravine. "No public relations were employed by the city here, where it really counts. The family was never consulted. They simply mailed an eviction notice." The Arechiga family was one of the last thirteen remaining families remaining at Chavez Ravine.

The crucial vote—to offer a definite deal to bring the Dodgers to Los Angeles—came before the Los Angeles City Council on September 7, 1957, following five hours of heated discussion. Mayor Norris Poulson made a dramatic plea for the council to approve the plan evolved by negotiator Harold C. McClellan. Poulson stated, "We are at the crossroads. Are we going to be a bush-league town or are we going to be major league in everything?" When Ed Roybal and the opposition attempted to delay the final action until the next day, the mayor jumped on his feet and shouted, "If we delay this, it goes out to the world that the city has lost its guts!" On a roll call, the resolution passed 11–3. The dissenting votes were cast by Ed Roybal, Earle Baker, and Patric McGee. Holland had initially voted no but got permission to change his vote with the hope that the issue would be reopened the next day. But that appeared impossible.[70]

Lucille Roybal-Allard recalled the struggle for Chavez Ravine. "God, that was a battle. I just remember the battle. We had meetings at our house constantly, and my dad led the fight. As I remember, it was to stop the building of Dodger Stadium, but the underlying goal was that it was probably going to be done and if it was going to be done and if it was going to happen, they had to give people fair market value for their home. That didn't happen, and to this day people are angry about that."[71]

On October 7, 1957, the Los Angeles City Council passed a resolution that transferred Chavez Ravine to the Dodger baseball team. On December 1, 1958, a referendum that could block the transfer of public to private land was put to the electorate. The baseball team won by a slight margin of less than 2 percent. However, more litigation continued. Los Angeles Superior Court Judge Arnold Praeger, ruling on the several lawsuits that nullified the City's contract with the Dodgers, declared the contract invalid because it was "an illegal delegation of the duty of the City of Los Angeles, an abdication of its public trust, and a manifest gross abuse of discretion."

However, on January 13, 1959, the California Supreme Court ruled in favor of the Dodgers. Finally, in May 1959, under the power of eminent domain, the police department of the city evicted the last remaining residents of Chavez Ravine. All remaining homes were summarily bulldozed. On September 11, 1961, the construction for Dodger Stadium began. The residents of Chavez Ravine formed an organization to maintain contact with each other. To this day, the many wounds of the land grab of Chavez Ravine have not healed.

According to Juan Gonzalez, sometime after eviction of the residents of Chavez Ravine, Walter O'Malley met Ed Roybal. "He asked Roybal to a luncheon with him and so they got together for lunch. [Walter O'Malley] was trying to get Roybal's support for developing Dodger Stadium. So Roybal knew that and they still had lunch. At the end of the lunch, O'Malley pulled out the money to pay for the lunch and Roybal said no, no. He [Ed Roybal] paid for it because he knew that just by paying the lunch he was going to feel that he would owe him a certain thing."[72]

Travels to Europe and the Middle East

Before the upcoming Mexican Independence Day weekend, Ed Roybal spoke on one similar experience of Mexicans and Jews. He stated, "As you know, about the same time Spanish conquistadores were ravaging Mexico, enslaving its people and trying to obliterate its fabulous culture, the co-de-spoilers of these gold-greedy conquerors were inquisitioning Jewish Spain."

The magazine *Heritage*, in its issue from September 5, 1957, commented of Roybal, "As a spokesman for human decency and the rights of man, he is in the forefront of public service in his time. Also, he is a man of astute understanding of forces of history, and we were profoundly moved last week to find his statement of mutuality that exists between Jewish and Mexican people—each with tragic memories of Spanish iniquities."

On September 16, Ed Roybal joined Los Angeles Supervisor John Anson Ford and County Parks and Recreation Director N. S. Johnson in an open car, along with a representative of the Mexican government, in a parade celebrating Mexico's 147th Independence Day anniversary. The parade chairman, Jose Jimenez Jr., a Belvedere businessman, stated that the prancing horse of Sheriff E. W. Biscailuz would lead the parade as Grand Marshall. The parade started at East First and Lorena Streets at 5:00 p.m. and then followed Brooklyn Avenue and then East First Street to Belvedere Park for an evening of festivities. Ed Roybal was a permanent fixture at the Mexican Independence Day parade and celebrations beginning with his first term of office in the Los Angeles City Council and later as U.S. Congressmen. His was held in genuine affection by the community, evidenced by the fact that the loudest cheers and most gracious applause was for him.

On September 13, 1957, Roybal announced that he would be going on a vacation trip to the Middle East and Europe on September 17. He stated, "I want to study at first hand the Middle East situation and get my own facts about that sensitive part of the world. This is my first trip abroad and I am going to travel with a commercial tour in order to get the greatest benefit from the short time I can be away from Los Angeles. In order to get a balanced view of actual conditions, I am including both Jewish and Arab countries on the itinerary in addition to brief stops in Copenhagen, Amsterdam, Rome, Madrid, Paris, and London. My visit is timed to include the Jewish high holidays, events and interviews with a number of leading business, labor and Government officials."[73] While in Rome, he had an audience with the Pope. He was scheduled to return to Los Angeles on October 19.

Upon his return, he was a guest speaker at the B'Nai Brith Lodge No. 1458 in East Los Angeles. Roybal provided an account of his trip to the Middle East. He followed this talk with two others, at the Westside Community Center and the Los Angeles Hillel Alumni Association, where his topic was entitled "Is the Public Getting the Truth about the Middle East?"

He told the press that the things that interested people the most in the countries he visited were the Little Rock school segregation crisis and the Russian satellite. He said, "Those I met questioned me at once about the integration trouble in Arkansas. They think the American people are lax in permitting such conditions to exist. They do not realize that Arkansas is a small part of the United States and that Little Rock is an isolated example. They wonder how Governor [Orval] Faubus[74] gets the power to be stronger than President Eisenhower...[The Russian] launching of the satellite gave the Middle East and Europe a strong impression about Russian strength and brought a cold chill of fear that another war could come."[75] About the newly-formed state of Israel, he noted, "In eight years Israel has worked wonders, although we cannot compare it with other countries, which have been attacking similar problems. There is much suffering and poverty but the spirit of Israel is great. While many European countries live in their glorious past, Israel is planning its glorious future."[76]

Roybal undertook the trip to the Middle East and the talks to inform himself on the increasingly controversial subject of Jewish-Arab relations, as his district contained a significant population of people of the Jewish faith. Many of these constituents followed closely events in the Middle East and were a powerful lobby on behalf of Israel's well-being. When this author was growing up in Boyle Heights, there were many animated street conversations both in English and Yiddish about events about the Middle East. The passionate concern of the Jews about Israel was not dissimilar to Mexicans in the United States about Mexico.

Another reason for Ed Roybal to be knowledgeable about the Middle East was that he was already considering running for a statewide or national elected position. He was looking ahead.

1958: Roybal's Run for the Los Angeles County Board of Supervisors

Between 1950 and 1960, the Eastside became more predominantly Latino (mostly of Mexican origin). In 1950, the Eastside had nearly 100,000 residents, of which 43 percent were Latino. By 1960, the number declined to nearly 91,000 but was 61 percent Latino (the majority still of Mexican ancestry). The U.S.-born Latino population meanwhile was declining. In 1950, 75 percent of the 9th District's Latino population was born in the United States. By 1960, it was 71 percent. As the 1950s ended, the African American community was becoming larger than the Mexican American community in Los Angeles, and was producing a larger voter turnout. Because the number of U.S.-born Mexicans was declining, so were Mexican American voter turnouts.

Roybal had considered public office beyond the Los Angeles City Council for several years. From his "safe district," he continued gaining supporters and encouragement to venture into higher political office. Accordingly, he ran simultaneously for re-election to city council and for the county supervisor position in 1957. He sought to replace the retiring supervisor, John Anson Ford. Two days after Ford announced he would retire, Roybal's campaign manager, Roger Johnson, made it known that Roybal would run for the position. Johnson told the *Eastside Sun*, "Although Councilman Roybal has no opponent for the April 2 election, a number of his supporters decided to band together in order to urge the voters of his district to give him a big vote of confidence as a tribute to his outstanding record."[77] In his press statement, Johnson mentioned the establishment of a fifty-member Roybal election support committee.

Roybal's main opponent for the county supervisor position was Los Angeles City Councilman Ernest E. Debs.[78] Debs, who served on the city council from 1947 to 1958, was a savvy politician. He pioneered the legislation that established the vast freeway system in the state and especially in Southern California.

On September 11, 1958, just before the Los Angeles County Board of Supervisors election, the Wilshire Press ran a cover story, marking the 177th anniversary of Los Angeles' founding. The story also focused on Edward R. Roybal as a symbol of the continuing Mexican presence in the city. The story said, "Edward R. Roybal and his family stand as this kind of symbol of the past, present and future" of the city that began as a pueblo and that had grown into the nation's third largest city.

By now, Roybal's children were adolescents. A daughter, Lillian Prudence (named for Lucille's mother), was fifteen years old, and Lucille Eloise (named for Roybal's mother), was seventeen. Both girls attended Ramona Convent School. Edward Jr. was seven years old. In September, Edward and Lucille celebrated their eighteenth wedding anniversary.

Edward Roybal Jr. would later recall, "I grew up right in the center of Chicano politics in the fifties. There was always a campaign going on, it seems. I remember my earliest memories of my parents were always of them lecturing me. The first thing that comes to mind is respect. He would say this to me, that you need to give people respect. If you expect to be treated with respect, you show your respect for someone."[79] Edward Jr. recalled that in politics men were overtly in the leadership roles, but women were very active behind the scenes. His parents taught him to cherish the cultural traditions. He recalled both his parents singing corridos and traditional ballads. His father played the guitar; Ed Jr. also knew the story of how his father serenaded his mother when they were courting.

Edward Jr. recalled, "I grew up around adults. My father wasn't around a lot. The phones would ring all day and night, and there were always things going on, groups of people coming to the house. I think I had a very loving family, and it was clear that I was loved by my parents."[80] He remembered his father teaching him how to box. He and his father had season tickets to the Dodger games. Although the elder Roybal had been opposed to taking Chavez Ravine from its residents, once the stadium was built, he put that behind him.

During campaigns, Edward Jr. licked and stuffed envelopes, ringing doorbells, and campaigning. When asked what role his mother played in the campaigns, he commented, "She was in charge with the campaign manager, but my father was often out, he had other things to do, and my mother was always there at the headquarters, she was the one in charge. She was holding it together."[81] He was also taught to behave in a certain manner. "I was supposed to be on my best behavior all the time. Everything you do reflects on your father. I think there was some notion that my parents are being judged by how I behave. So there was a lot of adult responsibility about being on your best behavior. We were never to give speeches, give interviews or answer questions."[82]

Lucille was indeed involved in Edward's campaigns, in addition to volunteering at the Well Baby Clinic and serving as a member of the Committee Concert. When asked about what role his mother played in his father's political career, Ed Jr. further stated, "I think she was just critical. You know, not only because of the role she played in his campaign but just being the support. I think at some point my mother decided to devote herself to my father's career. She was a bedrock. She was abreast of every issue, and they discussed everything, she wasn't just backbone support. She was central in strategies and organizing."[83]

Roybal based his bid for the Board of Supervisors on a platform that included opposition to oil drilling in residential areas without just compensation. He had taken the lessons of Bunker Hill and Chavez Ravine to heart.

In the June 1958 primary, Roybal lead his nearest opponent with 10,000 votes. He won the endorsement of the 51st Assembly District Democratic Council; Joseph Wolf, West Beverly Democratic Club; James Cristiano, West Pico Democratic Club; Manny Calof, Hollywood Young Democrats; Joe Wyatt, chairperson of the California Democratic Council; Bernard Selber, director of California Democratic Standing Committee for the 26th Congressional District; Don Rose, Chairperson of the Los Angeles County Central Committee; and Dr. Ralph Richardson, member of the Los Angeles Board of Education.

A series of tabulating irregularities occurred in the general election on November 4, manifesting all the features of voter fraud. When the tallying began, Roybal had a substantial lead. A second, third, and fourth voter tally each put Debs slightly ahead of Roybal. In the end, Ernest E. Debs was declared the winner by a 12,037 vote margin. Roger Johnson, Roybal's campaign manager, challenged the outcome. He said, after the tragic five-day comedy-of-vote-counting errors, "We cannot accept whatever new and different votes total is reported. There have been too many irregularities at the polling places, and in the counting, to give assurance of a report."[84]

Roybal later recalled, "The next day I found out that all of a sudden, 12,000 additional votes were found going for Mr. Debs. No one could understand how a thing like that could happen. Some years later I met the same deputy registrar of voters at a restaurant and he asked, 'Why didn't you have a recount?' I said, 'Well, I couldn't afford it.' It was $12,000, I said, but I couldn't afford $12,000. I told him what the committee's financial situation was but I think that thing [election] was stolen, which was the term that I used then, and I think I can use that term safely today because I still believe it."[85] Roybal told reporters after the final election returns, "If we find enough irregularities, I intended to go to court to ask for a new election."[86] In the end, however, for lack of money, the election was never contested in court.

Running for mayor crossed Roybal's mind, as might seem obvious considering his popularity in the city and the traction he was getting over challenging, controversial issues. But Roybal crossed it off his list because, as he said later, "Mayor was a position where you could go no place." He was already considering ascending the elected-position ladder to higher office. "It [the mayor's position] had no power, nothing," he said. "In those days, he [the mayor] was ceremonial," referring to the endless round of banquets, public occasions, and everything else that led to "a great time" but little else. That was not how Roybal defined public life.[87]

After losing the election to the Board of Supervisors, Roybal threw himself back into his city council work. Besides representing the 9th District politically, Roybal worked hard to bring economic development to the Eastside. During 1959, he became president of the newly formed Eastland Savings and Loan Association. It had been granted a charter early in 1959. The members of the board included Manuel Veiga, a mortician, and Dr. Hector M. Cruz, a dental surgeon, as vice presidents; Charles Goldring, an attorney and certified public accountant, as treasurer; and Jack Y. Berman, a motion picture exhibitor.[88] The Eastland Savings and Loan Association provided East Los Angeles residents and business people with accessible loans for economic development.

1959: Founding the Mexican American Political Association (MAPA)

In 1959, Roybal, with a group of long-time community activists—Bert Corona, Herman Gallegos,[89] Dolores Sanchez, Ramona Morin, and Francisca Flores—founded the Mexican American Political Association (MAPA). They met in Fresno to discuss the exclusion of Mexican-ancestry people as a force within mainstream politics, especially from the Democratic Party. The majority of Mexican ancestry people had voted for the Democratic Party since Franklin D. Roosevelt but had gained little in return in the form of services, federal jobs or appointments, or as the focus of concern in the area of civil rights. The new organization was meant to be a catalyst to address that exclusion within the Democratic Party. Roybal became the organization's first chairperson.

Bert Corona boldly said that MAPA was formed because of "the unwillingness of the Democratic Party to support in any real sense the needs and interests of Mexicans and other Spanish-speaking people in California and the Southwest." They intended to start in California and expand. Corona remembered that the Democratic Party gave only token support when Roybal ran for lieutenant governor in 1954, even though Ed had been overwhelmingly nominated at the Democratic convention. The party gave Roybal's campaign very little funding. "What money he obtained he had to go out and personally solicit from friends in the Spanish-speaking community," said Corona.[90]

The founding of MAPA and that of the Political Association of Spanish-Speaking Organizations (PASSO) in Texas in 1960 was a new strategy by Mexican American activists to assert their Mexican identity and marshal voters as a voting bloc. MAPA sought to get Mexican American candidates elected and from those successes to empower Mexican American communities by resisting gerrymandering and the poll tax. Both Republican and Democratic parties were pressured to include Mexican Americans in mainstream politics.[91] They also took on other issues besides electioneering. As noted by researchers Matt Meier and Margo Gutierrez, "MAPA's semi-autonomous chapters undertook to defend Mexican Americans in a wide variety of civil rights situations—police brutality, discrimination in schools, and public accommodations issues. It was particularly important to Mexican Americans in isolated rural areas."[92]

In reference to the participation of women within the Democratic Party during this time, Roybal stated, "Very few women were actually active participants. I don't remember very many Hispanic women, outside of my wife and maybe a few others. But I don't remember seeing any large number of women that were involved in the Party. I think MAPA was more open, and I think that other organizations within MAPA structure were also the same."[93]

But the Democratic Party was the main issue—specifically, its lack of adequate response to its constituents. As frustration was building at the end of the decade, with eight years of Dwight Eisenhower as president and Richard Nixon as vice president, a Democratic victory at the national level seemed remote enough that some began to wonder, wouldn't a third party make sense?

When asked whether he and the co-founders of MAPA had considered building a third political party, Roybal said, "I don't think a third party movement is a good way to go...I think the thing to do is to work within the party to bring about some changes. That is what we tried to do all along. These changes came about very, very slowly. But they take place because it was forced upon them."[94] MAPA was part of that forcing.

During the 1970s, MAPA attempted to evolve into a truly national organization, but it remained a largely California organization. At the start of the 1980s, the organization is said to have had some 5,000 members. By then, it had generally supported candidates running within the Democratic Party.

Chapter 6

Building Kennedy's Camelot
(1960–1962)

THE 1960S BURST ON THE SCENE, RELEASING THE TENSION OF THE SILENT Decade (the 1950s) and filling the air with it. The mainland communist Chinese were challenging the nationalist islands of Quemoy and Matsu. In 1959, the first socialist revolution in the Americas brought Fidel Castro to power in Cuba. In the United States, a series of unresolved murders of African Americans hastened the beginnings of the civil rights movement, which challenged segregation, exclusion, and racism. Within the Mexican community, the Chicano Movement, a new generation of activists who challenged the status quo and clashed with the Mexican American generation, finally put to rest the myth that Mexicans were the "invisible minority."

Kennedy Sets the Tone

The decade began with promise and expectation as a young President John F. Kennedy took office in 1961. He stated, "Those who possess wealth and power in poor nations must accept their own responsibility. They must lead the fight for those basic reforms, which alone can preserve the fabric of their society. Those who make peaceful revolution impossible make violent revolution inevitable."

However, those with wealth and power did not desist but sought to maintain and prolong their hold. Nationalist liberation movements flourished, challenging moribund empires, such the British and Portuguese in Africa and Asia, and newer hegemonies such as the United States in Latin America and Southeast Asia. In response to these nationalistic challenges, the United States invaded Cuba in 1961 and the Dominican Republic in 1965, and Soviet forces invaded Czechoslovakia in 1968. President Kennedy's Alliance for Progress gave way to Green Berets, military training, and advisors. In 1962, the Cuban Missile Crisis brought the world to the brink of nuclear annihilation.

Racial integration in the United States was met with increasing resistance, and Mexican farm workers began to organize around an incipient union led by César Chávez. In November 1963, President Kennedy was assassinated, bringing an abrupt end to Camelot and paving the way for President Johnson's Great Society and War on Poverty. Increasing United States involvement in Vietnam diverted funds from the social agenda. In 1968, Martin Luther King and Robert Kennedy were assassinated, hundreds of ghettos broke out into riots, and the antiwar movement shook the nation's assumptions of "business as usual" to its core. A wave of illegal activities escalated at the FBI, from harassment to wiretaps of dissidents and shootouts with the Black Panthers. The disparate voices of Mexican Americans, Native Americans, African Americans, women, gays, people with disabilities, and people living with hunger and poverty challenged the centuries-old national ethos and consensus of ethnicity and race, class and privilege, gender and gender orientation. The social phenomenon of the 1960s challenged long-held assumptions of the "melting pot" theory and the exceptionalism of United States society. However, the pendulum of history then swung in the opposite direction. By the end of the decade, Richard M. Nixon made a spectacular political comeback for "law and order" by winning the presidency.

In the meantime, the Mexican community was attempting to determine its own destiny. In 1967, Reies Lopez Tijerina of New Mexico led the Alianza de Pueblos Libres (Alliance of Free City-States) to struggle for the return of violated land grants. Mexican people made up some 10 percent of the population of the Southwest but accounted for 19.4 percent of casualties from that region in the Vietnam War. At the same time, relatives of Mexican American soldiers were accused of "stealing jobs" and were being deported. In December 1969, the National Chicano Moratorium Committee held its first mass antiwar demonstration. The Mexican American generation had taken the Mexican people to the very gates of equality, social justice, and inclusion by the end of the decade. The Chicano generation would take their peoples through those gates and challenge the institutional barriers to political empowerment. And although the Mexican people would now wander in the corridors of power, it would be decades before some would sit on the tables of political power.

The environment was thick with hope and expectation for social change. In 1960, Dwight D. Eisenhower was already the oldest person to hold the office of president. He had been born in the previous century. It seemed to many that the former general's administration suffered from a lack of intellectual agility when a more nimble perspective on the world and on domestic matters was needed. Remnants of McCarthyism lingered, although Joseph McCarthy had been defeated and did not return to the Senate. There was a sense that the country was lagging, and John F. Kennedy's theme, "let's get started again," hit a responsive chord.

Richard Nixon was elected to the U.S. Senate for California in 1950 and thereafter served two terms as vice president under President Eisenhower. He was from a working-class family in Whittier, California. A lawyer by profession, Nixon had served in the U.S. Navy during World War II, and had been elected to the House of Representatives in 1947 riding the wave of McCarthy and the House Un-American Committee witch hunt in the Hollywood film industry. As the incumbent vice president, forty-seven-year-old Nixon won the 1960 Republican presidential nomination by a ballot of 1321–10. His vice president running mate was Henry Cabot Lodge, U.S. ambassador, former senator, and member of the Eastern establishment.[1]

John F. Kennedy, the Democratic candidate, was forty-three years old in 1960. A World War II navy hero, he had been elected to the House of

Representatives from Massachusetts in 1947 and then to the U.S. Senate in 1953. Unlike Nixon, Kennedy arose from wealth and privilege. Like Nixon, he was an aggressive anticommunist. However, coming from Irish American ward politicians and organizations, his experience gave him compassion for the less fortunate and for civil rights.[2]

At a forum in Los Angeles right before the presidential campaign began, Kennedy told Ed Roybal and others present that he was a true friend of the Mexican community.[3] That was enough for Roybal. Coming from a Catholic, the words were binding. A true friend gets a true friend in return.

For Mexican Americans, it was not difficult to decide which of the two presidential candidates to support. Historically, the Democratic Party had been friendly to Mexican Americans and courted them for elections, but its elected officials were infamous for their inadequate responses to local needs and demands for public services. Mexican Americans felt they were being taken for granted. In 1948, Henry Wallace had included Mexicans in his campaign under the Amigos de Wallace organizations across the Southwest and concentrated in California. The Republicans had first started to court the Mexican vote with Dwight D. Eisenhower's candidacy in two campaigns. Under the Latin American Veterans and Volunteers for Eisenhower-Nixon, they had focused their efforts on middle-class voters, uncommitted voters, and particularly Mexican American veterans. The Eisenhower-Nixon ticket reaped votes for their efforts.

On a larger scale, however, Republicans had never much bothered considering Mexican American issues. As the party of business, their modus operandi of taking a slow, steady course was a mismatch for reform-minded people in a hurry for change. In fact, strong Republican elements were vehemently opposed to reaching out. Mexican Americans felt they had something at stake now and moved to find a place in the Kennedy campaign. At last, a national campaign claimed to look out for their interests—regional groups, pockets of voters, the disenfranchised, Catholic, anticommunist, social progressives.[4]

Viva Kennedy Clubs

Viva Kennedy Clubs sprang up mainly in California and Texas but also throughout the southwestern states—wherever a Mexican American political infrastructure existed. Ed Roybal and other Mexican American leaders, as well as leaders from national organizations such as League of United Latin American Citizens (LULAC) and the American GI Forum sensed an urgency for a marked presence in the 1960 national presidential campaign. Their followers were mainly Southwesterners and some Midwesterners, an important regional group but not yet a national constituency.

The Democratic National Convention was held in Los Angeles in July 1960. It attracted the largest presence of Mexican American delegates and spectators ever to a major party convention. Arizona, California, New Mexico, and Texas sent the most elected Mexican American officials. New Mexican U.S. Senator Dennis Chavez had initially backed Lyndon Johnson for president but now supported Kennedy. Prominent among the elected officials were Edward Roybal and Henry B. Gonzalez, a city councilman from San Antonio. Roybal had already committed to Kennedy a few months before the convention when the candidate went through a rigorous question-and-answer session in California. Roybal was introduced to John Kennedy by his brother-in-law, actor Peter Lawford, an activist in the California Democratic clubs, while at Lawford's Pacific Palisades home. Roybal's first impression was that Kennedy was "a very, very bright individual."[5] Kennedy was savvy about American society, the undercurrents, the so-called invisible America, and the problems of Mexican Americans with getting ahead. Roybal respected Kennedy, noting that he had the "the nerve that was required." At a time when the Democratic Party was trying to accommodate the party's Southern wing, Kennedy was opposed to that appeasement. He had the "nerve to oppose a Party position when everybody else is for it and you happen not to agree."[6]

Roybal looked on Kennedy as a Roosevelt-type politician, a reformist, with the "right answers to the right issues."[7] Ed Roybal Jr. noted, "I think once [John F.] Kennedy was nominated, my father really became enthusiastic with his support."[8] Roybal, Gonzalez, and Chavez could only give Kennedy limited local and regional support, but they hoped that a strong Mexican American showing in the national election would make an impression. These delegates pushed for certain party reforms at the convention: the creation of a pro-nominee electoral effort among and by Mexican Americans, a strong push for a civil rights plank in the platform, and recognition that Mexican Americans' economic and social conditions needed a political solution. These three approaches were unconnected, and no consensus in their favor was evident even among the Mexican American attendees. Mainly, the appeal was an ideological one. This was a mistake because no prior meeting had taken place to plan content and strategy."[9] This construction of a political infrastructure to form consensus became a basic lesson that all Latino efforts would have to learn.

The Mexican American leadership had high expectations about the Kennedy candidacy. Hector P. Garcia, the American GI Forum's founder, had not attended the Convention but sent a statement on July 12, 1960, to the Democratic National Convention Committee's Nationalities Division in which he underscored the limited participation by minorities in the Democratic Party, the advisability of using Latinos to sell democracy in Latin America, the need for inclusion of Mexican Americans in a significant way, and how Mexican braceros and Mexican American migrant workers were exploited. He called for an end to police brutality and a civil rights plank in the platform.

The document appears to have had limited circulation among the delegates. Again, Mexican Americans were between a rock and hard place. Their issues were not a central focus of concern. Then, as now, an ambiguity fostered by mainstream ignorance that alternatively perceived them as somehow "racial" but neither White nor Black. Frankly, said researcher Ignacio M. Garcia, "Mexican Americans were simply not an important part of the discussion at the convention, and up to that time no one apparently saw reason to include them." Despite the Supreme Court precedents set in education, the civil rights battles were in terms of a White/Black dichotomy. Mexicans and other Latinos were too regional, too small of a group, too unknown to reach the national conscience. The discrimination they experienced was considered "the result of individual acts, not social violence."[10]

Having failed to form a consensus on a Mexican American agenda with other delegates at the beginning of the convention, an effort was made to maximize their presence at the convention. Ed Roybal and Henry B. Gonzalez made a last-ditch attempt to discuss the role of Mexican Americans at the National Convention. They met with Senator Dennis Chavez. Then they approached the Kennedy campaign and the candidate's brother and campaign manager, Robert Kennedy. They emphasized the need for government jobs for Mexican Americans and concern for the continued segregation of Mexican school children.[11]

Robert Kennedy agreed with Roybal, Gonzalez, and Chavez about their suggestions to become part of his brother's national campaign. Someone was needed to actually head it, but Roybal, Gonzalez, and Chavez could not do so because of their pressing public duties. Carlos McCormick was selected to head the Viva Kennedy efforts. He was a native of Santa Barbara, California, had lived in Tucson, and was a Kennedy staff member. He was a senior-year law student at George Washington University who had taken a leave to work in Spanish-language public relations and Latin American affairs with the Kennedy campaign. McCormick obtained the support of Albert A. Peña Jr., Bexar County (Texas) commissioner and long-time activist, to head the Texas effort. Peña's conditions were that the Viva Kennedy Club would be a distinct political effort from the established state Democratic parties and would have direct contact to the Kennedy staff. He insisted that Mexican Americans be considered for high-level appointments and that the new president make a real effort to eradicate the poll tax. In turn, Robert Kennedy personally promised Peña these conditions.[12]

The American GI Forum gave their unofficial support to the Viva Kennedy efforts after expanding on Peña's conditions to include the plight of migrant workers. GI Forum veterans quickly became the backbone of the Viva Kennedy Clubs in Texas. Soon after the Democratic convention, McCormick appointed U.S. Senator Dennis Chavez and Representative Joseph Montoya (D-NM) as honorary chairmen. The co-chairpersons were Edward R. Roybal and Henry "Hank" Lopez of California; John Mendoza of Nevada; Jose Alvarado of Illinois; Filo Sedillo of New Mexico; Stanley Valadez of Pennsylvania; Henry B. Gonzalez, Hector P. Garcia, and Albert Peña Jr. of Texas; Joe Maravilla and Richard Rucoba of Indiana; Vicente Ximenes of New Mexico; Frank Rubi of Arizona; Agustine Olvera of Iowa; and Jesse Alvarado and David Vega of Kansas. Other chairs were appointed from the states of Florida, Ohio, New York, Colorado, and Michigan.

To augment their distinctness as a political group, they developed a symbol and a banner created by Ben Alvarado. It was a drawing of Senator John F. Kennedy wearing a large sombrero, with the words *Viva Kennedy* imprinted in blue. The brand, the identification, the public recognition became emblematic. The Viva Kennedy Clubs was the first major national partisan movement to join together under one candidate the notions of Democrat, liberal, empathy for the poor, and Latin America. The clubs were instrumental in bringing together a coalition of Mexican Americans, Puerto Ricans, Cubans, and other Latin Americans. The campaign gave the participating leaders exposure to each other's communities. This had the effect of educating them on their particular similarities and differences. They developed a heightened understanding, saw the range of political constraints, measured alternative approaches as solutions. In particular, the Mexican American and Latino middle class and labor representatives worked together.

In California, the Mexican American Political Association (MAPA) and the Community Service Organization (CSO) became responsible for the Viva Kennedy Clubs. The Kennedy Clubs' support staff came from the MAPA chapters, assisted by the CSO. The Viva Kennedy Clubs' effort within the CSO was directed by Ralph Guzman, a political science graduate student at UCLA. By the campaign's close, more than 130,000 Mexican American Democrats were registered to vote because of the Viva Kennedy Clubs, according to Carlos McCormick.[13]

Ed Roybal was selected as the leader of the Viva Kennedy Clubs in California. He went about this role with persistence, dedication, and meticulous diligence. In California, the Viva Kennedy Clubs maintained between themselves a loose relationship. Club leaders met to plan strategies and then forwarded these plans to Roybal for approval. Roybal was the liaison between the California Kennedy clubs and the Kennedy campaign. He also coordinated John Kennedy's visits to the state and those of other national figures. From state headquarters, the clubs published bulletins that kept chapters informed about meetings, rallies, speakers, and fundraisers. This autonomy from the state party allowed Mexican American leaders to focus on health, education, and employment—the same issues raised in Roybal's own campaigns.[14]

Roybal traveled widely and worked tirelessly for the Viva Kennedy organization. He stumped in Illinois, Kansas, Texas, and Arizona, reminding his audiences that discrimination had become more subtle but was still endemic. In these speeches, he shared his own experiences of discrimination and adversity and also his hopes and dreams for repairing the injustices. Time and again, he told audiences that Kennedy was the only presidential candidate who could change conditions by providing moral leadership behind government action. Roybal had little personal contact with Kennedy, yet felt connected, and he articulated to audiences that Kennedy had the gift of befriending everyone he spoke to. Roybal believed in Kennedy's sincerity.

John F. Kennedy won the presidential election over Richard Nixon with the smallest plurality in U.S. history, a mere 120,000-vote plurality of the popular vote, and 303 to 219 of the Electoral College votes. Mexican Americans nationwide were an important factor in the election, giving Kennedy more than 85 percent of their votes. In California, where Nixon was the native son, people of Mexican origin gave Kennedy 85 percent percent of their votes; in Texas, about 91 percent; and in New Mexico, 70 percent. The election had been decided in California by an infinitesimal two-tenths of 1 percent; in New Mexico, eight-tenths of 1 percent; and in Illinois, one-tenth of 1 percent.

The narrowness of the national victory led some to believe that the Mexican votes had made the difference for Kennedy. States with the largest Mexican and Latino populations coincided with the states where the election had its closest results. The president-elect sent a letter to Hector Garcia of the GI Forum congratulating him and other leaders for the "magnificent job turned in by the national Viva Kennedy Clubs."[15] Robert F. Kennedy told a Mexico City journalist that it was the "votes of Mexican Americans and other Latin Americans in the United States that elected" his brother. Kennedy went on to say that his brother's new administration would pay more attention to Latin America.[16] McCormick also credited the efforts of the Viva Kennedy Clubs for Kennedy's victory. He said that Kennedy's win "can be traced to the overwhelming one-sided votes in precincts inhabited by persons of Mexican and Puerto Rican descent."[17]

Unfortunately, this euphoria by Mexicans and Latinos alike would soon give way to a profound disillusionment with the Kennedy administration. In February, President Kennedy reiterated his desire to bring Mexican Americans into his administration. He informed reporters of the valuable talent in the Latin American community in the United States. He stated that a high position had been offered to a Mexican American who had not accepted it. The "high position" had been offered to Henry B. Gonzalez. It was an ambassadorship to a small Latin American country. Gonzalez apparently turned it down because he was considering at the time a possible run for Lyndon B. Johnson's vacated U.S. Senate seat, now that Johnson was elected vice president. Roybal was then considered, as were Raymond L. Telles, El Paso mayor, and Vicente Ximenez, a New Mexico scholar. The ambassadorship ultimately went to Arturo Morales Carrion, a Puerto Rican.[18]

A Rude Awakening to Political Reality

Roybal and other Mexican American leaders soon discovered to their disappointment that an IOU before November was not a check they could cash after Election Day. Promises are promises, not contracts. U.S. Senator Dennis Chavez criticized the Kennedy administration for taking too long to make appointments. Frustration began to cast its pall over the Mexican American leadership. McCormick himself voiced his own bitterness. Councilman Roybal made public his feeling that the Kennedy administration, while acknowledging the Viva Kennedy leaders' value, failed to come through with federal appointments.[19] No major appointments of Mexican Americans were ever made by President Kennedy.

A few minor appointments were made, however. Two went to Puerto Ricans who had not taken part in the Viva Kennedy Clubs. One Mexican American, Reynaldo Garza, who had been an Eisenhower Democrat, was appointed to a federal judgeship in Texas. The biggest appointment was probably that of Raymond L. Telles, who was appointed as ambassador to Costa Rica. He had only been marginally involved with the Viva Kennedy Clubs.

The disappointment with the Kennedy administration caused some Mexican American leaders to rethink the usefulness of competing among so many other pressing interests. Instead, the idea arose to stress their ethnicity and promote their native sons and daughters as local—not anointed—leaders. They would become politicians rather than reformers. Electoral politics would replace all other forms of activism.[20]

In March 1961, Texas leaders of the Viva Kennedy Clubs founded the Mexican Americans for Political Action (MAPA) organization. They selected Albert Peña Jr. as state chair and Hector P. Garcia as national organizer. Later in the month, they met in Phoenix, Arizona, to further strategize the political empowerment of Mexican Americans at the national political level. Roybal told the participants, "We find no consolation [in Kennedy's actions] and for that reason we must do something concrete about it." He said that the delegates must put aside the jealousies

175

that had arisen among the regional chapters and promote unity. Hector Garcia was chosen as president and Roybal as vice president.[21] However, unity proved illusory, as Roybal would say later, because they could not initially agree on the organization's name or what to call themselves.

The legacy of being a subjugated people manifested itself in a collage of self-identity. Underlying the naming dispute were mixed traditions about names and the regional identities and distinctions they implied. In Colorado, Mexicans called themselves Spanish Americans or Spanish-speaking; and in Texas, they called themselves Texans of Mexican descent. In New Mexico, they were Hispanos, while in California, they were Mexican Americans. Elsewhere, references were to Americans of Spanish descent or Latins. All the shibboleths seemed to deny the Mexican-ness that all of them had in common, and especially their Native American roots. Roybal and the Californians were the most adamant in promoting this aspect of Mexican-ness and native roots, and he suggested Mexican American Political Association (MAPA) as the name for the national organization (the same as the California organization). In the end, the organization was christened the Political Association of Spanish-Speaking Organizations (PASSO).

Ed Roybal, Henry B. Gonzalez, Albert Peña, Dennis Chavez, and Joseph Montoya did not attend the next meeting, held in Las Vegas, Nevada, reflecting a fracture in the leadership. Consensus on ethnic identity was failing, which doomed the organization as a unifying national entity. While PASSO encouraged community involvement in politics, it challenged the older, more conservative Mexican American leadership's accommodationist views.[22] The organization became mostly a Texas organization. By the 1970s, it split between the progressive wing of the Democratic Party and the emerging third parties, one of which was La Raza Unida Party.

The Viva Kennedy Clubs experience was an important benchmark for Ed Roybal, showing success at a pivotal moment in the presidential election. The Viva Kennedy Clubs were instrumental in making the

Mexican American community and its political leaders available for federal employment and appointment pools. The clubs showed for the first time that Mexican communities formed a national constituency. The clubs were not operating at a national level but were active in strategically important sections of the country. Their activism represented a new level of involvement where before they were held to a supporting role in party politics. However, Ignacio M. Garcia noted, "The dependence on Anglo American politicians by low-level Mexican American politicos and reformers made them vulnerable to the nationalism of the barrios in the 1960s and 1970s. It would create a schism between the nationalistic working class/student alliance and the accommodating, moderately liberal middle-class reformers."[23] Having to deal with some of the same unsavory local Democratic leaders who had shunned them and their issues before, people began showing the first signs of departure from the Democratic to the Republican Party.

The Viva Kennedy Clubs politicized the Mexican American reform agenda by emphasizing social welfare as a governmental action instead of a civic, mutual aid activity. However, these politics of inclusion forced the two major political parties to gradually move away from the strict government versus mutual aid dichotomy. There was some incremental change but it was too slow and ponderous for most activists. The clubs contributed to promoting an ethnic consciousness, although that identity was seen through prism of United States history instead of Mexican American history.

Roybal's 1961 Los Angeles City Council Race

In 1949, Ed Roybal's election campaign funding had largely been financed by small contributions from individuals and unions. By 1957, business was helping to underwrite Roybal's political campaigns. He had by now broadened his base to include businesses after the CSO withdrew from electoral politics and he could no longer count on their assistance. As a popular incumbent, Roybal supplemented small individual donations with generous and regular contributions from business elites.[24]

In 1961, Roybal ran for city council for the fifth time. His business support did not cost him his stalwart following, and he continued to be enthusiastically supported by labor unions, including the Joint Council of Teamsters No. 42, associated with the International Brotherhood of Teamsters, Chauffeurs, Warehousemen, and Helpers; the Los Angeles AFL-CIO COPE; and the Brotherhood of Locomotive Firemen and Enginemen. His multiethnic support continued through the Chinese American Citizens, the Italo-American Voters, Inc., and the Independent Voters League of California.[25]

Roybal's candidacy earned increasing support from the city's newspapers. The *Los Angeles Sentinel, Eastside Sun,* and the *California Eagle* endorsed Roybal's re-election with strong editorials.[26] The *California Eagle* said African Americans with their endorsement were giving unwavering support at a time when they were rapidly becoming the majority of voters in the redistricted 9th District. The *California Eagle* recognized that "Mr. Roybal has waged a long fight in city council to protect his constituents and to extend to them their rights. He was the only member of the Council to protect against this year's gerrymander which deprives Negroes of a seat in the Council. No person in California has done more than he to further civil rights."[27] During March 1961, 9th District African Americans held an afternoon social at the home of Mrs. Eloise Davis attended by 150 people.[28]

The city's largest Spanish-language newspaper, *La Opinion,* finally endorsed Roybal for the first time.[29] The *Examiner* also recommended Roybal's re-election. The *Mirror,* the *Los Angeles Herald & Express,* and the *Los Angeles Times* did not editorially endorse him; in fact, they did not make any recommendation in the race.[30] However, the *Los Angeles Times* singled out Roybal, noting his "many projects of citywide importance, projects which were largely supported by the business interests of his district," citing one measure that would allow a non-private group to operate the proposed new zoo, the Bunker Hill redevelopment, and the contract with Dodgers baseball team."[31]

Roybal faced two challengers: David Ruiz and Marion Carter. Neither had previously held office. Ruiz was a thirty-two-year-old Olvera Street merchant who promised "greater value" for the taxpayers' dollar, strictly supervised playgrounds, and a sympathetic ear for the advice of clergymen.[32] Carter was thirty years old, a writer and mother of four children. She told the *Eastside Sun* that she was concerned about the worn street conditions, inadequate street lighting, and crossing and safety signals in various areas. "I believe [in] the necessity for stronger representation," she said.[33] Without name recognition, a defining issue, or the support of the Democratic Party, both challengers met defeat.

Roybal kicked off his re-election campaign with an event at the Alexandria Hotel attended by more than 150 people. Roger Johnson was again Roybal's campaign manager. He made a pitch at the event for funds and recruits.[34] A couple of days before the election, the campaign organization held a dance at the Amalgamated Clothing Workers Hall.[35]

Election Day turnout was almost as low as in 1951. Still, Roybal won 67 percent of the votes, the majority from all four areas, out of a total vote of 26,319. Marian Carter obtained 11 percent and David Ruiz 7 percent. About 15 percent of the voters abstained from voting for any candidate. As in the previous election, the largest amount of roll-off voting (68 percent) took place in the South Central area.[36] More significantly, Eastside voting declined to its lowest level of only 9,652 voters, only about half of the votes cast by the Eastside in 1949. For the second consecutive election, votes from South Central (11,625) overshadowed those in the Eastside, even though the number of voters was smaller than in 1957.

Ed Roybal was gracious and humble about his victory. He stated, "I am grateful to the public-spirited citizens who gave of their time and efforts in making my re-election possible, thus giving me an opportunity to continue working not only on behalf of the people of my district but also on behalf of the people of Los Angeles."[37]

The spring election also saw changes in the Los Angeles mayor's race. A growing discontent with Mayor Norris Poulson was evidenced as ex-Congressman Sam Yorty forced the incumbent for a May runoff. Final semiofficial returns showed Poulson with 179,273 votes to Yorty's 122,273.

Despite the fact that he was the only councilman of color and the only liberal in the conservative, pro–big business Los Angeles City Council, Roybal gained the respect and admiration of his peers. In July, Roybal was elected president pro tem of the Los Angeles City Council over Councilman Timberlake by an 8–5 vote. Councilman Harold Henry was elected as council president. Later in September, Roybal became Acting Mayor when Mayor Yorty was in New York for a ten-day visit and vacation and the council president was in Seattle, Washington, attending a meeting of the American Municipal Association. It was the first time in the city's history that a Mexican American served as chief executive since 1868.

On September 4, 1961, Ed Roybal, as acting mayor of Los Angeles, presided over the 180th birthday of the city. More than 7,000 people attended the festivities at the heart of the Pueblo de Nuestra Señora la Reina de Los Angeles. In his speech, Roybal indicated the colonial-era buildings surrounding the Old Plaza and reclaimed them, saying, "This kiosk is the first of its kind in the United States. This is the dream come true for the Mexican American community. It was built in an effort to preserve the culture of Mexico and Spain and to leave, at the site of the city's founding, a history of the past and hope for the future of a city that is now No. 3 in the nation [in population]—soon to be No. 2." Cheers rang out. The Tipica orchestra serenaded the crowd. As part of the ceremonies, actor Bill Gaskin re-created the founding of the Los Angeles impersonating Felipe de Nava, the first governor of California, who had named the city in 1781. He arrived at the site on a beautiful white stallion. A religious parade then followed from the Mission Church that was led by Father Luis Bossi. City dignitaries such as Ernest Debs, chairperson of the Los Angeles Board of Supervisors, and Judge McIntyres Faries were on hand for the ceremonies.

By 1961, it was common knowledge in California political circles that Ed Roybal had the intention of running for higher political office, either for U.S. Congress or U.S. Senate. Observers of the political scene in California were already noting that the Democratic Party was not necessarily enthusiastic about having Roybal or another Mexican American leader run for higher office, even with the support of the party machine. These issues apparently came to a head on October 4, 1961, at a luncheon for Democratic Governor Pat Brown, which was held at Michale's Restaurant in Los Angeles. At the luncheon, Judge Leo Sanchez, an up-and-coming Mexican American leader, made a stirring speech criticizing how the Democratic Party was bypassing appointment for deserving Mexican Americans. However, it was Roybal who electrified the audience. In the process of introducing the governor, whom some thought he was protecting from Sanchez's sharp criticism, he made some unexpected and candid remarks. He commented, "I was invited to Governor Brown's home for dinner and the Governor asked me if I would like to run for U.S. Senator, Congress in the 30th District, or for Secretary of State and I told Pat that I would let him know later. Now, this is off the record, but I can I can tell him now at this luncheon what I have decided to do. I am going to run for Congress."[38]

Roybal's comments elicited a furor but also threw light on the contrast between Roybal's independence of mind and the condensation of the Democratic Party. He was thinking of the well-being of the Mexican American community first and the party discipline second. Roybal's decision put the governor on the spot because he knew that there were others with aspirations for the same seat in the U.S. Congress in the new 30th Congressional District. One known aspirant was Assemblyman Edward E. Elliot, a workhorse liberal who was instrumental in crafting the progressive bent of Brown's legislative program in Sacramento.

Brown, who was opposed to pre-primary endorsements, was flabbergasted, as was Elliot, who apparently had been cultivating his own support for the office. Judge Leo Sanchez also displayed a disposition to challenge Ed Roybal. The evening's events were evidence that the Mexican American community was increasingly impatient with the old party bosses and way of doing things. They were beginning to feel that justice delayed too long was indeed justice denied.[39]

In October 1961, Ed Roybal was selected to represent Los Angeles in the 400th anniversary of the founding of Madrid, Spain. He traveled to the city and was there October 12–18. Mayor Yorty had been invited to the event but could not attend due to pressing city government responsibilities. He informed J. D. Biddle, U.S. ambassador to Spain, that Roybal would be attending in his place.

He was accompanied on his trip by his wife, Lucille. He said later that Spanish officials inquired whether the Spanish missions in California were still functioning. He indicated to them that the best efforts were being made to preserve the historic sites. He also stated that he had seen much construction for low-income people in the city of Madrid. Conde de Mayalde, the mayor of Madrid, acknowledged Roybal by bestowing on him a Medal of Honor, the award given to a visiting political official.

He visited Berlin and saw firsthand what would be become known as the Berlin Crisis, when the Soviets shut down the roads to Berlin. Ed and Lucille also visited Rome and were able to visit the pope. The trip helped to educate Roybal further on issues of U.S. foreign policy and politics in Europe.

Speaking Out on Civil Rights

Among the key issues Roybal tackled during his fifth term were issues concerning city services equity, halting police brutality, support for antidiscrimination measures in city housing and employment, civil rights, and an end to social justice persecutions under the guise of anticommunism. He led several voter registration campaigns with the CSO and also opposed the displacement of low-income residents from Chavez Ravine (later Dodger Stadium) and Bunker Hill as a result of the freeway construction. His main concern was with the effects that unbridled development had on individuals and communities and on their quality of life.

During November 1961, Ed Roybal was the guest speaker at a gathering of Barstow's Community Service Organization, the local chapter of the National Association for the Advancement of Colored People, and the Independent Latin American Club on the pressing issue of civil rights. It turned out to be one of Roybal's most dynamic and rousing political speeches of his entire public career. He began by the noting the progress made by the Spanish-speaking people in the past few years and the native roots of Mexicans in the Southwest. He recalled to the enthusiastic and aroused audience the contributions of Mexicans in World War II and Korea. He reminded them of the fact that of all the Congressional Medals of Honor given, 32 percent of the recipients had Spanish surnames. Then, he touched on the turning point at the heart of the Mexican American generation. "Ladies and gentlemen, those of us who did go into the war and came back to the United States, came back to our home towns, forgot for some time that we did wear the uniform of the United States and that we did fight for this country. We also forgot, no doubt, that—perhaps on the battlefield itself—we promised ourselves that when we did get back to our home towns we were going to participate in civic affairs, that we were no longer going to be isolated or segregated, that we were going to come back and fight for those rights that were ours under the Constitution just as we fought for our rights to preserve democracy and to preserve liberty on the battlefields of Europe and the battlefields of the Pacific, and in Korea." He finished to rousing applause. For the Mexican American generation, the speech captured their hopes and dreams of an entire lifetime.

Chapter 7

Mr. Roybal Goes to Washington
(1962–1963)

MEXICAN COMMUNITIES IN THE UNITED STATES UNDERWENT DEMO-
graphic, political, and cultural changes in the 1960s. The decade also
witnessed the beginnings of the Chicano Movement—an assertive, more
militant movement than the patient one of the previous decade. The
Chicano generation clashed with the leaders of the previous generation
about the direction, strategies, and ideology of Mexican American political empowerment. It was also an identity movement, in the sense that
people looked to themselves for change instead of seeking acceptance
and accommodation. They turned against the hyphenation of citizens
and adopted their own unique name.

The Socioeconomic Status of Mexican Americans in the 1960s

In 1960, Mexican-origin people now numbered nearly 4 million. More
than 87 percent of this population lived in the southwestern states and 13
percent in all of the other parts of the country. Of these, 14 percent were
first generation, Mexico born.[1] Mexicans residing in the Southwest had
a $968 per capita income, compared to $2,047 for Whites and $1,044 for
non-Whites. Living conditions tended to be substandard as well. Nearly
30 percent lived in deteriorated housing; Mexican-descent families were
large, with 4.77 members on average, compared to Whites (3.39) and
non-Whites (4.54).[2]

Mexicans revered education and saw it as the main avenue to overcome low income and poverty. Public education was lacking in important ways. For example, Mexican-origin people over fourteen years of age averaged 8.1 years of schooling, compared to 12.0 for Whites and 9.7 for non-Whites.[3]

In Los Angeles County, the Mexican population in the 1960s grew from slightly more than 0.5 million to 1.2 million, an increase of 113 percent. Meanwhile, Whites decreased by 2 percent.[4] Mexican-origin people grew to over 80 percent of the Boyle Heights-East Los Angeles population. The postwar era had witnessed the exodus of middle-class Jews and European Americans, while working-class Mexicans moved in. As East Los Angeles became poorer and more Mexican, city and county authorities continued ignoring the socioeconomic needs of the expanding community. The increasing poverty, discrimination, school deterioration; the rise of street gangs; and the sense of hopelessness often manifested in the streets and in worsening community-police relations. Los Angeles Police Chief William Parker didn't help matters when he told the U.S. Civil Rights Commission in January 1960 that "some of these people [Mexicans] were here before we were but some are not far removed from the wild tribes...of the inner mountains of Mexico."[5]

Parker claimed that 28 percent of the city's arrests were of Mexicans and 40 percent of them African Americans. In response, some 500 people staged a demonstration against Parker following a Mexican American Citizens Committee meeting. Dr. R. J. Carreon Jr., the only Mexican American police commissioner, failed to attend the gathering and—incredibly—suggested that community leaders leave the issue of Parker's remarks alone. The Mexican American Citizens Committee, the American Civil Liberties Union, and the National Association for the Advancement of Colored People had earlier joined together to establish the Los Angeles Police Review Board. Councilman Roybal demanded Chief Parker apologize. The city newspapers censured Roybal. The *Los Angeles Times* accused Roybal of demagoguery.[6]

The United States Department of Justice, according to Dr. Armando Morales, received 1,328 complaints of police brutality nationally between January 1958 and June 1960. In 1965, the McCone Commission Report[7] noted that there were 412 complaints of police misconduct in Los Angeles. The CSO and Council of Mexican American Affairs alone had investigated sixty cases in the 1950s and 1960s from mostly Spanish-speaking complainants, all involving physical abuse by Los Angeles police.[8]

The *Weekly Outlook*, an East Los Angeles newspaper, noted, "In East Los Angeles it has been rather noticeable lately those police officers have taken it upon themselves to search individuals without first obtaining a search warrant. Citizens of East Los Angeles are being pushed to the point of rebellion." The newspaper reported on several altercations in which "citizens have chosen to involve themselves in fights with police officers."[9] Eighty-six percent of the police department was non-Hispanic, only the most obvious indicator of the department's scant willingness to adapt to the community's changing nature and likely an underlying cause for Mexican community-police conflict. The department had only a handful of Hispanic officers, and these had been previously in the military, according to Roybal. There were fewer still in positions above captain or assistant chief. The sheriff's department was perhaps slightly better, but those officers often served "at the will of a certain politician."[10]

"There was a lot of corruption. Los Angeles was a very corrupt city," said Roybal. "Not as bad as Chicago, but almost—a very corrupt city. There was a lot of organized crime, gangsters like Mickey Cohen and Bugsy Segal."[11]

There was a general public belief during these times, and especially in law enforcement, that the poor committed more crime than the affluent and that this tendency was magnified by dark skin and speaking a foreign language. Mexican Americans met those criteria. In fact, another general belief circulating at the time suggested that Mexican Americans were biologically prone to commit crimes.[12]

Councilman Roybal often spoke out against police abuse, at the price of arousing the media's wrath and that of the powers that be. He received several anonymous death threats for speaking up. Threats like that "happened quite often," he said, when asked about why he needed a bodyguard. "I even wore a bulletproof vest," he said, one made available by the LAPD. Inside the force there were some officers who favored his positions and not the chief's. "No one shot at me, but I was in danger."

Threats to Roybal would continue for many years. For example, in 1976, Roybal wore his bulletproof vest to the dedication of the Edward R. Roybal Comprehensive Health Center. He had received a specific threat, to be carried out during his speech. Police gunmen perched on tops of buildings, searching for the assassin and ready to respond. "It wasn't an easy feeling," said Roybal, "because what if they missed me and hit my wife."[13]

Roybal worked closely with the CSO, the Mexican American Political Association (MAPA), the League of United Latin American Citizens (LULAC), and the GI Forum throughout the 1960s to address police brutality and police misconduct. The issue would not go away, especially after the Watts Riot of August 1965. Gangs were increasing in number and at the same time more people were standing up. A growing number of Mexican Americans were demanding social justice on all fronts.

Roybal's 1962 Run for Congress

Edward Roybal was forty-six in 1962 and aspired to higher office, a federal office. Participating in Kennedy's presidential campaign had rekindled his desire for a national perspective on how government could effectively persuade opponents at the local level to resolve issues. President Kennedy's New Frontier policies sought a new kind of social justice that Roybal could agree with, by appealing to the idealism that was just now being defined for this generation. It was not the New Deal. It was newer.

By 1962, Roybal had already made two tries for higher office before he decided to run for the House of Representatives. In 1954, he had run for lieutenant governor and, in 1958, for the Los Angeles Board of Supervisors. He had failed to get elected both times.

Reapportionment in 1961 created the new 30th Congressional District. It included the 9th City Council District, the downtown area, the Macarthur Park and Wilshire Districts, and Southwest Los Angeles all the way to the Exposition Park border. Roybal let his supporters and others know he was interested in running. An inducement was that the new district's voters were 59 percent Democrats. In preparation, Roybal expanded his legislative agenda to include issues that would resonate beyond the Eastside and South Central, where he might gain a wider appeal among those outside his home district. Roybal included in his outreach creation of more job opportunities, civil rights, a new approach to assisting foreign governments, aid to education, health and hospital care for the elderly, an aggressive fight against narcotics addiction, concerns about business and industry, tax relief, provisions for easier home ownership, and an urban renewal approach that protected both individual and property rights.[14]

During the first week of March 1962, Roybal attended the retirement event of his long-time friend, Los Angeles Police Lt. Tom Bradley, at the Police Academy at Elysian Park. Bradley, a veteran officer of twenty-one years, planned to practice law as an attorney with the Charles Matthews law firm. Roybal presented Bradley with a resolution honoring his service and signed by every member of the Los Angeles City Council. No one could possibly predict at that time that Tom Bradley would become the first African American mayor of Los Angeles in the far-off future.[15]

In April 1962, more support for Roybal's congressional candidacy manifested itself. Gayle Collins, vice president of the AFL-CIO Committee on Political Action commented, "Labor decided to back Councilman Roybal for Congress because we felt that he would be the best candidate to help carry out the Kennedy program…because we believe the program will not only meet the needs of labor, but also all of the people." The AFL-CIO Committee on Political Action went on to endorse Roybal's candidacy. Los Angeles County Supervisor John Anson Ford praised Roybal's candidacy and emphasized Roybal's long and diligent support for the Fair Employment ordinance in the Los Angeles

City Council. He said, "I've never known Ed Roybal to back down once." Esteban Torres, by then an important organizer for the United Autoworkers unions, commented, "I recall that they endorsed him at each turn of his political endeavors, such as Supervisor, Lt. Governor, and Congressman. I was walking and knocking on doors working on the campaign. I was the chairman of my political committee in my local union. He [Roybal] was endorsed by labor. He believed very much in the labor union and working people."[16]

Even as he garnered more support, Roybal was busy in the Los Angeles City Council, where on March 13, 1962, he introduced an ordinance to provide nursing care for senior citizens in their own homes. The programs were made possible by federal funds available through one of the new laws secured by the Kennedy administration.

During April, the Japanese American community formed a citizens committee to help elect Councilman Edward R. Roybal for Congress in the 30th District and Governor Edmund G. Brown. A spokesman for the committee stated, "We believe that Governor Brown and Councilman Roybal deserve the all-out support of everyone because of their outstanding record." During the same month, Councilman Roybal was instrumental in Los Angeles City Council resolution to honor Daniel K. Inouye, the first congressman from Hawaii. Inouye was the first Japanese American to be seated in the House of Representatives. Roybal presented Inouye the city scroll.[17]

During early May 1962, the American Legion Post 826 withdrew its request to Roybal to review the Fourth of July Woodland Hills parade. John A. Gray, parade chairman, in a letter to Roybal stated that since the invitation had gone out May 8, "several items have come concerning your affiliations with several groups, amongst them your endorsement today by SANE [Sane Nuclear Policy]." Gray indicated that they would continue to investigate Roybal's affiliations. For his part, Roybal commented that this was "the most obvious and lowest kind of political smear. This is stooping to a new low. Since the parade isn't until the Fourth of July, but the election is next week, this makes it all the more obvious."[18] Not ironically, the parade marshal was G. Pappy Boyington, the top marine flying ace, who was running against Roybal for the 30th District.

Roybal's base of support, after thirteen years in office representing the 9th District, was highly diverse. It was just the type of following he needed for the congressional race. Organizations supporting him included the Council of Mexican American Affairs, the Southern Federation of Settlements and Centers, the Los Angeles County Conference on Human Relations, the Friendship Day Camp, the Memorial Jewish Community Center, tbe Medical Research Association of California, and the Workman's Circle, among others. However, the state Democratic Party was unsupportive and even disdainful of his run for Congress.

Roybal understood and almost expected the party to show no enthusiasm for his candidacy, even though he was the party's former candidate for lieutenant governor and had a statewide following. He knew Democrats were not enthused by someone who had a record of challenging some of their positions. "It was a general policy of these people that when they didn't like a particular position they just didn't support it in any way."[19] And in Roybal's case it meant not supporting him, especially since the new 30th Congressional District had been designed for someone else. Jesse Unruh,[20] the Democratic California State Assembly Speaker (1961–1969) and party leader, had designed it for William F. Fitzgerald.

Consequently, Roybal received no support from the party. Jesse Unruh, known to keep a firm control on the state, maintained party discipline. Unruh was one of the most powerful and colorful California politicians for many years. A tough and effective politician, and at times abrasive one, he first came to notice as the California State Democratic Party chairman. His most famous quotes were "If you can't drink a lobbyist's whiskey, take his money, sleep with his women, and still vote against him in the morning, you don't belong in politics" and "Money is the mother's milk of politics." Unruh had come up the hard way in politics, and he was reluctant to give anybody political favors. He had had two unsuccessful tries for the California State Assembly, in 1950 and 1952. He was finally elected as member of the assembly in 1954 but was an unsuccessful candidate for Presidential Elector of California in 1956, and in 1960 (until 1968) he was a delegate to the Democratic National Convention. In 1959, he authored California's Unruh Civil Rights Act, a far-reaching law that prohibited discrimination in housing and employment, which would become template for national legislation in the 1960s and 1970s. He ran against Ronald Reagan for governor in 1970 and for mayor of Los Angeles in 1973, but lost both elections. He was elected state treasurer in 1974, serving from 1975 until his death of prostate cancer on August 4, 1987.

Whatever Unruh said, in those days, party workers did. Roybal and Unruh were congenial to one another, but Unruh was never Roybal's supporter.[21] Lacking party support, Roybal's funding for the congressional campaign had to come increasingly from small businesses, to supplement the donations from working-class individuals and labor organizations.[22]

Roybal's campaign manager conducted a survey before the election. He was looking to identify the issues that most concerned voters. The survey wasn't to change an ideological point of view. Their position was generally liberal. But they needed to stake out positions as Democratic Party members. "Our position as liberals was different from the position that one would take if you just wanted to be with the party," Roybal clarified.[23]

Roybal's chief rival in the race, Loyola University professor William F. Fitzgerald, did not have the state Democratic Party's endorsement either. In April 1962, both Roybal and Fitzgerald attempted to get the California Democratic Council's endorsement but the board voted 23–18 to not recommend either candidate. Nonetheless, days before the June primary, California State Controller Alan Cranston, the California Democratic Council's founder, endorsed Roybal. Cranston said he saw Roybal as "a highly effective liberal." To Cranston, Roybal had already demonstrated an ability to win and hold office. "I have worked closely with Ed Roybal," he said, "and have watched him become the symbol of a new era of millions of people throughout California," adding that Roybal had already grappled with many of the issues that "equip him superbly for dealing with these fundamental issues on the national scene."[24]

During August, Lucille Roybal was named to the Democratic State Central Committee by Alan Cranston. Cranston, who was up for re-election as controller, was authorized by law to appoint five members to the governing group of the state Democratic Party. During this time, Lucille Roybal was active in the Parent Teacher Association, the League of Women Voters, and the Friendship Day Camp. She had been a former member of the YMCA board and was currently on the board of the Los Angeles Community Concert Association.

That same month, Ed Roybal traveled to Washington, D.C., where he attended a campaign briefing session. On the trip, he was compelled to use crutches due to a muscle injury from playing baseball. During the visit, he participated in a conference at the White House with President Kennedy and Vice President Lyndon B. Johnson. Roybal indicated that the conference had been attended by congressional nominees from twenty states. Among those attending were Attorney General Robert Kennedy; Secretary of State Dean Rusk; Commerce Secretary Luther Hodges; Majority Leader Carl Albert of the House of Representatives; Lawrence F. O'Brien, special assistant to the president; Sargent Shriver, Peace Corps director; and Director of the Budget David E. Bell. The Washington, D.C., visit would prove invaluable in meeting the key movers and shakers of the Democratic Party to Roybal for his future congressional activities.

Back home, Roybal garnered endorsements from an impressive and diverse group of supporters: the Property Association of Los Angeles, the Protective Owners Association, the Los Angeles County AFL-CIO COPE, the *Eastside Sun*, and *La Opinion*.

Despite the fact that his congressional district was beyond the confines of his old city council district, Roybal was able to maintain the crucial Jewish vote. Ed Roybal Jr. recalled, "I think the progressive Jewish community had a very good role model in identifying with my father, supporting him from the beginning. They had a very key role. In my father's campaigns there were always Jewish supporters who volunteered and were there from the beginning and throughout his career. When my dad first ran for Congress, he won in a congressional district that had had the lines drawn for a Republican to win. So my dad's first ten years, he represented Hancock Park, all that area, including Boyle Heights. This was part of that; a lot of [Jewish] folks had lived in Boyle Heights and moved to the Westside, and they continued to support him."[25]

Roybal defeated Democratic challenger William F. Fitzgerald by a nowhere-close margin of almost three to one.[26] By now, Roybal had refined his platform for the general election around eleven themes: peace, equal rights, employment, medical care, education, public welfare, housing, taxes, inflation, narcotics, and labor.

He proposed peace through strengthening the United Nations, arms control, and foreign aid. Employment should be created through public works and job training and retraining for those displaced by automation. He supported Kennedy's proposals of medical care for the aged and Social Security. Education should include supporting Kennedy's Aid to Education program and funds for teacher training. Public welfare should be streamlined, and recipients should have incentives to help themselves. Housing should be made more accessible, via low-interest loans and 200,000 new public housing units a year for senior citizens and others needing low-cost housing. He proposed tax relief for small business, property owners, and senior citizens. Inflation should be fought by stopping public spending waste in defense, agriculture, and foreign aid. Narcotics addictions should be treated as a public health problem rather than a crime. And border smuggling should stop. Roybal proposed removing the Landrum-Griffen and Taft-Hartley restrictive provisions that hindered organizing and bargaining rights, as well as opposition to federal right-to-work laws.[27]

Roybal's Republican opponent in the general election was Congressman Gordon McDonough. He had been a member of the Los Angeles County Board of Supervisors, 1933–1944, and had served as chairman for one year. He had been elected to the House of Representatives as a Republican and served between January 3, 1945, and January 3, 1963 (the 78th and the eight succeeding Congresses). He was a seasoned and astute campaigner and politician, which had served him well in his long political career.[28]

By fall, Roybal had the endorsements of the Los Angeles County AFL-CIO COPE; the two African American newspapers, the *Los Angeles Sentinel* and the *California Eagle*; as well as the *Eastside Sun*. Even the always-reluctant *La Opinion* gave him their endorsement.[29] The *Los Angeles Times* endorsed McDonough.

Roybal defeated McDonough with 57 percent of the popular votes (66,900–50,014). In his acceptance speech, Roybal recognized McDonough for campaigning "vigorously on a high level" and "without resorting to smear tactics."[30] Also running in the general election was Roybal's city council colleague Everett G. Burkhelter, who had served for nine and a half years, representing the 1 District. He was elected to represent the 27th Congressional District. Sam Yorty, the incoming mayor, praised both Roybal and Burkhelter, commenting, "There are some other members of the council I would be glad to send back to Washington," he said, "but not these two."[31]

Edward Roybal made history in winning the 30th Congressional District seat. He became the first person of Mexican ancestry in the California delegation to serve in Congress since the election of Romualdo Pacheco in 1876.

Serving in Kennedy's Camelot

Winning in the midterm election of John Kennedy's presidency, Roybal's victory was a gain for the administration and its effort to inaugurate a new liberal era. Kennedy represented the next generation in the tradition of President Franklin D. Roosevelt's New Deal. As such, Roybal was part of the 88[32] Congress (January 3, 1963–January 3, 1965) that was to set in motion what are now recognized as landmark laws. It was also an historic time for Mexican Americans. Henry B. Gonzalez[32] (D-TX) had been elected to the U.S. House of Representatives in 1961; and Joseph Montoya[33] (D-NM) was serving in the U.S. House of Representatives (1957 to 1964).

President John Kennedy, with the midterm elections behind him, was in his third year in office, a period often referred to as the "thousand days," before he was cut down by an assassin's bullets in Dallas, Texas, on November 22, 1963. His administration had still not succeeded in accomplishing passage of much of its promised social legislation but had laid out a blueprint showing what that new landscape might look like and had built up high expectations for the nation. His domestic agenda had been overshadowed by the Cold War and foreign policy issues.

A few weeks before Kennedy took office, Soviet leader Nikita Khrushchev referred in a speech to the "peaceful competition" in the Third World's "national liberation wars" and in "revolutionary struggles." Kennedy responded in his inaugural speech, saying the nation would "pay any price, bear any burden, meet any hardship, support any friend, and oppose any foe, to ensure the survival and success of liberty." Kennedy backed up his rhetoric with specific actions: forming the Green Berets for counterinsurgency and creating the Peace Corps to build infrastructure in underdeveloped countries by helping provide needed social services and planning. In some places, economic and military assistance was increased. In Latin America, the Alliance for Progress initiative was organized.[34] With Russians in space orbit by April 1961, ahead of the United States, Kennedy committed the nation to the Apollo Program in May to land a manned spacecraft on the moon before decade's end.[35] The Kennedy administration had also committed military advisors to buffer the growing conflict between North and South Vietnam. Kennedy was considering, in 1963, a long-term withdrawal sometime during his second term.

However, one of Kennedy's biggest challenges came from Cuba. Kennedy had inherited from the Eisenhower administration a plan for a covert operation against the island nation aimed to overthrow the regime. Cuba had experienced in 1959 a revolution led by Fidel Castro, which ended in the Communist Party's takeover of the government. The U.S. Central Intelligence Agency in April 1961 masterminded an invasion at the Bay of Pigs with a brigade made up of disaffected Cuban exiles. The insurgents were defeated within forty-eight hours of landing. Eighteen months later, the United States and the Soviet Union went to the brink of nuclear war when Cuba was quarantined, and the United States demanded that Cuba dismantle its Soviet-supplied missiles. The withdrawal of the missiles was obtained in exchange for assurances by the United States to not invade Cuba again.

Kennedy's domestic agenda garnered favor thanks to the Democratic majority in Congress. "If you were a Democrat," Roybal commented, "I'd say it was good. The Republicans didn't like him at all." It looked at the time, despite Kennedy's narrow victory over Nixon, that Democrats were unbeatable for the presidency. For that "we all thought he was great."[36] The key domestic issue was civil rights—reversing entrenched segregation, racism and prejudice. However, the Kennedy administration was hobbled by the "solid South," very much a part of the Democratic Party and part of the New Deal Coalition that made Democrats the majority party. Yet, the South was the locus of the practices that the administration sought to curb. President Kennedy spoke out forcefully against racism and in support of civil rights. However, legislation addressing both failed to pass through Congress.

Congressman Roybal and other new members of Congress were sworn in on January 9, 1963. President Kennedy sent Roybal a telegram. "Dear Ed," he wrote and congratulated him. In his message, Kennedy said he needed a Congress "committed to progress" that "meets the needs of today and future generations." Later, he greeted Roybal and the freshmen members of Congress in person when they went to the White House as a group.

During his first term in Congress, Roybal was assigned to the Interior and Insular Affairs Committee. The committee handled a wide variety of issues in the western and southwestern areas of the United States, including irrigation, reclamation, mineral resources, mining, management of Public Lands, Indian Affairs, National Parks and Sea Shores, conservation, and recreation. Upon his appointment Roybal stated, "I believe the work I will be doing on the Interior Committee will enable me to make a substantial contribution to the uninterrupted growth of the entire Pacific Southwest. The success of such projects as the Saline Water Conversion Program and the comprehensive water resource development of the Lower River Basin are vital to the future of Southern California."[37] Roybal was also named to the Post Office Committee. From this vantage point, he learned some of the intricate and complicated details about how the House of Representatives works.

In his very first statement on the floor of the House of Representatives, Ed Roybal noted the achievement of the late senator Dennis Chavez (D-NM) for his "courage and deep commitment to democracy and individual rights." He added, "His career gave pride, hope, and a place in the sun to three generations of Americans of Mexican and Spanish descent. And his tragic death is a great loss to several millions of Latin American descent, whose cause he championed for many years."[38]

Family Life in D.C.

Ed Roybal's move to Washington, D.C., changed the lives of his wife, Lucille, and his three children. Ed Roybal Jr. remembered, "When my father was elected to Congress, my sisters were already college age. I was the only one that was a minor. I was eleven years old. Even though they were in college, my father was so strict that we all went to Washington. My sisters fought to leave, and I think Lucille was only there for some six months. Lillian was there a year and half." Lucille went to live with her mother's sister and husband, Eddie Núñez, in East Los Angeles. Her father would not allow her to have an apartment. Ed Roybal Jr. recalled,

"I was the only one who lived in Washington a length of time. I mean, my whole adolescence was there. I was in the middle of sixth grade when I moved, finished sixth grade there, and then went on to junior high and high school in suburban D.C. The main thing I could say is that it was a whole lot different. In L.A. our house was the center of activity. The phones were always ringing, people were always there. It was very different in Washington and so the biggest impression when we were there was that my dad was never home as opposed to everything happening at our house. This was the big difference."[39] The Roybals bought a house in Kensington, Maryland, because they wanted the best schools for their son, Ed. The neighborhood was in a very exclusive and affluent area.

Despite Ed Roybal's busy schedule and exigencies of national and international events swirling about him, he remained at heart a very human and private man who took precious time for his family. On March 22, his young son Edward wrote him a letter to thank him for some precious hours spent together:

Dear Father,

Thank you very much for treating my class to a tour of the Capitol. I know you have made a big sacrifice paying for the thirty-three of us. Everyone in the class learned something from this tour. I am sure few people have the opportunity to see many of the places we did. It helped me [and] every one of us especially since we are studying government at school. I know that I learned many things from this tour. We all appreciate it very much.

Your grateful son,
Edward[40]

Ed's wife, Lucille, went through another type of culture shock and role evolution. Lucille Roybal-Allard recalled the tribulations and challenges of her mother this way: "My mother had a high school education and two years in a business college. She gets thrown into D.C., and they're from the barrio. We're like everybody else from the barrio. All our insecurities. All of a sudden my mother is dealing with wives of congressmen, who themselves are college graduates, Vassar, Harvard, and my mom felt extremely inadequate. The one thing my mother is, is she is very, very gracious. Every year my mother had the California delegation party, and my father would host it and in D.C. the tradition was you start at 6:00 p.m., you stand around a little cocktail, little antojitos, and then you say goodbye at 8:00 p.m., and it's over. My mother decided one year to make Mexican food. She cooked herself, and we helped her for days. Back then, my father would go back to Washington, D.C. with suitcases full of tortillas and chile sauce. And then she'd have Mexican music. So they came, and my mother was so gracious, making you feel so at home that you couldn't leave till one in the morning. My mother became famous because this was her niche. She became famous for this California delegation party every year. My father brought in musicians, tons of Mexican food, and this was the way my mother felt [a] part, this is where she could shine."[41]

However, not everything in Washington, D.C., was so pleasant for Lucille Roybal. Her niece, Irma Núñez, commented, "The thing that Aunt Lu always said is that she really loved being in L.A. because she felt that she was actively involved in the work Uncle Eddie did, but in D.C. she felt totally isolated."[42] Lillian Roybal Rose remembered Washingtonians' thoughtless slights. Once, when her mother went for a function to the International Club, Lillian recalled, "They were terrible to my mom…There were all Anglos, and they sat there with my mother there and talked about how they just couldn't get good Mexican help anymore. My mother said she sat there fuming. My mother threw a party for the neighbors, which was very common in that neighborhood, and one woman walked in and said, 'My goodness, the complexion of this neighborhood is really changing!'"[43]

On another occasion, Lucille recalled, "My dad goes to some fancy Mexican Embassy party and there's a million utensils, silverware, and glasses. My mother has no idea what to do, and my mother, being very patient, just sort of waited. Across from her there's a White woman, obviously very working-class, the spouse of somebody, who seemed to be as insecure as my mother, but this women was not patient. [The other woman] started talking a mile a minute, and then she saw them fill a cup with warm water and lemon hanging in there and she picks it up and drinks it. And it turns out that it's a finger bowl. And the woman realized what she had done. The woman was humiliated, and I remember Mother feeling so sorry for her that my mother reached over and just started talking with her, trying to make her feel better and my mother really related. My mother said, 'There but for the grace of God, am I, one more minute!'"[44]

Irma Núñez recalled Ed Roybal's consideration for all family members, "He was very devoted to my parents. My parents [Hortencia and Eddie Núñez] were very devoted to him and [my] aunt and to their children. I know there was a great love and appreciation and respect and devotion; no matter how busy his schedule was, he always made plans to include the family. The family was always invited to whatever events he was having, but also he made the time to have personal family ties, not only with his own family, but with his in-laws, his sisters-in-law, his brothers-in-law; the family was a very, very strong component for him."[45]

Pressing for Political Concessions

Through his involvement with the Viva Kennedy Clubs during the 1960 presidential campaign, Roybal had developed a strong friendship and connection to Vice President Lyndon B. Johnson. The aftermath of the election and the lack of forthcoming appointments of Latinos in the Kennedy administration brought growing discontent, especially within the Mexican American community. Roybal intended to press for some political concessions from President Kennedy or at the very least advocate in Congress on the plight of the Mexican American community.

In early August 1963, Johnson spoke to an audience of 1,000 at a luncheon sponsored by Mexican American Education Conference Committee at the Staler Hilton in Los Angeles. Johnson highlighted in his speech that as chairman of the President's Committee on Equal Opportunity, he had received 4,334 discrimination complaints in his two-and-a-half-year tenure but only ninety had originated from Spanish-speaking people. Johnson said, "I'm not asking for more complaints. I have plenty of those. But it seems to me that perhaps you have not been successful in making your needs known…and by that I mean facts, not mere grumbling."[46]

Although the audience listened politely, some felt impatient with him and the Kennedy administration. Roybal was instrumental in getting Johnson to speak after lunch to twenty Mexican American political leaders. The delegation met in the vice president's private suite. Roybal, Senator Clair Engle (D-CA), and Representatives George Brown and Chet Holifield, Democrats from California's 29th and 19th Districts respectively, were also in attendance. Dr. Francisco Bravo, Los Angeles police commissioner, said that Mexican American voters in California "have not received appointments to federal jobs even though we helped substantially in the 1960 campaign." Bravo walked out of the informal meeting when he was told that his presentation was out of order.

In turn, Manuel Ortiz, of the Planning Welfare Council, told the vice president that the greatest concentration of poor housing in the county was in and around East Los Angeles, "the hub of the Mexican American population." The Mexican American delegation presented Johnson with half a dozen concerns. Among them: that the administration recognize the Spanish-speaking community; give Spanish-speaking voters proper recognition and representation in the domestic branches of the federal government; give the Spanish-speaking population representation on the National Democratic Committee and other administrative and party policy advisory bodies; appreciate the fact that about 90 percent of Spanish-speaking Americans were registered Democrats and faithfully voted for Democratic candidates; recognize past appeals for representation and recognition on one of more than 100 applications presented; and finally, recognize that 90 percent of the nation's Spanish-speaking live in the Southwest and therefore should get the major share of the recognition.[47] Although at times stumped by the criticism, the vice president told the individuals present that his committee would "come in force" in November to hear the problems faced by Mexican Americans.[48]

Sponsoring and Influencing House Legislation

During his first term in the U.S. House of Representatives, Ed Roybal's goal was to get established in a new forum of politics. He was now in the center of national politics and the institution of the House allowed and permitted him to affect the lives of millions around the world: in cities, counties, states, the nation, and abroad, through the exercise of legislation in foreign affairs and policies. Because of the sheer volume of Roybal's issues and legislation (some sponsored, co-sponsored, voted on, or formulated behind the scenes) it would be impossible to cover everything in this book. As a consequence, here and elsewhere in this book I present only an overview and the highlights of Congressman Roybal's proposed and/or passed legislation.

From the House of Representatives, Roybal introduced a series of bills meant to expand civil rights for all and fight discrimination. At the time, his bills were not passed, but sections of them were included in bills introduced by others that passed. For Roybal, the main thing was not necessarily to get the credit or the glory. His strategy was to keep up the pressure on the Kennedy administration to move more quickly on this social legislation. For example, during June 1963, Roybal introduced his bill H.R. 6959, which would restrict federal funds for those educational institutions "not being operated and admitting students on a racially nondiscriminatory basis or which are not making progress toward that end with all deliberate speed." On June 3, from the floor of the House, he voiced what many people of color hoped for: that "]he mounting crescendo of sit-ins, stand-ins, knee-ins, freedom walks, and other racial demonstrations occurring across the country is, in many respects, an extremely healthy sign…. Now is the time for Americans in all walks of life to join in a noble crusade that will rid this country, once and for all, of the poison of racial and minority group discrimination."[49]

In July, Roybal introduced H.R. 7298, which was almost identical to the Administration's Civil Rights Act of 1963 but which included provisions strengthening voting protection for minority groups, extending and expanding the authority of the Civil Rights Commission. While acknowledging President Kennedy's initiative on civil rights, he stated, "But narrow sectional prejudice and short-sighted political considerations have so far prevented Congress from taking a strong, unequivocal stand in favor of the principle of equality."

Roybal candidly commented during his first terms in Congress, "A freshman congressman is sometimes advised to be seen and not heard until he has had a chance to gain a certain amount of legislative 'seasoning.'" In particular, Roybal was concerned with matters distinct from his specific committee assignments. "I was concerned about the mistreatment of senior citizens, for example, and also concerned about the fact that people coming from Latin American countries were not respected," he said.[50]

Ed Roybal supported President Kennedy's agenda. He informed his constituents of legislation in the House and how he voted on it, his visits to his district, his staff changes, and his thoughts on a diverse number of issues and concerns on local, national, and international levels. In March 1963, he began a monthly newsletter called *Congressman Ed Roybal Reports from Washington* as his main vehicle of reporting to the residents of the 30th Congressional District. In the first report he wrote, "Many times it may seem that the sheer size and complexity of today's modern government renders an individual citizen virtually powerless in the face of what appears to be an entrenched bureaucratic establishment. In my opinion, one of the most important jobs of a Representative is to serve as a vitally interested human link between his constituents and the multitude of government departments with which we have increasingly frequent contact, and which plays an increasingly important role in our every day lives."[51]

He supported the nuclear test-ban treaty (which was signed into law during August 1963), equal pay for women, a youth employment program (the 1962 Manpower Development and Training Act), a tax reduction, voting protection for minority groups, school desegregation, equal access to public accommodations, full and equal employment opportunities, and the extension of the Civil Rights Commission for another four years. He also voted against the extension of Public Law 78, also known as the Bracero Program, which provided 200,000 to 400,000 Mexican agricultural workers annually to work during the harvest time on United States cotton, sugar beet, fruit, and vegetable farms. About the law Roybal said, "In effect, the Mexican bracero program had been a multimillion dollar, cheap imported labor subsidy going to less than 1 percent of American's growers of food and fiber—generally operating large, profitable, corporation-like farms—at the expense of our lowest paid and most underprivileged citizens."[52] However, Congress did not end the Bracero Program until a later time.

An exhaustive review of the Roybal Papers from both his Washington, D.C., office and his district office reveals thousands of pieces of correspondence between Congressman Roybal and his constituents. It testifies to the thousands of people that the congressman touched and impacted though his intervention, assistance, advice, and recommendation. The letters offer heartbreaking stories of senior citizens who did not receive Social Security payments due them, veterans mistreated by the Veterans Administration, seniors being physically abused at retirement centers, high school students seeking a recommendation to college, military prisoners seeking adequate legal counsel, people denied equal access to housing, applicants seeking advice about admission to West Point and Annapolis, Mexican Americans and Mexican national legal residents disrespected and mistreated by the Immigration Service, tax payers harassed by the Internal Revenue Service, constituents unable to afford a funeral for a relative, among many others. Congressman Roybal served them all in some form, using his influence within the bureaucracy of a federal agency to straighten out a misunderstanding, an error, a form of prejudice. He offered advice, a referral to a more proper way to resolve the issue, or a sympathetic ear to a frustrated constituent. Over the years, constituents would write heartfelt thank-you letters speaking to Roybal's touch with the common man, his humanity, and his sense of dignity and nobility in helping others.

His staff worked diligently and with great dedication to respond to those who needed his help. His district office was located in Room 823, Federal Office Building, 312 North Spring, Los Angeles. His Washington office was in Room 140, Cannon Office Building, Washington, D.C. During March 1963, he appointed Alex Garcia as his field representative in his district office. Garcia would later on hold elected office.

An example of Congressman Roybal's timely intervention was in the case of Japanese American Tomoya Kawakita. Kawakita had been born in Calexico, California, of Japanese parents. He had grown up in Southern California, and in 1939, left for Japan to continue his studies. The outbreak of World War II left him stranded there, and later, he became an interpreter for the Japanese.

In 1946, Kawakita returned to the United States and was promptly arrested. A three-month trial followed, in which thirty-five American survivors of the Bataan Death March testified that Kawakita had abused them in a prison camp. Some of the witnesses stated that his treatment was so cruel that some of the war prisoners died or went insane. Kawakita nevertheless maintained throughout the trial and later that he had never committed any brutalities. Despite this, the court sentenced Kawakita to a long prison term in Alcatraz.

Reverend Howard Toriumi, when he was assigned to a parish in the city of San Francisco, made several visits to Alcatraz to visit Kawakita. Reverend Herbert Nicholson had also urged many of his influential friends to aid in the prisoner's release. Early in July 1963, a petition of 300 names had been submitted to President Kennedy to request a pardon for Tomoya Kawakita. Informed of the petition, Roybal expressed an interest in helping the Japanese American group with their efforts. Roybal asked for and was given all the documentation pertaining to the case by a committee of church leaders and interested friends.

In early November 1963, when the President's Committee on Equal Employment Opportunity Conference was held in San Francisco, Roybal told Kawakita's attorney, Jun Tori, that he had called the matter to President Kennedy's attention. Several voices nevertheless were raised in vociferous opposition to the pardon, including the Japanese American Citizens League, who had voiced a similar feeling years before. However, Kawakita's three sisters—Dorothy, Ruby, and Mary—persevered.

Changing the climate of the debate, World War II veteran and former prisoner of war Ellis Gordon, at that point an executive at the Bekins Van and Storage, Co., publicly stated that, despite his own bitter experience in the infamous Oeyama prison, he held no animosity toward Kawakita; Kawakita had suffered enough.

Tomoya Kawakita was granted a pardon. President Kennedy ordered his release for November 29, 1963. The order for his release had actually been made on Tuesday, a day after the funeral of President Kennedy. In all probability, President Kennedy had decided on parole much earlier, as evidenced by Kawakita's signature on a statement pledging to leave the country for Japan as early as November 1. It was perhaps Kennedy's last act of mercy.

The Kawakita family and the support committee expressed much gratitude to Congressman Roybal. Hiro E. Hishiki wrote in the *Kashu Mainichi*, a leading Japanese American newspaper, "The action of the late President was due primarily to the efforts of Congressman Roybal who consulted secretly with the group."[53] It was typical of Ed Roybal to work anonymously behind the scenes to get something done and claim no credit for himself.

Despite Ed Roybal's amicable relations and support for the majority of President Kennedy's policies and legislation, his manifested his discontent with the administration's unkept promises to the Mexican American community. On November 13, a little more than a week before the assassination in Dallas, at the fourth annual Convention of the Mexican American Political Association (MAPA), Roybal expressed the private thoughts of a public man. At the event, which was held at the Biltmore Hotel in downtown Los Angeles, Roybal said that President Kennedy had not kept his 1960 campaign pledges to Spanish-speaking Americans. He drew much applause when he stated that the Kennedy administration had failed to appoint a single Spanish-speaking American to a position of responsibility in the federal government. He warned that the votes of Mexican Americans in the Southwest would be essential for Kennedy's re-election in 1964. Roybal, however, also said that Kennedy had promised to name a Spanish-speaking American to the post of Coordinator of Latin American Affairs.[54]

Roybal's comments reminded Mexican Americans of the lingering unfulfilled promises of the Democratic Party. The theme would continue under Kennedy's successor to the White House.

During his first term in Congress, Roybal met Martin Luther King. In fact, they met at the Washington Memorial, during the civil rights demonstration when King made his famous "I Have a Dream" speech. Roybal was standing right behind him, next to Gus Hawkins of California. Roybal saw King as a man of exceptional ability to lead a movement; he saw an emotional speaker. "It came to the point where you liked him, and when you liked him, you really liked him."[55]

Roybal maintained and expanded his relations with the African American community. During mid-October 1963, he was the keynote speaker for a standing-room-only crowd at the final session of the 1963 state convention of the Virginia National Association for the Advancement of Colored People (NAACP) in Fredericksburg, which traced its history to the Revolutionary War and the Civil War. Roybal reminded the delegates that they were participating in a historic occasion. The NAACP convention marked the first time the city's public facilities and major public accommodations were opened for use on a desegregated basis to the members of minority groups. He cited the threat of prolonged Southern filibuster in a Senate civil rights bill, spoke of the successful August 28 March on Washington for Jobs and Freedom, and predicted the ultimate victory of those who struggled to end racism in the nation. He concluded, "Ours will be a better and stronger nation when we have finally abolished, once and for all, second-class citizenship in the United States." He was given a thunderous ovation by the highly enthusiastic crowd.

Roybal also got to know President Kennedy's brother Robert F. Kennedy better during this time. Roybal's recollection of the president's brother is illuminating: "He actually was the attorney for [Senator Joseph] McCarthy, and that to me was not good. But, when he started to work on behalf of Hispanics, he started to change; that's when I admired him. He was a very dynamic individual. I think he wanted to be president too, and I think that change came about for a very good reason. He fitted right in, and he was worth following, which we did."[56]

Founding the Congressional Hispanic Caucus

Henry B. Gonzalez of Texas, who became a member of Congress in 1961, preceded Roybal by one year as the first Mexican American congressional representative in the twentieth century. Later, in 1962, they jointly founded the Congressional Hispanic Caucus with Senator Joseph Montoya of New Mexico. The new organization's existence would be formalized during December 1976.

Roybal would joke later that when they announced to the Speaker of the House what they were up to, the Speaker asked them if they were going to conduct their meetings in a telephone booth—the three-man caucus being so small. The Congressional Hispanic Caucus as envisioned by its founders, sought to develop national policies that would reflect Latino concerns. Its principal role was to monitor legislative action, but it also focused on policies and practices in the executive and judiciary branches of government. A large part of its attention went into ways to expand Latino government employment and to strengthen the roles Latinos played in government. From the beginning, the Congressional Hispanic Caucus dealt with immigration and bilingual education issues and various civil liberties concerns such as housing discrimination and police brutality.[57] Roybal commented, "We were interested primarily in having Latinos become more active and get a better opportunity, not to be ignored completely as they had been."[58]

Roybal also founded the nonpartisan, nonprofit Congressional Hispanic Caucus Institute. Then, as now, it was made up of corporate representatives and community organizations, and its motto was "Developing the next generation of Latino leaders."[59] Lucille Roybal-Allard commented, "One of the things that he [Ed Roybal] saw when he was in Washington was that there was no Latino presence in terms of young college students or professionals who were coming to learn how policy is made so they eventually could become policy makers and get elected. [Today we] get Latino kids from all over the country coming to Washington, many for the first time to get a better understanding of how policy is made, how government works, and also one thing that's really important about [it] is that it helps to create a network that Latinos have not had in the past. So these young people coming from different parts of the country are getting to know each other in the early stages, so when they do succeed, they will already know who these potential leaders are."[60]

Gonzalez shared many similarities with Ed Roybal. He had served in the city council and the state legislature, run for governor, worked on the Viva Kennedy Club and was then appointed to a vacancy in a congressional seat, and later, won on his own. Roybal established a long-lasting friendship and collegiality with Henry B. Gonzalez. Roybal recalled, "I don't think there was any particular highlight in that relationship. We were colleagues, and we had certain objectives. The end result was that others followed us, and we did what we thought was a good job for the times."[61]

Although the Congressional Hispanic Caucus would grow significantly over the next forty years, it was in the 1960s still relatively insignificant in the context of the U.S. House of Representatives. Later, the Congressional Hispanic Caucus would have an impact on the congressional committees, where it has been instrumental in helping to place Latino congresspersons.[62]

Grieving and Continuing the Good Fight

Following President Kennedy's assassination on November 22, 1963, Lyndon Baines Johnson was sworn in as president. On December 5, 1963, Congressman Roybal spoke before the House of Representatives. He spoke from the well, saying, "because John Fitzgerald Kennedy has passed our way...[his] character, his vision, and his quiet courage" enabled the nation to chart "a safe course through the shoals of treacherous seas that encompass the world."[63] A commission of inquiry into President Kennedy's murder was appointed by Johnson, headed by Chief Justice Earl Warren. The Warren Commission concluded that Lee Harvey Oswald had assassinated President Kennedy and had acted alone.

President Johnson rallied the nation in this difficult time, meeting with a cross section of Americans in an effort to enlist their support and during the critical time of transition for the country. On one occasion, Johnson commented, "I am the only president you have. If you have me fail, then you fail, for the Nation fails."[64]

Ed Roybal and the rest of the nation in this time of national mourning put partisan politics aside and gave President Johnson their unequivocal support. Roybal noted, "President Johnson gives every indication of being a strong and dynamic Chief Executive who will continue with the plans and policies of John Kennedy while emphasizing the necessity of bringing all Americans together in support of the common good."[65]

Roybal himself mourned the passing of President Kennedy deeply. On December 5, 1963, he made a moving speech about what the fallen president had meant to him. Roybal stated, "With his compassion, his courage and his creative genius were blended a warm and good humor—a sparkling wit, a love for his fellow human beings…In international affairs, John Kennedy represented a force for reason, for strength, and for compassion. He sought to make a world safe for diversity, in a world that put a premium on conformity…Domestically, President Kennedy visualized his Nation as a young country striving to realize its full potential and secure for all its citizens the blessings of the great promise of America."[66]

Although the nation grieved, the business of Congress nevertheless continued. On December 12, 1963, Congressman Roybal introduced a bill, House Joint Resolution 845, which would prohibit discrimination, or denial or abridgement of any legal right, by either federal or state governments on account of gender. He commented on this occasion, "Over forty years ago, women received the right to vote. In my opinion, it is long past the time when similar equal rights should be granted in other fields…The California legislature, in its Assembly Joint Resolution 31 passed this year, has gone on record as favoring this Constitutional amendment and has urged Congress to take the lead in this important matter."

The constitutional amendment, which was very much ahead of its time, did not pass at that time or within Roybal's lifetime. However, the bill was a testament to his long-term vision of the full inclusion of women into the nation.

A young Ed Roybal outside his parents' house in Boyle Heights.

An adolescent Ed Roybal in the mid-1930s.

Lucille Beserra and Ed Royball were married on September 27, 1940, at St. Joseph's Catholic Church in downtown Los Angeles.

Ed Roybal during his service in the United States Army during World War II.

Lucille and U.S. Army serviceman Ed Roybal during World War II. They are accompanied by their daughters, Lillian and Lucille.

Lucille Roybal, daughter Lillian, and Ed Roybal campaigning for the 9th Los Angeles Council District in the late 1940s. The iconic Los Angeles City Hall Building is in the cloudless background.

Councilman Ed Roybal welcomes the Democratic presidential candidate Adlai Stevenson to Los Angeles. One the left is Roybal's young son, Ed Jr.

Ed Roybal teaches son Ed Jr. how to fish in a casual family moment during the mid-1950s.

Ed Roybal and former heavyweight boxing champion Joe Louis in the early 1950s. Roybal had boxed as an amateur in his adolescence and had a lifelong interest in the sport of boxing. He maintained a lifelong friendship with some boxing luminaries.

An article in the *Daily News* dated June 9, 1954, documents Ed Roybal's rising stature as a political leader.

A Roybal family moment in the mid-1950s: daughter Lillian, son Ed Jr., Mrs. Roybal, daughter Lucille, and Ed Roybal (playing his favorite guitar).

Lucille and Ed Roybal in the mid-1950s.

Ed Roybal; sister Eloisa Roybal Wilder; father Baudilio Roybal; brother Benny Roybal; sister Mercedes Roybal Verdugo; and uncle Luis Roybal.

Los Angeles Councilman Ed Roybal gives the legendary director and producer Cecil B. DeMille a Los Angeles certificate of recognition as a Hollywood film pioneer at the release of his biblical epic *The Ten Commandments* (1956, Paramount Pictures). Coincidently, DeMille was Anthony Quinn's father-in-law (Quinn was then married to Katherine DeMille).

President John F. Kennedy welcomes the newly elected Congressman Edward R. Roybal at the White House in late 1962.

Congressman Ed Roybal and President Lyndon B. Johnson in the White House Rose Garden in the late 1960s. Roybal became a vocal critic of Johnson's Vietnam War policy.

Senator Robert F. Kennedy and Ed Roybal in the mid-1960s. Kennedy by then had become a fervent support of César Chávez and the farmworker movement and the plight of Mexican Americans.

Ed Roybal and Senator Ted Kennedy in the mid-1950s. Roybal maintained a close relationship with the Kennedy family after President Kennedy's assassination.

Congressman Ed Roybal with actors Charlton Heston and John Gavin in the
early 1970s. Both Heston and Gavin served as Screen Actors Guild presidents.

Ed Roybal and actor Anthony
Quinn in the mid-1990s at a
function held at the Anthony
Quinn Public Library on César
Chávez Avenue (formerly
Brooklyn Avenue). Roybal and
Quinn were friends since their
adolescence.

Chapter 8

Envisioning the Great Society
(1963–1968)

AFTER THE ASSASSINATION OF PRESIDENT KENNEDY ON NOVEMBER 22, 1963, Vice President Lyndon Johnson assumed the mantle of President of the United States. Ed Roybal and the nation waited with hopeful anticipation for the country's wounds to heal and a return to normalcy.

Lyndon Baines Johnson was born near Stonewall, Gillespie County, Texas, on August 27, 1908. His ancestors were among the people who had revolted against Mexican Texas in 1836. Johnson attended Southwest Texas State Teachers College, where he is said to have learned compassion for the poor and the Mexican students that he taught during the depths of the Depression. In 1937, he ran for the U.S. House of Representatives on the New Deal platform.[1]

In 1960, Johnson was a candidate for the Democratic nomination but accepted the vice presidency when John F. Kennedy offered it to the Senate leader. After Kennedy's assassination, Johnson became president. In the 1964 presidential election the issues of debate were civil rights, nuclear proliferation, the continuing Cold War (which was heating up in Vietnam and Southeast Asia), poverty, the state of health care for senior citizens, and unfinished legislation of the Kennedy administration. Johnson soundly defeated Republican Barry Goldwater, with a landslide win, 43.1 million votes to 27.2 million. In the Electoral College, it was 486 for Johnson to Goldwater's 52.

LBJ's Great Society

During his first years in office, Johnson and a receptive Congress skillfully passed several of Kennedy's measures, specifically a tax cut and a new civil rights bill. Johnson then told the nation to build a great society: "a place where the meaning of a man's life matches the marvel of man's labor."

When he was re-elected, his administration became known as the Great Society. The legislation that followed was the most ambitious since Franklin D. Roosevelt's New Deal in the 1930s. Johnson's legislation included Medicare, urban renewal and redevelopment of depressed areas, a War on Poverty, aid to education, wilderness conservation and beautification, abolishing constraints to voting rights and removing desegregation, an accelerated space program, along with many other pieces of reform legislation.

Edward Roybal had developed a close relationship with President Johnson during the Viva Kennedy campaign. Johnson's Great Society, populist credentials, and his long-time support of Mexicans from Texas added immeasurably to Roybal's close relation with him. Lyndon Johnson was a consummate politician and Senate leader. Roybal remembered that he was the kind of person who would go right up and sit with representatives when they were having lunch in the House of Representatives dining room. "He sat next to us not because he wanted to have lunch with us, but because he had something to sell. And what he had to sell was the program…He was a very smart president, almost as smart as Clinton."[2]

Johnson was effective because of his "personal contact with Congressmen and his knowledge of government." He had a genuine grasp of the issues in the Mexican American community. "I think," said Roybal, that "he had a better grasp than that of anyone else up to that time." In particular, Roybal believed that Johnson's teaching experience among Mexican Americans in Texas had led him to conclude that the accepted curriculum was getting people nowhere and kids were not learning.[3] "While he wasn't perfect," Roybal added, "I have a lot of respect for him." The feeling must have been mutual, as President Johnson visited

Roybal's district. Johnson rewarded his political friends with his physical presence. "Anyone who was on his side, he would make a point to visit them when he came to California. He had very strong support of the community."[4]

Roybal actively supported much of the social legislation passed during this time, such as the Civil Rights Act of 1964, the Voting Rights Act of 1965, the 24th Amendment (which declared poll taxes unconstitutional), the Head Start Act (1965), the Higher Educational Act (1965), the Medicaid and Medicare Act[5] (1965) and the Older Americans Act (1965).[6]

The growing rift between the Mexican American community and President Johnson's War on Poverty[7] came down to funding in Los Angeles. In early September 1965, Congressman Roybal charged that almost two-thirds of the funds already appropriated were being spent in the Black community, although the Mexican American community, "with a larger population and similarly burdened with poverty problems, was not receiving equal treatment. Los Angeles poverty areas have a right to expect their full share of benefits from the new Economic Opportunity Program regardless of whether disturbances in another section of Los Angeles [a direct reference to the Watts Riot] may have temporarily highlighted an urgent need for aid."[8] During the 1965 fiscal year, the allocation was expected to exceed $75 million. The programs it funded included Operation Head Start, high school and college work training and work-study, legal aid, adult vocational training child care services, and small business development.

A continued disenchantment over the lack of appointments of Mexican Americans to significant government positions also plagued the Johnson administration. Likewise, the Democratic Party's reluctance to include Mexican Americans and the disproportionate rate of Mexican American casualties in Vietnam added fuel to the growing militancy of some. In October 1965, Congressman Roybal made some of his harshest criticisms of the Johnson administration, saying, "The Mexican American community wholeheartedly supports and applauds the progress made by the Negro, for we know only too well the legitimacy of his campaign to overcome generations of subordination. However, we are forced to risk criticism of our words because the pressure in the Mexican American community is mounting as our needs are becoming desperate. Our target should be the Johnson administration, which we support, but which does not seem to support us. This administration must be made aware of the appalling ignorance on the part of well-meaning administrators who continue to work under the false impression that Mexican Americans have more economic advantages than the Negro."[9]

President Johnson continued to court the support of Ed Roybal in the House for support of his social legislation. Johnson knew well that he could not afford to lose Mexican American support for his consensus politics when he was losing the South for the Democratic Party. Johnson still had plans to run for re-election in 1968 at the time of this strategic thinking.

President Johnson invited Roybal in October 1965 to the signing of the Immigration and Nationality Act of 1965,[10] taking place at the Statue of Liberty in New York Harbor. Roybal arrived at Kennedy Airport aboard Air Force One, accompanying Johnson. The Act represented the first major revision of immigration laws in forty years, eliminating some of the discriminatory national-origin quota system and setting up a more equitable first-come-first-served procedure based on preference categories."[11] Congressman Roybal looked on the bill as an historic reform.[12] The Immigration and Nationality Act had been proposed by Congressman Emanuel Cellar (D-NY) and co-sponsored by U.S. Senator Philip Hart (D-MI). However, Roybal had been actively involved behind the scenes, in his usual low-key style.

Delivering Federal Funding to the 30th District

Ed Roybal worked through a network of like-minded elected leaders, community organizations, government agencies (federal, state, city), and his staff in Washington, D.C., and Los Angeles to advocate, organize, and push for legislation and delivery of federal grants and monies. There were dozens of OEO (Office of Economic Opportunity) programs established in Los Angeles, one of the nation's fastest-growing urban centers. Many community leaders became program directors. The War on Poverty program experience also developed people's capacity to become activists as they organized to receive and maintain many of the program services.

The story of the War on Poverty and its many programs is beyond the scope of this book. I will therefore offer only a snapshot of some of the programs and efforts carried out by Ed Roybal in this regard. For example, on October 27, 1965, Roybal announced in Washington, D.C., that the Office of Economic Opportunity had allocated $1 million to assist some 5,500 families in the poorest areas of East Los Angeles. Congressman Roybal stated that one allotment of $145,890 was for an experimental project directed by thirty college-student leaders. Their mission was to divert the activities of 1,400 delinquent teenagers and gang members in East and South Central Los Angeles into more fruitful pursuits. Another $129,960 was allocated to three community centers to serve 300 families in the Princeton-Bonnie Beach, Duncan-Olympic, and Estrada Courts sections of East Los Angeles.[13]

By the winter of 1965, Robert F. Kennedy (D-NY), who had become increasingly distant from President Johnson, announced that he would challenge Johnson for the presidency in 1968. He made one of his first appearances outside of New York since his brother's assassination at a fundraising dinner for a massive voter registration and education drive in minority communities. Undoubtedly, Johnson watched the Roybal-Kennedy association with trepidation. Roybal welcomed Kennedy, who was feted with a $100-a-plate dinner at the Ambassador Hotel[14] and honored for his civil rights efforts. Roybal, Augustus Hawkins, and George E. Brown Jr., all representing Southern California, issued a joint statement in which they praised Kennedy's service as attorney general for enforcing civil rights laws in the South, his hard work as a senator, and his continuing efforts for equal rights.[15]

From August 11 to 16, 1965, large-scale riots took place in the predominantly Black neighborhood of Watts, in South Los Angeles. Some 34 were killed, 1,032 were injured, and 3,952 people were arrested. It was sordid reminder of the sorry history of racism, poverty, and frustration among Blacks in the United States. The McCone Commission, headed by John McCone, a former Central Intelligence Agency director and affluent Republican, was established to uncover the causes and make recommendations of how to improve social conditions. The commission was widely criticized. It recommended "compensatory" rather than equal treatment for racial minorities. Others, however, hoped that by providing War on Poverty programs and services the social conditions might be alleviated and other riots would be prevented. However, throughout the 1960s, other urban centers exploded into racial riots, leading to backlash and a hardened law-and-order mentality among the Right.

In the aftermath of the Watts Riot, federal monies and grants poured into the Los Angeles urban centers with the mission to improve the pressing social conditions. For example, in January 1966 a new $1.5 million federal grant for job training in East Los Angeles was announced. Politics now was not just for political posturing and photo opportunities but was an opportunity for demonstrable action for community good. According to Roybal, the grant resulted from urgent federal efforts to do something about the findings in the McCone Commission Report.[16]

A Medal for Peace

By the mid-1960s, Ed Roybal had become a widely respected legislator who would disagree with the opposition but never demonize them. He was recognized as a civil rights advocate, who established coalitions across different ethnic communities, and as man of peace, who abhorred violence and espoused reconciliation among individuals and nations.

For efforts like these, Roybal was awarded the Franklin Peace Medal in February 1966. The award and commendation recognizes outstanding citizens and leaders who make substantial contributions to the cause of world peace. Congressman Roybal, in accepting the award, reflected on his faith that "to survive in the dangerous, nuclear-space age" required "men and women of good will in every country" to reduce the causes of conflict in the world. Food, shelter, education, jobs, and health care—social justice, in other words—are the vital components here and elsewhere for those conditions.[17] It would be one of many such awards that Roybal would earn in his long career.

Congressman Roybal had been appointed to the House Foreign Affairs Committee in January 1965. The growing conflict in Vietnam and Southeast Asia, insurgencies in Latin America and Africa, and the continuing conflict between the United States and the Soviet Union made the Foreign Affairs Committee a very important one. Of this new post, he commented that it was "extremely gratifying to me in view of the vital leadership role our country has come to play in promoting the cause of freedom and international peace among the nations of the world...We have always been an outward-looking people, coming as we do from ethnic and cultural backgrounds—a true melting pot of strength and diversity which made America great... [I was] interested in being a good neighbor to the world, working in close harmony with others to promote international cooperation and expand our commercial trade contacts."[18] In order to become a member of the House Foreign Affairs Committee, Roybal had to relinquish his posts on the Insular Affairs and Post Office and Civil Rights Committees.

Johnson's presidency's great undoing was the Vietnam War. He began a significant escalation almost from the beginning. Opposition to Johnson's Vietnam policy sparked a national mobilization against the war. Roybal became increasingly outspoken in his opposition to the Vietnam War the longer the war advanced into the Johnson presidency. "We just can't continue to escalate [the war] and have...enough money for the Great Society programs. Taxes are already too high, so you certainly can't expect the people to pay more," he said. His opposition was separate and apart from his admiration for Johnson. Roybal recognized that Johnson's administration was responsible for more Spanish-speaking people being hired by the federal government than ever before. Johnson had also been responsible for bringing more awareness and attention to the problems of Spanish-speaking Americans than any prior administration. In that sense, President Johnson had made some inroads into the Mexican American community. He saw these as moments that needed to be leveraged as opportunities.[19]

The East Los Angeles High School Walkouts

In the first week of March 1968, thousands of Mexican American students walked out of Lincoln, Roosevelt, Garfield, Wilson, and Belmont High Schools in East Los Angeles in what would become known as the East Los Angeles High School Walkouts. Mexican American youth had become politicized by the entrenched discrimination against them, the disproportionate causalities of Mexicans and Chicanos in the Vietnam War, and the farm worker union movement. Chicano students at Lincoln High School were inspired by Sal Castro,[20] who educated them on the history of disfranchisement, the discrepancy between Eastside schools and those in the affluent Westside, and the rudiments of organizing.

However, students were further politicized by the alarming conditions of East Los Angeles schools: a dropout rate which exceeded 50 percent, the lack of Chicano teachers and counselors, the absence of Chicano studies courses, tracking of students into manual labor occupations, and punishment for speaking Spanish on campus, among other issues and concerns. Students had conducted a survey of the conditions and presented their data to the Los Angeles Board of Education, who basically ignored their concerns and demands for change. At that point, they took direct action and walked out. A long history of failed schooling for Mexican Americans had finally come to a dramatic turn.

The walkouts caught the imagination of the media. Ed Roybal, who himself had lived the experience of public education, was moved with concern, especially when the Los Angeles Police Department displayed their willingness to use force for the acts of civil disobedience. Congressman Roybal flew in from Washington to talk with students several times. On March 11th, he spoke at a special assembly at Roosevelt High School (his alma mater). In attendance were Dr. Julian Nava and Ralph Richardson, both members of the Board of Education. Roybal made a brief speech summarizing what had occurred and concluded saying, "I believe the leadership should come from the inside of school and not the outside. You can count on my support. I'm with you all the way."[21]

The East Los Angeles High School Walkouts was a turning point in the push to reform the public education of Mexican people. Soon after the walkouts in Los Angeles, Mexican students led walkouts across the Southwest and the Midwest. Parents, community organizers, and others came out in support of their students, having lived themselves the segregation, discrimination, tracking, academic failure, and disconnect from the learning process.

Ed Roybal was successfully re-elected in 1964 and 1966 with comfortable margins of victory. He continued to grow in national prominence as a congressional legislator during Johnson's presidency. However, his constituents back home lived the improved quality government services that Roybal fought for: federal job programs, Head Start clinics, senior citizen programs, summer youth programs and other programs were established in his congressional district and in the Los Angeles area. Increasingly, the Democratic Party recognized Roybal's was a "safe district," but what had made it so was responding to the needs of his constituents.

Roybal was running for his fourth term of office in June 1968. In the primary for the 30th Congressional District, he faced three Republican challengers: Cavner Calls, a businessman; Bill Lentz, a civil engineer; and Henri O'Bryant, a business executive. Roybal ran on his record and on his platform of favoring diplomacy over military, assuring the safety of U.S. allies, and providing educational and job opportunities. He emphasized accelerated housing construction, balanced mass transit systems, expanded park and recreational facilities, effective air and water pollution control, and the elimination of urban blight. Roybal went on to easily win the June primary and the November general election.

Family Marches On

In the decade following the campaign to elect John Kennedy and running all the way to the end of the Johnson administration, Edward Roybal's and Lucille Roybal's lives were filled with important family events. Daughter Lucille graduated from California State University, Los Angeles (CSULA), with a degree in speech and drama. She married Richard Olivarez in 1965. The wedding took place at St. Joseph's Catholic Church in Los Angeles, the same one where Ed and Lucille had wed in 1940. From Lucille and Richard's marriage a daughter, Lisa, was born.

The Roybals' second daughter, Lillian, graduated from CSULA in 1968 with a B.S. in sociology. She obtained a master's degree in education from the University of Southern California (USC) in 1970.

Edward Jr. attended junior and senior high school in the Washington, D.C., area. Ed Jr. would later attend the University of California, Los Angeles (UCLA), from 1969 to 1973 and then attend law school at University of California, Berkeley in 1973–1976.

Roybal's political life continued to be a family affair. Lucille Roybal-Allard recollected, for example, "We used to stuff [envelopes] and lick stamps. When I got a little older they used to call us 'bird dogs,' and we would do voter registration. So I was a bird dog for a few years."[22] Being the daughter of a public man also brought certain realities. Lucille Roybal-Allard commented, "I think for me the main part of it was the lack of privacy and lack of personal identity. When my sister and I would go to a dance where people might not know who we were, we used to decide on a different last name so we could just be anonymous and have fun... I remember as a freshman in college in a political science class I raised my hand to answer a question and after I finished the professor said, 'Well, now we know what your father thinks,' and went on to the next student."[23]

The typical day for Edward Roybal consisted of getting to his office at the Rayburn Building in Washington, D.C., between 8:00 and 9:00 a.m., where he caught up on paperwork, read, and prepared his schedule until the 10:00 a.m. committee meetings and sessions began. The House convened at noon and recessed for dinner about 6:00 p.m. Often the House reconvened at about eight o'clock for a night session.[24] Roybal saw Washington, D.C. as the world's hub where politics turns problems into policy solutions, those decisions in turn running economies and societies. He had six people working for him in Washington and four in the Los Angeles office. Alex Garcia was his local representative.[25]

Washington D.C., weather—hot and sticky in the summer and cold, rainy, and snowy in the winter—was not to Roybal's liking. Nor was the high cost of living. Roybal found the cost of rent outrageous. Still, these were small prices to pay for living in the world's hub and representing some of the U.S. people.[26] Edward Jr., at eleven years old, lived with his parents in Montgomery County, Maryland, a wealthy Washington suburb. The Roybals had a four-story colonial-style house there. He attended a junior high school "with only three or four Black kids," he said. Ed Jr. in particular remembered that because people thought he wasn't Black, they thought that, by default, he must be White. He remembered that, even though he could pass for White, "you know you're different."[27] During this period, Ed Jr. attended the Easter Egg Roll on the White House lawn and later viewed President Kennedy's body as he lay in state at the Capitol rotunda.

Roybal returned to the district at least once a month, making a cross-country commute. If he was going for only a weekend or a few days, Lucille would stay behind in D.C. If he was staying longer, she would travel with him. In Washington, Lucille was involved with other congressmen's wives, and she had to entertain quite often. She actually didn't enjoy that aspect of her life, even though she was very good at it and played the gracious hostess role quite well.[28] As a general rule, the family spent summers in Los Angeles.

During election times, Lucille Roybal ran the campaign headquarters in the district. Daughter Lucille Roybal-Allard would recall later, "My mother has been a tremendous role model…She's really the one who has helped to support and spearhead my father's career. She used to run his headquarters, which used to be our home when we were kids because they couldn't afford a headquarters. So she has always been there, helping him get elected, walking precincts, registering voters, doing all the things that needed to be done. At the same time, she'd be at his side whenever she needed to be at public events. She worked very hard and is greatly responsible for his success, because it really does take a partnership. In politics it takes the cooperation of family, otherwise it's impossible to succeed."[29]

For relaxation, Ed Roybal took up karate in the 1960s. He eventually earned a black belt. He also played the guitar and liked to sing and dance. For the serious man that he was taken to be, the one who didn't smile easily and nearly always had some serious message, this was out of character and contrasted with his public persona. Both Ed and Lucille Roybal enjoyed dancing.

In addition to his congressional obligations, Roybal was involved with many organizations, including the Boy Scouts, American Legion, United States-Mexico Health Association, County Commission on Human Relations, Metropolitan Recreation and Youth Services Council, Welfare Planning Council, Council of Mexican American Affairs, Belvedere, Hollenbeck and Downtown Coordinating Councils, Knights of Columbus, and East Los Angeles Rotary Club.[30]

Political Wrestling in the Los Angeles 9th Council District

When Roybal was first elected to Congress, he requested that the Los Angeles City Council defer appointing anyone and, instead, hold an election in the spring of 1963. Mayor Sam Yorty supported Roybal's proposal. However, the city council ignored the request and, instead, appointed Gilbert Lindsay, the first African American to serve in the Los Angeles City Council, to fill the 9th District vacancy.

A dramatic contest followed in the primary and general elections of 1963 between the incumbent Lindsay and Richard Tafoya, Roybal's first cousin. Many Mexican Americans were angry about Lindsay's appointment and saw it as another example of a White majority superimposing its will by pitting two minorities against each other. In the end, Lindsay was elected to the seat. He was already sixty-two years old when he won the election. Lindsay kept the position until his death in 1991 at the age of ninety-one. No Mexican-descent person or Latino would be elected to the Los Angeles City Council until 1985.

During that long twenty-two-year hiatus, Mexican Americans debated and argued about how they might become politically extinct. The Lindsay appointment left a trail of bitterness and division between the Mexican and African American communities. The general sentiment was that the groups had been played off by a dominant majority of conservative Republicans and Westside liberals, who had effectively eliminated Mexicans from competition for more than two decades from the city council.[31] In the next apportionment for council districts, three Blacks were elected, and the election of a Mexican American was made nearly impossible. Lacking local city leadership, the Mexican community was once again made vulnerable to schemes from politicians who did not have top-most the interests of the neighborhoods and communities that were majority Mexican American.[32]

Two main barriers prevented the incorporation of these minority communities in city governments throughout the United States: urban political machines and minority group fragmentation.[33] Fragmentation happened in the 9th District. Lindsay's appointment was to some extent diluted, for the coalition that had masterminded the maneuver gained Mayor Sam Yorty's hostility. Yorty, though elected in 1961 with minority support, became a foe of minorities and progressives.[34]

A power struggle was underway at city hall at the time of Lindsay's appointment. Demographic changes in the district and differences in political organization there played into Lindsay's political strategy. To no small extent, the long-term exclusion of African Americans from political representation at city hall contributed to the outcome.[35] One reflection of city hall politics was the appointment of Joe Hollingsworth, a White real estate businessman to fill the vacancy in the 10th Council District; Lindsay's appointment to the 9th made Hollingsworth's appointment a lot easier and more palatable to the district with a marked African American presence. The City Council had ignored pleas from African American community leaders who earlier presented a number of qualified African American candidates for consideration for the 9th District seat.

Mayor Sam Yorty had his own agenda for the 9th District. Following Lindsay's appointment, the mayor attempted to remove council members who had opposed him on other issues and then played the Mexican community against the African American community. Gilbert Lindsay was a field deputy for County Supervisor Kenneth Hahn. In turn, Councilman Gordon Hahn (Kenneth Hahn's brother) lobbied hard for Lindsay's appointment.

Kenneth and Gordon Hahn were part of political dynasty in Los Angeles politics. Kenneth Hahn, the younger of the two brothers, served in the Los Angeles City Council until 1963, when he was elected to the Los Angeles County Board of Supervisors. A maverick liberal, he had often sided with Edward Roybal in the city council and was at odds with him on several issues. The bitterest disagreements came over two issues. First, Kenneth Hahn approved the removal of the predominantly Mexican residents of Chavez Ravine to clear the way for the new Dodger Stadium. Second, he supported Gilbert Lindsay, an African American, to Roybal's city council seat.[36]

Gordon Hahn served in the California Assembly from 1947 to 1953.[37] He was appointed to the Los Angeles City Council in 1953 and served until 1963. Like his brother, he supported the building of Dodger Stadium and the appointment of an African American to Roybal's former council seat. It would appear that the motivation of both Kenneth Hahn and Gordon Hahn to support Gilbert Lindsay's appointment was to establish a new Los Angeles political coalition of White liberals, Westside Jews, and African Americans. Politically, it would prove to be an astute move, as their support for Lindsay would cement their African American support base, one that Kenneth Hahn Jr. would continue to capitalize in the early 2000s.

For the Los Angeles City Council, Lindsay's appointment became one more round in the power struggle with Yorty. It also signaled the beginning of a new coalition that diminished the political voice of the Mexican American community. This coalition led to further elaboration and cabals in which Mexican Americans were incidental players, until the emergence of Tom Bradley in the 1980s.

Demographic changes had indeed been occurring in the 9th District. The district was becoming increasingly overcrowded and impoverished, and fewer Mexican Americans voted. In turn, the number of African Americans voters eclipsed Mexican American voters. Meanwhile, the Los Angeles Mexican American population rose from 9 percent in 1950 to 14 percent in 1960. Redistricting, then, also contributed to a larger African American presence in the 9th.

Lindsay was challenged by four candidates from the Eastside in the election of 1963. In the May general election, the contest was down to Lindsay and Richard Tafoya. Lindsay won with 16,459 votes to Tafoya's 13,171. According to scholar Katherine Underwood, "Lindsay institutionalized Roybal's representative style and stressed his firsthand knowledge of the district's problems, opposition to discrimination, made his office accessible, and advocated equitable distribution of services."[38] However, now his core constituency was African American.

For his part, Congressman Roybal continued to practice the politics of inclusion much as he had as a councilman. In August 1963, he appointed African American Del Coffey as his personal coordinator of the 25th Congressional District, with primary responsibility for organized labor and the African American press. Roybal said, in making the appointment that he was "extremely fortunate to have a man of Del Coffey's caliber to work with."[39]

The loss of Councilman Roybal was, for the Mexican American community, a return to the lack of political representation in Los Angeles City Hall. Once having been united, they were now adrift again. Criticism in the guise of observation would question whether Mexican Americans had the capacity to organize or why they could not decide on a leader and why was there no unity. Few, if any, political realities were taken into account. Simply put, there were new difficulties, new hurdles, and a new threshold to transcend. Roybal's old coalition would not hold. Most Jews went over to side with African Americans and joined with the Black civil rights struggle. In the new era, the Jewish and African American partnership began to be seen in terms of excluding others. Political scientist Jaime Regalado noted that in this time, "Latinos became kind of isolated." With isolation, the district became susceptible to the scourge that had afflicted the Mexican American democracy movement ever since the preceding century: gerrymandering.[40]

Chapter 9

The Chicano Movement and Nixon's First Term
(1969–1971)

DURING THE 1960S, THE MEXICAN AMERICAN GENERATION WAS, AS MOST generations are, challenged by the next generation, in this case, the Chicano Movement generation. The passion, idealism, impatience, and aspirations of that generation were part of the worldwide youth movement that sought to change the world and castigate the adults for not doing so. The Chicano Movement was characterized by cultural nationalism, political empowerment, and a renaissance in the arts that drew themes from lesser-known histories, political struggles, and Mexican indigenous roots. This chapter is not meant to be a comprehensive or in-depth history of the Chicano Movement. Rather, the following is only an overview. It is also an effort to contextualize the social forces around Edward R. Roybal in the 1960s and 1970s.

Among the movement's key sociopolitical elements were César Chávez and the United Farm Workers Union's organizing efforts, Reies Lopez Tijerina and the land struggle in New Mexico, Corky Gonzalez and the inner-city movement, La Raza Unida Party's founding, the East Los Angeles High School Walkouts of 1968–1971, and the region-wide Chicano moratoriums against the Vietnam War over disproportionate Chicano and minority casualties.

Chicanos: Claiming Youth, Identity, and Cultural Roots

Some historians have assumed that the Chicano Movement, as the Mexican

American civil rights movement, emulated and followed the African American civil rights movement of the 1960s in origin and substance. This was of course not true. The two movements had different origins and themes, key events and outcomes. However, at every turn, the Latino-themed rights movements have been downsized in the chronicles of the times. Both, however, were civil rights struggles, and the need for social and economic justice was felt urgently by members of both groups. Both channeled pent-up frustrations into an emergent capacity to elect representatives. Although the Chicano Movement coincided in time, sometimes in theme, and often in manner of protest, rhetoric, and public expression with the African American civil rights movement, the roots and causes were distinct. For Chicanos, it emanated from the historical dynamics between indigenous people and the mainstream United States. In short, it was and continues to be a struggle to overcome a damnable marginalization.

The issue of self-identity became an important factor in the lives of young Mexicans. It was manifested in a cultural renaissance in art (especially murals), music, film, theater, literature, and other forms of cultural expression throughout the Southwest and the Midwest. In the yearning to rediscover their cultural and historical identity, they called themselves Chicanos. The term had existed for many decades, especially in the border regions. It was usually used to refer to lower-class Mexicans. It was similar to the word *pocho*, which was used to describe deculturalized, English monolingual Mexicans and Mexican Americans living in the United States. The word *Chicano* comes from pre-Colombian times and id derived from the Aztec tribal name Mexica, with the *x* pronounced like *sh*.[1]

Jose Angel Gutierrez defined the experience of being Chicano this way: "Chicanos occupied, often side by side, and the same general physical space as that of Anglos. We definitely were not, however, a part of their reality. We existed, but did not matter to them."[2]

The United Farm Worker union organizer and playwright Luis Valdez, founder of the Teatro Campesino, wrote in more detail of the relationship between Chicanos and Anglos: "The gringo is trying to impose the immigrant complex on the Chicano, pretending that we 'Mexican Americans' are the most recent arrivals. His melting pot concept is a sham…The Anglo cannot conceive of the Chicano, the Mexican, the Mestizo, in all his ancient human fullness…He accepts Mexican culture only to the extent that is has been Americanized, sanitized, sterilized, and made safe for democracy."[3] Further emphasizing the importance of identity and self-identity in the Chicano Movement, Carlos Munoz Jr. wrote, "The Chicano movement was a historic first attempt to shape a politics of unification on the basis of a non-White identity and culture and on the interests of the Mexican American working class. The movement rejected all previous identities, and thus represented a counter-hegemonic political and cultural project."[4]

The Chicano generation's emergence had a special significance in Mexican American social development. It represented a direct challenge to the previous generation's dedication to political empowerment and social justice. Some Mexican American leaders, such as Henry B. Gonzalez, rebuked and became hostile to the goals of the Chicano Movement, while others like Congressman Edward R. Roybal maintained cordial relations with the younger and more radical leaders.

The difference in strategy and ethos between the Chicano Movement generation and the Mexican American generation was the degree of radicalization. Previously, Mexican American organizations had served or were co-opted into serving as patient agents of social control, establishing accommodation as the public norm. They essentially served as brokers for community interests that demanded too little and settled for even less.

The Black Power Movement, which paralleled the Chicano Movement, influenced Chicanos' notions about cultural authenticity to the extent that it encouraged respect for national differences and diversity within the ethnic group, and suspension of unachievable cultural images, such as looks and complexion and even behaviors, by people of color. Black Power helped the Chicano Movement articulate its cultural nationalism—an antithesis to adaptation and conformity, or assimilation and acculturation.

Militant and activist youth, women, and some disaffected elements were skeptical that traditional methods of advocacy would lead to direct action and results fast enough. They also questioned the leadership's legitimacy.[5] Chicanos were turned off by "happy times" notions of cultural pluralism and an oversimplified "old-time, Fourth of July" sense of unity. The emerging Chicanos reclaimed their pre-Columbian past and indigenous roots. In their search for a homeland, they found Aztlán, the ancestral home of the home of the Nahua peoples. The word *Aztec* is the Nahuatl word for "people from Aztlán." Aztlán is thought to have been located in what today is the U.S. Southwest. Because Chicanos accepted their mestizo origins (*mestizo* refers to people of mixed race), the idea of racial purity was questioned, its criteria for purities of any kind challenged. The Chicano generation also questioned the nation's ideological foundations: they despaired of the American dream, in contrast to the Mexican American generation's hopes of achieving it. In attitude, the Chicano generation was skeptical, pessimistic, and sometimes cynical. They were the sons and daughters who had already seen through false hopes of their immigrant parents and grandparents. The landscape was that of youth alienation and a rebellion that looked for an alternative way to be effective and make a way for themselves in a post-industrializing America.[6]

For Carlos Munoz Jr., a leader in the Chicano Movement, it "represented a new and radical departure from the politics of past generations of Mexican American activists. It called for new institutions to make possible Chicano self-determination…It opposed racial, political, and patriarchal domination and economic exploitation…It called for the expansion *of the democratic process* and individual rights for Mexican Americans; and emphasized direct political action."[7]

Chicano activist José Angel Gutiérrez wrote, "My generation of Chicano activists made events happen…We asserted our right to a homeland, Aztlán. My generation began the struggle to make a reality of Aztlán, building community in a serious way…We created more organizations and programs for all Chicanos than any previous generation of activists.

Our record as builders of the Chicano community remains unmatched and unchallenged by the present generation of Hispanics."[8]

Radical change like that witnessed in the 1960s occurs when rising expectations are dashed or betrayed. This seems to have been the common experience in the many and diverse Mexican American communities. For instance, good-paying jobs required increased educational attainment. The professions and high-tech manufacturing production in a modernizing Southwest required well-educated workers. Almost by definition, most poor Mexican Americans and other minorities were excluded from this benefit pool. Their numbers grew more incompatible with the nation's labor demand. The education and employment gap between Mexican Americans and mainstream Americans was widening.[9] As mentioned in chapter eight, thousands of Los Angeles high school students in 1968 walked out of their schools in protest, calling national attention to the plight of Mexican American education. Similar walkouts spread throughout the Southwest and the Midwest.

Ed Roybal saw the activism of the Chicano Movement as a natural outcome from political leaders' social unresponsiveness in the past. "I was not surprised really, but pleased," he said. The Chicano Movement was the progeny of the prior generation's efforts. "It was happening after we did the same thing in a much smaller scale in Boyle Heights," he added.[10] However, he was opposed to some of the methods of the Chicano Movement. According to his niece, Irma Núñez, Roybal "was already so experienced in politics that when the saw the Chicano Movement, he just couldn't understand why they were doing it, the way they were doing it. He always communicated that instead of marching and protesting that if you go out door to door to register voters, you could get more done because you get these people to vote, for issues. He understood the political process and how things could be done in the long-term basis if you did it within the system. But…our generation, the Chicano Movement generation, did not have access to information; we didn't have books written about Chicano political leaders. And because youth is very limited, because we didn't suffer the way the generation before us suffered…we didn't realize how far we had come along; many people didn't understand what he had accomplished."[11]

Diverging Forces in the War on Poverty

President Johnson's War on Poverty included the creation, in 1964, of the Office of Economic Opportunity (OEO) to create job-training programs and related initiatives, such as Job Corps, VISTA, Head Start, and Upward Bound. Most of the community-level strategies and approaches were designed and implemented with African American communities in mind.[12] Not surprisingly, the Equal Employment Opportunity Commission itself did not have a single Mexican American on its staff until 1967, when Mexican activists walked out of the March 28, 1966, meeting the commission held in Albuquerque, New Mexico.[13] The United Civil Rights Committee, which was formed in Los Angeles in 1963 even refused to admit Mexican Americans. The poverty, low school-completion rates, segregation, high unemployment, and political marginalization among Mexican Americans remained overlooked in the country at large. Not until 1970, in the Cisneros case,[14] did a Federal court determine that Mexican Americans were an "identifiable ethnic minority with a pattern of discrimination."

The escalating war in Vietnam diverted funds from poverty programs to the conflict. Office of Economic Opportunity programs were farmed out to other agencies and departments. The Head Start program became part of Health, Education and Welfare and the Job Corps part of the Department of Labor. A scaled-down program called Model Cities took the place of OEO. Model Cities became very controversial because of the "urban renewal" features. The election of Republican Richard Nixon in 1968 marked the beginning of the end of the War on Poverty as a policy. Almost all of the programs would continue, but poverty ceased to be a stated priority, in Nixon's administration as in all those that followed.

Political scientist Jaime Regalado in turn noted about the Chicano Movement, "I think the movement generation tended to want things now and didn't necessarily trust the structures of organized America through which to achieve in a radical revolutionary change. How do you change a system that's horribly structured against you? Not by participating in the structures of that system."[15]

The Chicano Movement did not propose policy alternatives but did publicly react to the adverse effects of some policies. It was an agitation movement that prompted political leaders to action. Scholars of this era also note that some aspects of the movement focused on entitlement, which ultimately caused its demise. Most of all, it was a youth movement that percolated to all age groupings and inspired many who would have otherwise stayed in the sidelines.

Coloring all aspects of the Chicano Movement was the plight and growing visibility of a Mexican and Mexican American underclass. Prior to the 1960s, this group was concentrated in the rural districts, occupied as agricultural workers (some undocumented). Modernization and mechanization in Mexico displaced millions of peasants that the national economy did not absorb, even though Mexico had the fastest-growing gross national product (GNP) in Latin America.[16] The result was dramatic increase of Mexican immigration to the United States so that a larger percentage of the workforce was undocumented than before. Mexican migrants rapidly filled the ranks of the low-skill agriculture, light industry, and service sectors.

The Chicano Movement, like other movements of that time, had a place and a moment in history, but changed or fell apart when the next current pushed through. Students for a Democratic Society (SDS), Yippies, Black Power, Teach Ins, National Mobilization Against the Vietnam War, the McGovern Campaign: people of these movements as well as the Chicano Movement folded into other activities that became transformative, such as the women's movement, ecology movement, self-actualization, self-help/community action, electoral politics, education reform and opportunity, and overall the expansion of nonprofit civic action.

Chicano Movement Icons and Leaders

The Chicano generation developed leaders, icons, and organizations that were in general more radical than the Mexican American generation. These new leaders shared the political stage with the prior generation of leaders and they broadened the spectrum of applicable ideologies and strategies, from nonviolent disobedience to militant Marxism.

One of these leaders, who made his cause known broadly throughout American society, was César Chávez. César Estrada Chávez (1927–1993) was born in Yuma, Arizona, and spent his childhood on the migrant trail. He and his father, Librado Chávez, were members of the National Farm Labor Union in 1939, founded by Ernesto Galarza. After military service in World War II, César went to San Jose, California, where he married Helen Fabela, and joined the local Community Service Organization. There, he met Fred Ross and soon began work on voter registration.

Roybal remembered meeting Chávez when he was studying as an intern under Fred Ross. Clearly, Ross had already spotted those character traits that go into a good community organizer. Roybal commented that for Chávez "to be able to come up in the union the way he did, you had to have something special to do it, and he had it."[17]

Chávez became a prominent leader in the CSO but left in 1962 to dedicate himself to forming a new farm workers union. Along with his wife and a group of dedicated followers, he founded the National Farm Workers Association, which later became the United Farm Workers (UFW). In 1963, Chávez led the Delano grape strike. Workers' rights gradually began to be seen in the context of the civil rights movement's quest for social justice. In April 1966, Chávez led a march to the California state capital to demand full civil rights and justice for the farm workers.[18]

Chávez stressed high moral and spiritual strength as the basis for his movement; he endured jail sentences, and went on fasts. This act of faith in the people, in justice prevailing, and in the correctness in the cause was constantly reinforced. Chávez gave the civil rights movement, as a social and political vanguard, a new depth previously unknown, in places and among people previously unaccounted for. His ingenious protest methods, carried out by legions of loyal followers, brought laborers' rights to the attention of even passive Americans and highlighted the need to correct the wretched practices they suffered to bring food to the table for everyone.[19]

Congressman Roybal and César Chávez knew each other well and for a long time, and their relationship was, as Roybal said, "a very good one." They had both been Saul Alinsky students. "Because of that, I think our relationship was rather close and there was no difference in what we were seeking, what we thought we should have, but there was a difference in the way the approach was made. I think that César Chávez articulated his reason for organizing and the need of the farm workers better than anyone else."[20] Roybal's approach became elected office and Chávez's that of a labor leader.

Lillian Roybal Rose recalled, "I always heard nothing but positive things from my dad about César Chávez. I was involved in the grape boycott, and I did go to Delano with different college kids. Every time he [César Chávez] saw me, he'd say, 'How's your father? Please give my best to your father.' I know that they did disagree on one main thing and that was during the Simpson-Mazzoli [hearings]... They wanted to go after the employers that hired illegals because the illegals were breaking back the strike and my father was against that. That's the only time I ever heard them at odds with each other."[21]

Richard Santillan, at that time a young Chicano activist who had done volunteer work for the UFW from 1965 to 1970, went to see César Chávez in 1970 about running for office within the newly formed La Raza Unida Party. Santillan recalled, "[Chávez] looked at me and said two things. That as much as he supported the notion of La Raza Unida Party, that he was not, he didn't see himself as a Chicano leader, that he was a labor leader, that [being a labor leader did not]... diminish him being Chicano. He could not endorse a party that he thought was exclusively for Chicanos with a union that was comprised of Blacks and Whites, and Arabs, and Mexican, and Filipinos, he couldn't do it. And I remember leaving the meeting, not so much angry, [but] so disappointed because that was part of my political processing."[22] César Chávez did send Santillan a letter supporting, but not endorsing, La Raza Unida Party. Santillan asked himself at that time, "Why doesn't the Congressman [Roybal] come over? Why doesn't César come over? Why are they staying on that side?" However, many years later Santillan realized that "there were very legitimate reasons and I think very practical and political reasons why both the Congressman and others did not promote La Raza Unida Party."[23]

Many years later, Lucille Roybal-Allard noted, "Being a political leader as an elected official is one thing, and being an activist is something else, and I think both are important. And they both have a purpose. But I think there are times where there is confusion on the part of political activists who don't understand the political process from the inside and have certain expectations of their elected political officials, and when they don't meet those expectations become very critical and in some cases actually undermine their efforts that are being made within the political system."[24] Ed Roybal Jr. said of his father's role in the political system, "My father always firmly believed in working within the system and to a certain extent had a great deal of faith in the system or that the system would be made to work. He had no illusions about it being perfect by any means, without racism or any of the obstacles. But, still he believed that the system, that you could work within the system and that was the most effective way of bringing change.... Another important thing for my father was respect. If you want to work within the system, you have to treat people, even though opposed to your views, with respect and demand that in return. So, the kinds of tactics that we often saw in the '60s, the confrontation and so forth, were very adverse to my father's practice and civility."[25] Lillian Roybal Rose underscored one final difference between her father and some of the activists of the, 1960s: his firm stance on nonviolence.[26]

Reies Lopez Tijerina (born 1926) was another important Chicano Movement leader. He was born to a family who lived a marginal existence by the farm fields of Fall City, Texas. He became a nondenominational preacher along the Mexican border, with a concern for social justice. After traveling many dusty trails, he settled in northern New Mexico, where the status of Spanish and Mexican land grants became the focus of his efforts. He founded the Alianza Federal de Mercedes in 1963 to work for the restoration of the land grants. In the group's demand for civil rights, it filed lawsuits against the government, organized marches, and occupied the Kit Carson National Forest. Tijerina was arrested and then freed on bail. The organization took on a more militant, more defiant position thereafter and was renamed the Alianza Federal de Pueblos Libres.[27]

Roybal had met Tijerina but did not call himself a follower, nor did Tijerina make much effort to enlist Roybal's support. Roybal thought Tijerina "was a bright guy" but "tried to lead a movement without actually being able to keep it together."[28] "Tijerina was successful in getting the land grants that were made available to those people by the King of Spain. Recording those grants was difficult because the records were not well kept. But the truth of the matter is that the grants actually took place...I supported the findings of Senator [Dennis] Chavez (Chavez had previously attempted to investigate the legitimacy of the land grants)."[29]

Lillian Roybal Rose recalled that her father supported Tijerina's cause but not his tactics.[30] Ed Roybal Jr. commented, "My father's family being an old New Mexico family, some of our family were Tijerina's border constituency. I still remember my father talking negatively about Tijerina's tactics. I think he was sympathetic to the issue of people getting compensation for the lands that were stolen. We did have ancestors who were once wealthy and lost their land. We did have people who were swindled out of their land basically with the collusion of the government and so there was sympathy with the cause."[31] By the 1990s, Reis Tijerina had all but disappeared from public view.

Another nationally known Chicano Movement leader was Rodolfo "Corky" Gonzalez (1928–2005). Born in Denver, he was the son of a migrant sugar beet workers.[32] In 1970, he founded the (Colorado) Raza Unida Party and moved from Chicano nationalism to class struggle and internationalism (the concept of solidarity with other liberation movements in the Third World). By the late 1970s, incessant police harassment and litigation severely hampered his organization. In October 1987, a serious traffic accident left him physically limited. Corky Gonzales is recognized for "stitching into the Chicano fabric urban issues."[33] Ed Roybal and Corky Gonzalez never met, nor did Gonzalez ever make any known effort to enlist Roybal's support. That they would not have contact is odd because both men shared in common an urban focus for community organization. Part of their formation included a love of the ring. Roybal was aware of Gonzalez's prowess and referred to him "as a former boxer . . . from what I gather, and I understand pretty good too."[34] There was respect there, Roybal knowing from indirect sources that Gonzalez was "a very smart individual and tenacious in his position." Otherwise, said Roybal, "I don't think I ever had any impression of him either way."

Jose Angel Gutierrez was born in 1944 the son of a physician in Crystal City, Texas. At twenty-two years of age he co-founded the Mexican American Youth Organization (MAYO) in San Antonio and was elected its first president. In 1969, he co-founded La Raza Unida Party as a Texas independent political party that sought to bring to fruition the political self-determination of Mexican people. Between 1970 and 1972, the party had some success in electing several Chicanos to the Crystal City government, including Gutierrez himself, who became a Zavala County commissioner (referred to as a judge in the state) in 1972.[35]

Political scientist Richard Santillan, a young Chicano activist and La Raza Unida organizer, reflected on what the party signified, "The ideology of La Raza Unida Party was the fact that it was going to be the political arm of the Chicano Movement and it was a time when in the 1970s, the international movements had their political arms."[36] Despite the political failures of the La Raza Unida Party, Santillan commented, "One of the things La Raza Unida Party did for a brief time was I think that it warned the Democratic Party that Chicanos were disillusioned...It told the Republican Party that the Mexican American vote was open....[So] people had to begin competing for that vote."[37]

Santillan cited several reasons for the demise of La Raza Unida Party. First of all, it was sexist: "There were a lot of women who left the party." A second reason was that "the government engaged itself in a host of illegal activities to destroy the party." Third, Santillan also mentioned that the party was too open, "too democratic. It was comprised of everybody who wanted to come in, from people who were Marxist to people disillusioned who wanted to make a statement. By allowing everybody to come in, it never could build consensus. The party also lacked any type of political understanding or consciousness of the fact that there were differences among Chicanos from Texas to California, New Mexico, and Arizona. It actually saw the Chicano Movement as male, as young, as heterosexual, as able-bodied, as some would even call it college educated; that's how the party saw the community. And never saw the community I think in all its complexity."[38]

According to Congressman Roybal, "I was asked to join La Raza Unida Party which I never did." About the experiment of La Raza Unida Party, Roybal commented, "They had a cause and began to organize, and they did very well. But not well enough for Mexican Americans elsewhere because of the difficulty in the Mexican community as to what to call ourselves."[39] Ed Roybal Jr. recalled, "I remember my dad talking about that [La Raza Unida Party] a lot. He actually agreed that the Democratic Party was condescending, patronizing. They didn't help my dad at all. But he did not think that a third party would have any clout. We just didn't have the numbers, we didn't have the power, and what we would do is end up letting the Republicans win; then things would be worse."[40]

Other leaders in the Chicano Movement, though they may not have considered themselves as such, included artists. The movement inspired many to struggle for better opportunities and improved images in both film and television, as well as visual art. One of these organizations, called Nosotros, was co-founded by actor Ricardo Montalban in order to address discriminatory hiring practices and stereotyping concerns in the movie industry. Roybal recollected that Montalban's organization was "successful because of the political pressure. The motion picture industry finally gave in a little bit."[41]

Ed Roybal was a strong supporter of the visual arts, especially Chicano art. Juan Gonzalez, one of the first Chicano muralists and founder of the Goetz Art Gallery, said that Roybal was instrumental in providing monies for a host of artistic projects in East Los Angeles. Irma Núñez (Roybal's niece and Juan's wife), recalled that after the Goetz Gallery moved to Olvera Street, they invited Ed and Lucille Roybal to the inauguration. "My aunt and uncle walked through and were in awe of the beautiful art, to see beautiful, positive images, quality works of art that were of our culture. My aunt called me and said, 'I want to redecorate our entire house in Pasadena with this art,' and so I sent my whole 300-print collection to their house, and she handpicked [several] limited edition prints, and they're still in their home today. They were definitely lovers and supporters of the arts even though his focus was helping education. But, when the opportunities were there for him to actively support us, I saw how it really fed his spirit."[42]

Friction Between Chicanos and the Establishment

The Chicano Movement challenged the leadership of the Mexican American generation in several ways. The Chicano Movement attempted to fill the political vacuum that existed due to the small number of Mexican American elected or appointed officials. In the 1960s, for example, only four Mexican Americans served in Congress: Ed Roybal, Dennis Chavez, Joseph Montoya, and Henry B. Gonzalez. The representation of Mexican Americans at the local and state levels was similarly small. In Los Angeles, the city with the largest Mexican population (second only to Mexico City), no Mexican American served in the city council from Roybal's departure to Congress in 1962 until 1985.

Ultimately, however, the movement disregarded the federal government, especially having seen little of the benefits from President Johnson's War on Poverty programs, which focused primarily on the African American community. Chicano leaders learned some difficult lessons; for example, they came to see that Roybal's job was not to hold up high the Chicano banner but to represent and benefit his district. They learned that representative government does not respond to who is the neediest. It responds to who is best organized. Chicano youth decided consciously to hinder the governmental process because "responsiveness," as they defined it, could not be obtained by sharing power. To accomplish their goals they had to make their leaders look inept. The few elected leaders that there were (and the important ones were at the local level, not Congress) leveraged the Chicano Movement to a wider benefit, to expose the plight of the Mexican community and their dashed expectations.

There was a high rate of Mexican American casualties in the Vietnam War, disproportionate to population size. Elected officials, moreover, seemed unable to end the conflict. When President Nixon and Secretary of State Kissinger expanded the war into Cambodia, many felt further galvanized to seek alternative methods of protest. War protests became a new platform in the civil rights movement, expanding the definition of social and economic justice. With a few notable exceptions, Latinos were marginalized in the antiwar effort. Thus, Chicano leaders had additional fuel with which to challenge the political strategies of the Mexican American generation. Long-established organizations led by middle-class leadership, like LULAC, and the former serviceman-led GI Forum saw themselves supplanted in influence by working-class leadership and community-based organizations.

The Chicano Movement challenged political patronage, lobbying, elected office methods, and other traditional methods of bringing about change. The process of demanding change in the 1960s was often dramatic and confrontational; it involved direct action such as pickets, marches, demonstrations, pilgrimages, sit-down occupations of buildings, and walkouts. As a consequence, participants captured more media attention and served to publicize or pressure for a demand more immediately. The new political strategies and the search for a third party forced both major parties to reconsider and gradually become more inclusive of Mexican Americans and their issues.

In sum, the Chicano Movement did not fill a political vacuum so much as it filled a protest vacuum. While the movement fashioned itself to be about asserting ethnic pride, its protests were mainly against unresponsive government. The movement was successful in that it alerted potential voters to unfulfilled political promises and empty government rhetoric, and made them realize that getting more Latinos elected was indeed a necessity. Likewise the Chicano Movement raised consciousness about the importance of holding elected representatives more accountable to the community.

Conscientious elected leaders like Congressman Roybal worked with great diligence and dedication to acquire more concessions in terms of programs, services, jobs, and civil rights. He was also part of the effort to elect Latinos, especially at the local level. Edward Roybal Jr. recalled that in the 1960s people who identified with the Chicano Movement "lashed out at my father." Their complaint was that he represented "the establishment." The establishment, at the time, was taken to mean those people who had social, political, and economic power and influence. The period was characterized by frequent and incendiary antiestablishment accusations. "I grew up," he said, "hearing a lot of stuff in the '60s and '70s that my father hadn't done anything for the Chicano community and this and that." Congressman Roybal had become a target, but the Roybals attributed the attacks to lack of information. "Those were hard times," added Ed Jr. "My father has a hard skin, and I do think a lot of these things healed, and in fact, a lot of the radicals then, are, you know, more established [now]. [Some are] educators and in other fields [where they] are reevaluating the position of my father."[43]

Ed Roybal, unlike other Mexican American leaders of his generation, was open to the ideas and perspectives of the Chicano generation. Irma Núñez recalled, "One of the key things [Ed] learned from [Saul] Alinsky was that the key to organizing was personal relationships. Making friends and having personal relationships opens dialogue and when you have communication, you can resolve problems. When you have a person who may not agree with you in the beginning, but they're willing to listen and they're willing to take your viewpoint into consideration, that's when you start winning the hearts and then the minds of individuals. And it's gaining the support of one person at a time that's going to develop that broad base; that's going to give you the power to back the issues that you are fighting for."[44]

Over time, some Chicano activists, like Richard Santillan, came to see the historic role played by Ed Roybal. "When I started teaching Chicano studies is when I really got down about the contributions, the legacy of the Congressman [Roybal] in terms of being a pioneer." Santillan undertook much research about Chicano history to discover the contributions of Ed Roybal and the Mexican American generation. In 1972, when he began teaching, Chicano history had yet to be written. Most of the youth of the Chicano Movement did not know their own history, through no fault of their own. Schools had failed to even acknowledge their history, least of all to teach it to them. Santillan reflected in hindsight that Roybal's generation "has never been given due credit."[45]

Congressman Roybal in Nixon's First Term

In 1968, Ed Roybal was elected to a third term in Congress. It was a time when youth movements throughout the world challenged both socialist and capitalist establishments. They were antiwar and pro-peace, anti–nuclear bomb, for the environment, and for the inclusion of minorities, women, handicapped, and gays. From Peking to Paris to Mexico City, this unprecedented youth movement shook the status quo to the very foundations. Like the Children's Crusade of the Middle Ages, the youth movement failed to take power, but it altered the world forever with regard to political consciousness, the empowerment of those formerly excluded from societies, sexual mores, and popular culture.

Richard Nixon was elected president of the United States in 1968. The Democratic Party, plagued by internal divisions and strife that year at its convention in Chicago, nominated Hubert Humphrey for the presidency. Ed Roybal and other Latino leaders were involved in Humphrey's presidential campaign, but it did not have the excitement of those of 1960 and 1964. The nation at large was divided and in turmoil. That year saw urban riots, anti–Vietnam War protests and mass movements against the war, and the assassinations of Robert Kennedy and Martin Luther King.

Nixon's political comeback in 1968 was remarkable. After his defeat by John F. Kennedy in the presidential election of 1960, the public and the media had all but given him up to political death. In 1962, he had run for governor of California and been trounced by Democrat candidate Pat Brown.

Nixon had always had a dark side and was known to engage in demagoguery, name calling, and opportunism. It had manifested long before in red baiting his political rivals, most notably Congresswoman Helen Gagahan Douglas. Nixon had served in the on the House Un-American Activities Committee. This dark side was also in evidence when things did not go his way, and he became frustrated, embittered, and venomous with his critics and detractors.

In the aftermath of Nixon's defeat for California governor, he lashed out: "Just think how much you're going to be missing. You won't have Nixon to kick around anymore because, gentlemen, this is my last press conference."[46] He returned to private law practice. However, after the disastrous defeat of Republican Barry Goldwater in 1964, the Republican leadership took a second look at Nixon. They felt he was an experienced mainstream candidate who measured up well against the liberal Lyndon

B. Johnson. Boosting his chances even more, Johnson chose not to run for re-election; moreover, the 1968 Democratic Convention in Chicago was a disaster. The Democratic Party was divided from within over the Vietnam War, and it was besieged from without by divergent dissident groups, which included Students for a Democratic Society (SDS), Yippies, student militants, antiwar activists, and Black Power militants, among others. A major riot ensued at the very gates of that convention, which was covered eagerly by the media. Roybal was concerned with the effect that the disruptions would have on the Democratic Party. "The convention took a hit," he said, realizing that "any party or gathering of any kind that has a riot has to suffer the consequences of that riot. So I was not surprised that it would damage the party as a whole. But to be able to defend that action is something I can't do."

Ed Roybal was a change agent. But there was method to what he proposed and even method to how those changes would come about. His grinding struggle in Congress, though not recognized as such, involved the meticulous production of words for the laws and regulations that make governing a stabilizing act. Mob rule was an authoritarian form, in its essence. It was like a whim. An impertinence. An imposition over reasonable methods of governing. But these were not reasonable times; instead, passions were taken to have the same logic as reason and consensus. The events and their consequences were disturbing, even to a change agent like Roybal.

Three formidable Democratic candidates sought the presidential nomination in 1968. Before serving with Lyndon Johnson as vice president, Hubert Humphrey was a senator from Minnesota. While under normal circumstances he would have been the hands-down favorite, two other popular senators campaigned for the nomination: Robert F. Kennedy (President Kennedy's brother) and Eugene McCarthy. Roybal was very impressed with all three candidates, expressing this with a term that he reserved for influential people who fully captured their times and were fully engaged in them: *colorful*. In the final analysis, Roybal felt "they were very colorful individuals and very intelligent, the top of the line...Choosing between the three was made difficult because their platforms and principles they stood for were so similar."[47]

Eugene McCarthy took an antiwar stance. He had initially launched a protest campaign against Lyndon Johnson's re-nomination and succeeded in helping force Johnson to withdraw. Robert F. Kennedy overtook McCarthy in the primaries, and Humphrey entered the race for the nomination. After winning the crucial California primary and appearing well on his way to the nomination at the Democratic Convention, Kennedy was assassinated, on June 5, 1968, in Los Angeles.

The Democrats nominated Hubert Humphrey as the party's standard-bearer for president, with Ed Muskie as his vice presidential running mate. "I knew him well. We all talked about the same things. I liked him because he was actually trying to promote the programs of President Kennedy," said Roybal. "Knowing him as well as I did, I supported him. I knew was an honest man and didn't play around. And that was significant. I thought he could win, but I was wrong."[48] Humphrey proved an effective campaigner, but the voting public that was fed up with youth protestors and riots tipped the close numbers in Nixon's favor. President Johnson gave Humphrey almost no support, but on balance, it is likely that Humphrey wanted to distance himself from Johnson's liabilities.

On April 4 of that same year, Reverend Martin Luther King was assassinated. Roybal had supported and had marched with King. Roybal stood right behind him at the Lincoln Memorial when King gave his famous "I Have a Dream" speech. Roybal commented, "I also supported those leaders who had been the support structure to King, like Dr. Ralph Abernathy, those persons and groups that maintained the civil rights movement after King was gone."[49]

On Election Day, Nixon won with 31.8 million popular votes. Humphrey came in a close second with 31.3 million votes. Former Alabama governor and avowed segregationist George Wallace siphoned nearly

10 million votes for the American Independent Party. In the Electoral College, Nixon had a commanding lead over Humphrey, 302–191. Wallace received 46 electoral votes. Nixon acquired 10 percent of the Mexican American/Latino vote. However, Nixon had made a fundamental political error even in victory; he had chosen Spiro Agnew as his running mate. Agnew, the right-wing governor of Maryland, had a long history of dishonesty and crassness and would prove to be Nixon's Achilles' heel.

Agnew headed the president's Cabinet Committee on Opportunities for Spanish-Speaking People, which got the ball rolling for many of Ed Roybal's important activities. Despite this, Ed Roybal and the new president had parted company long before. Their differences were irreconcilable in the big picture. Nixon's involvement in the red scares of the 1950s and his involvement with the infamous Senator Joseph McCarthy gained him no respect from Roybal. How much of it was his values and what part was political opportunism, Ed Roybal did not know. All he was sure about when Nixon won the presidency was that "I was surprised. I didn't like what I saw, but that's as far as I went with it."[50] He could distinguish among Nixon, the man, and his politics. In fact, Roybal even found Richard Nixon "very nice and he made you feel at home." Roybal remembered Nixon was a gracious host, charming even, and so was his wife, Pat. "You could really like him as an individual but not enough to follow his lead."[51]

Congressman Roybal recalled actually meeting Nixon way back in 1947: "Well, we were both in uniform, and I was called by the Women's League of Voters if I would take a debate that was already announced, and I told them that I didn't have any money to buy a suit. And they said, 'Well go in uniform.' I did, and as I was approaching the school, going up the stairs was Richard Nixon. I saluted him, and he saluted back, and then we went into the debate. The debate was based on housing, and their right in Whittier to promote a program that did not exclude anybody based on their particular racial background."[52]

1969: A Silent Minority No More

By 1969, Ed Roybal had developed a Latino agenda of legislation and the making of a national constituency. The Chicano Movement had dispelled the myth of Latinos as the "silent minority." Events such as the farm worker movement led by César Chávez, the East L.A. High School Walkouts, Reies Tijerina's struggle for land grants, and Corky Gonzalez's Crusade for Justice had received national media coverage and brought visibility to the plight of the Mexican community. Similarly, the struggle of Puerto Rican organizations for social justice and the prominence of Cuban immigration had begun to evolve into a national Latino presence and constituency. Ed Roybal and other elected officials were instrumental in giving a voice in Congress to this growing constituency.

By this time, Roybal was also beginning to be acknowledged by both his peers and colleagues in Congress. On a visit to the offices of U.S. Senator Alan Cranston (D-CA), Ed Roybal was moved and inspired by a copy of a poem that he found there. It was a poem written by Chinese philosopher Lao-Tsu some two thousand years before. Cranston sent Roybal a copy of the poem. The untitled poem in a very real and ironic sense encapsulated the type of political leader Ed Roybal was. The poem read:

> A leader is best
> When people barely know that he exists;
> Less good when they claim him
> Worse when they despise him.
> Fail to honor people,
> And they fail to honor you.
> But of a good leader,
> When his work is done,
> His aim fulfilled,
> They will all say,
> "We did this ourselves."[53]

Ed Roybal's unassuming and egalitarian style, open mind, and practical approach to his legislative duties were confirmed the very same month in a letter to a constituent, Mrs. S. C. Crane. She had asked him whether he would support the candidacy of Congressman Morris K. Udall for Speaker of the House. Roybal wrote, "As you may know, I am most frequently lined up with the Members who seek to streamline operations and make way for innovations and fresh ideas. Even though 'Mo' Udall was late in making his bid and gaining the necessary momentum to win the contest, he did win concessions that should create a greater involvement of energetic recent arrivals. This should widen and vitalize legislative attacks on the problems that face our Country."[54]

Roybal did not have the ego or temperament for political grandstanding; rather, he exercised his altruism in taking care of business. During late January 1969, Roybal was assigned to the powerful Veterans Affairs Committee, which enabled him to work on providing assistance to armed forces veterans. Their readjustment into society and treatment by the Veterans Administration had been one of his long-term concerns. California had nearly 3 million veterans. They were all affected directly or indirectly by activities of the Veterans Affairs Committee in such areas as housing, education, and training programs; VA hospitals and medical care; GI insurance; compensation and vocational rehabilitation; and veteran's pensions. Roybal was able to continue serving on the Foreign Affairs Committee at the same time.

During late January, Roybal sponsored a bill to set Dr. Martin Luther King's birthday aside as a national holiday. He wrote to a constituent, "I am among those who greatly admired him for his dedication to human rights and his courageous efforts to promote racial equality; I mourn our Country's loss through his tragic and untimely death."[55]

Also in January 1969, Los Angeles City Councilman Thomas Bradley, a long-time close friend of Ed Roybal, began seeking to establish a coalition of Mexican Americans and Blacks. Bradley was running for mayor.

At this time, Blacks were 18 percent of the electorate in Los Angeles and Mexican Americans, 13 percent. Bradley had for years been vocal about his proposal that the Los Angeles City Council be enlarged from 15 to 17 members to "increase the potential" for Mexican American representation. Bradley was also a consistent supporter of the struggle of César Chávez and the United Farm Workers Union.

However, within the Mexican American community, the feeling about a "Brown and Black" coalition ranged from reluctance to opposition. Early on, some leaders like Bert Corona, Dr. Julian Nava, and Richard Calderon worked to establish such a coalition. However, the key Mexican American leader was Ed Roybal, and there was much speculation about whether he would back the proposed coalition. The *Los Angeles Times* wrote, "Proponents of the coalition hope that Rep. Edward Roybal" will support "Bradley and, in effect, the coalition. Roybal, an extremely careful politician, however, probably will not show his hand until the issue is clearly resolved, if at all."[56]

Roybal was instrumental in establishing the La Raza Por Bradley Para Mayor Committee, which was fully active by March. The support committee included J. J. Rodriguez, Bert Corona, Dr. Julian Nava, Richard Calderon, Richard Alatorre, Reverend Yahac Mardirosian, Reverand Father John B. Luce, Dr. Rodolfo Acuna, Joe Sanchez, Soledad Alatorre, and Larry Ramirez. Roybal announced, "I urge all my friends and supporters in the City of Los Angeles to vote and work for Tom Bradley for Mayor because he is the most qualified candidate who understands all of our needs and will govern for all people."[57]

In mid-March, Congressman Roybal introduced H.R. 8416, which would give the Inter-Agency Committee on Mexican American Affairs statutory authority from Congress to continue its work on a permanent basis. He received the bipartisan support of more than fifty legislators in the U.S. Senate and the House of Representatives. Roybal stated, "Establishment of the Committee on a permanent basis would be a major contribution toward achieving the Committee's goals of increased jobs, better housing, improved health care, and wider educational opportunities for members of the Spanish-speaking community."[58]

The Inter-Agency Committee had been created by Executive Memorandum in June 1967 and had as its members the secretaries of Health, Education, and Welfare; Housing and Urban Development; Labor; Agriculture; and Commerce. Vicente T. Ximenes continued to serve as his chairperson.

Roybal's Commitment to Peaceful Change

On April 7, 1969, Roybal was invited to make a speech on the topic of urban problems at Occidental College, in the northeast area of Los Angeles. Roybal's speech captured the pulse of that passionate time of the nation's history but even more displayed his sense of hope, compassion, and commitment to peaceful change, and the transformative power of tolerance. He said in his speech, "A few weeks ago I met with a group of students who were walking out of an East Los Angeles school to urge them not to follow the Watts example. I told them that one's right to protest does not include the burning of our communities and the destruction of our society and institutions." He told of how a high school student asked him, "What institutions and what society are you asking us to preserve? The society that polluted our air and water or the society whose greed and disregard for human dignity condemned fellow man to a condition of poverty, squalor, and disease?"[59]

Roybal then told his audience what he thought needed to be done urgently. He acknowledged that all Americans must "examine carefully our institution, our fragmented and overlapping governments and our fiscal and social disparities." He said that to make changes "does not mean the establishment of a new government, but rather the coordination of existing governmental facilities in planning together to solve common problems...We must realize that what is needed is a strategy for the imposition of priorities that puts your most talented people and your financial resources precisely in those parts of the city and suburbs were the need is most pressing." He reminded them that residents of barrios and ghettos had heard promises before and "later found themselves living in a worse slum" than before. "The words *eminent domain* are most feared by people in lower income groups." He described the how the poor and minorities had suffered under eminent domain in the building of the freeway system and Dodger Stadium in Chavez Ravine. He called for the inclusion of ghetto residents: "They must be given an opportunity to participate fully, and be listened to, as they speak loud and clear of their ideas for changes."[60]

He concluded, "Our mission and strategy must be to strengthen capable political institutions. Communities must be given the opportunity to identify their own problems and together organize an appropriate combination of programs that will help solve their social ills...We can answer the questions of the younger, restless generation, if we really care."

During his first term, Nixon focused on U.S. foreign policy, especially the Vietnam War and a rapprochement with communist China. In Vietnam, he began to reduce the U.S. troop presence from 550,000 to 24,000 and war spending from $25 billion to less than $3 billion.[61] In his plan to push the Vietnamese to the peace table in Paris, Nixon had Cambodia secretly bombed, thus expanding the conflict in Southeast Asia despite the apparent pullback. In the issue of China, he invoked the old Chinese proverb, "The enemy of my enemy is my best friend." Nixon was working a wedge between the Chinese and the Soviets. As early as the 1960s, evidence of a Sino-Soviet conflict was appearing. Military clashes had even occurred along the long Russian-Chinese border. Mindful of the fact that mainland China possessed more than half of the world's population and the huge possibilities of an economic market, Nixon and Secretary of State Henry Kissinger decided to work for rapprochement.

Articulating his feelings about the normalization of relations with communist China, Congressman Roybal stated, "Well, I will always be interested in any movement that is designed to bring about peace but without violence, and when I support the movement for peace, I do not support a movement that has as its main objective the violent overthrow of a government."[62]

Raising Standards

Ed Roybal was honored at a testimonial dinner on September 19, 1969, at the Biltmore Hotel in Los Angeles for his twenty-year anniversary of distinguished public service. At the dinner he called for a $2.00 minimum wage level. His bill, H.R. 13145 would raise the federal minimum wage from $1.60 to $2.00. The bill would also require overtime pay to employees after eight hours in a day and forty hours in a week; it would also eliminate special wage and hour exemptions in the law, which then denied millions of workers any protection under the Fair Labor Standards Act.

Roybal said that the "long overdue improvements" would offset the inflationary increases in the cost of living, while fulfilling the "humanitarian goal" of the wage and hour act. He further commented, "It is clear to me that preventing poverty and reducing the welfare burden, by assuring a decent wage is much better—and much less costly—than attempting to repair the human damage caused by substandard wages and living conditions, after that damage has already been done."[63]

While Congressman Roybal was busy carrying out his congressional duties in the nation's capital, events back in Los Angeles once again reminded him how difficult it was to change the minds of some. On September 2, 1969, Judge Gerald S. Chargin of Santa Clara Juvenile Court passed sentence on a seventeen-year-old Chicano who had allegedly committed incest. Judge Chargin commented, "Mexican people, after 13 years of age, think he is perfectly all right to go out and act like an animal. We ought to send you out of the country—send you back to Mexico. You belong in prison for the rest of your life for doing things of this kind. You ought to commit suicide. That's what I think of people of this kind. You are lower than animal and haven't the right to live in organized society—just miserable, lousy, rotten people. Maybe Hitler was right. The animals in our society probably ought to be destroyed because they have no right to live among human beings."[64] Once again, the entire Mexican community had been smeared and defamed for the alleged actions of one person. Congressman Roybal denounced his racist remarks and called for his removal. He and Senator Joseph Montoya also called for an investigation. Despite Roybal's and Montoya's denunciations, Judge Chagrin was merely transferred to the civil division of the Superior Court.

Roybal also held his own staff members to high standards of behavior, and many exceeded his expectations. Clara Ignatius was one of the remarkable staff members in Ed Roybal's office in Washington, D.C. She was his executive secretary, part of a staff of five. According to one staff member, "We all have our own responsibilities, but she's really his sidekick. She's the head gal."

She lived most of her life in Los Angeles. She claimed she had been born in a train moving from Philadelphia to Los Angeles. She would never say her age. She stated, "I'm not a day over 39, although I've been 39 for a number of years." She first worked for the Los Angeles Board of Public Works. She then worked a few years as a secretary to the Board of Commissioners and then joined the general secretary's office of Los Angeles city hall. She was assigned to Roybal after his 1949 election to the Los Angeles City Council. She recalled, "I had to be sort of a social worker. His district is one with a lot of problems of low-income families...juvenile delinquency, lack of education...I would sit and listen. I couldn't always help, but I would always listen." She took the initiative to take a Spanish course in Mexico for six weeks. She said, "I wanted to help and felt more of a rapport with these people if I spoke their language." She apparently not only won their gratitude but also their respect. She recalled that when Roybal's constituents left his office they would tell her, "*Usted es muy amable y simpática* (You are very kind and sympathetic)."[65]

On the day after Roybal won his election to the House of Representatives in November 1962, he approached Clara Ignatius about going to Washington, D.C., with him. She recalled, "I really had no desire to go to Washington. I didn't want to leave Los Angeles or City Hall. It seemed as if I'd spend my life there." She informed Roybal that she would think about it. Her uncle eventually talked her into coming to the nation's capital, much to Roybal's satisfaction.

She recollected in 1969, "I've seen three decidedly different administrations. When I first came here, it was one of the most exciting periods, when President Kennedy was president. It was such a glamorous administration. Young people just stampeded to Washington. Then came the Johnson era. It was not as exciting or as young. It was more homespun, less dynamic. Today, things are rather low-keyed, Mr. Nixon has taken an efficient, businesslike attitude as if he were trying to calm things down." Clara Ignatius was one of many loyal, hardworking, and dedicated staff who worked in Ed Roybal's office and provided his constituents compassion and effective assistance.

On October 8, 1970, Congressman Roybal from the floor of the House of Representatives called national attention to the continuing disproportionate casualties of Mexican Americans in the Vietnam War. He cited an article entitled "Mexican American Casualties in Vietnam" written by Ralph Guzman, Ph.D., a professor of political science at Merrill College, of the University of California, Santa Cruz. Roybal stated, "These somber statistics prove once again, as similar experience in World War II and the Korean War conflict showed, that the Spanish-surnamed community in the United States has traditionally shouldered its share, and more, of the burden of military service in the United States." He cited the study's findings that during the period between January 1961 and February 1967, 19.4 percent of war casualties had Spanish surnames; and between December 1967 and March 1969, 19 percent of the total had Spanish surnames.

Roybal concluded, "Only a relatively small number of Mexican Americans have been able to circumvent obligatory military service by attending college." He noted the underrepresentation of Mexican Americans in institutions of higher learning. At the University of California, Mexican American students numbered less than 1 percent of the total number of the total student population of 97,000.

Nixon and Mexican Americans

President Nixon, who had grown up in Whittier, California, near Mexicans and other poor people, was not sensitive to the plight of Mexicans or the underprivileged. Nixon moved to decentralize social programs with the launch of New Federalism. Under this initiative he gave block grants to municipalities to spend as they wished. In 1973, Congress passed the Comprehensive Employment and Training Act (CETA). It altered the focus of job training programs. Whereas before they targeted low-income working-class recipients, they now focused on White, upper-working-class individuals. The consequence of the CETA block grants resulted in giving local politicians and the private sector more control, effectively reducing services to the poor. One of Nixon's advisors, Arthur Burns, whom the president later appointed to the Federal Reserve Board, defined poverty as an "intellectual concept."[66]

Nixon also had no tolerance for the United Farm Workers Union (UFW), founded by César Chávez, despite the fact that he was heavily indebted to the California agricultural growers. During 1971 and 1972, Nixon helped the grape producers by sponsoring a bill that required farm workers to give ten days' notice before striking and outlawing farm worker secondary strikes. The bill further called for a thirty-day cooling-off period before some type of binding arbitration could be brought in. It was an attempt to end the ability of farm workers to stop production during the harvest season. Although Nixon failed, the American Farm Bureau Federation sponsored like-minded legislation in Oregon and Arizona. In May 1975, the California state legislature passed the California Agricultural Labor Relations Act, which established the Agricultural Labor Relations

Board (ALRB) to supervise elections and resolve appeals. It also permitted unions to call for secondary boycotts when employers refused to negotiate after a strike had been won.

In 1969, Nixon replaced the Inter-Agency Committee on Mexican American Affairs with the Cabinet Committee on Opportunities for Spanish-Speaking People. It broadened the focus of concern from Mexican people to Hispanics in general. In 1972, Nixon appointed some fifty Mexican Americans to high federal positions. They included Romana Bañuelos, a Los Angeles food manufacturer. She served as treasurer of the United States from 1971 to 1974. In 1970, Nixon also helped start the National Economic Development Association (NEDA), which was funded by federal and state agencies.

1970: Building a Re-election Platform

Congressman Roybal was instrumental in the creation of the Cabinet Committee on Opportunities for Spanish-Speaking People, which replaced President Johnson's Inter-Agency Committee on Mexican American Affairs. The former committee had been created by a presidential memorandum but had no regular authority for obtaining or spending money.

Ed Roybal and Senator Joseph Montoya (D-NM) had introduced bills, which gained the support of the majority of both parties. The House bill passed 314–81 and went directly to President Nixon for signature into law. The newly created committee now had the power to function for years to come. However, it had a small budget, the initial appropriation being around $500,000 a year. The committee would be composed of the secretaries of seven departments: Agriculture; Commerce; Health, Education, and Welfare; Housing and Urban Development; Labor; Treasury; and Justice. Other membership would include the director of the Office of Economic Opportunity, the administrator of the Small Business Administration, the chairperson of the Civil Service Commission, and a commissioner of the Equal Employment Opportunity Commission. The measure also set up an Advisory Council on Spanish-Speaking Americans composed of nine members appointed by the president, which would represent all the Spanish-speaking communities in the United States (Puerto Ricans and Cubans, for example, had not been represented at this level before). The head of the new committee was expected to be Los Angeles attorney Martin Castillo.[67]

Roybal commented on the new committee, "Spanish-surnamed Americans, along with all other citizens, must be offered a real chance to enter into the mainstream of our nation's life—to obtain a full share of the great economic, social, and educational benefits of this land. By establishing a statutory Committee on Opportunities for Spanish-speaking People as a cabinet-level voice within the executive branch—designed specifically to represent the significant segment of the population in the highest government councils—we are going a long way toward realizing these worthwhile goals."[68]

During February, Ed Roybal announced his intention to run for a fifth term in the U.S. House of Representatives. During the same month, Michael L. O'Brien, an advertising/marketing executive and president of the California Republican Assembly, 30th Congressional District, also announced his candidacy for the 30th District seat. O'Brien, a former amateur boxer, came out swinging at Roybal, labeling him as a "captive of the radical left." He charged that Roybal "does not really represent the district" and that he was "constantly supporting the same types of fanatics."

Roybal's campaign in turn emphasized his significant legislative accomplishments. In the last session of Congress, he had voted for reform of the U.S. income tax, providing rate reduction for all individual taxpayers; an appropriation measure for public education and health care programs bringing more than $150 million to California; draft reform, which offered a more equitable lottery system; and a bill on drug abuse education, which had passed the House and was awaiting Senate action. He introduced the bill that created the Cabinet Committee on Opportunities for

Spanish-Speaking People and a bill calling for the repeal of the Emergency Detention Act, which had been used to round up Japanese Americans during World War II. He co-authored a bill banning the use of gas and bacteriological warfare. In the campaign, Roybal could also point to his continuing legal efforts in conjunction with Los Angeles County and California state officials to have the big four automakers produce cars with less emission pollution.

Despite these efforts, during mid-February, the Congress of Mexican American Unity, held at East Los Angeles College, voted not to endorse Ed Roybal for the June primary. He was the only Mexican American legislator not to win the group's endorsement. Roybal was not present at that gathering, and he had not sent a representative. Upon losing the vote for endorsement, Roybal supporters placed a motion before the convention to suspend the rule in order to allow the endorsement of the absent congressman. The motion, which required a two-thirds majority vote for its passage, was defeated by a vote of 217 to 134. Student delegates were the core of the opposition to Roybal's endorsement, with the exception of members of Católicos Por la Raza, who abstained from voting because it was a "political issue." Raul Ruiz, one of the leaders of the opposition, stated, "The issue is not that he is not present [today]. It is that he has not been present on the issues affecting the Chicano community."[69] This statement was refuted by Alejandro Trujillo, of the Mexican American Youth Organization (MAYO), who went on to document Roybal's many efforts on behalf of the Mexican American community and added, "If any Chicano is not in tune, then we have to cultivate him. We, the people, have to guide him."

The issues and passions at the convention were reflective of the Chicano Movement era. Chicano history was taught in neither high schools nor universities. Even community activists did not often know the struggles, sacrifices, and achievements of the previous generation.

A few months later, Los Angeles City Councilman Thomas Bradley enthusiastically endorsed Roybal's re-election. Publicly addressing

Roybal, he said, "Your record in the Congress of the United States is one of which all of us are proud...Matters of concern to you have been creating jobs, providing decent housing, guaranteeing civil rights, providing care of our senior citizens and improving education for our youth. You have worked hard to restore peace in this very troubled world."[70]

Tackling Racial Integration in Schools, the Community, and Government

The issue of school bussing became a hot issue in California, and Ed Roybal received many letters from constituents raising this emotional issue with him. The California Superior Court had rendered a mandate to integrate the Los Angeles public schools starting in September of 1970. In one letter to a constituent, Roybal commented, "Although affirmative steps must be taken to relieve the existing racial imbalance in our public schools, I am inclined to agree with you that forced bussing is not the answer to this tumultuous problem."[71] At that time, the Los Angeles Board of Education took the position of appealing the court's decision.

A survey conducted by the *Los Angeles Times* during March 1970 found that mandatory bussing of school children to end racial segregation in public schools was opposed by a ratio of 3:1 by the California's thirty-eight congressional delegates. The study revealed that Democrats were moving away from support of school bussing as well. The survey indicated a shift from achieving integration to a focus on improving schools in minority neighborhoods.

Roybal at this point stated, "It would seem reasonable that bussing could be considered as at least one of many devices in an effort to overcome a situation of unconstitutional racial or ethnic segregation in schools. I don't believe that bussing should ever be the only, or ever the primary, method employed to achieve this goal."[72] Roybal was only one of seven in Congress to favor bussing under reasonable circumstances.

In mid-February 1970, the California state senate announced it would redraw the state legislative and congressional districts. Chairman of the Senate Elections and Reapportionment Committee Melvyn Dymally (D-Los Angeles), held the hearings at East Los Angeles College. Roybal stated that the legislature did not know where Mexican Americans lived. He blamed the resulting disenfranchisement of Mexican Americans on the U.S. Census Bureau, saying that they had asked only one in every twenty persons if they were Mexican Americans. He added that "the Mexican American community remains the most underrepresented."

At that time in California, there was only one Mexican American in the congressional delegation (Roybal), one state assemblyman, and no state senators. Roybal commented that the committee recognized that Mexican Americans were underrepresented and that he had made the same argument to a reapportionment committee in 1961 and had been ignored. He stated that he was "disgusted at the way the committee, controlled by Democrats, ignored the community."[73]

During February, Roybal announced a federal grant of $988,258 to the White Memorial Hospital at 1730 Brooklyn Avenue in East Los Angeles. It was authorized by the Health, Education, and Welfare Department's Hospital Survey and Construction Act. The funds would go to a new three-story rehabilitation center. The White Memorial Hospital, a private facility, and the County General Hospital were the only two that serviced the East Los Angeles area. Roybal commented that "it is essential that we expand our hospital facilities in order to meet the spiral demand for adequate medical treatment."[74]

Ed Roybal continued to press for constructive changes in the East Los Angeles public schools in the aftermath of the historic walkouts the previous years. During mid-March, on a visit to Los Angeles, Roybal took the initiative to arrange a meeting with Chief of Police Ed Davis, and invited Perez, principal of Roosevelt High School, along with the student body president of Roosevelt, a representative of the Parents Association, and Reverend Margirosian of the Mexican American Education Committee.

Roybal later met with the acting superintendent of schools and negotiated the creation of new guidelines designed to include community participation in the prevention of violence and elimination of factors that fostered unrest. Roybal promised to continue to work toward a solution to the problems and expressed his continued support of students' efforts as long as they were nonviolent and did not violate the rights of others. He believed that worthwhile results could be achieved by the exercise of their rights to protest in a firm, but peaceful way.

Transforming the Vietnam War and Other Priorities

In March 1970, Roybal was appointed to the Appropriations Committee, which was then under the leadership of Chairman George Mahon (D-TX). The Appropriations Committee is one of the most powerful in Congress; it has the authority to review all phases of how the taxpayers' money is spent by the federal government and is also a watchdog against inefficiency and waste in government. Within Appropriations, Roybal served on the General Government Subcommittee. He remained in both the Federal Operations and Treasury Post Office Committees, which oversaw foreign affairs, civil service employment, the effectiveness of representation, control of narcotics smuggling, and the efficiency of the newly redesigned U.S. Postal Service.

Roybal's busy legislative agenda included several pending bills. One called for the withdrawal of U.S. forces from Vietnam and Laos and another for the establishment of a volunteer army. He co-sponsored the Public Works Acceleration Project, which would provide 80 percent of grant-in-aid to local communities' badly needed public works; another bill called for the authorization of $4.77 billion for educational programs administered by the Office of Education and related agencies; another would authorize $30 million for the National Endowment for the Arts.

However, Nixon's political intransigence at home and his intolerant rhetoric against the antiwar movement continued to polarize the nation. On April 30, 1970, Nixon announced a draft extension on account of the expansion of conflict in Cambodia. The next day, Nixon lashed out at student activists: "You see these bums, you know, blowing up the campuses. Listen, the boys that are on the college campuses today are the luckiest people in the world, going to the greatest universities, and here they are burning the books... Then out there [in Vietnam] we have kids who are doing their duty. And I have seen them. They stand tall and they are proud."[75] Clearly out of touch with the aspirations of many young people, Nixon clung to the thesis that the "silent majority" shared his feelings. Hundreds of student demonstrations broke out, some turning into rioting. At Kent State University, in Ohio, disturbances resulted in the National Guard being called out. Four students were killed by guardsmen. The National Guard was called out to restore "law and order" in twenty-one campuses in some sixteen states. Soon thereafter, some 450 colleges were closed down.

Roybal was greatly concerned about the expansion of the Vietnam War. He wrote to a constituent, "President Nixon's distressing decision to send Americans into Cambodia strongly confirms my belief that our objective of closing down communist sanctuaries in Cambodia will result in the prolonged involvement of American troops in a quagmire so dangerous that it could envelop all of Indo-China."[76]

Ed Roybal joined other congressmen in the signing of a resolution (H.R. 964) that called for the United States to refrain from any military action in Cambodia, and a wire to President Nixon protesting further United States involvement in Southeast Asia. In addition, Roybal introduced H.R. 986 to stop funds for war in Cambodia and Laos and to limit funds for war in Vietnam to that amount required to carry out the safe and orderly withdrawal of all United States combat and support troops from South Vietnam by June 30, 1971.

As the election primary for 1970 neared, Ed Roybal's many loyal supporters joined his re-election campaign. One of these was Thomas Bradley, an old friend from his Los Angeles City Council campaigns. A former Los Angeles police officer, he had become city councilman for the 10th District.

Bradley endorsed Roybal "without reservations," a "wholehearted endorsement." In a private letter to Roybal, Bradley wrote, "You have concerned yourself with the problems of the 30th Congressional District, as well as the entire nation." Bradley cited Roybal's congressional efforts to create jobs, provide health care for senior citizens, provide decent housing, guarantee civil rights, and improve education for youth.

Bradley commended Roybal for never being "too busy to see and talk to the many persons I have sent you" and taking the time to "get out among the people and lend a helping hand wherever possible."[77]

During May, Roybal urged the Defense Department not to award contracts to aerospace companies with discriminatory employment practices. He specifically cited the North American firm Rockwell, based in Los Angeles, as one of the main culprits.

Roybal cited the 1965 executive order that required companies with a pattern of racial discrimination to submit "affirmative action programs." He indicated that the company's figures for Mexican Americans were not acceptable. He charged that Mexican Americans made up only 3.3 percent of the company's office and clerical staff, 4 percent of the technicians, 1.2 percent of managers and officials, and 1.9 percent of other professional categories. Mexican Americans were concentrated in warehousing and maintenance. Roybal called for an affirmative action program that specified a time frame in which the company had to ensure that at least 25 percent of its new hires would be from a minority groups.

Congressman Roybal continued to keep a busy legislative schedule. During late May, he introduced H.R. 1040 in order to establish a Select Committee on Nursing Homes and Homes for the Aged. He had received hundreds of reports of the abuse of senior citizens in nursing homes and in homes for the aged.

He was instrumental in obtaining a $700,000 job-training award from the U.S. Department of Labor to continue the 150-trainee New Careers Project. The Mexican American Opportunity Foundation in East Los Angeles operated the project.

On April 3, four candidates were announced to replace Congressman Roybal for the 30th Congressional District for the June 2, 1970, direct primary election. They included Blasé Bonpane, Republican; Samuel M. Cavnar, Republican; and Boris Belousov, American Independent.

In June, Ed Roybal once again was in the lead in battling another Mexican stereotype campaign, this one sponsored by the Elgin Watch Company. The company had ignited a firestorm of protest when they launched a national campaign for their Elgin Watch, which stated, "Our new Elgin is better than the Elgins Zapata was willing to kill for in 1914." The ad prominently featured a photo of Emiliano Zapata, the revered Mexican Revolution icon.

Roybal joined several individuals and organizations to express indignation: Ruben Salazar, Alex Garcia, the Congress of Mexican American Unity, the Mexican American Political Association, and several Chicano studies departments at various universities. Soon thereafter, the Elgin Company made a retraction and withdrew the advertisement campaign. Roybal sent a letter to the Elgin Company in which he wrote, "In thanking you for withdrawing this public notice from the news media, may I say this type of stereotyping is degrading and insulting to those of us of Mexican ancestry as it merely substantiates and perpetuates the often polarized misconception of the Mexican American people. Moreover, it is inaccurate and misleading and an affront to the dignity of a socially disadvantaged people who have sacrificed their lives for our country."[78] Roybal indicated that his constituents had written to him regarding this matter.

The Elgin Watch incident was a reminder that despite the social policy advances of the 1960s, media images of Mexicans remained the same. At a time when Ed Roybal was one of a handful of Latino elected officials at any level of government, he found himself like a fireman trying to put out the multiple fires of racism, prejudice, government inaction, and defamatory images.

Mexicans Are Shut Out of Los Angeles City Council Representation

The absence of a single Mexican American in the Los Angeles City Council since the departure of Ed Roybal in 1962 continued to be an important concern for Roybal and the Mexican American community. In 1970, the City of Los Angeles had fifteen districts. There were two Black councilmen, Gilbert W. Lindsay (7th District) and Thomas Bradley (8th District). However, the city, which had been founded mainly by Mexicans (most of them mestizos) and in which the largest minority was Mexican, continued to languish without better representation.

Thomas Bradley had long supported the addition of more council districts in order to provide some Mexican representation. In late July, Roybal sent a telegram to all the members of the Los Angeles City Council urging the expansion of the city council from fifteen to seventeen and to put the proposal in the November 1970 ballot. Roybal joined others in sending a letter to the Los Angeles City Council reiterating the expansion of the council and the placement of the proposal on the November ballot. The letter stated, "Failure to assure representation for Mexican Americans will increase the dangers of very grave social dislocations and tensions between groups in the City."[79]

The proposal was defeated by the council by a vote of seven to six and never made it to the ballot in November. One strong opponent of the measure was Councilman Ernani Bernardi, who charged that it was "legalized mandatory gerrymandering." He said that it would "build false hopes" of electing Mexican American lawmakers and scoffed at the implication that "we're going to cut up a particular district for Mexican American representation."[80] The Mexican American community would tread in the political desert for another decade.

During July, Ed Roybal focused part of his attention on the issue of police misconduct once again. Seven officers of the Los Angeles Police Department were charged with manslaughter and assault in connection with the killing of two Mexican nationals in a downtown apartment. The district attorney's office filed charges after numerous complaints by a wide array of Mexican American organizations. The shootings had taken place during a raid by police on a skid row apartment at 826 East Seventh Street as they searched for a murder suspect. Guillermo Beltran Sanchez, twenty-three, and Gilardo Sanchez, twenty-two, were killed by police officers. The police claimed that the two had run from the apartment during the raid. The actual suspect later surrendered to the police.

Following the shootings, Congressman Roybal held a press conference and called for an investigation by the U.S. Civil Rights Commission and a federal grand jury. Roybal commented, "It is high time that the Los Angeles police commissioners see their duty as first to protect the citizens they serve against police abuses rather than protect the police against citizen complaints as seems to be the policy now. No longer is it advisable to leave this grave crisis in the hands of local authority."[81]

The Community Service Organization (CSO) followed the case with a resolution requesting the state attorney general investigate the incident. The state attorney general subsequently charged the seven police officers with manslaughter and assault in connection with the incident. The issue of police misconduct in the Mexican American community continued to be an issue that would not go away.

In early August 1970, Ed Roybal introduced H.R. 18615, which ended military inductions after June 30, 1971. Essentially, the bill called for an all-volunteer army. Sixty members of Congress joined him in this bipartisan effort. Roybal indicated that an all-volunteer army would cause only a small budget increase and in the long term would be cheaper in real economic terms. The transition could be achieved without impairing the nation's ability to meet existing and anticipated troop-level requirements; the new army would not differ greatly in ethnic, racial, and economic makeup from the present system.

The Chicano Moratorium

Many Chicanos opposed the war in Vietnam. While middle-class students could obtain a college deferment that excluded them from the military draft, most young Mexican Americans did not attend college. Consequently, they were drafted into the military in high numbers.[82] Those figures, understood in impressionistic terms—someone's friend, someone's relative killed and wounded—led to Mexican Americans organizing several national moratoriums to oppose the war, beginning in 1969.

On August 27, Roybal announced his support for a proposed march and stated, "I congratulate the organizers of the Anti–Vietnam Moratorium March who are committed to combating the increasing use of violence by both government and by individual citizens as a solution to complex social and political problems...It is tragic that our minority communities, who share so few of the total benefits of American life, are forced to sacrifice so much more for the right to live in this country...With so few Mexican Americans able to afford college it is clear why so many of these youths are forced to join the military in order to obtain some form of specialized training. Yet is not the possible loss of one's life too high a tuition to ask any young man for his education?"

On August 29, 1969, an estimated 30,000 people assembled at Laguna Park in East Los Angeles as part of a moratorium. Their purpose was to protest the war, and particularly the continued disproportionate rate of Mexican American casualties in the conflict. Police overreaction and use of excessive force resulted in rioting on the part of some Chicano activists. Three deaths resulted, including that of noted *Los Angeles Times* correspondent and newsman Ruben Salazar. Many participants and observers were injured.

Roybal, who had developed a warm relationship with Salazar, was very moved and touched by his death. He said of Salazar, "Violence has deprived us of the man who best articulated the necessity for the peaceful pursuit of long overdue social reforms for the Spanish-speaking community in the United States. One thing we know, however, is that Ruben Salazar's burden passes on to each of us who remain behind, and we must continue to peacefully pursue his goals of social reform with steadfast determination."

During a press conference, Roybal expressed his sadness over the tragic events of the August 29 moratorium in East Los Angeles. He commented, "I find the growing reversion to violence in response to social and political problems a tragic indictment of all those concerned (whether they be members of the Mexican American community or law enforcement) and urge all parties involved to come to recognize that the behavior which leaves one person dead and more than twenty others wounded offers no answer to anyone's problems."

He called upon "the most responsible elements in the Mexican American minority, law enforcement, and the society at large" to join in addressing the crisis in East Los Angeles. Roybal also confirmed that Chairman Emanuel Celler of the House Judiciary Committee would appoint a special subcommittee to review the issue of police-community relations around the country, including Los Angeles.

A few days later, Roybal told the *Los Angeles Times*, "There has to be a change in attitude on both sides if we are not to repeat the senseless bloodshed. The police attitude toward minority groups is abusive, just as it was 40 years ago when I was a boy in Los Angeles."[83]

After the deaths, Roybal spoke to Assistant Attorney General Jerrie Leonard and requested a federal investigation of the entire matter. In addition, he wrote a personal letter directly to President Nixon, again requesting a prompt and full-scale independent federal investigation of all the facts surrounding the disturbances in East Los Angeles—with public disclosure of the findings to ensure an objective inquiry.

On October 27, Ed Roybal was again endorsed by the *Los Angeles Times* for re-election to the 30th Congressional District. The *Los Angeles Times* wrote that Edward R. Roybal "has long been an eloquent, effective spokesman for minorities, since he went to Congress from the Los Angeles City Council."[84]

During the latter part of the year, Ed Roybal during a press conference charged that the federal government operated a de facto occupational caste system against Spanish-Speaking Americans. Roybal cited data of the past two years in which less than 3 percent of the 2.6 million federal workers were Spanish speakers; one-third of 1 percent were in the top positions. The Spanish-speaking population in the country was at that time estimated to be 6 percent. He called the federal government "seriously inept in pushing to hire more Spanish-speaking Americans." He stated that "by its indifference it had perpetrated this occupational caste system and turned the ideal of equal employment into another American myth."

He cited the exclusion of other minority groups as well. He accused the Civil Service Commission, which under Executive Order 11478 was obligated to carry out an equal employment program for the federal government, of acting "immorally and illegally." He indicated that the employment rolls of the Department of Commerce, Labor, Health and Human Services (now HHS) and the Department of Housing and Urban Development (HUD) included less than 2 percent Spanish-surnamed individuals. Another violator was the Office of Employment Opportunity, which was mandated to serve the poor. While the Spanish-speaking made up some 24 to 27 percent of the poor, they made up only 3.6 percent of OEO's payroll.

Roybal warned that if "this pattern of exclusion is not reversed," litigation in the federal courts would be the only recourse.

Chapter 10

Voting Rights, Immigration Reform, and Koreagate
(1971–1979)

DURING THE 1970S, ED ROYBAL ENTERED HIS THIRD DECADE OF PUBLIC service. He was now a seasoned congressman and still only one of a handful of Latino congressmen. The decade witnessed several political scandals, including one that toppled a presidency. Another scandal, Koreagate, almost destroyed Roybal himself. It was a decade marred by contentious issues such as revolutions in Central America and the Middle East, a domestic economic recession, continued East-West nuclear rivalry, and a resurgence of the political Right. Roybal weathered the decade and continued his commitments to alleviate the plight of the poor, to push for the inclusion of minorities and women, to advocate for senior citizens and people without health care, and to address the challenges of an immigrant underclass.

Revising the Social Contract

Richard Nixon set out to decentralize most of the social programs begun under the New Deal, altering forever those parts of the Kennedy-Johnson legacy that Edward Roybal had championed. Nixon followed up with a major federal restructuring, called New Federalism, which moved social priorities down to the local level. This was done by giving states and municipalities the responsibility to make grant and contract awards to local groups using money from federal government–issued block grants. In this way, Nixon was able to distance the federal government from more social welfare responsibility.

As an example of how New Federalism worked, in 1973, Congress passed the Comprehensive Employment and Training Act (CETA). CETA block grants gave local politicians and the private sector more control over federal monies, effectively reducing services to the poor. Whereas previously the federal government's various job training programs targeted low-income working-class recipients, the effect that CETA ultimately had was to channel money toward White, upper-working-class individuals instead.[1] One of Nixon's advisors, Arthur Burns, who was later appointed chairman of the Federal Reserve Board, defined poverty as an "intellectual concept."[2]

Roybal's political philosophy on poverty differed considerably. In addition, his actions were guided by the idea that "you always do the right thing" regardless of what others may do. He was not interested in getting credit. If he proposed a bill and only part of it became law, or if a part was incorporated into somebody else's bill, he believed that was okay the main thing for him was to pass legislation that was beneficial to people.

Among many legislative actions that exemplified this philosophy, in May 1972, Roybal introduced House Resolution 946 in support of Title I under the Elementary and Secondary Education Act with additional funding in low-income areas. His resolution sought to add $2.5 billion to the $1.59 billion already committed. On September 14 of that year, he reported to Congress that he had cleared the way for a $4.7 million two-year extension of federal antipoverty programs (Job Corps, Head Start, legal aid, and other social welfare programs). He noted that with some 25.6 million Americans living in poverty, "we must redirect ourselves in helping our fellow Americans escape poverty and gain access to decent jobs, housing, and educational opportunities…This country must move away from a situation where the size of a person's pocket books determines not only legal representation one receives, but whether one receives any at all."[3]

In like manner, Congressman Roybal hailed House passage of the Roybal-McFall Accelerated Public Works Impact Act in September 1972.

The legislation authorized a $4.4 billion economic development bill, which passed on a 285–92 vote. The bill authorized $500 million a year through 1974 to areas where unemployment was above the national average. The funding was designed to assist communities seeking to build public facilities—libraries, hospitals, and water and sewer lines—with 80 percent matching grants.

The bill, introduced by Congressman Roybal and fellow Californian John J. McFall, was, as Roybal said during a debate, "an effective tool in attacking joblessness and relieving the unemployment-inflation crises which have gripped this country since President Nixon took office four years ago. First, it has helped local governments in building needed facilities, which drain the taxpayer's pocketbook. Second, it has created immediate employment in the building trades, which are among the hardest hit unemployment groups in the country."[4]

Roybal continued with his long-term commitment for passing legislation creating health care accessibility and was the subject of an editorial in the *Grass Roots Democrat*, where he was quoted as saying, "There has been a growing public concern over the high cost of health care. In a poll conducted in my district, an overwhelming majority endorsed the idea of national health insurance program to reduce our rising medical expenses. Along these lines I am supporting efforts to create a national health system that would provide quality health care for all Americans on a prepaid basis, regardless of a person's income, employment or age."[5]

In November 1972, Roybal traveled to Del Rio, Texas, for a ribbon-cutting ceremony at a new Democratic Party storefront. He expressed his optimism for the Democratic challenger, George McGovern, in the upcoming presidential election against President Richard Nixon. About the Nixon administration, Roybal stated, "This administration has double-crossed the poor and the oppressed of the U.S.A."[6] He singled out three Nixon vetoes on Education, Health, and Welfare bills. He charged that the Bilingual Education Bill of 1970 had lost $25 million. A deep political cleavage between the working class and the middle class was in the making.

Turmoil Abroad and at Home

During 1968 to 1974, Congressman Roybal served in the House Committee on Health, the Committee on Education, and the Committee on Foreign Affairs. In the latter committee, he traveled on many fact-finding missions. During this time, civil wars raged in Guatemala, Nicaragua, and El Salvador, with the United States government predictably supporting the entrenched oligarchies and militaries. About these fact-finding missions he recollected, "I was in El Salvador. I went there with a Catholic priest from Los Angeles and we got to meet both sides and talk to them about their particular position. We saw an opportunity for whatever we could do here to be beneficial first of all to us and beneficial also to them."[7]

Roybal's tenure in Congress was also replete with domestic travel. He would often crisscross from one coast to the other when issues of concern arose in his congressional district, the city of Los Angeles, or the state of California.

In February 1971, Roybal proposed a subcommittee under the House Judiciary Committee be set up to investigate the practices of civil rights law enforcement nationwide, including a review of Chicano-police relations. Hearings were undertaken in Los Angeles, in the aftermath of the Chicano Moratorium and three deaths. Roybal stated that the subcommittee would "get into the entire problem of police-community relationships, both with the county and the city police, and then make recommendations to both sides to better relations." He indicated that he expected the subcommittee to also investigate the deaths of two Mexican nationals by police the previous summer, *Los Angeles Times* journalist Ruben Salazar, and Mexican Americans deemed suicides in county jails. He added, "There has to be a change in attitude on both sides if we are not to repeat the senseless bloodshed of last summer and last month. The police attitude toward minority groups is abusive, just as it was 40 years ago when I was a boy in Los Angeles."[8] Roybal and other Chicano leaders expressed dismay at the few gains since the riot.

During October 1971, growing ethnic conflicts required Ed Roybal's attention. Some fifty-two of the sixty-seven Chicanos employed by the Economic and Youth Opportunities Agency of Greater Los Angeles (EYOA) walked out, citing vast irregularities within the antipoverty agency's personnel practices and policies. Some Chicano activists claimed that the agency was being steered to Black control. Ed Roybal urged all parties to resolve once and for all the crisis and said that the "solution cannot be left to EYOA discretion; for it involves serious federal and statutory issues and charges of racial inequality in EYOA staffing and funding practices." He noted that Mexican Americans held only four out of EYOA's twenty-two policy-making positions. Roybal urged immediate resolution so that further conflict between these groups could be prevented.[9]

Ed Roybal was not above addressing the concerns of the most marginalized and forgotten segments of society. The concerns of Chicano inmates in prison institutions was not something many congressmen would become involved with. However, Roybal was aware the long history of discrimination against Mexicans and Latinos in all walks and strata of life. In April 1972, Roybal called for a state probe of the penal system in California concerning Chicano prisoners, in response to complaints from inmates and the Mexican community at large. He wanted a probe at San Quentin, a prison where Chicanos were in the majority. Many of the complaints forwarded to him originated from San Quentin. The congressman focused his attention on inmate treatment, security control, segregation, isolation, and parole and revocation procedures and practices, especially when issues of race discrimination arose.[10] Roybal sought more financial support for inmate rehabilitation, training, and bilingual programs. During August, Congressman Roybal visited San Quentin to meet with Chicano inmate representatives and in support of the EMPLEO school project, a federal educational program for Chicano inmates. He expressed support in a taped interview for radio station KSQ.[11]

On November 27, 1972, Congressman Roybal announced his opposition to California Proposition 17, which sought to return the death penalty to the state. To make his point, he brought a dummy miniature gas chamber as a prop to the Los Angeles Press Club, where he made the announcement.

The Watergate Scandal

At one moment, Nixon was basking in a historic election victory and in the next, his presidency was unraveling. Nixon's not entirely submerged dark side became increasingly visible. Nixon became paranoid, secretive, and increasingly distrustful of the media and of the federal government's checks and balances. Upon publication of the Pentagon Papers by the *New York Times* on June 13, 1971, a political firestorm blew up. The Pentagon Papers consisted of a 7,000-page overview of U.S. involvement in Vietnam from the end of World War II to 1968, commissioned by Defense Secretary Robert McNamara while he served under Presidents Kennedy and Johnson. Daniel Ellsberg, a RAND Corporation employee and researcher, leaked the top-secret documents to the press. In response, Nixon established an anti-leak unit called the Plumbers, which conducted a series of covert activities. One of them was to burglarize Daniel Ellsberg's psychiatrist's office for material about Ellsberg.

In late May 1972, during the re-election campaign, the Plumbers broke into Democratic Party headquarters at the Watergate Hotel, in Washington, D.C. They did so a second time on June 17, 1972. On the second occasion, the five burglars were caught. Increasingly paranoid, Nixon had been taping his private conversations. Congressional investigators insisted that Nixon turn over the tapes. This evidence was, of course, the "smoking gun" linking Nixon to the break-ins. Soon thereafter, on October 10, 1973, Vice President Spiro Agnew pleaded no contest to criminal charges of tax evasion (one of forty indictable counts stemming from allegations of accepting kickbacks from contractors, criminal conspiracy, tax fraud, and bribe taking while he was Maryland's governor). Nixon was now facing impeachment charges of his own stemming from the Watergate investigation.

Gradually, Congress began to hold the Nixon administration more accountable for unethical behavior. For example, during mid-June 1974, Congressman Roybal asked the General Accounting Office (GAO) for a report on spending for White House domestic intelligence, specifically, an audit of the White House Plumbers unit and the Intelligence Evaluation Committee for the last four fiscal years. Roybal stated that he was asking for the GAO study because the White House and Office of Management and Budget had repeatedly ignored his earlier requests. Roybal said that the withholding of this information bordered on "arrogance and contempt" toward the appropriations process and the public's right to know how their money is being spent. "There is little doubt that the White House obsession with domestic surveillance resulted in serious threats to due process and our basic right to privacy," Roybal commented.[12]

Nixon and Roybal Re-elected

Despite unrest on American college campuses, antiwar protests, and scattered reporting on Watergate, most people voted for Nixon in his 1972 re-election. Nixon benefited from the fact that the Democrats had nominated a left-of-center candidate, George McGovern of South Dakota. McGovern was considered an ineffective speaker and campaigner and was portrayed by Republicans as an appeaser. His platform included immediate and unconditional withdrawal from Vietnam and an increase in welfare spending. Nixon also benefited from the fact that inflation was down 2.7 percent in the summer of 1972; also, real incomes were rising by 4 percent annually and since 1969, federal taxes had been cut some 20 percent for the average family.

On Election Day, Nixon garnered 60.7 percent of the popular vote to McGovern's 38 percent (one of the lowest numbers ever obtained by a major-party candidate). Nixon beat McGovern in the Electoral College with 520 electoral votes to McGovern's 17 (his only electoral victories came in Massachusetts and Washington, D.C.). Nixon got 31 percent of the Mexican American vote nationally. Despite the low showing in the presidential race, Democrats gained control of both chambers of Congress.

Nixon was unhappy with the lower-than-expected Mexican American vote. In 1972, he had appointed several Mexican Americans to high federal positions. Among the appointees was Romana Bañuelos,[13] a Los Angeles food manufacturer, who served as U.S. Treasurer from 1971 to 1974. Regarding Nixon's boast that he had appointed forty-three Mexican Americans to key government positions,[14] Roybal stated, "Forty-three appointments out of almost 15 million [Spanish-speaking] people is nothing to brag about."[15] He said that Mexican Americans were not making gains in federal employment; only 2.9 percent of government employees were Spanish surnamed when Nixon had first taken office, and the figure remained at 2.9 percent. Mexican Americans were being hired to about 2,300 new civil service jobs a year when Nixon took office; thereafter the number went down to 1,307 per year.

Nixon appointed Ann Armstrong as his White House aide on domestic Latino affairs. Despite the ethnic incongruity, Nixon stated that she was qualified because, "Mrs. Armstrong and her husband own a large ranch at Armstrong, Texas, an area populated extensively by Mexican Americans."[16] The same logic would have been unacceptable in reference to any other minority community, such as African Americans or Asian Americans.

While Nixon made a concerted effort to win the Latino vote from the Democrats, he displayed a singular mindset not to respect the democratic process in Latin America. Both Nixon and Secretary of State Henry Kissinger were complicit in supporting the military overthrow on September 11, 1973 of the democratically elected socialist president of Chile, Salvador Allende. Allende, elected overwhelmingly in 1970, designed a progressive nationalist program for his country. Nixon commented angrily, "I'm not going to permit a Communist leader in Chile, just because [of] the stupidity of the Chilean electorate."[17]

In the November 1972 election, Congressman Ed Roybal beat two challengers to his 30th Congressional District seat: Republican State Assemblyman Bill Brophy and Peace and Freedom candidate Lewis McCammon. Neither candidate made much of a dent in Roybal's political base. The Vietnam War and the cloud of scandal brewing over President Nixon's head hobbled the Republican challenger. The second challenger was unknown and ineffective. Roybal was comfortably re-elected with his traditional allies of labor, minorities, and working-class voters.

Coalescing Latino Interests

Throughout the Nixon, Ford, and Carter administrations, Congressman Roybal remained committed to the concerns of Mexican Americans and Latinos, the poor, the physically challenged, and the elderly. In 1971, one year before Nixon's reelection, he gave up his previous committee assignments for a seat in the powerful Appropriations Committee, where he served until he retired. During this time also, Congressman Roybal worked on behalf of Vietnam veterans and their health care needs, especially those of the disabled and handicapped. There was growing evidence that the Veterans Administration provided less than adequate assistance to Mexican Americans and African Americans.

Roybal indicated his own increasing "disgust" with the Democratic Party, which Mexicans had historically supported, because it often exerted its control of the legislature not by making good legislation but rather by gerrymandering district lines, reapportioning congressional and California Assembly seats in 1950 and 1960. Reapportionment never seemed to benefit Mexican Americans, however. Roybal stated that there was a resignation among some community members that "regardless which party is doing about gerrymandering the Spanish-speaking community is always second best."[18]

During September 1971, Congressman Roybal called for a conference of Spanish-speaking Americans in Washington, D.C. He was supported by U.S. Representatives Herman Badillo (D-NY) and Manuel Luján (R-NM),[19] and Senator Joseph Montoya (D-NM). They invited some 500 Latino national and regional leaders. Roybal outlined the reason for the gathering this way: "The purpose of the conference is to develop national strategies which directly represent the needs and priorities of the Spanish-speaking; and to explore the formation of a continuing nationwide coalition of Spanish-speaking groups... What we are beginning today can only intensify the quest of Spanish-speaking Americans for national solidarity and political effectiveness."[20]

This was important because it was the beginning of a joining together of Hispanic organizations (Cuban, Puerto Rican, Mexican American, Chicano, etc.) to form a broader Latino coalition. Others moving in this direction were the Cabinet Committee, the Barbazon Terrace Agreement, the Democratic Latino Officeholders group, the Congressional Caucus—and the idea here was to bring them all together. Such a convergence of Latino communities working together for common goals had never happened before. The fast-growing communities of Mexican Americans, Puerto Ricans, Cubans, and the emerging Central American communities in the United States were beginning to claim a national presence.

A major concern of elected Latino leaders was the accurate count of their communities by government agencies. Roybal and others challenged the 1970 U.S. Census, charging that it inaccurately counted Spanish-surname residents. In December 1971, he sought a recount of the Spanish-speaking population after receiving numerous constituent complaints. He said the Census Bureau was deliberately "naive" to rely only on mailed-in responses from a sample size representing about 5 percent of Spanish-surnamed residents. The form contained over 150 questions in English. The Census Bureau ignored the fact that more than half of the people receiving the form spoke Spanish and considered Spanish their mother tongue. "The underlying problem in the Bureau is its total lack of training and expertise in reaching [the] ghetto and barrio poor," Roybal said. "This is discriminatory and certainly involves constitutional issues of due process, equal protection of the laws and denial of federal benefits."[21]

Roybal proposed that the Census Bureau hire more minority people and have closer contact with the communities. The census had become increasingly important as a result of the New Federalism policy, whereby governmental programs and the distribution of federal funds relied on census population figures.

Over time, Roybal and other Latino elected leaders developed a Latino agenda (e.g., bilingual education, the Voting Rights Act of 1975, founding the Hispanic Congressional Caucus, MAPA, NALEO) and brought together a national Latino constituency. With the advent of the Chicano Movement, Roybal incorporated the concerns and issues of the new Chicano and Latino generation (e.g., education reform, ending the Vietnam War). However, Roybal always worked for what was good for the most people. Thus, his push for legislation for health care, senior citizens, funding AIDS and the Centers for Disease Control, and civil rights reflected these concerns.

When I asked Roybal what, on a personal level, were some of the most important things he did during the years of 1968 to 1970, he said, "Number one was the passage of the Bilingual Education Act and the agreement by the [Congressional Hispanic Caucus] to include one Republican member that we had left out (Manuel Luján), and that was significant because of the fact that we were trying to bring about an atmosphere of including the various ethnic groups that in fact had the same need and suffered the same fate." During the same interview, I asked him if he worked closely with the Congressional Black Caucus, and he commented, "Yes, I did and voted for their budget every time because their budget was based on a more reasonable assumption, but it never went through."[22]

During this period, Roybal played a key role in the passing of legislation that outlawed discrimination based on age. He also worked with his characteristic dedication to provide numerous government benefits and opportunities for the physically handicapped.

During 1972, Congressman Roybal was appointed chairman of the Housing and Consumer Affairs Subcommittee of the Select Committee on the Aging, the House committee solely devoted to issues affecting senior citizens. The Consumer Affairs Subcommittee was intended to investigate aspects of legislation relating to consumer and housing needs and to work closely with the Banking Currency and Housing Committee to seek out solutions to problems to protect living standards for the elderly.[23]

During 1973, Ed Roybal once again campaigned for re-election, this time to the 25th Congressional District. He continued to be a member of the Committee on Appropriations and to serve on the Foreign Operations Subcommittee and the Treasury, Post Office, and General Government Subcommittee. His platform included several key issues. He indicated he had voted for increases in non-service pensions for veterans and their widows; supported the territorial integrity of all in the Middle East; sought a more efficient Medicare and Medicaid; voted for the bill to extend federal aid to colleges and students, creating the National Institute of Education; voted for the continued authorization of the Cabinet Committee on Opportunities for Spanish-speaking People; and voted for a 10 percent increase in old-age survivors and disability insurance coverage under Social Security.

During the year, he also urged the establishment of a national office for migrant and seasonal farm workers within the Department of Health, Education, and Welfare, which would affect some 4 million farm workers. The federal office would be responsible for the development of a national farm worker policy, which would include setting programs priorities and goals and allocating funds to meet the needs of agricultural workers.

Roybal stated that low wages forced parents to put young children to work in the fields, and that one-fourth of farm workers were under sixteen years of age. He cited studies indicating that 1.6 million farm workers existed solely on their farm wages, earning an average annual income of $1,095, among the lowest in the nation.

During the 93rd U.S. Congress (January 3, 1973 to January 3, 1975), Ed Roybal introduced legislation to provide bilingual proceedings in the court system. He presented extensive evidence on longstanding discriminatory practices, such as denial of equal protection under the law in the administration of justice toward Mexican Americans and pervasive police misconduct.

Increasingly, during the 1970s, Ed Roybal and other Latino elected leaders worked in conjunction with Mexican and Latino organizations to pass the Latino legislative agenda. One of the more important was the Mexican American Legal Defense Fund (MALDEF). It was founded in 1968 in Texas as a nonprofit civil rights organization to protect the rights of Mexican Americans and Latinos.

Roybal worked closely with MALDEF on several pieces of legislation. Antonia Hernandez, who became MALDEF's president and general counsel between 1985 and 2003, recalled arriving in Washington, D.C., in 1978 to work for the Senate Judiciary Committee, where her responsibility was immigration and refugee policy in addition to Latino, civil rights, and related issues. That's when, she said, she began working closely with Roybal. At first the focus was on immigration. Mainly, she singled him out because he was one of the very few Latino members of Congress, and there were none serving in the Senate. After she left the Senate committee job, she headed MALDEF's Washington, D.C., office. Hernandez remembered working closely with Roybal on the Voting Rights Act of 1975 and the Civil Rights Act of 1982.[24]

Antonia Hernandez reflected that Roybal "always carried himself with a great deal of dignity. He has this unique quality that few leaders have—to feel and connect with the common folk. When you see him, you see it in his comfort level. He listens, he connects, he understands. He's the type of person that feels, that's comfortable representing his district."

Roybal was known for his persistence with a kind of confidence that his participation could make a difference, and that was how he applied himself to politics. He persevered when other might have given up. Whatever the issues, he did not limit himself, and, said Hernandez, "that's the other attribute, that Mr. Roybal has a real deep sense of connection with humanity and I think that's what makes him unique."[25]

Ford as Caretaker President

On August 9, 1974, with the House of Representatives readying to vote on the articles of impeachment, to be followed by a trial before the Senate, Nixon resigned. Gerald R. Ford[26] assumed the presidency. Ford had served as House minority leader and was a representative from Michigan before his appointment as vice president when Agnew resigned on October 10, 1973. Ford's other noteworthy service was as a member of the controversial Warren Commission investigating President Kennedy's assassination.

President Ford pardoned Nixon immediately for "all crimes he might have committed or may have committed." The pardon effectively ended the possibility that Nixon would undergo criminal prosecution. When I asked Congressman Roybal whether Nixon would have been able to survive in his presidency if he had admitted his wrongdoing or asked for forgiveness from the United States public, Roybal commented, "Well, perhaps he should have done that, but he didn't. There was failure in the final results. But Nixon could have been successful in keeping his presidency if he had apologized and come clean with the American people."[27] The popular assumption was that Nixon could not have survived. It seems that Roybal thought otherwise.

In 1974, Congressman Roybal ran unopposed and was re-elected to serve in the U.S. House of Representatives for a sixth term. It was a dangerous time in the world. There was a worldwide oil crisis and a recession. Iran's revolutionary government had taken U.S. hostages. Revolutions were taking place in El Salvador, Nicaragua, and Guatemala, and Russian troops were moving into Afghanistan.

President Ford did his earnest best to create his own political persona while still under Nixon's shadow. Historian Paul Johnson said that Ford served in the U.S. House of Representatives "without much notice or achievement but growing approbation from his colleagues, in twelve succeeding Congresses, emerging as minority leader by virtue of seniority and lack of enemies."[28] President Johnson is said to have joked disparagingly of Ford, "The trouble with Jerry Ford is that he used to play football without a helmet."[29] Ford's legendary lack of physical balance, the butt of many jokes, was due to a bad ear, which apparently affected his equilibrium. In turn, Roybal recollected about Gerald Ford, "First of all, he was a good Republican leader. He actually tried to carry out the orders of [President Nixon]…I knew him. I liked him as an individual."[30]

Ford was seen by many as a caretaker president, despite his attempts to be more. He also had the misfortune to occupy the presidency as the Congress made a concerted effort to limit the powers of that office. Nixon's excesses and abuses of power were still fresh in everyone's mind. Congress asserted itself even before Nixon's resignation through passage of the War Powers Act, which passed over the president's veto on November 7, 1973.[31] The trend to curb the imperial nature of the presidency continued into the late 1970s, by which time there were some seventy congressional amendments that curbed the president's power in the conduct of foreign policy.[32]

Under President Ford, the United States' military presence in Vietnam finally ended. Military assistance to South Vietnam declined significantly throughout 1973, and almost immediately the South Vietnam government unraveled. On April 21, 1975, the South Vietnam government abdicated.

Aiming for some foreign policy progress before the 1976 election, Ford jump-started the Strategic Arms Limitation Talks (SALT), which Nixon had begun in 1972. SALT II resulted in the Helsinki Accords, by which the Soviet Union renounced the right to use force in its sphere of influence, Eastern Europe.

Ford selected Kansas Senator Robert Dole, a World War II hero, as his vice presidential running mate in 1976. Neither Ford nor Dole were blessed with charismatic personalities, and they failed to fire up voters at a time when the public was ready for change, following eight years of Republican administration, scandals, corruption, and polarization.

The Voting Rights Act of 1975

The National Voting Rights Act of 1965 outlawed the discriminatory practices that had caused African Americans to be disenfranchised. The act permitted the federal government to observe elections, banned literacy and other tests, and required the states to get federal approval before enacting new voting laws. A formula in the law made it apply to states where a large Black population experienced a small voter turnout in proportion to their numbers (primarily the Southern states). It had been signed by President Lyndon B. Johnson, who had earlier signed into law the Civil Rights Act of 1964. During March 1975, the act was up before Congress for renewal. For Roybal, this presented an opportunity to expand its coverage to Hispanic Americans and Native Americans.

Roybal stated that more than 3 million Mexican Americans in California experienced serious impediments to voter registration and voting participation. Many local authorities held at-large school board elections[33] that made it virtually impossible for Mexican Americans to be elected. Redistricting, registration and voting irregularities, and changes in polling places without notifying people, as well as the lack of bilingual registrars and election officials, were also to be counted among the discriminatory practices. In the city of Los Angeles alone, with a Spanish-speaking population larger than the population of some states, there was not one city councilman of Spanish descent.[34]

Roybal stated that Mexican Americans were approximately 16 percent of California's total population and 12 percent of its voting population, but held only 0.7 percent of the state's elected offices. He included in his proposed revisions to the Voting Rights Act any "political subdivision" where more than 5 percent of the voting-age population was of Spanish origin and where the total voter turnout was below the 1972 national average.

The Voting Rights Act of 1975 was passed by the U.S. Congress and signed by President Ford. In Section 203 it incorporated a requirement for language assistance to speakers of Native American and Alaska native languages, Spanish, and Asian languages. Language assistance is mandated when one or more of the language groups has limited English proficiency and makes up at least 5 percent of the voting-age population or when one of the groups has more than 10,000 voting-age individuals in a county. Limited proficiency is defined in the act as an illiteracy rate higher than the national illiteracy rate.

In the aftermath of the Mexican-American War and the Treaty of Guadalupe Hidalgo in 1848, all Mexicans living in the Southwest became U.S. citizens. However, English language and literacy tests, poll taxes, and coercion prevented most Mexican Americans from exercising the right to vote. The Voting Rights Act of 1975 went a long way toward rectifying their exclusion.

The Voting Rights Act of 1975 was one of Roybal's proudest legislative achievements. However, not everyone supported the inclusion of language minorities in the renewal of the Voting Rights Act. This included conservatives but also some members of the civil rights coalition, who thought it would dilute the original intent of the Voting Rights Act of 1965.

During 1976, Ed Roybal readied himself to run for his seventh term in Congress. At that time, the district had 464,972 people, of whom approximately 95,000 were voters. Roybal described his district as "a district of great wealth and of serious economic and social problems." In a letter to constituents announcing his re-election bid he stated, "I realize that my efforts in Congress make only a small contribution to the total effort. But I do enjoy the challenge and want to keep trying to help continue the nation on a steady course."

A law authored by Roybal to improve census and data-gathering activities for Latinos was signed into law by President Ford on June 16, 1976. Roybal indicated that the action was necessary in "light of substantial failures by the government to correctly represent this second largest minority group." He commented that the purpose of the law was to "ensure that the federal government provides a fair and current reporting of the social, health and economic conditions affecting the more than 12 million Spanish-origin population of this country."[35]

In February 1979, the U.S. Census Bureau revealed that the Hispanic population in the United States made up approximately 12 million. Of these, Mexican Americans numbered 7.2 million; Puerto Ricans, 1.8 million; Cubans, 700,000; and Central and South Americans, 900,000. The Congressional Hispanic Caucus held its annual fundraising dinner at the Washington Hilton Hotel in Washington, D.C., with First Lady Rosalynn Carter as a special guest. The theme was progress and unity. Ed Roybal in the keynote speech commented, "There was a time when Hispanics of this country were referred to as the silent minority…the invisible minority. But you were never invisible, you were not silent. It is only those who could not see, those who could not hear. For if they had, they would have seen, as we see today, our rich and vital community."[36]

The Carter Years

On Election Day, November 2, 1976, Jimmy Carter,[37] the governor of Georgia and a Washington outsider, was elected president with 40.8 million votes to Ford's 39.1 million. Carter won 297 electoral votes to Ford's 241. The Democrats remained in control of Congress. Carter had unseated a weak incumbent in a somewhat-close election, but an array of unexpected challenges lay ahead for the new president. Carter had won the Democratic nomination over Jerry Brown, supported the United Farm Workers Union in California, and won the presidency (possibly for the first time since John Kennedy) because of the Latino vote.

President Carter introduced human rights as a major foreign affairs policy variable and as a consideration in how the Cold War would be conducted under his administration. His even-handedness and fairness in diplomacy did much to win the confidence of the peoples of the Third World. He signed the Panama Canal Treaties, which returned the canal and Canal Zone to Panamanian sovereignty. In Nicaragua, he recognized the Sandinista government that came to power in July 1979 after overthrowing the U.S.-supported Anastasio Somoza dictatorship that had ruled for forty years. Upon the governments of nearby El Salvador and Guatemala, Carter imposed standards for human rights as conditions of U.S. support. In the Middle East, Carter signed the Camp David Accords in 1978 and a peace treaty between Israel and Egypt in 1979. Diplomatic relations with the People's Republic of China were established, and the SALT II treaty was signed with the Soviet Union.

Carter's domestic achievements included deregulation of the energy, transportation, finance, and communications industries. Congress passed a comprehensive energy program under the auspices of the new Department of Energy. Carter's administration shepherded major environmental protection legislation through Congress, such as the Alaska Lands Act. The Department of Education initiated new programs.

In 1976, Roybal continued to bring federal grants for community programs, especially through the Housing and Community Development program, which provided annual support for local improvement programs. It funded redevelopment, recreation centers, and neighborhood programs. In July of that year, Ed Roybal presented a sampling of his public papers to Morris Polon, Cal State Los Angeles librarian, and John A. Greenlee, university president. Roybal announced he was presenting the CSULA Archives with all his public papers and memorabilia. Some 76 boxes of official materials were being catalogued by the library staff.

During early 1977, Ed Roybal and the Congressional Hispanic Caucus worked hard to recommend Latinos for Carter to appoint to his administration. The caucus submitted more than 600 qualified Latino nominees. In early March, Roybal and other caucus leaders met with President Carter to further make their case for Latino appointments. Soon thereafter, Carter made some significant appointments to his administration. They included Commissioner of the Immigration and Naturalization Service Leonel Castillo, Assistant Secretary of Commerce Favian Chavez, Director of the Community Services Organization Graciela Olivarez, Assistant Secretary of Housing and Urban Development William Medina; and Assistant Administrator of the Bureau of Latin American Affairs Abelardo Valdez. He also appointed Dr. Julian Nava as ambassador to Mexico. All together, President Carter named eleven Latinos to top positions in his administration.

Ed Roybal took the opportunity when the appointments were announced to give an overview of the economic status of Latinos in the nation, declaring, "While total unemployment for 1976 was 7.7 percent, Hispanic unemployment was 11.2 percent. In the short span of two years, Hispanic unemployment is up to 35 percent. Last year the jobless rate for Latino teenagers, ages 16 to 19, was even worse at 23 percent."[38]

Carter's chances for a second term were doomed with the seizure of U.S. embassy in Teheran, Iran, near the end of his first term. Embassy staff were held hostage for fourteen months. The revolution in Iran, which precipitated the hostage taking, was linked to a United States–initiated coup in the early 1950s and imposition of the Shah Mohammed Reza Palavi. Iran's oil crisis led to an energy crisis in the United States, which exacerbated inflation and the recession. Carter's standing in the polls dropped dramatically and made him appear weak before the election challenge from the resurgent right wing of the Republican Party led by Ronald Reagan. The fifty-two U.S. hostages were finally released from the Iranian Embassy, on the same day Carter left office and Ronald Reagan was sworn in. The coincidence has raised questions about possible backdoor deals between Ronald Reagan–George Bush and the Iranian government.

Founding the National Association of Latino Elected Officials (NALEO)

By 1975, with Congress having passed the revised Voting Rights Act, Roybal could see that the number of Mexican American elected officials from the Southwest would increase dramatically. The issue for him was not so much the number now but how to maintain some discipline among so many levels of government. How long would it take a school board member to relate to the state representative or to a congressional representative staff person? How would novice officials know how to negotiate a large decentralized organizational structure to become effective advocates for the community concerns that they shared with other Hispanic officeholders? How would they know where the pivotal decisions were made? How would they know how to read a complex budget? And how would Hispanic priorities stay topmost in their minds as they looked after their local interests?

Ed Roybal had an idea of how to create more effective unity within Latino elected officials and also develop an infrastructure that would help mobilize community participation. The idea that Roybal birthed would eventually become the National Association of Latino Elected Officials (NALEO), in 1976. The organization was co-founded by Harry Pachon, Robert Garcia, and several others who shared a vision of a national network for the Latino community. Ed Roybal served as president of NALEO from 1976 to 1991, after which the NALEO board of directors designated him president emeritus. He additionally served as the chairperson of the NALEO Educational Fund (1981–1994).

He envisioned NALEO as a nationwide association that was also a network for Latino elected officials who mutually pursued civil rights, voter education and registration, educational and social welfare goals, economic betterment, and issues of mutual interest. "That organization," said Roybal, "was founded by others and myself... [as] an effort to bring about representation as well as provide representation to the government process."[39]

The nonpartisan organization educates newly elected officials through seminars on how the system works in their respective areas—school boards, city councils, mayors, etc. It also focuses on issues by monitoring and analyzing institutional policies and often proposes original legislation. It supports itself through dues and sponsorship fees. Membership is available for all elected and appointed government officials and associate members willing to work to achieve the organization's goals. The organization has been effective in Latino voter education and registration.[40]

Antonia Hernandez said that NALEO was particularly effective in mobilizing hundreds of thousands of people to become citizens. The direct consequence of this process was the growing voter turnout of Latino communities.[41] By the 1990s, NALEO was instrumental in Hispanic social development and political evolution. Hernandez called this nonpartisan organization "neutral." "It is important," she said, "because it is not partisan but serves a public interest."[42]

Immigration Reform

Unlike any other ethnic community in the United States, Mexican Americans comprise both new arrivals (border crossers) and natives to the United States Southwest (those who stayed in place while the border crossed them). To address this reality, several efforts were made during the Carter administration to reform immigration law and immigration policy. Congressman Roybal was in the forefront of the major bills that were proposed, including one of his own. Each bill had a different solution to immigration, but it was widely agreed that immigration was emerging as a nagging issue to an increasingly intemperate nation.

Urgency for immigration reform in the late 1970s and early 1980s was fueled by the increasing number of Mexican workers immigrating to the United States, as well as thousands of Salvadorans, Guatemalans, and Hondurans fleeing civil war, guerillas, death squads, and right wing, repressive regimes (many of which were supported by the United States). Because of the disruptions, they were unable to make a living. The increasing numbers of these poor, mestizo, and indigenous populations in some parts of the United States encouraged xenophobia and nativism. William Colby, a former CIA director, commented in 1978 that Mexican migration created a greater threat than the Soviet Union. Dallas Mayor Pro Tem Jim Hart warned voters that these aliens had "no moral values" and were destroying the neighborhoods. He said that women could be "robbed, raped or killed."[43] During the fall of 1988, California passed the "English Is the Official Language" proposition that other states began to emulate.

The road to immigration reform was a contentious one. The Rodino Bill (H.R. 8713) proposed to fine and jail employers who knowingly hired "illegal aliens." The bill sought to eliminate the incentive to hire undocumented workers. Roybal and other critics argued it would have a number of serious unintended consequences. For instance, it would increase discrimination against American citizens who merely looked like Mexican foreign nationals. It would also impact the union movement. Roybal noted there were many undocumented workers of Western European origin in the United States but that the Rodino bill would not affect their ability to move easily into "mainstream America."[44]

Congressman Peter W. Rodino Jr. (D-NJ), chairman of the House Judiciary Committee, said his bill would provide job opportunities and job security to American workers and that they "will no longer have to compete for jobs with a docile and exploitable undocumented workforce."[45] Roybal countered that the Hispanic Congressional Caucus was prepared to offer seventy-five amendments to the Rodino bill and would request a roll-call vote on each one.[46] Roybal indicated that U.S. workers would not take the low-paying jobs that undocumented workers occupied. "This is definitely not a jobs bill," he said.

During early April 1983, Roybal introduced his own immigration bill, H.R. 4909. "The legislation I have introduced," he said, "recognizes the U.S. commitment to family reunification." The legislation also called for increasing funds for stepped-up border-control measures and for improved efficiency in processing applications for legal entry.[47] The bill would impose stiff penalties on employers who exploited undocumented workers by violating existing minimum wage and health and safety laws. Roybal criticized Representative Romano Mazzoli's (D-KY) proposed immigration bill for failing to advocate strict labor law enforcement.

Roybal's bill simplified the legalization process for undocumented workers who had resided in the United States for several years. Under the Mazzoli bill, and the companion bill sponsored by Senator Alan Simpson (R-WY), the status of long-term residents would be adjusted by a complicated two-tier process that many critics said would consequently create a large sub-class of undocumented workers who would stay in the country but who were unprotected by the law. The *Miami Herald* praised Congressman Roybal's bill, saying, "The proposal deserves serious consideration. INS needs more resources to patrol the Southwest border where more than 80 percent of the illegal aliens enter the country. Furthermore, stricter enforcement of existing labor, health, and safety laws will make it harder for employers to continue to hire illegal immigrants with impunity."[48]

The U.S. Senate passed the Simpson bill in early May 1983, 78–18. Both California senators, Democrat Alan Cranston and Republican Pete Wilson, voted against the bill. Cranston called the bill "a major step toward a police state" in setting up a national worker identification system that would "require every person in the U.S. to have some form of authorization by his or her government in order to work."[49] Dolores Huerta, vice president of the United Farm Workers Union, stated that the union was "solidly behind" the Roybal proposal and termed the Simpson-Mazzoli bill "destructive and fraudulent."[50] The *San Diego County Union* wrote, "By moving forward with Simpson-Mazzoli, the House leadership ignores a major alternative for immigration reform—Rep. Edward R. Roybal's bill…For those who impugn Hispanic motives in offering an alternative immigration bill, let us set the record straight. Hispanics view immigration reform as both important and necessary, but see Simpson-Mazzoli as a continuation [of the status quo] under the guise of immigration reform. Our views have been brutally shaped by the mass deportations which our communities experienced during the 30s, the excesses of 'Operation Wetback' during the 50s, and the now legendary factory raids we have witnessed in recent years." Democrat presidential candidate Gary Hart praised Roybal's bill. Vice President Walter Mondale, the presiding officer in the U.S. Senate, stated he needed more time to study it. However, House leadership did not even give Roybal's bill public hearings.

During May 1985, Roybal introduced a modified immigration bill. Roybal stated, "Let there be no doubt that Hispanic Americans want immigration reform. However, let there also be no doubt that any bill that creates discrimination, barriers to employment or other forms of suppression will meet strong opposition."[51] Roybal's bill now included a one-tier legalization system with an eligibility date of January 1, 1982, increased INS and Border Patrol personnel, a protection system for those seeking legalization, continuation of provisions for family unification, and prohibition of the establishment of a national identification card. A complementary bill, sponsored by Senator Edward Kennedy (D-MA) in the Senate, would grant amnesty to undocumented workers already within the United States.

The Rodino-Simpson bill became law during the fall of 1986. Called the Immigration Reform and Control Act, it had three goals: to reduce jobs available to undocumented workers by imposing sanctions on their employers, to reduce undocumented immigration, and to provide an amnesty program. It also included a section to end employer abuses of workers' rights. The new law included features of the previous bills (such as employer sanctions, a guest worker program, amnesty for undocumented workers who had arrived before January 1982, and increased funding for the INS). It also gave farmers special privileges by granting legal status to anyone who had worked in agriculture for at least ninety days in the previous year.

Koreagate: Roybal Fights for His Political Life

Ed Roybal faced the hardest moment of his political life during the Koreagate scandal. The events in question occurred during 1976 and were investigated in 1978. They involved several South Korean political figures trying to influence Democratic members of the U.S. Congress. It appears that the goal of the alleged conspirators was to reverse President Nixon's decision to remove U.S. troops from South Korea. The South Korean Central Intelligence Agency (KCIA) allegedly sent bribes and favors through a South Korean businessman, Tongsun Park, in order to gain influence for the South Korean objectives. It is alleged that some 115 members of the U.S. Congress could have been involved. Among those South Korean figures suspected to have been involved were Sun Myung Moon, founder of the Unification Church; South Korean Prime Minister Chung Il Kwon; and Kim Hyung Wook, former KCIA director.

The two main figures in the Koreagate scandal were Tongsun Park, who was the key individual on the South Korean side, and Richard Hanna, who operated objectives within the United States. In accordance with their agreement, the two men would share in the commissions of the United Sates sales of rice to South Korea and would utilize that money to influence members of Congress to the benefit of the South Korean government. Hanna was also responsible for developing an effective lobbying strategy for Park and Kwon similar to his prior successful lobbying of Taiwanese and Israeli interests in the U.S. Congress. Park is said to have been responsible for providing ample funds to curry the favor of congressmen with monetary incentives of $100,000 to $200,000 for each individual who helped them pursue their objectives.

The conspirators' objectives formed a web of political, economic, and social factors. Some South Korean political leaders, including President Chung-hee Park and Tongsun Park, were upset with President Nixon's decision to withdraw United States troops from South Korea. They intended to preserve a strong United States presence in their nation. A second objective was that President Park was concerned about a promised United States economic package of assistance to modernize the South Korean military and wanted to make sure it would be forthcoming. A third objective appears to have been to counter increasing criticism of President Park's human rights violations and other policies.

The U.S. Department of State detected the illegality of Park's activities as early as 1970 and notified the South Korean embassy in Washington concerning them. There were efforts to return Tongsun Park to South Korea and/or to have him register as a lobbyist, both which proved unsuccessful. U.S. Ambassador to South Korea Philip Habib and U.S. Attorney General William Saxbe warned embassy personnel to cut their ties with Park; they warned visiting congressmen to avoid Park as well.

The Koreagate scandal became public in 1978. Consequently, relations between the United States and South Korea became shaky and difficult. South Korea thought that Koreagate was exaggerated by the United

States media. The United States expected its counterparts to cooperate with the investigation. Many political experts on both sides suspected that Koreagate was part of President Gerald Ford's election strategy. They proposed that Ford was actively attempting to neutralize the Democratic Party's political exploitation of the Watergate scandal and Ford's pardon of Nixon. This perspective further proposed that by linking Democratic congressmen to Koreagate, Ford would weaken the Democratic Party in the next congressional and presidential elections.

In 1976, the Justice Department appointed Leon Jaworski as special prosecutor. (Jaworski had been the special prosecutor in the Watergate scandal as well.) After much stonewalling by the South Korean government, Tongsun Park finally came to testify before the U.S. House of Representatives in a hearing regarding the scandal. During Park's testimony, he admitted handing out cash payments to some thirty members of Congress. Ultimately, only ten members were implicated seriously with the scandal. Most of these members resigned, and for three, the statute of limitations expired. During July 1978, the Koreagate investigating committee began to finalize its findings. After thirty-three months of investigating the scandal the House Ethic committee voted to begin disciplinary action against four Democrats on charges that they knowingly allowed Tongsun Park to buy their votes. Specifically, Edward R. Roybal and two other U.S. representatives from California, Charles H. Wilson and John J. McFall, were charged with not reporting a $1,000 cash gift from Tongsun Park and converting it to use and lying about it. Congressman J. Patten (D-NJ) was also charged but found not guilty, while Otto Passman (D-LA), a former congressman, escaped prosecution due to illness. Leon Jaworski expressed frustration with the investigation's meager findings. He stated that "the amount of wrongdoing or the amount of poor judgment or unethical practice has not turned out to be what was predicted by some." He noted however, that the "investigations put congressmen on notice for some time to come that they ought to exercise the greatest caution."[52] Richard Hanna was eventually convicted and sentenced to six to thirty months in prison. For testifying in Koreagate, Tongsun Park was granted full immunity; however, in 2005, Park was accused of having been an intermediary with some corrupt United Nations officials in Iraq's oil-for-food conspiracy. He was arrested and, in 2007, sentenced to five years in prison.

This was the hardest and most difficult crisis of Roybal's entire public life. At the end of July 1978, Ed Roybal was welcomed by some 400 well-wishers. He stated that there was no bribery involved in the accusation made against him and that if he had known the contribution had come from Park, he would not have taken it. He said the contribution had come from an unknown donor and that the money had been used to buy tables at a fundraiser for senior citizens. He indicated that he had received the money in the office of former Congressman Otto Passman of Louisiana, who had introduced him to a man in his office, but Roybal had not caught the man's name. Roybal claimed he was being scapegoated and pointed out that similar probes had been dropped (including one against Tip O'Neil).[53]

On September 13, 1978, Roybal issued a formal statement to the Committee on Standards of Official Conduct of the House of Representatives. He once again stated that he had met a man at Congressman Passman's office in 1974, that Passman called the man "his very dear friend." The visitor told Roybal that he wanted to help him with his campaign for re-election and gave Roybal $1,000, which was unsolicited. On March 1978, Park named Roybal as a recipient of a campaign contribution. Roybal stated, "I firmly believe that the money I received from Park was part of the monies deposited in my campaign account in February 1974, but I cannot now independently prove it with documentary evidence since I did not personally attend to this matter but delegated them to volunteers. This, however, does not deter me from my conviction that the monies were used for my campaign, regardless of whether there is evidence to indicate that the campaign contributions may have been made in August and not February." He concluded, "I can assure you that I have too much respect to willfully or intentionally lie to a member of this or any other Committee and there isn't enough money around to make me throw that away, much less for one thousand measly dollars."[54] It should be noted that Mr. Roybal had voted against every piece of legislation that Tongsun Park had supported or lobbied for. This is a matter of public record, as a review of the *Congressional Record* can verify. This evidence completely discredits allegations that Mr. Roybal was even remotely involved in vote buying or any other related scheme.

On September 19, 1978, the nine-member Committee on Standards of Official Conduct voted that Roybal should be censured because he had used the 1974 contribution from Tongsun Park improperly. The committee voted 6–2, with one member voting Present to clear Roybal of another charge of lying. If approved by the full House, he would have had to stand and listen to findings of guilt.

John McFall, who served as majority whip from 1973 to 1977, was censured for not reporting to the House clerk $4,000 in contributions from Park and for making personal use of the funds. Charles Wilson was censured for lying to the House committee that he had not received worth more than $100 in value since January 1, 1970, after accepting $1,000 from Park.

During the last week of July 1978, the House committee cleared eight other congressmen of misconduct and wrongdoing. These included House Speaker Tip O'Neil and Majority Whip John Bradermas. O'Neil had allowed Park to throw two birthday parties for him at a supposed expense of about $7,500. Brademus accepted $2,950 from Park. Nonetheless, the committee found that had violated no law.

On September 27, 1978, Ed Roybal issued a statement regarding the committee's findings. Regarding Count 1 (failure to report a campaign contribution from Park), Roybal said that "has never been in dispute" and that he was not surprised by the findings on Count 2 (lying about the contribution). About Count 3 (originally an accusation of perjury, in violation of federal criminal law), Roybal stated, "The committee found that I had violated not Federal laws, but Rule 1 of the Code of Conduct of the House of Representatives. I am disappointed even at this lesser charge." In reference to Count 4, he noted, "in which I was charged with perjury and violation of Rule 1, was completely rejected by the Committee and I stand fully exonerated. The Committee's recommendations of censure are regrettable." Records indicate that at the time the House had censured only eighteen of its members, most of them in the nineteenth century.

In a letter dated November 29, 1978, Thomas H. Henderson Jr., chief of the Public Integrity Section of the United States Department of Justice, stated regarding Ed Roybal and Koreagate, "Roybal admitted in later testimony (April 25, 1978) that he did receive $1,000 in cash from an Oriental who he assumes was Tong Sun Park. The House Committee found that this change of testimony and other facts testified to on April 25, concerning the incident was not intentionally untruthful as originally charged."[55]

Roybal indicated that his disciplinary action would not affect his seniority rights or his position in the Appropriations Committee. He said, "A reprimand is like a slap on the wrist and censure is like a kick in the pants." His attorney, Richard Hilbey, addressed the Ethics Committee before the vote, stating that Roybal was "an honest man enjoying a good and an excellent reputation who made an honest mistake—a mistake in judgment."

The Mexican American community rallied to Roybal's defense in what they saw as scapegoating a minority and liberal congressmen. The National Council of La Raza on October 10, 1978, issued a formal statement characterizing the proceedings against Roybal as "a pattern of discrimination against Hispanic public figures and elected officials" and the "seeming racist and witch-hunt tactics of the Committee staff investigators give us strong reason to suspect an element of conspiracy to render ineffective the leading Hispanic voice in the House." The *East Los Angeles Tribune* on October 5, 1978, noted, "Scores of congressmen, including the former and present Speaker of the House of Representatives, also accepted campaign gifts from the same Korean national. Apparently they are off the hook and Roybal isn't because he forgot, neglected, or didn't know he should report it."

The article noted Roybal's generosity to the downtrodden and poor. "The woman without money to bury her husband, the father without the dollars to save his family from eviction, the mother without funds to put food on the table, the family with a child in need of an operation—all turned to Ed Roybal. And where the wheels of welfare couldn't meet the sudden emergency, Roybal did. Ed was a giver, not a taker!"

Another group, The Coalition of Mexicanos/Latinos Against Defamation issued a formal statement on October 6, 1978, commenting that the "Hispanic community of the United States is incensed at the most recent attack by the House Ethics Committee against our congressman and chairman of the National Hispanic Congressional Caucus, Edward R. Roybal." Members of both the Congressional Hispanic Caucus and Congressional Black Caucus mounted a campaign to stop the censure against Roybal. Congressman Henry B. Gonzalez (D-TX) and Congressmen Charles Rangel (D-NY) and Parren J. Michell (D-MO) met with the Ethics Committee to challenge the recommendation of censure against Roybal. However, the Ethics Committee decided to keep the censure recommendation.

Other Latino leaders also spoke out against the Ethics Committee charges, including Mario Robledo, head of the California Health and Welfare Agency; Eduardo Peña, president of the League of United Latin American Citizens; and Carmen Delgado, president of the National Conference of Puerto Rican Women.[56] Congressman Phillip Burton stated to the press, "As you say in California, you can't buy Ed Roybal for money, marbles or chalk."[57]

Roybal's Exoneration

However, on October 13, the House voted only to reprimand Ed Roybal, as well as Charles H. Wilson and John L. McFall. Roybal stated it was a "victory for me, for the civil rights of all Congressmen, and for all Americans who believe in the Constitutional rights to equal justice." He said he was relieved and thanked his many supporters for rallying to his defense. He added, "The decision today shows the potential strength of the Hispanic community when it unifies behind a cause. This is, then, not only a personal victory for me, but for all Hispanics throughout the nation."[58]

Roybal easily won re-election to the U.S. House of Representatives in the November 1978 elections. During December, California's twenty-five delegation members united to have Roybal and Charles H. Wilson retain subcommittee chairmanships. The amendment, sponsored by Representative James C. Corman (D-CA), passed 161–73.[59] Roybal was able to retain his chairmanship of the House Select Committee on Aging and Wilson his House Post Office Subcommittee position.

Not all were happy with the House decision or the amendment that allowed Roybal and Wilson to retain their positions. A *Los Angeles Times* editorial dated December 8, 1979, said, "We cannot condone a buddy system that winks at unethical conduct of a seriousness that warrants official reprimands." On December 28, 1978, a columnist wrote in the *Washington Weekly Globe*, "What the Roybal matter proves thus far is that the charge of racism has replaced patriotism as the last refuge of scoundrels. Presumably the Justice Department won't be buying such nonsense. We'll see."

Ed Roybal survived his severest political ordeal thanks to his lifelong integrity, dedicated work for his constituents, and the support of many who saw through the political intrigues and chicanery. The following anonymous poem made the rounds at that time. It exposed some of the reasons of why Ed Roybal and other were charged:

> The four little scapegoats,
> To the leadership's glee,
> Inherited unfairly
> The guilt of the three.

> But the shameless Committee
> The scapegoats they'll hang,
> Make a sham of all justice
> As their self-praise they sang.

O'Neill's son was in business
With Korean Park.
Whose parties were frequented
By the set that was smart.

The Committee on Ethics,
All this they ignored,
As they found four old scapegoats
They knew they could gore.

For old brother Brademas,
O'Neill and Breaux,
Excuses they made
For the lies they unfold.

The unethical staff
As they run all the show
Made saps of the Members
Who did as they were told.

What has happened to justice?
In the land of the free?
Where you're innocent always
Until guilty you'll be.

The shame of this nation
Under ethics you'll see
When the scapegoats are punished
And the leaders go free.

One is left wondering why Ed Roybal and others were hounded by
the House Ethics Committee. Looking back with the hindsight of many

years, this writer proposes that the Koreagate scandal most likely was part of a larger strategy by the Ford administration and others in the Republican Party to cripple the Democratic Party in the coming presidential elections. They hoped to draw attention away from the Watergate scandal and Ford's pardon of Nixon. Coincidently, Tongson Park and Richard Hanna set events in motion that attempted to win favor with the Democratic Congress to counter the Republican pressure to remove U.S. troops from South Korea and diminish military assistance.

Both Park and Hanna appear to have been less than successful in their objectives. It appears that the Democratic House chairpersons (O'Neill and Brandemas) were actively courted by Park. However, once they realized the ulterior motives of both Park and Hanna, they removed themselves from complicity and association. But some members of the Democratic Party were already implicated. The Democratic Party leadership was compelled to find some sacrificial lambs and appease Republicans who were already making cries of a double standard and going for the jugular. Because Koreagate did not turn out to be a political scandal in the magnitude of Watergate, Democratic leaders were not directly endangered, but sacrificial lambs they indeed gave up.

Political expediency dictated that Ed Roybal be one of the sacrificial lambs. He was a lone Mexican American in the House, low-keyed, had no political machine, and he was a liberal (long tied to civil rights and social programs legislation, and was against the Vietnam War). Many questions are left unanswered. For example, during the time of the House Ethics Committee investigation, Roybal's office in Washington, D.C., was twice burglarized. Nothing was taken, "but could [it have been] an illegal clandestine examination of his records and files, or was it to plant bugging devices?"[60] The makeup of the Ethics Committee is also in question. It was handpicked by the Speaker of the House (O'Neill). It was made up of twelve congressmen: three who were retiring, three who were seeking another office, and six who seldom showed up to make up a quorum. Were they serving merely to repay old political debts?

At the end, those making the charge against Ed Roybal miscalculated. His constituents, political colleagues, community leaders, and other members of the Latino community rallied to his defense, bringing the Latino community together as they had never been before. Roybal's integrity, hard work, social legislation, and collegial spirit of respect and bipartisanship of many decades served to deliver him from his political ordeal. He became stronger because of it and only grew in stature thereafter.

Despite the time and stresses of the Koreagate scandal, Ed Roybal continued to carry out his congressional duties and responsibilities. Roybal received the 1978 Health Service Award from the National Association of Community Health Centers and the National Minority Health Consortium. In making the award, the association's president, Louis Garcia stated, "Mr. Roybal has consistently served as a spokesman and leader in improving health care to medically unserviced communities."[61]

During April 1978, Roybal spoke against the "apparent conspiracy being waged by the Teamsters Union and the California grape growers against the farm worker movement." After visiting César Chávez and the Coachella Valley, Roybal stated that a poll of thirty-one farms "clearly demonstrates strong worker support" for César Chávez's Farm Workers Union.[62]

Advocating for Senior Citizens

A few years before the Koreagate scandal, Roybal and three other congressmen came together to create a U.S. House Permanent Select Committee on Aging to advocate for senior citizens. Rep. Claude Pepper[63] (D-FL), Senator Spark Matsunaga[64] (D-HI), and Senator Jan Yagi-Buen (D-HI), along with Roybal, were the four Congress members who went about proposing the new committee to the leadership.

The U.S. Permanent Select Committee on Aging was established with the intent of conducting investigations and hearings. The idea was to jumpstart legislation and other actions through the regular House committees. The committee was approved as such on October 8, 1974, by a

299–44 vote in the House. The committee conducted its first business in June 1975 and had thirty-five members.[65]

All four founders of the committee held similar seniority, which meant that all were eligible but only one of them would become the committee's chair. Matsunaga said he did not want to become the committee's chairman because he planned to run for the U.S. Senate. So it became a choice among Yagi-Buen, Pepper, or Roybal. They drew straws, and Pepper won.

Pepper was a very strong advocate for seniors, and he drew a lot of publicity. Sometimes he was confrontational on issues. Roybal was more methodical and was known to tell staff, "Lets find out what we need to do and let's do it. Let's not tell anybody. We'll just work behind the scenes and then we'll just get it done." He would also say, "I don't care who takes the credit, as long as it gets done."[66]

When Claude Pepper left the Committee on Aging, it was widely assumed that Congressman Roybal would become the new chairman, since he had been the ranking member, the number two person on the committee. However, that was not necessarily a done deal. Some machinations behind the scenes prevented Roybal from becoming chairman. Side talks took place with Speaker Tip O'Neil, who would appoint the Committee on Aging chair. The scuttlebutt asserted that because Roybal was Latino, someone else would be more knowledgeable about what was going on. "I would call that discrimination," said Roybal staff member Jorge Lambrinos. But Tip O'Neil stayed the course and upheld the rule that the next person in line becomes chair. In the meantime, there were concerns expressed about what would happen to the committee with Roybal as chairman. He was following a man of wide and deep reputation, esteemed by many, and considered irreplaceable. "Keep in mind that [Claude] Pepper had been, I mean, Mr. Aging by the mere fact that he was on television every other day," said Lambrinos. Roybal, in contrast, was very low key. There were even rumors that the committee was now only going to deal only with Latino issues. "In fact," added Lambrinos, "somebody came and asked me, 'If Mr. Roybal becomes chair…do we have all have to learn Spanish?'"[67]

The House Select Committee on Aging was instrumental in major reforms in nursing home operations, the reduction of abuse against senior citizen patients, increased home care benefits for the aging, and the establishment of developing research and care centers for Alzheimer's disease.

The committee met with President Carter during August 1976 to propose specific legislation to address various aging concerns. Roybal stated, "I stressed the growing need for congregate housing, a residential setting for elderly residents which includes services such as meals, housekeeping, routine health care and transportation. With this type of federal emphasis on this type of housing, many senior citizens would be able to lead independent lives and avoid unnecessary institutional care."[68]

During October 1978, Ed Roybal was presented with a special award from the national Council of Senior Citizens (NCSC) recognizing his record of voting 100 percent on the issues of vital concern to older Americans. The NCSC had more than 3.5 million members. House members were rated on their votes on such legislation as social security, the Legal Services Corporation, and a national consumer cooperative bank.

The U.S. Congress had passed several major legislation earlier in the year to improve the service delivery and increasing funding for federal programs benefiting the elderly. The House Select Committee on Aging had been a major force in spearheading the passage of these bills. These included increasing the mandatory retirement age from 65 to 70 (which Roybal opposed). The law was already in effect for federal workers and would be applied to most private employees on January 1, 1979.

In April 1979, the Los Angeles Board of Supervisors named a new county health center on East Los Angeles' Fetterly Avenue in Roybal's honor. Naming the center in recognition of Roybal's contribution to community health was approved 4–1; with only conservative Baxter Ward's vote objecting. Roybal had not only consistently supported improved community health care but had played a major role in planning this health center.[69]

One often unheralded resource that all elected leaders need to have is a good office staff. Ed Roybal was effective to a large degree in responding to the needs of his constituents in a timely manner due to a seasoned, dedicated, and responsible staff.

In 1977, Congressman Roybal hired Henry Lozano[70] to be his chief of staff in his congressional district office. Lozano would remain in that position until Roybal's retirement in 1992. Lozano met Roybal through his union work. "I think one of the most unique things about Mr. Roybal," commented Lozano, "was the fact that he never changed...He was very, very down to earth. He never lost his touch, the common touch with the folks here. He always would comment, 'Now, I know it is so easy for these things go to your head.' He was just involved in about every issue you can think of regarding Latinos—be it housing, employment, you name it—he was there, with the veterans. This guy was always there."[71]

As chief of staff, Lozano was the eyes and ears from the district to the Washington, D.C., office. The fact that Roybal kept getting re-elected term after term reflected his popularity within his district and that was so because he responded to the specific needs of his constituents. His popularity made his re-elections possible with little expenditure. I asked Henry Lozano about how Roybal kept in touch and remained cognizant with the district's pressing issues. Said Lozano, "He'd tell us, 'I don't want no meetings, no nothing scheduled, and I'm just going to be out and about.' So he would go to different places [with] people he hadn't seen for fifteen or twenty years and just go around the community and have coffee or beer with some of these folks and all over the place and get it directly from the people. There would be no schedule, no media, no nothing...He'd get in his car and go to some meeting unannounced, not preset. I guess he sort of got his juices going around or they'd tell him some of the problems that we didn't hear...They called him Eddie. You know, Mexicans are very proper in terms of addressing the title. It didn't bother him; whereas some other folks may get all bent out of shape about a title, he didn't."[72]

Jorge Lambrinos[73] was another important addition to Roybal's staff. Roybal hired Lambrinos as his chief of staff in Washington, D.C., and director of the House Select Committee on Aging. Lambrinos would remain with Roybal until 1992.

Right after the job interview, on a Tuesday morning, Roybal telephoned Lambrinos. Roybal asked him to put together a paper on the needs of the elderly by Thursday night before he left for Los Angeles. Lambrinos put together the paper. A week later, Roybal telephoned again, asking Lambrinos to defend the paper. Then, three weeks later, Harry Pachon, then Roybal's chief of staff, called Lambrinos to tell him Roybal wanted to see him again. "That's when he called me up and offered the staff director's job, with a warning, 'You're representing me now,' said Roybal. 'Just watch your back because there's people here that are going to try to get you. They're going to try to get you to get to me.'"[74]

Roybal told Lambrinos, "We do things because they're right, not because they are politically expedient. If it's not politically expedient but it's right, then do it because it's right. Then we fight the battle as to why—let me worry about the people who are not supporting this thing. We're going to do this because it's right." Lambrinos recalled, "Sometimes, Roybal took positions that were not popular in the district and he explained to people why he took a certain action. Usually, by the end of the meeting, he generally would have people in agreement with him, and you could hear them say, 'Yeah, Eddie, you did the right thing.'"[75] After 1992, following the congressman's retirement, Jorge Lambrinos became director of the Edward R. Roybal Center for Applied Gerontology.

During February 1979, Ed Roybal was re-elected chairman of the Housing and Consumer Interests Subcommittee of the House Select Committee on Aging. The fifteen-member committee made recommendations on federal funding levels for housing programs for the elderly. In fiscal year 1979, the City of Los Angeles received $14.8 million in federal funds for housing programs, most of which benefited elderly residents. Within the previous three years, more than 6,000 elderly residents in

Los Angeles had received rent subsidies through Section 8 funds. Of the 1979 funding, more than $700,000 was earmarked for Section 202 programs for the construction and rehabilitation of housing for the elderly and handicapped.

During Roybal's tenure as chairperson, he led the successful fight to restore some $15 million in funding for low-cost health programs for senior citizens. He was also able to expand the housing program for senior citizens. During 1982, he fought to preserve the Meals on Wheels program[76] and the preference of veterans in hiring practices.

In his retirement, Jimmy Carter would earn worldwide recognition as humanitarian and progressive elder statesmen. He would publish several highly praised books[77] and through the Carter Center, in partnership with Emory University, in Atlanta, Georgia, he continues to work with fellows and associates to resolve international conflicts, protect human rights, and promote democracy. The Jimmy Carter Work Project (JCWP) for Habitat for Humanity International (HFHI) works to provide hundreds of low-cost houses for the poor.

Congressman Roybal worked well with and admired President Jimmy Carter, saying, "First of all was a very good politician. He was very bright and well-liked by both Democrats and Republicans. I remember the meeting that was held of the leadership of the House where the President would come and shake hands with everyone."

Beginning in 1979 and through the early 1980s, Congressman Roybal was chairman of the Treasury-Postal Service House Committee and co-chair of the Subcommittee on Appropriations and a senior member on the Labor, Health, and Education Appropriations Committee. Through senior committee positions, Roybal became one of Congress's most powerful members. His ranking on committees strongly influenced how Congress disposed of issues dealing with aging, labor, health, and education. Roybal held legislative power—referred to as "a lot of clout"—and was sometimes considered "one of the Cardinals" of the House. What that meant in practical terms was that Roybal could go up to the chairpersons of other committees and tell them he needed a favor, saying something like, "this is important to me." Those chairs would also approach him in the same way. That is how Congress, much like a club, works. "A lot of people don't realize the power that Mr. Roybal had when he was in Congress," said Jorge Lambrinos. "I mean, he was one of the key members and one of the most powerful members in Congress."[79]

Lambrinos remembered Roybal telling him about his approach to working inside a complex legislative system, where so much hangs in the balance. "He told me that you need to be frugal, you needed to make sure that whatever you do has a purpose. You don't just do things because they were there to be done or because you want to get credit for this or that. If we put monies into a program, you put those dollars there because they were going to have an impact." Edward Roybal was very careful in how much public investment was made in programs. He picked his spots, he was patient, then he waited for the results to produce the outcome everyone knew was right.[80]

Chapter 11

The Elder Statesman
(1980–1988)

ON ELECTION DAY, NOVEMBER 1980, REPUBLICAN CANDIDATE RONALD Reagan[1] won 43.9 million popular votes to Jimmy Carter's 35.5 million. Illinois Congressman John Anderson, a Republican-turned-Independent, won 5.7 million popular votes. The Electoral College results magnified Reagan's victory: he received 489 electoral votes to Carter's 49. However, among Mexican Americans, African Americans, and Jews, Reagan was less than successful.

At the time of Reagan's election, the nation faced an oil crisis, sizable inflation, and revolutions abroad—all of which contributed to a right-wing resurgence. Among the policies that Roybal found objectionable was escalating U.S. involvement in Central America. He supported proposals for peaceful resolutions to the conflicts there. Roybal remained active in his opposition to the xenophobic and exclusionary policies against undocumented workers. He continued to press for quality care for seniors, the expansion of educational opportunities, job creation for the poor, federal funds to fight the new disease called AIDS, and the establishment of a national disease control center.

Grounded in Reality Amid Illusions of Grandeur: The Reagan Years

President Ronald Reagan and Vice President George Herbert Walker Bush were inaugurated on January 20, 1981. Only sixty days into his first presidential term, Reagan survived an assassination attempt.

Once in office, Reagan proposed an economic policy he termed "trickle-down economics." It called for drastic government deregulation, budget cuts, and tax breaks for corporations, strong national defense, and union-busting policies. These measures were presented in terms of their ability to trickle down to the very poor in the form of job creation and economic stimulus. Reagan's election platform was anchored in the philosophy of "supply side" economics,[2] which became the benchmark for other neoconservative[3] economic approaches that followed.

Reagan raised defense spending 35 percent during his two terms in office and built up the largest deficit in the nation's history. Reagan is remembered as a popular president, although that assessment is not consistently supported by his popularity polls from the time. The media called him the "Teflon president" because criticism and scandal seemingly never stuck to Reagan personally. Such affairs were never ascribed to him as the intellectual author. Reagan was also known as the Great Communicator. He was effective at playing the wise, kindly, grandfather offering ideological recipes to the nation for all its maladies. He maneuvered public opinion on the imperialist misdeeds of the "evil empire," the Soviet Union, and warned how socialist welfare deterred investment and personal initiative. His homespun humor gave some Americans the feeling of national renewal and self-confidence.

Roybal and other liberal Democrats attempted to curb the excesses of the right during the Reagan years. Roybal had met the new president right before the election and thought Reagan was a very pleasant man. He saw Reagan as someone who could charm an individual, whether or not he was predisposed to his line of thought. Roybal referred to Reagan as the type of individual you can't forget once you've met. He recognized Reagan for his charisma and his reputation as the Great Communicator. "I think most of the time he was taking advantage of his acting," said Roybal.[4]

In 1980, Roybal led an effort to restore public funds to programs aiding the elderly, including a community-based alternative to nursing homes. In the same year, he voted to further strengthen fair housing laws and to establish a Department of Education. During the 97th Congress (1981–1982), Congressman Roybal chaired the Congressional Hispanic Caucus, leading the opposition against the Simpson-Mazzoli immigration bill, which proposed sanctions against domestic employers who hired undocumented workers.

During the 1980s, Roybal continued to hold important congressional posts. He was chosen as chairman of the Treasury, Postal Service, and General Government Subcommittee. In addition, he served in the Labor, Health and Human Services, Education, and Related Services Subcommittee. He continued to serve in the Select Permanent Committee on Aging, becoming its chairman in 1983 (during the 98th Congress).

Between 1979 and 1983, Congressman Roybal pressed to have health legislation passed. He directed Jorge Lambrinos and committee staffers to draft health legislation. Reflecting on that time, Lambrinos commented, "People would say, 'Well that's never going to pass,' and 'Why are you wasting your time?' But it goes back to his saying, 'Don't talk about it, just do it.'" And that's what they did. Roybal's staff drafted a bill called U.S. Health. Roybal's thinking was that the bill had a chance of being passed. Even if someone else's bill won out, components within his bill could still gain favor, and others might take one piece out, and that part would see the light of day and would become legislation. Roybal's strategy was to provide a road map from which others could design onramps, frontage approaches, more lanes and alternative routes.[5]

In 1982, Roybal ran unopposed in the primary and easily won re-election to an eleventh term. In the same month of his re-election, Roybal drafted an amendment to a House Committee on Appropriations bill to restore funds for bilingual education. The Reagan administration had requested a 41 percent cut in that funding. A reduction of that magnitude,[6] said Roybal, meant that hundreds of schools would lose financial support to continue programs for children who had limited English proficiency. Roybal used reports to show that the program was a proven, effective approach. Surveys pointed out that Hispanic students who participated in bilingual education improved in reading, math, and scientific skills. Roybal's proposal would increase, not decrease, grants to local school districts and expand parent participation in all phases of the bilingual education program.

A record number of Latinos won elected office in November 1982, four of whom went to Congress. They were Esteban Torres and Matthew Martinez of California, Solomon Ortiz of Texas, and Bill Richardson of New Mexico. Re-elected to Congress were Kika de la Garza and Henry B. Gonzalez of Texas. Roberto Garcia, of New York, the only Puerto Rican serving in Congress, was also re-elected. Manuel Luján, of New Mexico, was the only Republican Latino in Congress. Hispanic members of Congress numbered eleven. Joseph Berrios, a Puerto Rican, became the first Latino elected to the Illinois state legislature. Mexican American Gloria Molina (from Los Angeles) was elected to the California state legislature, joining several other Latinos and Latinas at that level. Many have attributed the gains in 1982 and thereafter to several causes: the increase in citizenship among Latinos, the various efforts for voter registration, the efforts by organizations such as the National Association of Elected officials (NALEO) and others; and the growing awareness among the Latino communities that they needed to translate their demographics into votes.

Eighty percent of Latinos voted Democratic in the 1984 presidential election that returned Ronald Reagan to office for a second term. The increase in Latino voter turnout was generally ascribed to discontent with the effects of so-called Reagonomics policies. In addition, the Southwest Voter Registration and Education Project and NALEO had undertaken a nationwide voter registration effort, allowing people to express their discontent through their votes.

Regarding the increased Latino voter turnout, a *Santa Fe Springs News* analysis noted, "That indicates not only greater awareness, but also more active participation on the part of young people who are seeking good careers and equal rights of franchise...However, the main issue in the Hispanic community is still employment...To ease the problem throughout the coming decade, we must convince corporate America that there are well-trained Hispanics ready to assume significant responsibility."[7]

Economist Ben Fernandez, a Republican, commented, "From coast to coast I'm seeing much more political action than ever before."[8] According to the 1980 U.S. Census, the Latino population in the Southwest grew by 61 percent and the national Latino population numbered 14.6 million, not including a significant undercounted, undocumented worker group. The Voting Rights Act provisions were only now being felt. A number of people who had been constrained or prevented from voting before were now able to exercise their right. The population was growing; expectations were high—but unrealistic—because most of the population was below voting age or fell into the younger demographic age range (which tends to vote least). It was, however, not a bad showing for Latinos in 1982 and 1984.

Ed Roybal was a longtime advocate for the rights of women. Women had played important roles in the founding and organizing of the CSO and MAPA, Roybal's campaigns for Los Angeles City Council and U.S. Congress, and all the legislation that he had sponsored and supported. In 1983, he voted to support the passage of the Equal Rights Amendment.[9] Unfortunately, like many times before, it failed to get ratification.

In May 1983, Roybal supported Congresswoman Mary Roe Oakar's (D-OH) legislation to end gender bias in Social Security payments. The legislation's eight parts were drawn from recommendations by the Aging Committee's Task Force on Social Security and Women, which Oakar chaired. Roybal promoted the conviction behind the legislation that marriage is a partnership in which benefits are to be shared equally. However, Social Security payments rules allowed women who worked in the home to become eligible for a fraction of their husband's benefits. About 85 percent of the single women over sixty-five years of age were living near or below poverty.

Inequities in the Social Security system were only partly to blame. Women who worked and paid into the system received $335 per month on average at that time, while the national average for all workers—men and women—was $405 per month. Roybal asserted that the Social Security system bias against women occurred "in part because the regulations were drafted at a time when there were far fewer women in the workforce."[10] The package he supported would establish a system where earnings were viewed as being shared equally by husband and wife; provide four months of benefits to a surviving spouse after age fifty; allow full benefits for disabled surviving spouses, regardless of age; restore the minimum social security benefit; and eliminate the Government Pension Offset, which reduced spousal benefits.

As far back as the 1950s, Ed Roybal had proposed a metro rail system for large urban centers like Los Angeles. At that time, however, a series of massive freeway building projects was initiated instead. In Los Angeles, the freeway building resulted in the dislocation of entire communities like East Los Angeles.

However, Ed Roybal was able to witness the shift in the mindset regarding mass transit. In early June 1983, the House Appropriations Committee approved a bill to contribute an extra $17.5 million for the first section of the Los Angeles Metro Rail system. The amount approved was less than the requested $127.5 million, for the projected seven-year transit project intended to bring traffic relief to metropolitan Los Angeles with a line from Downtown Los Angeles to the Wilshire and Fairfax districts, Hollywood, and North Hollywood.[11] Los Angeles Mayor Tom Bradley acknowledged that "this is the first time a full Congressional committee has approved funding for the beginning of a Los Angeles subway project."[12]

Beginning in the 1980s, Ed Roybal began to receive long-overdue recognition for his selfless efforts on many issues and concerns. One example was his long-standing concern for health care, dating back to the tuberculosis epidemic in his childhood. In his young adulthood, before and after World War II, Roybal had worked as a health educator. Thereafter, as a Los Angeles city councilman, he had worked tirelessly to provide his district and the city accessible and quality medical resources. Throughout his tenure in Congress, he had been a dedicated advocate for health care. On June 8, 1983, Roybal was commended by the Los Angeles County American Lung Association for leading the fight in the House of Representatives for special TB block grants and for urging continuation of existing postal rates favorable to the American Lung Association and other nonprofit agencies. The honors recognized that Roybal had gone a long way, as an employee of the California TB Association in Oakland and as the health education director with the Los Angeles County TB Association (both organizations now part of the American Lung Association), before he was elected to the Los Angeles city council in 1949.

In 1984, Ed Roybal prepared to run for re-election again. During June 1984, Congressman Roybal faced a Democratic rival, Tim Pike. He handily beat Pike for the nomination with 86 percent of the vote. Among the Republicans, Roy D. "Bill" Bloxom (a businessman) and Howard Steninger contended for their party's nomination. Bloxom beat Steninger, 55 percent to 45 percent. In the November general election, Roybal obtained 74,261 (71.7 percent) votes to Bloxom's 24,968 (24.1 percent).

In June 1984, Secretary of Health and Human Services Margaret Heckler, submitted to Congress proposals to raise the Medicare benefit eligibility age from sixty-five to sixty-seven. A federal advisory panel aimed to produce $300 billion in new revenues and savings to keep the Medicare program from going bankrupt. Congressman Roybal, as the House Aging Committee's chair, stated that the panel's recommendations were "not an acceptable solution to our Medicare problems." Senior citizens were already paying twenty cents out of every one dollar of their income for medical care. "We need a plan that controls health costs, not one that cuts medical coverage," he said.[13] According to a Congressional Budget

Office forecast, Medicare would remain solvent up to 1988 but would then run into deficits by the early 1990s.

Another of Reagan's money-saving strategies involved closing some small Social Security offices, those with fewer than fifteen staff members. The proposal was to go into effect after March 1985. Roybal thought that this was only an opening move, one leading to the closing of other offices, ones with fewer than twenty-five workers. "The proposal would mean that more than half of the 1,340 offices could be closed," he said. Roybal pressed Health and Human Services Secretary Margaret Heckler at hearings about the memo regarding the proposed closings. He recommended that, should the closings be approved, each Social Security field office be reviewed on a priority basis before any actual closing took place.

In May 1985, Roybal sought to counteract another Reaganomics strategy, this time by proposing a tax cut of his own. Roybal introduced H.R. 2471, which would reduce Social Security taxes for American workers earning less than $40,000 per year. These earners made up 94 percent of taxpayers.

Roybal could see behind the Reagan charade. Tax cuts did not mean tax cuts but tax savings for those in the higher income brackets, business owners, and investors with capital gains—savings that would unlikely be passed on to consumers and workers, the real victims of inflation-led earnings deterioration. Social Security recipients, too, needed protection from being hurt by inflation. The Reagan administration, Roybal reasoned, really wanted "to cut benefits for old people and keep taxes high on young people so that they can build huge Social Security surpluses to finance the deficits they created by big spending on weapons and tax breaks for the wealthy." He believed that if the administration was going to use Social Security to balance the budget, it should reform the Social Security tax system and make it more equitable. That meant that corporate executives with six-figure incomes should pay at the same effective tax rates as their employees. By Roybal's estimate, the government could afford to pay the cost of living adjustments, cut the tax rates, and still reduce deficits by more than the Senate plan that was under discussion.[14]

Roybal's bill would repeal the Social Security tax increases due in 1988 and 1989 and reduce tax rates by 2 percent per year in 1986, 1987, and 1988. He said that self-employment rates would be reduced even more. All Social Security taxpayers would then be taxed at equal, across-the-board reduced rates on all income from wages and salaries.

Also in May 1985, Roybal, as chair of the House Select Committee on Aging, conducted hearings in Los Angeles on Alzheimer's disease.[15] Roybal and the committee heard a lot of heartrending testimony about the disease's effects. One of the witnesses was Maria O'Brien, daughter of the Oscar-winning actor Edmond O'Brien, who had died earlier that month of complications from Alzheimer's. She stated, "Ironically, a man who once could hold an audience in the palm of his hand towards the end had great difficulty expressing even his most basic feelings of affection, recognition, and love."[16]

At that time, Roybal's call for federal efforts to research and treat the disease were met with little enthusiasm. It was not until several years later when President Ronald Reagan began to suffer some of the disease's symptoms that it drew greater public attention. Roybal had had the foresight to call attention to it earlier. He pioneered the first public policy advocacy to provide funding for Alzheimer's disease, of which President Reagan would later die. The funding went a long way to assisting research into finding ways to combat the deadly disease.[17]

In mid-1985, Ed Roybal drew his attention to the growing concern of drug cartels, especially those located in Colombia, and their smuggling into the United States.

In June 1985, a House subcommittee on Treasury, Postal Services, and General Government held hearings in Los Angeles to investigate drug smuggling into the United States. The hearings coincided with President Reagan's proposal to cut the number of customs inspectors from the federal budget (an attempt at cost cutting to balance the spiraling deficit). Roybal was the only one of the eight subcommittee members to be at the hearings. Other hearings were scheduled in Texas and New Mexico.[18]

Funding AIDS Research

Congressman Roybal's lifelong concern for health issues brought him center stage in the early 1980s. Research funds were needed to combat a new disease, Acquired Immune Deficiency Syndrome (AIDS). The very uniqueness and deadliness of the disease caused widespread fear, panic, and paranoia. Roybal sprang into action when the disease's consequences were still barely comprehended.

In 1978, gay men in Sweden and the United States and heterosexuals in Haiti and Tanzania began showing signs of skin infection from a rare kind of cancer. Their lungs developed a type of pneumonia that destroyed their immune system. The new disease, initially named the Gay Related Immune Disorder (GRID), was soon also found among drug addicts who shared needles. Women, children, and hemophiliacs became infected through blood transfusions. The disease became a source of grave concern, as infected people were assumed to put others at risk. The disease was renamed AIDS. It was deemed to be incurable as the death toll rose dramatically. In 1980, 31 deaths had been attributed to AIDS in the United States; in 1981, 234; in 1982, 853; in 1983, 2,304; in 1984, 4,251; and in 1985, 5,636.

Homophobia at the highest levels of leadership nurtured indifference to AIDS. In 1985, after film star Rock Hudson died of AIDS, President Reagan mentioned the word *AIDS* for the first time in the context of public health. However, three years earlier, Roybal had taken the initiative to address AIDS as a health issue and public policy concern. In 1982, he fought and obtained the first funding ever focusing on AIDS research, which was far from a popular position to take at the time.

In September 1983, Roybal supported an increase of $12 million of federal funding for prevention and AIDS research as part of a supplemental appropriations bill. Roybal made it clear that AIDS represented a frightening epidemic that needed an all-out effort to find the cause and to invent a cure.[19]

In 1983, scientists at the Pasteur Institute in Paris, France, isolated a virus that they linked to AIDS. In 1984, United States researchers also isolated a similar virus. And by 1986, the viruses were found to be the same. They named it the Human Immunodeficiency Virus (HIV). A major breakthrough occurred in 1995 clinical trials, known as the Delta Trial, that proved conclusively that the use of two drugs together were better than using one. The resulting treatment became known as Highly Active Antiretroviral Therapy, or HAART. Soon thereafter, deaths from AIDS began dropping in the United States and in England. However, ignorance, stigma, and government indifference around the world allowed AIDS to spiral out of control in the developing world.

By championing research and development, Roybal was the first policy leader in the United States to shepherd funding for AIDS at a time when AIDS was just beginning to break out, 1979–1980. He thought about it as a health issue but soon found it overlapped with cultural and sexual orientation issues. His office would receive calls from the public complaining that Roybal was trying to get funding for AIDS. Criticism was plentiful from colleagues and from constituents. Everybody was afraid of AIDS but willing to ignore it, as if it that would make it go away. Being the man he was, Roybal stuck to his guns and argued the fact that it was a health issue that needed to be addressed.

Roybal was a very private man. He did not make friends easily, but he made some in the House over the years. Among them, in the late 1970s and early 1980s, were Phil Burton[20] and John Burton.[21] John had been one of the most effective political leaders in California for some forty years. He was a dedicated advocate for the disabled, aged, and marginalized.

Ed Roybal and John Burton worked very closely on health issues, as John was a member of the Subcommittee on Aging and one of the subcommittee chairs on the Health Committee. Phil Burton joined Roybal as one of the early supporters of AIDS research funding. The men were sufficiently close that they used to play cards together on a regular basis, when they would make cases and strategize and support each other on issues.[22]

Both Phil Burton and John Burton were close to labor unions and liberals. In political circles they were said to be the last of the San Francisco political machine. They were also said to play poker and smoke cigars as pastimes. John resigned from the U.S. House of Representatives in 1983 citing an addiction to cocaine and alcohol.

Over the years, the push for legislation on a variety of health issues was leading up to national health insurance. The two long-term advocates for health legislation and, ultimately, national health care were Ed Roybal in the U.S. House of Representatives and Ted Kennedy in the U.S. Senate.

Ed Roybal shape the nation's acceptance of extending health coverage to all, though he found that, as with Latino civil rights, the national public was not ready to have a serious discussion about national health insurance. However, Roybal and like-minded others chipped away at popular discriminatory practices until the need for change was accepted. He was a pathfinder in this respect. He was also one of the first legislators to introduce legislation to establish a national health care plan.

Funding the Centers for Disease Control (CDC)

Congressman Roybal played another historic role with his timely support for funding of the Centers of Disease Control and Prevention (CDC). His concern emanated from his lifelong concern for health, but also from the AIDS epidemic and other new diseases that were devastating entire continents.

The CDC, founded in 1946 as the Communicable Disease Center, was renamed the Center for Disease Control in 1970. In the early 1980s, the CDC tackled the new diseases such as AIDS using the same strategies as with its traditional epidemiological work against malaria, typhus, and other communicable diseases. Much later, in 1992, it was renamed again as the Centers for Disease Control and Prevention.

Roybal's initiative in the early 1980s led to CDC funding for tuberculosis. Roybal was prompted to action after visiting the CDC campus in Atlanta, Georgia, with other members of Congress in 1980 during the Democratic Party Convention. The facility was built mainly from leftover World War II–era dilapidated military barracks, which were like Quonset huts, with metal plates on the floor to patch the rotted places. Roybal liked telling the story that when he was walking through on his visit he came across a refrigerator. He said, "This refrigerator looks like the one my grandfather had, you know with the motor up on top." He was astounded at this. Here was one of the world's major health disease prevention agencies working with antiquated equipment. Roybal said at that point, "We've got to do something about it."[23] And that he did.

Three weeks following Roybal's visit to the CDC, Jorge Lambrinos, his staff assistant, obtained a set of photographs documenting the dilapidated conditions. They took note that the CDC was spread out over three campuses. Roybal wanted to have the facilities concentrated in one location to minimize the cost of operation and to make it easier for researchers, lab workers, and all personnel to be able to work better.[24] As usual, Congressman Roybal's vision was not shared at large by others in Congress, especially when it came to the monies he wanted for new CDC buildings. Nonetheless, keeping to his own adage of doing something if it was right, he persevered and was able to add an appropriation to a bill for the General Services Administration.

In 1999, the CDC named its new location the Edward R. Roybal campus and the Edward R. Roybal Laboratory. During his career, Roybal secured $100 million for the CDC, helping to make it one of the world's premier research and disease intervention institutions. In recent years, CDC has extended its scope to bioterrorism and weaponized disease, such as anthrax.

Roybal's Further Efforts to Counter Reagonomics

President Reagan's economic policies continued to have devastating effects on working-class families and individuals. Ed Roybal became one of the most vocal and courageous critics of the president's policies.

The policies that collectively made up Reagonomics were supposed to produce a $28 billion surplus by 1986 but instead resulted in a $1,193 billion deficit over a five-year period. The deficit averaged $137.3 billion per year when Reagan left office. The public debt had gone up to $2.684 trillion.[25]

"I think he had a very poor record of dealing with the poor and with other people in need," Roybal believed, even though Roybal recognized that Reagan had succeeded in selling his ideas to the public. He saw the policies as part of the politics to benefit Reagan and his supporters. He persuasively sold them, but they did little for the general public good.[26]

Roybal was very upset about the Reagan budget cuts. As part of his work on the House Select Committee on Aging, he put together a briefing book on the impact the Reagan cuts were having and distributed this information to all the committee members and to organizations as his way to provide ammunition for arguments about how the cuts were adversely impacting people. "He was very concerned, incensed even, with what was happening to older adults and poor people."[27]

Reagan was re-elected in 1984, defeating former Vice President Walter Mondale 54.4 million votes to 37.5 million votes. Reagan won everywhere except Minnesota, Mondale's home state, and the District of Columbia. Reagan received 525 electoral votes to Mondale's 13.

After Regan was re-elected, the Iran-Contra scandal, covert U.S. involvement in Central America (Nicaragua, El Salvador, Guatemala), and the skyrocking deficit jeopardized Reagan's credibility with the electorate.

The Iran-Contra Scandal

President Reagan's administration, after secretly selling arms to Iran, diverted the proceeds to the Contras—the counter-revolutionaries fighting the Sandinistas in Nicaragua. Iran was publicly acknowledged as a

U.S. enemy, responsible for official hostage taking of U.S. embassy personnel. The weapons sale to Iran was prohibited by the U.S. Congress and United Nations sanctions.

In 1985, Israel volunteered to be the intermediary, shipping weapons to Iran in exchange for U.S. hostages held in Lebanon. In January 1986, President Reagan decided to approve the sale and divert the profits to the Contras despite its violation of the 1982–1983 Boland Amendment, which made the act illegal. One thousand TOW missiles were sent to Iran in February 1986, with miscellaneous weapons and parts following between May and November of the same year. The diversion of the proceeds from the arms sale to the Contras was arranged by Colonel Oliver North, an aide to U.S. National Security Advisor John Poindexter. The covert operation was exposed when a plane was downed over Nicaragua and the weapons and funds were revealed. Oliver North had his secretary shred documents that implicated them in the Iran-Contra scandal. On November 25, 1986, U.S. Attorney Edwin Meese admitted the appearance of prosecutable wrongdoing.

The scandal forced Reagan to appoint the Tower Commission to investigate the affair. Reagan, on television, stated he couldn't remember whether he had approved the arms sale. The commission implicated North, Poindexter, and U.S. Secretary of Defense Casper Weinberger, stating that it could not conclusively determine the level of President Reagan's involvement because many documents had been shredded. Nonetheless, on February 26, 1987, the Tower Commission rebuked Reagan for not being in control of his national security staff.

Roybal reacted with disgust to the Iran-Contra scandal. He felt the administration was knowingly breaking the law. He would work behind the scenes to address the issue. He was not one of the key players but instead joined with others in investigating the administration. Roybal's premonition of presidential involvement proved warranted.

On November 18, 1987, the United States Congress issued a final report that declared Reagan bore "ultimate responsibility" for the misconduct of his aides and that his administration had exhibited "secrecy, deception, and disdain for the law."[28]

Revolution in Central America

Reagan failed to understand the historic shift in Central America of popular movements that would address the region's grinding poverty, illiteracy, misery, and social injustice. He saw the movements in terms of the Cold War. President Reagan imposed an economic embargo in the aftermath of Nicaragua's Sandinista Revolution in 1979. He then apportioned $20 million to train and arm the Contras opposing the Sandinistas.[29]

Roybal was very concerned about the hostilities in Central America, but he was more involved with the situation in El Salvador than he was with Nicaragua. He nonetheless followed events there and did not support many of Reagan's initiatives. At Archbishop Oscar Romero's[30] invitation, Roybal went to El Salvador and tried to get a caucus to support and speak on what was happening there (e.g., the death squads, etc.) and cease unconditional U.S. support for the Salvadoran military.[31] Tragically, no peaceful resolution was found in the next six years, between 1979 and 1985. Some 75,000 Salvadorans died in the conflict.

In Guatemala, Reagan increased assistance to military cliques who fought a barbarous war that inflicted massacre, torture, and disappearances among the Maya Indian majority. The United Nations in the mid-1990s estimated at least 250,000 Mayas were murdered.[32]

In 1999, to his credit, President Bill Clinton apologized for the past U.S. support of some Guatemalan military regimes. "For the United States, it is important that I state clearly that support for military forces and intelligence units which engaged in violence and widespread repression was wrong, and the United States must not repeat that mistake."[33] However, United States media routinely consigned the magnitude of the Central American war to the most obscure pages.

Chapter 12

Retirement and Legacy
(1989–2005)

As President's Reagan's second term came to an end, Vice President George Herbert Walker Bush[1] ran again for the presidency (he had run unsuccessfully in 1980). On Election Day in 1988, Bush was elected president. He had selected Indiana Senator Dan Quayle for his vice president. His Democratic opponent was former Massachusetts governor Michael Dukakis. Bush won the election with 48.9 million votes to Dukakis's 41.8 million votes. In the Electoral College, Bush won 426 electoral votes to Dukakis's 111 electoral votes.

During Bush's conservative administration, Roybal and other liberal leaders in Congress continued to press for legislation that protected the poor, the elderly, and minorities. In the 101st Congress (1989–1990), Roybal played a key role in helping to pass legislation that reversed a 1989 Supreme Court decision permitting age-based discrimination in employee benefits. In the same Congress, Roybal pressed for legislation on health care issues. He was instrumental in renewing legislation for medical services to individuals with Alzheimer's disease. With the elderly population increasing, he understood how extremely important it was to the country to advance research to prevent and treat the disease.

The George H. W. Bush White House

President Bush's honeymoon with the U.S. Congress was short-lived. The previous eight years of Republican presidential leadership (which some called misleadership) had taken their toll on the tolerance of Democrats and others.

In March 1992, executive branch perks came up at a subcommittee hearing on General Government Appropriations. The subcommittee discussion, chaired by Roybal, included expenses for the executive residence. The issue of government perks had become a hot topic the previous summer when White House Chief of Staff John Sununu's extensive travels led to an investigation of government expenses. Roybal had asked the executive branch for information on all the free privileges extended at the White House, and their costs. With the nation in economic recession, public anger focused on Congress's perks—such as free mail, free health care, free travel, subsidized food, low-cost gyms and child care, free parking at the airport, and discount barber and gift shops. President Bush, in reaction, derisively referred to members of Congress as a "privileged class of rulers" and made similar attacks on Congress a cornerstone of his re-election campaign.

For more than half a century, part of the ethos of the Republican Party had been an intense and rabid anticommunism. During the Bush presidency, however, the communist bloc collapsed. After years of the United States funneling millions in assistance to the non-communist movement in Poland, a non-communist government came to power on September 12, 1989. During November 9–10, 1989, the Berlin Wall came down, and in mid-1991, the Soviet Union was dissolved. George H. W. Bush now faced a new world and a new set of quickly changing opportunities.

The fall of the Soviet Union left the United States as the sole superpower in the world. The first country to experience the United States' unconstrained unilateralism in the post–Cold War era was Panama. President Bush ordered the invasion of Panama in 1989, dubbed Operation Just Cause, in order to restore democracy there. It was the same type of intervention the United States had used throughout the twentieth century to make and undo presidents and leaders.[2] Bush built the case for the invasion on democracy, an incident in which U.S. servicemen and their wives had been disrespected, and that Panamanian leader Manuel Noriega was involved in drug running. Previously, Noriega had been a useful ally to the United States in the 1980s when revolutions swept through much of Central America.[3]

The 1991 U.S. military invasion of Iraq was a different matter. Iraq possessed the world's second-largest oil reserves and had long been a client state of the United States. The United States had provided Iraq's nationalist leader, Saddam Hussein, unconditional support with war material and weaponry for its war against Iran in the early 1980s. That war of attrition left more than a million dead and widespread economic and human devastation. On August 2, 1990, Iraq invaded a disputed area claimed by the oil-rich nation of Kuwait. Iraq also argued that Kuwait was undermining its economy by underpricing oil sales.

President Bush and Secretary of State James Baker organized a coalition (made up mostly of U.S. troops) and with the support of Congress and the United Nations launched the invasion of Iraq on January 16, 1991. However, despite the impressive show of U.S. power in the invasions of Panama and Iraq, President Bush's popularity was fleeting. At home, a growing national deficit, inflation, budget cuts, and high unemployment signaled re-election trouble.[4]

Congressman Roybal Retires

Ed Roybal had begun considering how he might leave Congress. It had occurred to him before, but now he was certain. He decided to not stand for re-election at the end of the 102nd Congress (1991–1993). He would not run in the 1992 federal elections. He was seventy-six years of age and wanted to retire for many reasons. He wanted to spend more time with his family, especially his wife. He knew and understood what happened when age took over. It was happening to him too.

"I had been in Congress long enough," Roybal said. His health was a consideration. He also wanted to participate in health and health education at a deeper level, and he needed time to explore. He said, "In particular, [then as now] health issues are important to me, especially in those centering on taking care of the senior citizens and how to interest more men and women in gerontology."[5]

He acknowledged that some issues and concerns would remain unattended upon his leaving office. "These are the things," he said, "that are important to me and we hope that we get more and more [still done] so that it becomes a real legacy that can be left behind. I don't think that I can say that I was most happy with anything in foreign policy because a great deal of it included violence and I'm against violence...One of the regrets is that I became ill. I wish I had been able to delay that a few more years."[6]

By the end of 1992, the wear and tear of responsibilities, a bi-coastal existence, marathon committee meetings, constituent issues, pressing policies, and maintenance of a public profile mixed with personal issues caught up with the congressman.[7]

The end of his public career marked the beginning of a long-overdue recognition of his many accomplishments. After the long march to gaining equitable political representation for Latinos, Roybal's retirement also marked the end of one pioneering era and the beginning of the next.[8] His daughter Lucille Roybal-Allard was of that new generation coming on the public scene.

Congressman Edward Roybal's first daughter, Lucille, was the only one of the Roybal children to run for office. She was elected to the California State Assembly in 1987. She won by a wide margin.[9] In the state legislature, she was a strong advocate for several issues, especially women's rights and environmental equity. She was very successful in leading a campaign against the location of a toxic waste incinerator in a low-income area within her district. Her energetic and inclusionary style reminded many of her father. Her leadership was commended by a number of diverse groups, including the California Sierra Club, which honored her with its first Legislative Environmental Achievement Award. The California chapter of the National Organization for Women (NOW) named her Legislator of the Year in 1991.

On Election Day, November 1992, the Democratic candidate, William Jefferson Clinton,[10] defeated George H. W. Bush in his bid for re-election. Clinton trounced Bush 43.3 million votes to 37.7 million. A third candidate, Ross Perot, had 19 million votes. It was the first time in 43 years that Edward Roybal had not been on any ballot for elected office.

Lucille Roybal-Allard ran in 1992 for the newly redrawn 33rd Congressional District, which stretched to the south of her father's old 30th Congressional District.

The 33rd Congressional District included Downtown Los Angeles, portions of Boyle Heights and East Los Angeles, and the southeastern communities, which included the cities of Commerce, Vernon, Huntington Park, Bell, Bell Gardens, South Gate, Cudahy, and Maywood. The district had the highest concentration of Latinos of any congressional district in the nation: 84 percent. Roybal-Allard had no major Latino opposition in the race. Among voters, 61 percent were registered as Democrats and 22 percent as Republicans. Roybal-Allard was elected in November 1992 and has since been re-elected several times.[11] Her newly reconstituted 40th Congressional District does not contain Boyle Heights and Downtown Los Angeles.

Edward Roybal served for forty-three years in public office—thirteen years in the Los Angeles City Council, between 1949 and 1962 and thirty years in the U.S. House of Representatives, from 1963 to 1993. For almost half a century he was an active member in the history-changing process that drives this country. He met with the powerful and the powerless, the famous and the infamous, the noble and the ignoble.

He could look back proudly to the distance Mexican and Latino communities had come. Mexicans and Latinos were significant voting blocs at the local and national level, and hundreds of Mexican and Latino-origin leaders had been elected to local, state, and federal offices. Organizations and groups that he had founded—the Mexican American Political Association (MAPA), the National Association of Latino Elected

Officials (NALEO), and the Congressional Hispanic Caucus—were educating, training, and mentoring a new generation of Mexican and Latino political leaders, as well as helping to provide their community with social justice and services.

Over the years, Edward R. Roybal received numerous awards and honors. Among them were two honorary doctorates of law, from Claremont Graduate School and Pacific States University. In 1973, Yale University honored him with a visiting Chubb Fellowship; and in 1976, the County of Los Angeles inaugurated the Edward R. Roybal Comprehensive Health Clinic in East Los Angeles. On January 8, 2001, President Bill Clinton presented him with the Presidential Citizens Medal. The Presidential Citizens Medal had been established by executive order in 1969 to recognize the exemplary service of U.S. citizens.

Transitioning from Public to Private Life

Upon his retirement, Congressman Roybal's service was further recognized with the establishment of the Edward R. Roybal Institute for Applied Gerontology at California State University, Los Angeles (CSULA). The mission statement came from Roybal himself. He stated, "Through caring for the elderly, we are rewarded with the joy of giving dignity, security and comfort to those who taught us the meaning of such things." He served for several years as president of the Edward R. Roybal Foundation, which is dedicated to provide scholarships and internships to students wanting to attend college in the field of health.

Both the University of Southern California (USC) and the University of California, Los Angeles (UCLA), the two most prestigious universities in the area, wanted to host the gerontology center. Roybal wanted the center located at an institution that was more accessible to the local community, with the type of ebb and flow that is difficult for elite institutions. California State University, Los Angeles, was selected on that basis. Besides, CSULA was closer to the district Roybal had represented.[12] It was near the heart of the Mexican community in East Los Angeles and Boyle Heights. Presently, the Edward R. Roybal Institute on Aging is located at the USC campus in the USC School of Social Work.

From 1998 to 2002, six Edward R. Roybal Centers for Research on Applied Gerontology were established throughout the United States. Their mission was to keep older people independent, active, and productive in later life. The centers were established to encourage the application of existing basic knowledge about cognitive and psychosocial changes with aging to a wide range of important practical problems facing older people. The Roybal Centers are funded by the Behavioral and Social Research Program at the National Institute on Aging at the National Institutes of Health. The centers are located at Boston University, Cornell University, the University of Alabama at Birmingham, the University of Illinois at Chicago, the University of Michigan, and the University of Miami.

On July 12, 1999, the Centers of Disease Control and Prevention (CDC) dedicated and named its main campus in Edward R. Roybal's honor and presented him with the center's most prestigious award, the Champion of Prevention Award. "All his life, no matter where or at what level he sat, Edward R. Roybal has made the public's health his personal and professional priority," said CDC Director Jeffrey P. Koplan at the ceremony. Roybal's leadership, he said, "has prevented the illness and death of many Americans."

Ed Roybal once said that he would like to be known simply as someone who provided opportunities for others. He especially wanted that legacy to be known for opportunities in health and education. That would satisfy him, he said, "because to me they are still the most important things." To be remembered as someone who cared for humanity was important to him. In fact, it was all connected. Public service through elected office was an outlet in which to express those problems and issues that were critically important, too important for a citizen to let stand. From this level of engagement came the satisfaction of knowing "when things are done to better the situation," Roybal said.[13] Now, his great satisfaction would come from being involved in a different way in health and education.

Congressman Roybal's retirement in 1993 marked the end of an era of those political leaders who were responsible for building today's Hispanic political tradition. Many of his contemporaries began to retire or pass away.

One of his contemporaries was the legendary union organizer Bert Corona, who had also been one of the co-founders of MAPA. A few years before Corona's death, Congressman Roybal reminisced about him, "He is a good union man and he does his job well...I would say he's a close friend of mine, yes."[14] Bert Corona died on January 15, 2001, at age eighty-two due to a series of ailments.

Many of the elected political leadership from Congressman Roybal's generation also disappeared from the scene during this time or even before. Senator Dennis Chavez of New Mexico died in 1962; U.S. Congressman Joseph Montoya of New Mexico, in 1978; and U.S. Congressman Henry B. Gonzalez of Texas, in 2000. Many leaders with whom Roybal had worked with as a councilman or congressman for civil rights and social justice had also succumbed. Saul Alinsky passed on in 1972; Carey McWilliams, in 1980; César Chávez, in 1993; and Anthony P. Rios, in 1999. The ranks of that generation were thinning. But their achievements endure.[15]

Roybal suffered a heart attack in 1998, and his wife also became ill. He died at the age of eighty-nine, at the Huntington Memorial Hospital in Pasadena, California, of respiratory failure after complications of pneumonia on October 24, 2005. His wake was held at Resurrection Church, one of the poorest parishes in Los Angeles. His funeral mass was held at the new Los Angeles cathedral, Our Lady of the Angels. He was buried in Calvary Cemetery, in the heart of East Los Angeles.

On March 25, 2008, the Los Angeles Unified School District's Board of Education voted to name Central Los Angeles High School #11 (formerly the Belmont Learning Center) as the Edward R. Roybal Learning Center. The school opened on September 3, 2008.

Ed Roybal's beloved wife, Lucille Beserra Roybal, passed away on Sunday, December 23, 2012, at approximately 3:00 a.m.. She died peacefully in her sleep, just two weeks before her ninety-sixth birthday. She was buried next to her husband in Calvary Cemetery.

Epilogue

It is often said that the past is prologue and that an epilogue is the summary of its many parts. When a person passes from the scene it is common for family and friends, peers and colleagues to find words to summarize the meaning of that person's life. It is also an attempt to understand the many parts of a man's life (especially one in the public limelight) and to come to terms with his death. While we mourn, we grapple with the absence of the man. We begin the healing, and from the pain comes at last the wisdom to endure.

As I attended the funeral at Resurrection Church in Boyle Heights, I saw the faces of Chicano, Black, White, and Asian people of the past and present. They were from labor, politics, the arts, education, and the law, and some were common people of the community who remembered Mr. Roybal from back when they were an invisible minority. They did not have clean and smooth faces; they did not wear three-piece suits or Rolex watches, nor did they look around to catch the eye of the media cameras or well-connected friends. I saw the history marked in their faces, the tribulations of daily life, the low-paying jobs, and the burdens of poverty. These common people remembered how far they had come in their history, and they remembered that Mr. Roybal had led them to a new place and time. They were no longer invisible but had agency born of their own history. At the rosary and at the funeral mass the next day, they came by the thousands to walk the last mile with Mr. Roybal to his final resting place in the heart of his old council district where it had all begun.

They all came, the high and the low, to pay their respects and to mourn the passing of part of what they knew about the man. His family was there, his beloved wife, Lucille, who with extraordinary reserves of discipline and strength manifesting spoke eloquently of the man she had loved forever. His children attended, Ed Jr., Lillian Roybal Rose, and Congresswoman Lucille Roybal-Allard, as did their children, and cousins, extended family, and friends. At the funeral, Edward Roybal Jr. spoke about his father's legacy: "I don't think the political legacy has been recognized or appreciated. I don't think most Chicanos, let alone most Anglos, have any information about what things were like fifty, sixty years ago and how things have changed. The level of struggle that it took to get to where we are now."[1] When asked about what he respected about his father and mother, he commented, "Certainly, a great sense of pride and integrity. A certain passion and commitment."[2]

I recalled the years of research I had spent on the life of Mr. Roybal. I remembered at the conclusion of my long interview with him that, regarding the assignment to write the book, that he had said he could not tell me his entire life story or its meaning. That, he said, I had to look for. It was a daunting prospect then, even with the resources of Harvard University at my command at that time. However, I had set out into that journey of discovery about the man and determined to finish it.

Colleagues and scholars provided some of the meaning of the man and of his legacy. His former chief of staff, Henry Lozano, commented about Congressman Roybal's legacy, "I believe he was probably the first coalition builder in Los Angeles. I mean there's one thing in terms of building coalitions, not only in terms of getting himself elected but getting other Latinos elected that is also being in the forefront...So I guess he's leaving a great legacy we can be proud of."[3]

According to Henry Lozano, Congressman Roybal's longevity as an elected political leader was easily explainable: "Well, he was very astute politically. He never put on airs about who he was and stuff like that, just a common respect. He had respect for other people. People respected him. I think that's probably the key word, *respect*. Integrity, but respect overall; no question he had integrity, and he respected other people's views and opinions. Even though he may have disagreed many times, he respected that person's right to say it." Lozano added another factor that earned Roybal widespread support among working-class people and laborers: "It was always there. He was always a strong labor vote."

Former MALDEF president and general counsel Antonia Hernández stated, "Mr. Roybal's legacy will be, I think, three-fold. First, the pioneer. He opened the door for a lot of us and set an example. Secondly, his legacy would be one of a very ethical, humane individual. The third legacy is that he's going to be a legacy not just for the Latino community. If you talk to people, and just to use the issue of AIDS but there's a lot of other issues, he was ahead of getting money to look into this awful disease way before anyone."[4]

Political scientist James Regalado commented on Congressman Roybal's legacy, "I think it's already here. He is the dean of Latino politics in the Southwest and more specifically in California, and by deed he seemed to be the first one, the pathfinder, the symbolic first, and so he has almost regal status in terms of his legacy. It's already a legacy. He stayed his guns. He took on the city council. He saw death threats. He was called a communist, but he stood tall. And I think standing tall was very much part of his legacy in that very, very difficult time."[5] Professor Rodolfo Acuña offered his acknowledgement of Edward R. Roybal in the history of Mexican Americans: "Eddie Roybal is the first person in the modern era that Latinos have who was a hero."[6]

In the expanding literature of the Mexican American experience, Edward R. Roybal is recognized and acknowledged as one of the most important and unique leaders in the struggle for the political empowerment of Mexican people. Ignacio M. Garcia noted, "While ethnic solidarity had always been part of electoral rhetoric in the barrios of

Southern California, the CSO under Roybal's leadership, created an ethnic agenda that identified 'Mexican' issues. This meant that Mexican American candidates could not simply request support because of their personal ethnicity; they now had to promote a Mexican American agenda. This strategy sought to eliminate barrio opportunists and those who were political lackeys of Anglo American power brokers."[7]

Politics have changed significantly since Congressman Roybal served, especially the role of special interests. Henry Lozano commented on this issue, "I think that if you look at it they're probably more pronounced. I don't think you'll ever take them out completely because they fuel all the money to fuel political gain. I think the ones that have made out the most are political consultants. They have more competitive races than ever before. That's full employment for consultants, political consultants. There's a lot more polling done now. Every race you can think of, there's a poll. They predict more or less the outcome of the race often times just by spending some money on polling. Campaigns are more expensive." In reference to the new Mexican American political leadership, Antonia Hernández commented, "It's the people we fought to get into the best colleges and universities who have gotten their education, who have come out and are devoting their life to public interest. In Xavier Becerra, I see Mr. Roybal. I can say the same thing with Ciro Rodriguez in Texas. Henry B. Gonzalez, his son took over his congressional district. Gutierrez, out of Chicago, is young, just got elected in 1992. Mr. Roybal paved the way. I don't want to mislead you to think that all of our elected officials are glorious and ethical and clean and share the values that Mr. Roybal had, however."

Congressman Roybal's long tenure in Congress was the subject of much admiration, especially in light of the multiethnicity of his congressional district. Henry Lozano commented, "Again, because he took care of business in terms of constituent problems, you know, issues and stuff like that from the Asian community, he took very good care of them, Little Tokyo, Chinatown were in his district. He had very, very strong support there and in Washington; look into his record and how he voted on issues affecting those folks. He was right on top of the issue, and again we go back to respect. He respected them, they respected him." Jorge Lambrinos recalled, "For the most part, Mr. Roybal's campaigns were low-key. He was at a couple of fundraisers in the park and he never raised a lot of monies for a lot of his campaigns, so they were pretty much low-key events. Even when he had opposition, once or twice there was a potential for a strong candidate. The feeling was that these individuals were not going to be a major threat. That's also one of the considerations that they take when they select members to be on the Appropriations Committee. They want to ensure that members that are on the Appropriations Committee are coming from safe districts. Whether it be Republican or Democrat because they want to make sure that these people stay on."

However, even the words of colleagues and scholars could not capture the full measure of the man.

At the rosary and the funeral, I remembered the recollections of his surviving brothers and sister and other relatives. I imagined the young Ed Roybal, fighting for a place to belong in Boyle Heights, fresh from New Mexico. I remembered Roybal the fighter and recollected Mr. Roybal reminiscing happily about his boxing days, complete with his fighter's stand and jab. From that same clay of a fighter had evolved the adolescent who protested before the city council the "Mexican night" at the park; the young man who traveled to UCLA and worked at several jobs during the Great Depression; the health care worker with the TB Unit who witnessed the deprivations of the poor; the young man who ran for the Los Angeles City Council and won, changing the way business was done in the "good ole boy" network; and the solitary congressman who educated an entire nation about the "sleeping giant," the segregation of Brown and mestizo people, bilingual education, the disproportionate rate of Chicano casualties in the Vietnam War, police brutality, Alzheimer's disease, AIDS, and the plight of seniors and who expanded the debate about race and ethnicity beyond Black and White. They say that fighters think with their hearts. Mr. Roybal was like that, but he also used his mind and repaired the social fabric that too often left many to fall through where it was frayed: the poor, people of color, aged, and disabled.

His efforts to build the first grassroots and multiethnic coalition in Los Angeles politics was unprecedented and even since his retirement in 1992 have continued to impact how politics are conducted. Edward Roybal epitomized the hopes and dreams of the Mexican American generation during pivotal periods in contemporary history, the Great Depression, World War II, the Cold War, the civil rights movement, the Chicano Movement, and the post–Cold War transition and the mentoring of another generation of political leadership.

In this long journey to find the man and the meaning of his life, through research and writing this book, I encountered a host of challenges and adversities. I would like to thank the many people who contributed in every conceivable manner, in good times and bad times. Finally, I wish to humbly thank Mr. Roybal, for asking me to seek his life and meaning as I saw it, and for having seen the heart in me able to do so.

Notes

Prologue

1. Movimiento Estudiantil Chicano de Aztlán (MEChA) is a student organization that promotes higher education, culture, and history.

Chapter 1

1. U.S. Census data show that in 1910, Texas had 125,016 Mexican-born people; in 1920, 251,827; and in 1930, 262,672. California in 1910 had 33,694 Mexican-born people; in 1920, 88,771; and in 1930, 191,346. New Mexico appears to have been only the fifth point of destination for Mexican immigrants. In 1910, New Mexico had 11,918 Mexico-born people; in 1920, 20,272; and in 1930, 15,983.

2. In the farmlands, labor was in short supply due in part to legislation that curtailed imported labor: Japanese (the Gentlemen's Agreement of 1907 with Japan); Chinese (Chinese Exclusion Act of 1882); and Europeans (the Immigration Acts of 1917, 1921, and 1924). The outbreak of World War I in 1914 increased the labor shortage when young men left the farms for the army.

3. Lillian Roybal Rose, author interview, April 29, 2005.

4. Evelyn Verdugo, author interview, September 23, 2006.

5. Edward R. Roybal (United States Representative, 30th District of California 1963–1975 and 25th District of California 1975–1993), author interview, July 28, 1999.

6. Louis Roybal, author interview, September 23, 2006.

7. Irma Núñez, author interview, September 23, 2006.

8. The mutualistas were benevolent organizations, which helped community members as a clearinghouse for employment, housing, funeral arrangements, medical assistance, legal aid, and as an institutional buffer that eased the transition for past and new immigrant arrivals to the United States. They were also instrumental in replicating Mexican cultural traditions such as celebration of Cinco de Mayo and Mexican Independence Day (September 15th). Membership was voluntary. For example, one of these mutualistas was the Liga Protectiva, which was founded in Phoenix, Arizona, in 1914 and by 1919, had founded chapters in New Mexico. One important religious organization, especially in New Mexico, was the Penitentes, founded in the 1880s.

9. Elsie Roybal Wilder, author interview, September 23, 2006.

10. Joseph C. Tardiff and L. Mypho Mahunda, eds. *Dictionary of Hispanic Biography* (Detroit, MI: Gale Research, Inc., 1996), 780.

11. Tardiff and Mahunda, 780.

12. Esteban Torres (United States Representative, 34th District of California 1983–1998), author interview, March 20, 2007.

13. Ruth Finney, "A Backer for Valle Grande," *Los Angeles Times*, February 27, 1963. The most important nonagricultural employer of Mexicans during the early 20th century was the railroads. During the 1920s, Mexicans became a significant workforce on the western railroad system. The Union Pacific; Southern Pacific; Atchison, Topeka, and Santa Fe; Western Pacific; Colorado and Southern; and Denver and Rio Grande provided employment to between 32,000 and 42,000 track workers, who made up 75% of the total workforce. Railroads were ecstatic with the efficiency and cheap cost of Mexican railroad workers. For example, R. A. Rutledge, chief engineer of the Santa Fe, commented on one occasion, "The Mexican cannot be driven like the Negro, but anyone who knows how to manage the Mexicans can get more work out of them than any other class." Railroads generally paid Mexicans the lowest industrial wages, from

$0.35 to $0.39 an hour. The packinghouses paid between $0.45 to $0.47 an hour, while the steel mills paid $0.45 to $0.50 for eight hours or $0.44 for 10 hours. Mexicans were excluded from the building trades by unions who demanded citizenship for membership. The American Federation of Railroad Workers did not employ a single Mexican tradesman. Organized labor itself often stereotyped Mexicans as lowering wages, and people of other ethnicities were antagonistic towards them. Often, these tensions would carry over into the streets and the neighborhoods.

14. Rodolfo F. Acuña, *Occupied America: A History of Chicanos*, 3rd ed. (New York: Harper & Row), 178–190. For example, during 1919–1920 and 1920–1921, the Arizona Growers Association spent some $325,000 in recruiting and in 1920 there was a heavier importation of Mexican laborers. The transporting of Mexicans to cotton areas was carried out by train. Then, suddenly, in early 1921, the bottom fell out of the economy, and a subsequent depression brought heavy unemployment. Mexican labor was caught in a dilemma. In times of prosperity, their numbers aroused hostility, and in times of bust, they became convenient scapegoats of the failure of the national economy. Some nativists wanted to include Mexicans in the Immigration Act of 1921, but the railroads and agribusiness were too heavily dependent on cheap Mexican workers. In New Mexico and elsewhere, a series of mass deportations of Mexican workers and labor strikes followed.

15. Evelyn Verdugo, author interview, September 23, 2006.

16. Most of the Mexican population of Los Angeles, which had settled around La Placita (the original site of the city's founding in 1781), was pushed eastward in the direction of the Los Angeles River. The area east of La Placita and the river became known as Sonoratown or the Cornfield. Later, Mexicans were pushed farther, across the river, where there were no city services (such as water, sanitation, electricity, and gas) and few improved roads. The largest concentration of Mexicans

resided in this section of town and later, the numbers increased with other recently arrived immigrants who went to East Los Angeles.

17. *Fortnight Magazine*, October 24, 1954, 21.

18. Until the late 1800s, the district was a dairy center and had vineyards growing. Andrew Boyle became its largest landowner when he bought the plot known as Old Mission Vineyard. Boyle's son-in-law, William H. Workman (later a Los Angeles mayor), subdivided the land into lots, from which the name "Boyle Heights" sprang. At the turn of the century, Armenians, Molokan and Orthodox Russians, Jews, Italians, and Eastern European immigrants settled in the area. Later, African Americans occupied the margins of Boyle Heights, and Asians (mostly Japanese) had a community presence. Ethnic interaction, intermingling, and fusion were mainly at a low level.

19. Katherine Underwood, "Process and Politics: Multiracial Electoral Coalition Building and Representation in Los Angeles' 9th District, 1949–1962" (Ph.D. dissertation, University of California, San Diego, 1992), 56.

20. Underwood, "Process and Politics," 58.

21. Edward R. Roybal, author interview, July 28, 1999.

22. In 1924 for example, 64 schools in eight counties reported their ethnic makeup as between 90 and 100% Mexican. In 1931, another study found that 80% of school districts with significant Mexican American enrollments practiced segregation. In Los Angeles, as with other districts with large Mexican enrollment, the attendance zones were manipulated by officials in order to make sure that Mexicans went to separate schools. This de facto segregation was until 1935 imposed by a long-standing state educational code, which permitted the segregation of Mexicans (defined as part Native American), Chinese, Japanese, and Mongolian students.

23. George Sanchez, *Becoming Mexican American: Ethnicity, Culture, and Identity in Chicano Los Angeles, 1900–1945.* (New York: Oxford University Press, 1993), 258–259.

24. Edward R. Roybal, author interview, July 28, 1999.

25. Edward R. Roybal, author interview, July 28, 1999.

26. Edward R. Roybal, author interview, July 28, 1999.

27. Edward R. Roybal, author interview, July 28, 1999.

28. Edward R. Roybal, author interview, July 28, 1999.

29. Elsie Roybal Wilder and Louis Roybal, author interview, September 23, 2006.

30. Elsie Roybal Wilder, author interview, September 23, 2006.

31. Elsie Roybal Wilder, author interview, September 23, 2006.

32. Elsie Roybal Wilder, author interview, September 23, 2006.

33. Elsie Roybal Wilder, author interview, September 23, 2006.

34. Evelyn Roybal Verdugo, author interview, September 23, 2006.

35. Louis Roybal, author interview, September 23, 2006.

36. Lucille Roybal-Allard (United States Representative, 40th District of California), author interview, April 29, 2005.

37. Ernesto Galarza, "Life in the United States for Mexican People: Out of the Experience of a Mexican" (proceedings of the 1929 National Conference of Social Work, Chicago: University of Chicago Press, 1930), 402.

38. The zoot suit's origins have been disputed and have been attributed either to the African American jazz musicians or to Clark Gable's alternately hot-and-cool Rhett Butler character in the 1939 film *Gone with the Wind*, who wore a proto–zoot suit in the second half of the film.

39. Octavio Paz, *The Labyrinth of Solitude: Life and Thought in Mexico* (New York: Grove Press, 1950), 13. The noted Mexican writer Octavio Paz, who spent two years living in Los Angeles during the mid-1940s wrote of the zoot suiters, "They have lived in the city for many years, wearing the same clothes and speaking the same language as the other inhabitants, and they feel ashamed of their origin, yet not one would mistake them for authentic North Americans…What distinguishes them, I think is their furtive, restless air, they act like people wearing

disguises, who are afraid of a stranger's look because it could strip them and leave them naked."

40. Elsie Roybal Wilder and Louis Roybal, author interview, September 23, 2006.

41. Edward R. Roybal, author interview, July 28, 1999.

42. The ordeal of the Okies caught the sympathy of the nation. This was partly due to the fact that they were White, in contrast to the Mexican and (and to a lesser degree, Filipino) migrant workers who were the backbone of the agricultural industry in the Southwest, and to the fact that the Okies traveled in family groups.

43. Acuña, *Occupied America*, 202.

44. George J. Sanchez, *Becoming Mexican American: Ethnicity, Culture, and Identity in Chicano Los Angeles, 1900–1945* (New York: Oxford University Press), 223–224.

45. Esteban Torres, author interview, March 20, 2007.

46. Edward R. Roybal, author interview, July 28, 1999.

47. Elsie Roybal Wilder, author interview, September 23, 2006.

48. Edward R. Roybal, author interview, July 28, 1999.

49. Louis Roybal, author interview, September 23, 2006.

50. Sanchez, *Becoming Mexican American*, 225.

51. Edward R. Roybal, author interview, July 28, 1999.

52. Elsie Wilder Roybal and Louis Roybal, author interview, September 23, 2006.

53. The CCC was under the U.S. Army's control. Camp commanders possessed disciplinary powers and corpsmen were required to address their superiors as "sir." By September 1935, more than 500,000 youth had lived in CCC camps, many of them staying from six months to a year. The workforce focused on reforestation and soil conservation. They also dug canals and ditches, built more than 30,000 wildlife shelters, restored historic battlefields, stocked rivers and lakes with almost a billion fish, and cleared campgrounds and beaches. The CCC was supposed to operate under a nondiscriminatory policy.

Although there was rigid segregation and hiring quotas, especially in the South, Blacks made up some 10% of the workforce by 1936. Mexican American and Native American youth also benefited from the CCC, although not as much as Blacks. The CCC employed young men between the ages of 17 and 23 years. An enrollee was paid $30 a month, of which $25 were sent to the enrollee's family. By the end of the CCC in 1942, almost 3 million young men had participated in the CCC. For the army, the experience in managing such a large labor force and the paramilitary discipline learned by corpsmen provided preparation for the massive call-up of civilians in World War II. For the young men who participated, they benefited in terms of better health and economic standing. Equally important in their experience was that of realizing the power and efficiency of the federal government and its active compassion for victims of the Great Depression.

54. Individual Record, Civilian Conservation Corps, Serial number CC9-178708 and Certificate of Discharge from Civilian Conservation Corps, Edward R. Roybal; National Archives, College Park, MD.

55. Edward R. Roybal, author interview, July 28, 1999.

56. Lillian Roybal Rose, author interview, April 29, 2005.

57. Luis Angel Firpo (1894–1960) was a legendary Argentine heavyweight boxing contender who almost beat heavyweight champion Jack Dempsey in 1923. Known as the Wild Bull of the Pampas, he amassed thirty-one wins, seven ties, and four losses in a career that lasted from 1917–1936.

58. Joe Louis (1914–1981) is considered by many to be the greatest heavyweight champion of all time. During a boxing career that spanned from 1934 to 1951 he won 68 fights, lost 3, and had 54 knockouts. He held the heavyweight title for almost 12 years and had a record 25 successful title defenses.

59. Ramon Novarro was born Ramon Samaniegos, in Durango, Mexico, in 1899. He was a second cousin of Dolores Del Rio, who achieved

Hollywood stardom in the mid-1920s. Navarro's rags-to-riches experience took him through the entertainment industry's ranks. He began in 1917 as a dancer, film extra, and bit actor until his breakthrough came in 1922 when he portrayed the villain in *The Prisoner of Zenda*. Ramon Novarro was the first Latino film star in Hollywood to also direct, produce, and script films. He was arguably for a decade (1924 to 1934) the biggest movie star in the world. He was, all the while, very active in fundraising to help those being repatriated to Mexico, while contributing to the Mexican community through charities and scholarships. He remained active in these pursuits until his death in 1968.

60. Edward R. Roybal, author interview, July 28, 1999.

61. Dolores Del Rio (1905–1983) was born in Durango, Mexico, and was the second cousin of Ramon Novarro. She was the first Mexican female star in U.S. cinema beginning in 1926 until 1942, when she began a second career in Mexican films. Although a breathtaking beauty, she became a versatile actress in comedy, drama, and musicals in cinema as well as in theater. For more information on the history of Latinos in U.S. cinema, see Frank Javier Garcia Berumen, *Brown Celluloid: Latino/a Film Icons and Images in the Hollywood Film Industry, Volume I (1894–1959)* (New York: Vantage Press, 2003).

62. Lupe Velez (1908–1944) was born in Mexico and became the second Mexican female star in Hollywood films, beginning in 1927. She excelled especially in comedy and was the first Latina to star in her own film series, *The Mexican Spitfire*. She committed suicide on December 14, 1944, after a broken romantic relationship.

63. Gilbert Roland (1905–1994) was born Luis Damasio Alonso in Chihuahua, Mexico. He became the second Mexican male star in Hollywood films, beginning in 1927. He played romantic lovers, villains, the Cisco Kid (in six films), and character roles in film and television until his death of cancer on May 16, 1994.

64. Jose Mojica (1896–1974) was born in Jalisco, Mexico. A tenor, he was under exclusive contract with the Chicago Opera between 1921 and

1930. He made 14 Spanish-language Hollywood films between 1929 and 1935. In 1942, after making a few more Mexican films, he retired for the priesthood. He died of hepatitis on September 20, 1974.

65. Lupita Tovar (b. 1911) was born in Mexico and began in Hollywood films in 1928. She played in every type of film venue: both English-language and Spanish-language films, westerns, Mexican films, and British films. She starred in the first Mexican talking film, *Santa*, in 1931. She retired in 1945 to be with her family. She is the mother of actress Susan Kohner and producer Pancho Kohner. Her grandchildren are directors, producers, and screenwriters.

66. Sanchez, *Becoming Mexican American*, 180.

67. Sanchez, *Becoming Mexican American*, 179.

68. Sanchez, *Becoming Mexican American*, 185–188.

69. Robert Emmet Lucey (1891–1977) was born in Los Angeles, California, on March 16, 1891. He was ordained as a priest in 1916 and spent the next 18 years working in the Archdiocese of Los Angeles. He served as director of Catholic Charities, as director of Catholic hospitals, as president of the Catholic Conference of Social Work, and as a member of the California State Department of Social Welfare. He was consecrated bishop in 1934 and began programs to educate the laity in social activism and in forming social-activist organizations. He was appointed archbishop of San Antonio, Texas, from 1940 to 1969. He became the chairman of the Bishop's Committee for the Spanish-Speaking, which integrated all Catholic schools under his jurisdiction, and continued to work for social change. He died on August 1, 1977.

70. The Catholic Church subsequently established settlement house and recreational centers. In 1922, Father Lucey received permission to establish the Confraternity of Christian Doctrine (CCD), an organization of lay volunteers to instruct Catholic children attending public schools. The center was located in a movie theater on the corner of Riggin and Mariana Streets, between Boyle Heights and East

Los Angeles proper. In the 1930s, the Catholic Church continued to build its outreach to the Mexican community through the many churches and parochial schools, especially in East Los Angeles.

71. Lucille Roybal-Allard, author interview, April 29, 2005.
72. Elsie Roybal Wilder, author interview, September 23, 2006.
73. Elsie Roybal Wilder, author interview, September 23, 2006.

Chapter 2

1. Edward R. Roybal (United States Representative, 30th District of California 1963–1975 and 25th District of California 1975–1993), author interview, July 28, 1999.
2. Mario T. Garcia, *Memories of Chicano History: The Life and Times of Bert Corona.* (Berkeley: University of California Press, 1994), 77–78. Corona, who arrived in L.A. from El Paso, Texas in 1936, lived with an aunt and her husband on Echandia and Brooklyn Streets in Boyle Heights. It is not unlikely he ran across the young Ed Roybal in the neighborhood at some point and that the lifelong friendship between these two dynamic young men began there.
3. Richard A. Donovan, "Roybal Rouses the Ninth: A Los Angeles Mexican-American District Learns How to Make Its Political Voice Heard," *Reporter* (January 17, 1950), 8.
4. Edward R. Roybal, author interview, July 28, 1999.
5. Elsie Roybal Wilder, author interview, September 23, 2006.
6. Elsie Roybal Wilder, author interview, September 23, 2006.
7. Lucille's parents both died of heart attack, her mother in 1954 at the age of 75 and her father in 1958 at the age of 78.
8. The Casa Lopez in Old Town San Diego is named for Lucille Beserra Roybal's ancestors.
9. Matthew Brown, later Matias Moreno, married Dolores Carrillo, whose cousin was film actor Leo Carrillo.
10. Irma Núñez, author interview, December 10, 1999.
11. "Part 2: The Struggle in the Fields," *Chicano!; the History of the*

Mexican-American Civil Rights Movement. DVD documentary, National Latino Communications Center, 1996.

12. Lucille Roybal went on to graduate from California State University, Los Angeles. She worked in the field of public relations and as a fund raising executive for the United Way. In 1986, she was elected to the California State Assembly by a wide margin. She served for three terms.

13. Juan Gomez-Quinones, *Roots of Chicano Politics, 1600–1940* (Albuquerque: University of New Mexico Press, 1994), 400.

14. Robin F. Scott, "The Mexican-American in the Los Angeles Area, 1920–1950: From Acquiescence to Activity." (Ph.D. dissertation, University of Southern California, 1971), 156, 195, 256, 261.

15. Alonso Perales, *Are We A Good Neighbor?* (New York: Arno Press, 1974), 79.

16. Rodolfo F. Acuña, *Occupied America: A History of Chicanos*, 3rd ed. (New York: Harper & Row), 260.

17. Richard Griswold del Castillo and Arnoldo De Leon, *North to Aztlán: A History of Mexican Americans in the United States* (New York: Twayne Publishers, 1997), 102–103.

18. Under the terms of the Bracero Program, transportation, housing, and wages ($0.30 an hour minimum) were regulated. The law provided an exemption from military service, a condition that foreign workers would not displace domestic workers, and a prohibition of racial and ethnic discrimination against migrant workers. Many growers did not like the concessions, as they were accustomed to having a free hand in exploiting cheap Mexican labor, but they acquiesced, given the labor shortages and the war conditions. Under the program, some 220,000 braceros worked in the United States between 1942 and 1947. In rural Texas, notorious for racial discrimination, Mexicans were not permitted onto the farms as braceros until October 1947.

19. Griswold del Castillo and De Leon, *North to Aztlán*, 85.

20. Arthur F. Corwin, ed. *Immigrants and Immigrants: Perspectives on Mexican Labor Migration to the United States (Contributions in*

Economics and Economic History) (Westport, CT: Greenwood Press, 1978), 117.

21. Acuña, *Occupied America*, 261.

22. Elsie Roybal Wilder, author interview, September 23, 2006.

23. Evelyn Verdugo, author interview, September 23, 2006.

24. Lillian Roybal Rose, author interview, July 28, 1999. Lillian, one of Roybal's daughters, said, "I can't remember the time exactly, where there was a community meeting in East Los Angeles, in Boyle Heights, and I remember an elder Japanese man stood up and recounted a story that had happened years prior…before my father was in politics. This older Japanese man, who is gone by now, recounted that story to this meeting and thanked my father for the stand that he took."

25. Ronald Takaki, *Strangers from a Different Shore: A History of Asian Americans* (New York: Penguin Books, 1987), 400–402. Two-thirds of all Japanese people were not immigrants but had been born in the United States. Thousands of these U.S.-born Japanese, known as *Nisei*, joined the armed forces and eventually saw action in the European theater. Most of them fought in the 100th Battalion and 442nd Regimental Combat Team. They earned some 18,143 individual military decorations, which included 1 Congressional Medal of Honor, 350 Silver Stars, 47 Distinguished Service Crosses, 810 Bronze Stars, and more than 3,600 Purple Hearts.

26. After the war, the Japanese American Citizens' League (JACL) continued to litigate for compensation. In 1965, Congress authorized a compensation of $38 million, which was actually less than a 10th of their actual losses.

27. "Sleepy Lagoon" was also the title of a popular song recorded earlier in 1942 by big band leader Harry James.

28. Acuña, *Occupied America*, 255.

29. Carey McWilliams (1905–1980) was a lifelong progressive and activist lawyer and writer. In 1955, he became the editor of the journal

The Nation. In 1949, he wrote one of the earliest and most highly respected books on Mexican Americans, *North from Mexico: The Spanish-Speaking People of the United States.*

30. Acuña, *Occupied America*, 256.

31. In the late 1970s, Chicano playwright Luis Valdez wrote, produced, and directed a popular play entitled *Zoot Suit*, which chronicled the events of the Sleepy Lagoon case and the subsequent Zoot Suit Riots. The play was made into a film in 1981 and is available on both video and DVD.

32. Acuña, *Occupied America*, 259.

33. The FBI report was entitled "Racial Conditions (Spanish-Mexican Activities in Los Angeles Field Office Division)," Acuña, *Occupied America*, 261.

Chapter 3

1. Rita Hayworth (1918–1987) was born Rita Cansino to members of a Spanish dance team in New York City. She was a singer and dancer from an early age. Beginning in Hollywood films in 1935, she rose to become a legendary sex symbol, as well as an excellent actress in varied drama, comedy, and musical roles. She died of Alzheimer's disease on May 14, 1987.

2. Maria Montez (1920–1951) was born in the Dominican Republic. During the 1940s, the striking beauty became a popular star in a series of Technicolor costume films for Universal Studios. In the late 1940s, she left to make films in Europe after her studio refused to give her an opportunity to play more varied roles. She died of a heart attack at the age of 31 a few days after Universal beckoned her to return.

3. Ramon Novarro was semiretired by now, and his second cousin Dolores Del Rio began a film career in Mexico after 1942. Jose Mojica joined the priesthood. Lupe Velez committed suicide in 1944. Only Gilbert Roland and Lupita Tovar continued from the first group.

In the early 1940s, a new galaxy of Mexican and Latino film stars appeared on the screen.

4. Anthony Quinn (1915–2002) was born Antonio Oaxaca Quinn in Chihuahua, Mexico, to a Tarahumara Indian mother. His grandfather was Irish. He moved to the United States when he was an adolescent and grew up in Boyle Heights. He broke into films in 1936 and became a major film star in the early 1950s. He was the first Mexican actor to win an Academy Award (Best Supporting Actor for *Viva Zapata!* in 1951). He won a second Best Supporting Actor Academy Award, in 1956 for *Lust for Life,* and thereafter was nominated several more times. A prolific and legendary life force, he also acted in the theater, sculpted, and wrote two autobiographies.

5. Tito Guizar (1908–1999) was born in Guadalajara, Mexico. He was already established in his native country as an actor and singer when he made his Hollywood film debut in 1935. After the late 1940s, he worked for the most part in Mexico.

6. Arturo de Cordova (1908–1973) began as a journalist and radio broadcaster. He broke into films in 1935 and soon became a romantic and dramatic leading man. He starred in 10 Hollywood films between 1940 and 1949.

7. Ricardo Montalban (b. 1920) made his Mexican film debut in 1941 and soon became a romantic leading man. In 1944, MGM Studios brought him in as their resident Latin lover. Later, the versatile actor branched out into film, theater, and television roles. In the 1960s, he co-founded Nosotros, an organization dedicated to eradicating Latino stereotypes and creating better opportunities for Latino talent.

8. Hector Lopez Garcia (1914–1996) obtained his medical degree at the University of Texas School of Medicine in 1939. He volunteered during World War II, serving in the infantry, with the engineers, and in the Medical Corps as a combat surgeon. Returning home, he practiced family medicine in Corpus Christi, Texas, and also worked

with veterans at the local Veterans Administration (VA) facility. There he soon saw how discrimination toward Mexican American veterans was playing out. The refusal of the Three Rivers, Texas, mortuary to bury Mexican American war hero Felix Longoria in the town cemetery led to his involvement in the widespread protest and the founding of the GI Forum. He was increasingly drawn to the political arena and the struggle for the civil rights of Mexican Americans. He was an active member of the Viva Kennedy Clubs in the early 1960s and was appointed to the U.S. Commission on Civil Rights by President Johnson. In 1984, he was awarded the Presidential Medal of Freedom by President Reagan. He continued with his private medical practice until his 70s. He suffered with cancer for more than a decade towards the end of his life. He died in July 1996 from pneumonia and congestive heart failure.

9. Edward R. Roybal (United States Representative, 30th District of California 1963–1975 and 25th District of California 1975–1993), author interview, June 30, 1999.

10. Edward R. Roybal, author interview, June 30, 1999.

11. Edward R. Roybal, author interview, June 30, 1999.

12. Edward R. Roybal, author interview, June 30, 1999.

13. Edward R. Roybal, author interview, June 30, 1999.

14. The Hollywood Ten, a group of uncooperative film directors and screenwriters, were blacklisted and sentenced to prison for contempt of Congress. In 1951, a second wave of HUAC hearings began when Missouri senator Joseph McCarthy began demanding the "naming of names." It created a Mexican community that was constantly under suspicion. These were often people who organized or participated in organizations for social justice, civil rights, and collective bargaining rights for labor. They came under severe scrutiny, surveillance, and red-baiting suspicion. These circumstances were even more difficult for people of color in the entertainment industry or writers and social critics pursuing social justice and equality. Hundreds of writers,

union organizers, actors, screenwriters, film directors, and ordinary citizens were blacklisted or gray listed, deemed suspect and unemployable.

15. Edward R. Roybal, author interview, June 30, 1999.

16. Mario T. Garcia. *Memories of Chicano History: The Life and Narrative of Bert Corona* (Berkeley: University of California Press, 1994), 155–156.

17. Sanford D. Horwitt, *Let Them Call Me Rebel: Saul Alinsky, His Life and Legacy* (New York: Alfred A. Knopf, 1989).

18. *Fortnight Magazine*, August 18, 1954, 9.

19. Edward R. Roybal, author interview, July 30, 1999.

20. Maria Linda Apodaca, "They Kept the Home Fires Burning: Mexican-American Women and Social Change" (Ph.D. dissertation, University of California, Irvine, 1994), 73.

21. Parley P. Christensen was born on July 19, 1869, in Weston, Idaho, and moved to Newton, Utah, as a child. He became a schoolteacher and principal in several schools in Murray and Grantsville. In 1895, he graduated from Cornell University Law School, practiced law in Salt Lake County, and then was elected Salt Lake County City Attorney in 1900. He died in Los Angeles, on February 10, 1954.

22. Katherine Underwood, "Process and Politics: Multiracial Electoral Coalition Building and Representation in Los Angeles' 9th District, 1949–1962" (Ph.D. dissertation, University of California, San Diego, 1992), 96.

23. Anthony P. Rios (1914–1999) was better known as Tony Rios. He was one of the co-founders of the Community Service Organization (CSO) in 1947. He was born in Calexico, California, and moved to Los Angeles in the 1930s. He began as a farm worker organizer and later was a community organizer. He believed in using the ballot to evolve what he termed "barrio power" in order to obtain Raza rights. He weathered gracefully the coming of the Chicano generation but cautioned confrontational activists that organizing barrio power was

a long, patient, and arduous endeavor. Although involved in many causes and Mexican-American organizations, his political devotion remained to the very end with the CSO.

24. *La Opinion*, April 1, 1947, 8.

25. Richard A. Donovan, "Roybal Rouses the Ninth: A Los Angeles Mexican-American District Learns How to Make Its Political Voice Heard," *The Reporter* (January 17, 1950), 7–9.

26. Underwood, "Process and Politics."

27. Donavan, "Roybal Rouses the Ninth," 7–9.

28. Saul David Alinsky (January 30, 1909–June 12, 1972) was born in Chicago, Illinois, of Russian Jewish immigrant parents. He came to prominence organizing the Back of the Yards neighborhood in Chicago and laid the foundation for modern political grass roots, or community, organizing. His key books include *Reveille for Radicals* (1946) and *Rules for Radicals* (1971).

29. Horwitt, *Let Them Call Me Rebel*.

30. Horwitt, *Let Them Call Me Rebel*, 228.

31. Underwood, "Process and Politics," 98.

32. Edward R. Roybal, author interview, July 30, 1999.

33. Beatrice W. Griffith, "Viva Roybal—Viva America," *Common Ground* 10, (Autumn 1949), 61–70.

34. Donovan, "Roybal Rouses the Ninth," 8.

35. Fred Ross (1910–1992) graduated from the University of Southern California in 1936. Unable to get a professorship due to the Great Depression, he became employed by the California State Relief Agency and in the late 1930s administered a migrant worker's camp for the U.S. Farm Security Administration. During World War II, he held an administrative position in an internment camp for Japanese Americans. After the war, he returned to Southern California where he helped organize the Unity League for the American Council on Race Relations. Through his acquaintance with Saul Alinsky and thereafter Edward R. Roybal, he became part of the founding of the CSO. Later, he joined former

CSO member César Chávez and the United Farm Workers union.

36. Apodaca, "They Kept the Home Fires Burning," 34.

37. Garcia, *Memories of Chicano History*, 164.

38. The CSO often supported complaints and litigation. Later, housing projects such as Wyvernwood and Pico Aliso were desegregated due to CSO involvement. In 1964, the CSO chartered its own credit union.

39. Apodaca, "They Kept the Home Fires Burning," 40.

40. The CSO conducted citizenship classes that included education on U.S. history and government. In 1952, an immigration law permitted that people over age 50 could take their citizenship exam in Spanish. The CSO mobilized and became involved in a campaign that resulted in some 3,000 becoming U.S. citizens.

41. Apodaca, "They Kept the Home Fires Burning," 37, 82. The CSO took up the issue of pensions for noncitizens in 1953. Through its efforts in 1961, Governor Pat Brown signed into law California Legislative Bill AB-5 that removed the citizenship requirement for state assistance to the retired and to the disabled.

42. Apodaca, "They Kept the Home Fires Burning," 34.

43. Apodaca, "They Kept the Home Fires Burning," 83.

44. Garcia, *Memories of Chicano History*, 166.

45. Garcia, *Memories of Chicano History*, 166.

46. Kaye Lynn Briegel, "The History of Political Organization Among Mexican Americans in Los Angeles since the Second World War," (master's thesis, University of Southern California, 1967), 18.

47. Apodaca, "They Kept the Home Fires Burning," 74.

Chapter 4

1. David G. Gutierrez, *Walls and Mirrors: Mexican Americans, Mexican Immigrants, and the Politics of Ethnicity* (Berkeley: University of California Press, 1995), 170.

2. Under the McCarran-Nixon Act, any immigrant found to be guilty of what the government called "subversive activities" could be arrested

and deported. Between 1950 and 1952, some 1 million Mexicans were repatriated or deported the law. Thousands of U.S. citizens had their constitutional rights violated when the Immigration and Naturalization Service entered private homes or detained people without probable cause during mass roundups. In 1952, the McCarran-Walter Immigration and Nationality Act went further and allowed naturalized citizens to be deported on the mere government suspicion that these people were involved in subversive activities.

3. Gutierrez, *Walls and Mirrors*, 171.

4. Lucille Roybal-Allard (United States Representative, 40th District of California), author interview, April 29, 2005.

5. Ed Roybal Jr., author interview, April 29, 2005.

6. Gutierrez, *Walls and Mirrors*, 169.

7. Beatrice W. Griffith, "Viva Roybal—Viva America," *Common Ground* 10, (Autumn 1949), 65.

8. Richard A. Donovan, "Roybal Rouses the Ninth: A Los Angeles Mexican-American District Learns How to Make its Political Voice Heard," *Reporter* (January 17, 1950), 9.

9. Griffith, "Viva Roybal—Viva America," 61–70.

10. Edward R. Roybal (United States Representative, 30th District of California 1963–1975 and 25th District of California 1975–1993), author interview, July 30, 1999.

11. Kenneth C. Burt, "The Power of a Mobilized Citizenry and Coalition Politics: The 1949 Election of Edward R. Roybal to the Los Angeles City Council," *Southern California Quarterly* 85 (2003): 418.

12. Melvyn Douglas (1901–1981), was born Melvyn Hesselberg in Macon, Georgia. He made his stage debut in Chicago in 1919 and went on to play Shakespeare and every type of role on Broadway. He made his Hollywood film debut in 1931 and soon reached stardom, excelling in sophisticated comedies as well as dramas. He was married to Congresswoman Helen Gahagan Douglas. Both she and the actor were effectively blacklisted in the early 1950s. In order to survive, he

returned to the theater. He made an impressive film comeback in the early 1960s, winning two Best Supporting Actor Academy Awards for *Hud* (1963) and *I Never Sang for My Father* (1970).

13. Helen Gahagan (1900–1980), was born on November 25, 1900, in New Jersey. She was a Broadway leading lady and opera star in the 1920s and 1930s. She had one memorable film title role, in *She* (1935). She got into politics and was twice elected to the U.S. House of Representatives, as a congresswoman for the 14th Congressional District in California from 1945 to 1949. In 1950, however, she was defeated by Richard M. Nixon in her bid for the U.S. Senate in an especially red-baited campaign by her opponent. She married actor Melvyn Douglas in 1931.

14. Roger Johnson died in 1984 at the age of 81. He had stored decades of his own life remembrances, including Ed Roybal's campaign documents, as well as photos, films, and newsreels in his garage. Upon his death, however, the material was discarded.

15. Donovan, "Roybal Rouses the Ninth," 8.

16. Katherine Underwood, "Process and Politics: Multiracial Electoral Coalition Building and Representation in Los Angeles' 9th District, 1949–1962" (Ph.D. dissertation, University of California, San Diego, 1992), 101.

17. Maria Linda Apodaca, "They Kept the Home Fires Burning: Mexican-American Women and Social Change" (Ph.D. dissertation, University of California, Irvine, 1994), 78.

18. Irma Núñez, author interview, December 10, 1999.

19. Lucille Roybal-Allard, author interview, April 29, 2005.

20. Underwood, "Process and Politics," 102.

21. Donavan, "Roybal Rouses the Ninth," 9.

22. Griffith, "Viva Roybal—Viva America," 66.

23. The advent of World War II brought some decisive changes. In 1942, labor leader Philip Randolph and the African American community were able to exert pressure on President Franklin D. Roosevelt. The

president issued an executive order forbidding discrimination in the defense plants. Later the same year, the Southern Pacific Railroad began bringing thousands of African American workers into Los Angeles. They, like other African Americans before them, were restricted by housing segregation. Nevertheless, the African American community grew. In 1940, they were 3.1% of the city's population; in 1950, 8.7%; and in 1960, 13.5%. African American political representation was almost nonexistent. The exception was the election of State Assemblyman Augustus Hawkins, who was elected as a Democrat in 1934. Ironically, Hawkins had defeated the only other African American official, Republican Fred Roberts. In the city of Los Angeles, the three council districts with a large African American population had none of their own as representatives.

24. "The California Eagle Recommendations for Election, April 5," *California Eagle*, March 31, 1949.

25. Griffith, "Viva Roybal—Viva America," 66.

26. Editorial, *Daily News*, May 10, 1949.

27. "Roybal for Council," *California Eagle*, May 26, 1949.

28. "Roybal Names Committee to Spur Campaign," *Eastside Sun,* May 19, 1949.

29. Underwood, "Process and Politics," 108.

30. Samuel Goldwyn Jr. would also become a prominent film producer in his own right.

31. Underwood, "Process and Politics," 108.

32. Griffith, "Viva Roybal—Viva America," 68.

33. Donovan, "Roybal Rouses the Ninth," 7.

34. Fletcher Bowron (1887–1968) was born in Los Angeles, California. He was a Superior Court judge in California and then mayor of Los Angeles, 1938–1953.

35. Underwood, "Process and Politics," 113.

36. Edward R. Roybal, author interview, July 30, 1999.

37. Lucille Roybal-Allard, author interview, April 29, 2005.

38. Lucille Roybal-Allard, author interview, April 29, 2005.

39. Lillian Roybal Rose, author interview, April 29, 2005.

40. Lucille Roybal-Allard and Lillian Roybal Rose, author interview, April 29, 2005.

41. Ed Roybal Jr., author interview, April 29, 2005.

42. Jaime Regalado, author interview, January 10, 2000. Regalado worked at the Pat Brown Institute, California State University, Los Angeles.

43. Representative Chet Holifield of California, "Election of Roybal—Democracy at Work," 81st Cong., 1st Sess., *Congressional Record* (August 9, 1949).

44. Burt, "The Power of a Mobilized Citizenry," 433.

45. J. Blake, "Roybal Victory Shows L.A. Minorities' Power," *The Militant*, June 30, 1949.

46. R. E. G. H., "The Latin One-Eighth." *Daily News*, July 1, 1949.

47. Edward R. Roybal, author interview, July 30, 1999.

48. Burt, "The Power of a Mobilized Citizenry," 433.

49. Harold Harby (1894–1978) was born in Gjovik, Norway, and came to the United States in 1910. He and his wife moved to the West Coast in 1918, where he worked for two oil companies. He was elected to the Los Angeles City Council in 1939 but left office in 1942, when he was convicted of using a municipal car for an out-of-state trip. He was re-elected to the Los Angeles City Council in 1943 and served until 1957. His was the swing vote that defeated a measure to build a $100 million public housing project in Los Angeles.

50. Edward R. Roybal, author interview, July 30, 1999.

51. Edward R. Roybal, author interview, July 30, 1999.

52. Lucille Roybal-Allard, author interview, April 29, 2005.

53. "Protest Condemnation for Juvenile Hall Addition," *Eastside Sun*, August 31, 1949.

54. "City Councilman Takes Steps Toward Fair Employment Act," *Westlake Post*, August 11, 1949.

55. "The Council and FEPC," *Los Angeles Times*, September 23, 1949.

56. Harold A. Henry (1895–1966) was born in Virginia City, Nevada. After military service in World War I, he became a reporter for the *Los Angeles Examiner*. He established his own newspaper, the *Wilshire Press*, which ran from 1925 to 1941. He was elected to the Los Angeles City Council in 1945 and served as its president for four terms during 1947 to 1962. He is often confused with Harold Harby, who was another Los Angeles city councilman during the same era.

57. "Council Turns Down FEPC Ordinance by Vote of 8 to 6," *Daily News*, September 28, 1949.

58. "Racial Bigotry Flared at City Hall to Defeat FEPC," *California Eagle*, September 29, 1949.

59. Lucille Roybal-Allard, author interview, April 29, 2005.

60. "Roybal Refused Home Because of Race, Charges Real Estate Firms Here Are Discriminating," *Eastside Journal*, September 7, 1949.

61. "Councilman Charges He Was a Victim of Minorities Ban," *Daily News*, September 2, 1949.

62. "Repairs Begin on East Side Streets," *Eastside Journal*, November 2, 1949.

63. "Work Started on Play Center on Bunker Hill," *Los Angeles Times*, November 15, 1949.

64. "Community Medical Foundation Fund Campaign Opens Saturday." *California Eagle*, March 30, 1950.

65. "History Made in Council; Roybal Speaks to Local Youngsters in Native Language." *Eastside Journal*, January 11, 1950.

66. "Plan East Side Receiving Hospital," *Eastside Journal*, January 11, 1950.

67. "Los Angeles 'Red-Hot City,'" *Citizen News*, September 13, 1950.

68. Joseph Eli Kovner, "Ed Roybal Merits 'Badge of Courage,'" *Eastside Sun*, September 14, 1950.

69. *Citizen News*, September 13, 1950.

70. *Herald Express*, September 13, 1950.

71. Lillian Roybal Rose, author interview, April 29. 2005.

72. Lucille Roybal-Allard, author interview, April 29, 2005.

73. "Southland Leaders to Honor City Councilman Roybal," *Daily News*, November 4, 1950.

Chapter 5

1. Paul Johnson, *A History of the American People* (New York: HarperCollins Publishers, 1999), 808–809. With only 7% of the world's population, the United States of America had some 42% of its income and half of the manufacturing capacity. The United States produced 43.5% of the world's electricity, 57.5% of the steel, 80% of the automobiles, and 62% of the oil. It also owned some 75% of the world's gold. Its per capita income was $1,450, while the next group of countries (Great Britain, Canada, Switzerland, and New Zealand) had a per capita income of only about $700 to $900. The consumption of calories was about 3,000 per day, which was about 50% more than in Western Europe.

2. Rodolfo F. Acuña, *Occupied America: A History of Chicanos*, 3rd ed. (New York: Harper & Row, 1988), 269.

3. Under the Federal Employee Loyalty Program, a loyalty review board investigated government employees and dismissed those deemed disloyal to the government of the United States. Consequently, the U.S. attorney general came up with a list of 91 "subversive organizations." Membership in any of these was grounds for suspicion of disloyalty or guilt by association. Between 1947 and 1951, the federal government investigated 3.2 million employees and fired 212 as security risks. Another 2,900 employees resigned. Some wanted to avoid being investigated; others did not fear their associations would be questioned but simply felt their constitutional rights were being violated.

4. See: Patrick McGilligan and Paul Buhle, *Tender Comrades: A Backstory of the Hollywood Blacklist* (New York: St. Martin's Press, 1997). State and local governments followed suit and passed laws requiring loyalty oaths and other infringements of free speech (i.e., removal of the right to associate, violation of due process, and a culture that

now assumed guilt of the accused). Thousands were investigated, hounded, dismissed, slandered, and had their lives destroyed.

5. Lt. Col. Miguel A. Garcia, "Roots of Hispanic Servicemen," *La Luz*, September 1978, 26–27.

6. Acuña, *Occupied America*, 299.

7. U.S. Department of Commerce, Statistical Abstracts: 1942, 1953, 1973, 1984, 1991, and 1992. Washington, D.C.: Government Printing Office.

8. Leo Greber, Joan W. Moore, and Ralph C. Guzman, *The Mexican American People: The Nation's Second Largest Minority* (New York: Free Press, 1970), 68.

9. Ignacio M. Garcia, *Viva Kennedy: Mexican Americans in Search of Camelot* (College Station: Texas A & M University Press, 2000), 14.

10. Garcia, *Viva Kennedy*, 15.

11. Arthur O'Sullivan and Steven M. Sheffrin, *Economics: Principles in Action* (Glenview, IL: Pearson Prentice Hall, 2003), 233. Mexican union membership also declined during the 1950s. Red baiting weakened many unions, and some conservative union leadership was cowed by business, government, and even its own rank and file. By mid-decade, the agricultural unions (the National Farm Labor Union, the National Agricultural Workers Union) and industrial unions (the International Unions of Mine, Mill, and Smelter Workers; the United Cannery, Agricultural, Packing, and Allied Workers of America) who were more progressive and active in recruiting Mexican workers were in sharp decline or no longer existed. Their base of support and political infrastructure were in decline.

12. Garcia, *Viva Kennedy*, 17.

13. Garcia, *Viva Kennedy*, 25.

14. Garcia, *Viva Kennedy*, 28.

15. Roberto E. Villareal, Norma G. Hernandez, and Howard D. Neighbor. *Latino Empowerment: Progress, Problems, and Prospects* (Westport, CN: Greenwood Press, 1998), 4.

16. Henry B. Gonzalez (1916–2000) began elected office as a San Antonio city councilman (1953–1956). He then became the first Mexican person since the mid-1880s to serve in the Texas state senate (1956–1960) and also in the U.S. House of Representatives (1961–1998). Matt S. Meir and Margo Gutierrez described him as having "consistently supported and advanced the interests of the poor and the powerless. The economic and civil rights of his constituents have always been his primary concern." Along with Edward R. Roybal, Gonzalez co-founded the Congressional Hispanic Caucus. A moderate Democrat, he came to vehemently oppose much of the Chicano nationalism of the Chicano generation of the 1960s, and specifically the Mexican American Youth Organization (MAYO) and La Raza Unida Party, both founded in Texas.

17. Joseph Montoya (1915–1978) was born in Pena Blanca, New Mexico. He was still a student at Georgetown University Law School when he was elected to the New Mexico Assembly as an assemblyman in 1938 and served until 1940, when he was elected to the New Mexico State Senate (1940–1947). He served as lieutenant governor (1947–1957) and served two additional terms in the state senate. He was elected to the U.S. House of Representatives (1957–1964). Upon the death of Dennis Chavez, he was elected to the U.S. Senate (1964–1976). A moderate Democrat, he was a strong advocate for education, the rights of undocumented workers, agriculture, and health care.

18. Dionisio "Dennis" Chavez (1888–1962) was born in New Mexico. He had obtained his law degree by attending night classes at the age of 32 and set up practice in Albuquerque in 1920. He served in the U.S. House of Representatives (1930–1935). He was appointed to the U.S. Senate (1935–1962) upon the death of New Mexico Senator Bronson Cutting. According to Meier and Gutierrez, "In the U.S. Senate Chavez worked without respite and consistently supported the rights of his Nuevomexicano constituents. His most important contribution, especially to the Hispanos of his state, was

his advocacy and support of civil rights and education." He wrote and pushed to establish a permanent Federal Fair Employment Practices Commission and was also one of a few to denounce Senator Joseph McCarthy.

19. *Eastside Sun*, March 11, 1951.

20. Roybal's newspaper scrapbook, Los Angeles County Library, East Los Angeles branch.

21. Richard A. Donovan, "Roybal Rouses the Ninth: A Los Angeles Mexican-American District Learns How to Make Its Political Voice Heard," *The Reporter* (January 17, 1950), 9.

22. *Los Angeles Times*, April 1, 1951.

23. *Eastside Sun*, March 29, 1951.

24. *Eastside Sun*, March 29, 1951.

25. Newspaper accounts from 1951.

26. "League Analyzes Councilman Races." L.A. Fire and Police Protective League newsletter, March 26, 1951.

27. Katherine Underwood, "Process and Politics: Multiracial Electoral Coalition Building and Representation in Los Angeles' 9th District, 1949–1962" (Ph.D. dissertation, University of California, San Diego, 1992), 122.

28. Underwood, "Process and Politics," 127.

29. "50 Complaints Reported by Councilman Roybal," *Daily News*, February 26, 1952.

30. "Jury Votes All-Out Brutality Probe," *Daily News*, March 18, 1952.

31. Lillian Roybal Rose, author interview, April 29, 2005.

32. Underwood, "Process and Politics," 128.

33. Ed J. Davenport (February 9, 1899–June 24, 1953) served in the Los Angeles City Council from 1945 until his death.

34. "Knife Threat 'Just Quip'—Davenport." *Los Angeles Examiner*, September 11, 1953.

35. "Knife Threat 'Just Quip'—Davenport." *Los Angeles Examiner*, September 11, 1953.

36. Manny Hellerman, "Our Fighting Councilman," *Eastside Sun*, September 11, 1952.

37. Richard Graves began his professional roots in the Bureau of Public Administration (formerly the Institute of Governmental Studies). He was the star student of Director Sam May. After graduate studies, Graves went to work for the League of California Cities and later became its executive director. He was a friend and ally of Governor Earl Warren. Graves was very active in the formulation of state policy as one of the leading members of Warren's brain trust. When he ran for governor, he resigned his post in the League of Cities. After his defeat for governor, he began a successful career in economic and urban development. He lived in San Francisco and Pebble Beach until his death in 1989.

38. Lillian Roybal Rose, author interview, April 29, 2005.

39. Lucille Roybal-Allard (United States Representative, 40th District of California), author interview, April 29, 2005.

40. "Dick Graves and Ed Roybal," *AFL Committee For Graves & Roybal* newsletter, 1954.

41. "LA's Councilman from 'The Wrong Side of the Tracks,'" August 18, 1954.

42. "Eagle Tells Choices in Tuesday Election," *California Eagle*, October 28, 1954.

43. Esteban Torres (United States Representative, 34th District of California 1983–1998), author interview, March 20, 2007.

44. Goodwin J. Knight was considered a Republican Party "regular." He moved from Utah to Los Angeles in 1904, attended Stanford University, served in the U.S. Navy during World War I, and returned to finish his studies at Cornell University. He married Arvilla Cooley, who died before 1954. He was appointed by Governor Merriam and served for 12 years as a Superior Court judge in Los Angeles County. He was appointed governor of California by President Eisenhower when Earl Warren left for his appointment to the U.S. Supreme Court. He won re-election in 1954, but lost to Democrat Pat Brown in 1958.

45. Harold J. Powers had served as president pro tempore of the California Senate from 1947 until October 5, 1953. He then became lieutenant governor replacing Goodwin J. Knight (who resigned upon being elected California governor). Powers would serve two terms as lieutenant governor, from October 5, 1953, to January 4, 1959.

46. Davie Soibelman, "$40 Million Bunker Hill Housing Up," *Daily News*, November 15, 1954.

47. Walter L. Scratch, "Bunker Hill Plan Okayed by Council," *Citizen News*, April 26, 1955.

48. "Against Their Own," *Citizen News*, April 25, 1955.

49. Lucille Roybal-Allard, author interview, April 29, 2005.

50. "Council Asked to Pass Fair Job Practices Bill," *Los Angeles Times*, May 12, 1955.

51. Lillian Roybal Rose, author interview, April 29, 2005.

52. "Roybal Eyes Ford's Post," *Eastside Sun*, October 6, 1955.

53. John Hunt, "Roybal Blasts Plan to Charge for Services at Baby Clinics," *The Mercury*, May 16, 1956.

54. Fred Arnold, "Dem. Chiefs Confuse Liberals, Moderates," *Los Angeles Herald & Express*, February 10, 1956.

55. "Hawkins, Roybal Heading Stevenson Vote Campaign," *Los Angeles Sentinel*, May 3, 1956.

56. "Council Denies Plea for Report on Integration," *California Eagle*, April 26, 1956; "Council Blocks Bid for report on Integration," *Herald-Express*, April 26, 1956.

57. "L.A. Councilman Thinks State Will Turn to Adlai," *Sacramento Bee*, October 1956.

58. *The Free Press*, October 1956.

59. Sid Hazeur, "Council Move Blocks Negro Representation," October 25, 1956.

60. Ed Roybal Jr., author interview, April 29, 2005.

61. "2 More Members on Council Urged," *Los Angeles Examiner*, November 28, 1956.

62. "New Chapter Formed in East Los Angeles," *The Open Forum*, December 1956.

63. Underwood, "Process and Politics," 135.

64. Irma Núñez, author interview, December 10, 1999.

65. Dick Walton, "Five L.A. Candidates Certain of Re-Election—No Opposition," *Los Angeles Herald & Express*, March 29, 1957.

66. Underwood, "Process and Politics," 136.

67. "NAACP Aide Says State Lacks Minorities Rights," March 24, 1957.

68. Fred Takata, "CSO 10th Anniversary," *Pacific Citizen*, August 2, 1957.

69. "Family Won't Budge for the Dodgers," *Mirror-News*. August 21, 1957.

70. Paul Zimmerman, "L.A. Council Votes Dodgers Deal, 11–3," *Los Angeles Times*, September 7, 1957.

71. Lucille Roybal-Allard, author interview, April 29, 2005.

72. Juan Gonzalez, author interview, December 10, 1999.

73. "Roybal to Make Tour of Europe, Middle East," *Los Angeles Citizen*, September 13, 1957.

74. Orval Faubus (1910–1994) was governor of Arkansas from 1955 to 1967. He became well-known for his opposition to the desegregation efforts at Little Rock High School ordered by the U.S. Supreme Court. He ordered the Arkansas National Guard to prevent African American children from attending the school. He would later moderate his stand regarding desegregation.

75. "Roybal Tells of Middle East Trip," *Eastside Sun*, November 1957.

76. "Roybal Tells of Middle East Trip," *Eastside Sun*, November 1957.

77. *Eastside Sun*, March 21, 1957.

78. Ernest Debs (February 7, 1904–March 17, 2002) was born in Toledo, Ohio. He attended public schools and then moved to Los Angeles to work in the movies as a dancer. In 1942, he was elected to the California Assembly for the 56th District and served until 1947, when he was elected to the Los Angeles City Council (serving until 1958). He was elected to the Los Angeles Board of Supervisors in 1958,

1962, 1966, and 1970. He is credited with pioneering legislation for the freeway system in California.

79. Edward Roybal Jr., author interview, July 20, 2001.

80. Edward Roybal Jr., author interview, July 15, 2001.

81. Edward Roybal Jr., author interview, July 15, 2001.

82. Edward Roybal Jr., author interview, July 15, 2001.

83. Edward Roybal Jr., author interview, July 15, 2001.

84. "Count Again in Debs Lead Over Roybal," *Valley Tribune*, November 20, 1958.

85. Edward R. Roybal, author interview, July 30, 1999.

86. "Count Again in Debs Lead Over Roybal," *Valley Tribune*, November 20, 1958.

87. Edward R. Roybal, author interview, July 30, 1999.

88. "Eastside Savings to Open on 1st Street, Roybal President," *Eastside Sun*, February 5, 1959.

89. Herman E. Gallegos (b. 1930) was born in the Colorado mining town of Aguilar. He was educated in two California state universities (1948–1952) and the University of California, Berkeley (1955–1958). During the 1950s, he worked on the creation and development of the CSO, serving as its national president 1958–1960. In the 1970s, he became one of the first Mexican Americans to serve in the board of directors of a private corporation.

90. Mario T. Garcia, *Memories of Chicano History: The Life and Narrative of Bert Corona*, (Berkeley: University of California Press, 1994), 195. Bert Corona (1918–2001), the legendary labor and community organizer, was the inspiration and/or co-founder of several civil rights–oriented organizations, including Asociación Nacional Mexico-Americana, the Congreso de los Pueblos de Habla Espanola, the Community Service Organization, and the Mexican-American Political Association.

91. David Gutierrez, *Walls and Mirrors: Mexican Americans, Mexican Immigrants, and the Politics of Ethnicity* (Berkeley, CA: University of California Press, 1995), 181.

92. Matt Meier and Margo Gutierrez, *Encyclopedia of the Mexican American Civil Rights Movement* (Westport, CT: Greenwood Press, 2000), 148.

93. Edward R. Roybal, author interview, July 30, 1999.

94. Edward R. Roybal, author interview, August 4, 1999.

Chapter 6

1. Richard Nixon (1913–1994), although a moderate conservative, brandished a bullish anticommunism that justified Eisenhower's interventionist policies in Latin America (e.g., Guatemala in 1954). This foreign policy justified covert or overt intervention in the affairs of Latin American nations whenever they did not put U.S. interests ahead of the interests of their own people, as in issues such as nationalizing industry and land reform. In domestic race relations, Nixon, like the Republican Party, appeared unperturbed and insensitive to the demands of minorities and women for inclusion and for change.

2. John F. Kennedy (1917–1963), was well aware of the long history of discrimination against the Irish, and as a Catholic, he had experienced the same anti-Catholic biases that Mexican Americans dealt with. He had learned to empathize for other people who suffered discrimination. Back wounds he had suffered in the war limited his physical activity and caused him excruciating pain for the rest of his life. From this he had learned humility about the physical handicaps of others. His older brother Joe, the apple of his father's eye, had been killed during World War II. From this John Kennedy had learned to live intensely in the brevity of life. Because he had a sister who was born with an intellectual disability, he understood the necessity of health care for all. Kennedy was moreover an intellectual whose had published a book entitled *When England Slept*, and the Pulitzer Prize winning *Profiles in Courage*.

3. Ignacio M. Garcia, *Viva Kennedy: Mexican Americans in Search of Camelot* (College Station: Texas A & M University Press, 2000), 94–95.

4. Some Mexican Americans felt a certain romantic affinity with the candidate's Irish heritage. During the Mexican-American War (1846–1848), some recently arrived Irish to the United States who had enlisted to fight against Mexico for the promise of U.S. citizenship went over to the Mexico side after they witnessed numerous deprivations against Catholic churches and clergy. They became known as the San Patricios (the Saint Patrick Battalion), and many of them were subsequently executed upon capture by U.S. forces. A second affinity was Catholicism. Third, a powerful sense of optimism had taken hold, making the choice between the status quo and Kennedy's "New Frontier" theme an easy one. His very youth and vitality held the prospect that an orderly transition to local and national social acceptance was possible for Mexian Americans.

5. Edward R. Roybal (United States Representative, 30th District of California 1963–1975 and 25th District of California 1975–1993), author interview, August 4, 1999.

6. Edward R. Roybal, author interview, August 4, 1999.

7. Garcia, *Viva Kennedy*, 44.

8. Ed Roybal Jr., author interview, April 29, 2005.

9. Garcia, *Viva Kennedy*, 33.

10. Garcia, *Viva Kennedy*, 41.

11. Garcia, *Viva Kennedy*, 44.

12. Garcia, *Viva Kennedy*, 45.

13. "Forerunners Participate as Individuals in 'Viva' Clubs," *Forum News Bulletin*, December 2, 1960; "Forerunners and Sen. Kennedy Ride into White House on the Mexican Burro," *Forum News Bulletin*, December 1, 1960.

14. Garcia, *Viva Kennedy*, 93–95.

15. Garcia, *Viva Kennedy*, 106.

16. "Mexicans Pleased by Election of Kennedy," *Kansas City Star*, November 21, 1960.

17. Garcia, *Viva Kennedy*, 106.

18. Garcia, *Viva Kennedy*, 109.

19. "Kennedy Patronage, Latin American Policies under Fire," *Congressional Quarterly*, January 23, 1961.

20. Garcia, *Viva Kennedy*, 122.

21. Garcia, *Viva Kennedy*, 126.

22. Matt S. Meier and Margo Gutierrez, *Encyclopedia of the Mexican American Civil Rights Movement* (Westport, CT: Greenwood Press, 2000), 184.

23. Garcia, *Viva Kennedy*, 172.

24. Katherine Underwood, "Process and Politics: Multiracial Electoral Coalition Building and Representation in Los Angeles' 9th District, 1949–1962" (Ph.D. dissertation, University of California, San Diego, 1992), 140.

25. "More Groups Come Out for Roybal," *Eastside Sun*, March 30, 1961; "AFL-CIO Endorsements," *L.A. Citizen,* March 31, 1961.

26. "Vote for Richardson, Tinglof, Roybal," *California Eagle*, March 23, 1961, p. 4; "Sentinel Recommends," *Los Angeles Sentinel,* March 30, 1961, p. A1; Kovner, Joseph Eli, "Roybal Endorsed by Eastside Sun," *Eastside Sun*, April 2, 1961, p. 1.

27. *California Eagle*, March 23, 1961, p. 4.

28. "150 attend Roybal Fete," *Los Angeles Sentinel*, March 23, 1961.

29. *La Opinion*, April 2, 1961, Section 2, p. 1.

30. "The Decisions for Tuesday," *Los Angeles Times*, April 2, 1961, Section C, p. 4; "Examiner's Recommendations," *Examiner*, April 2, 1961, p. 12.

31. "City to Face Important Job at Polls: Great Decisions on L.A. Future Loom for New Council," *Los Angeles Times*, April 2, 1961, p. 1.

32. "Rundberg, Roybal Face Tough Rivals," *Los Angeles Evening Herald & Express*, March 15, 1961, p. A10

33. *Eastside Sun*, February 2, 1961.

34. *Eastside Sun*, April 2, 1961.

35. *Eastside Sun*, April 2, 1961.

36. Roll-off voting is when a voter participates in the top-of-the-ballot election, but does not vote on the rest of the measures or elections on the ballot.

37. "Incumbents on Council Re-elected," *Los Angeles Times*, 1961.

38. "The Observations on Governor Brown, Judge Sanchez, and Councilman Ed Roybal." Eastside Sun, Novemebr 12, 1961.

39. "The Observations on Governor Brown, Judge Sanchez, and Councilman Ed Roybal," *Eastside Sun*, November 12, 1961.

Chapter 7

1. U.S. Department of Commerce. Statistical Abstracts. Washington, D.C.: U.S. Government Printing Office, 1942, 1953, 1973, 1984, 1991, and 1992.

2. Leo Gebler, Joan W. Moore, and Ralph Guzman. *The Mexican-American People: The Nation's Second Largest Minority*, 106, 126, 185, and 251.

3. Gebler, Moore, and Guzman. *The Mexican-American People*, 143, 150, 236. Without sufficient education, most of the Mexican population was stuck in low-paying jobs, or in poverty, and often facing a bleak future. Students of Mexican descent were plagued by segregation, tracking into lower-tier academic classes, and unequal funding, as well as living in housing that were often dilapidated and over-crowded.

4. Rodolfo F. Acuña, *Occupied America: A History of Chicanos,* 3rd ed. (New York: Harper & Row), 319.

5. Acuña, *Occupied America*, p. 319.

6. Acuña, *Occupied America*, p. 320.

7. The McCone Commission Report (1965) was prepared by the McCone Commission, which was established to study and analyze the causes of the Watts Riot of 1965. It was headed by a wealthy Republican businessman. It advocated "compensatory" rather than "equal" treatment for minorities. It made modest recommendations to avoid police-community conflicts, but they were generally ignored.

8. Armando Morales, *Ando Sangrando (I Am Bleeding)*, La Puente, CA: Perspectiva Publication, 1972, 24.

9. *The Weekly Outlook*, April 6, 1964.

10. Edward R. Roybal (United States Representative, 30th District of California 1963–1975 and 25th District of California 1975–1993), author interview, July 30, 1999.

11. Edward R. Roybal, author interview, July 30, 1999.

12. Morales, *Ando Sangrando (I Am Bleeding)*, 33.

13. Edward R. Roybal, author interview, July 30, 1999.

14. *Eastside Sun*, February 8, 1962.

15. "Wilshire Division Honors Retiring Lt. Tom Bradley" *California Eagle*, March 8, 1962.

16. Esteban Torres (United States Representative, 34th District of California 1983–1998), author interview, March 20, 2007.

17. "Japanese-American Leader Given City Scroll," *30th District Democrat*, April 2, 1962.

18. "American Legion Withdraws Roybal W.H. Parade Bid." *San Fernando Valley Times*, May 1962.

19. Edward R. Roybal, author interview, August 4, 1999.

20. Jesse Marvin Unruh (September 30, 1922–August 4, 1987) was born in Newton, Kansas, and served in the navy during World War II. After the war, he earned a B.A. in political science and journalism from the University of Southern California in 1948.

21. Katherine Underwood, "Process and Politics: Multiracial Electoral Coalition Building and Representation in Los Angeles' 9th District, 1949–1962" (Ph.D. dissertation, University of California, San Diego, 1992), 255–256.

22. Underwood, "Politics and Process," 256.

23. Edward R. Roybal, author interview, August 4, 1999.

24. *Eastside Sun*, May 27, 1962.

25. Ed Roybal Jr., author interview, April 29, 2005.

26. *Los Angeles Times*, June 8, 1962.

27. "Roybal Outlines Constructive Platform in Congress Race," *Southern California Teamster*, May 23, 1962.

28. Gordon Leo McDonough was born in Buffalo, Eric County, New York, January 2, 1895. He moved with his parents to Emporium, Cameron County, Pennsylvania, in 1898 and attended public schools. There he worked as a chemist from 1915 to 1918; he moved to Los Angeles and resumed that career, 1918–1933. After retiring from politics, he died in Bethesda, Maryland, on June 25, 1968.

29. "Hay Cinco Candidatos de Origen Mexicano," *La Opinion*, November 4, 1962, sec. 2.

30. *Eastside Sun*, November 15, 1962.

31. "2 Councilmen Resign to Assume House Seats," *Los Angeles Times*, December 27, 1962.

32. Henry B. Gonzalez (1916–200) was born in San Antonio, Texas, to Mexican parents. He served in the San Antonio City Council from 1953 to 1956 and was elected to the Texas State Senate, serving from 1956 to 1961. He served in the U.S. House of Representatives from 1961 to 1999.

33. Joseph Montoya (1915–1978) was born in Pena Blanca, New Mexico, to descendants of Spanish settlers. He served in the U.S. House of Representatives from 1957 to 1964 and in the U.S. Senate from 1964 to 1977.

34. Paul Johnson, *A History of the American People* (New York: Harper Perennial, 1998), 857.

35. On July 20, 1969, Apollo 11 landed Edwin Aldrin and Neil Armstrong on the moon.

36. Edward R. Roybal, author interview, August 4, 1999.

37. "Roybal Named To House Interior Affairs Group," *Wilshire Press*, February 7, 1963.

38. "Rep. Roybal Lauds Sen. Chavez," *Los Angeles Times*, February 13, 1963.

39. Ed Roybal Jr., author interview, April 29, 2005.

40. Edward Roybal Jr. to Congressman Edward R. Roybal, March 22,

1963. Edward R. Roybal papers, California State University, Los Angeles Library.

41. Lucille Roybal-Allard (United States Representative, 40th District of California), author interview, April 29, 2005

42. Irma Núñez, author interview, April 29, 2005.

43. Lucille Roybal-Allard, author interview, April 29, 2005.

44. Lucille Roybal-Allard, author interview, April 29, 2005.

45. Irma Núñez, author interview, December 10, 1999.

46. Ruben Salazar, "Latin Citizens to Report Bias," *Los Angeles Times*, August 10, 1963.

47. "Lyndon in Town: Seeing 'Everybody.'" *Los Angeles Herald-Examiner*, August 9, 1963.

48. Salazar, "Latin Citizens to Report Bias."

49. U.S. Congress. House of Representatives. 88th Cong., 1st sess., *Congressional Record*, (June 3, 1963).

50. Edward R. Roybal, author interview, August 4, 1999.

51. *Congressman Ed Roybal Reports from Washington*, March 1963.

52. *Roybal Reports*, June 10, 1963.

53. Hiro E. Hishiki, "Across the Editor's Desk," *Kashu Mainichi*, November 29, 1963.

54. "MAPA Parley Pledges Mexican American Aid," *Belvedere Chronicle*, November 14, 1963.

55. Edward R. Roybal, author interview, August 4, 1999.

56. Edward R. Roybal, author interview, August 4, 1999.

57. Matt S. Meier and Margo Gutierrez. *Encyclopedia of the Mexican American Civil Rights Movement* (Westport, CT: Greenwood Press, 2000), 63.

58. Edward R. Roybal, author interview, August 4, 1999.

59. Currently the Congressional Hispanic Caucus Institute offers a two-year fellowship and a summer institute.

60. Lucille Roybal-Allard, author interview, April 29, 2005.

61. Edward R. Roybal, author interview, August 4, 1999.

62. More recently, the Hispanic Congressional Caucus has also represented the interests of a host of Latino/a organizations. The group served to advise and consult with Presidents Carter and Clinton regarding political representation and educational issues of urgent concern to Mexican American and Latino communities.

63. U.S. Congress. House of Representatives. 88th Cong., 1st sess., *Congressional Record* 109, (December 5, 1963).

64. "Congressman Ed Roybal Reports from Washington." *Mexican-American Sun*, December 12, 1963.

65. "Rep. Ed Roybal Reports." *Eastside Journal – Belvedere Citizen*, December 5, 1963.

66. Speech of Hon. Edward R. Roybal" 88th Cong., 1st sess., *Congressional Record* 109 (December 5, 1963).

Chapter 8

1. Lyndon Baines Johnson (1908–1973) served for a short time in the U.S. Navy during World War II, where he reached the rank of lieutenant and won a Silver Star during action in the South Pacific. After serving six terms in the House of Representatives, he was elected to the U.S. Senate in 1948. In 1953, he became the youngest Minority Leader in the Senate's history. In 1954, the Democrats took control, and he became the Majority Leader. In that position, he became legendary for his persuasive powers.

2. Edward R. Roybal (United States Representative, 30th District of California 1963–1975 and 25th District of California 1975–1993), author interview, August 6, 1999.

3. In tune with Johnson's agenda, Roybal authored the 1968 legislation that established the National Bilingual Education Act to assist schools in meeting the educational needs of children whose main language spoken at home is not English.

4. Edward R. Roybal, author interview, August 6, 1999.

5. Medicaid was created on July 30, 1965, through Title XIX of the

Social Security Act. Each state administers its own Medicaid program and the federal Centers for Medicare and Medicaid Services (CMS) monitors the state-run programs and establishes requirements of delivery, funding, and eligibility. The mission of Medicaid is to be the United States' health program for low-income individuals, their children, and people with disabilities. Medicare is a social insurance program administered by the U.S. government and provides health coverage for people aged 65 and over who meet the criteria (citizens or permanent residents) or under 65 years of age and disabled.

6. The Older Americans Act of 1965 established the Administration on Aging (AoA). Its mission is to provide continuing care for older people and help them maintain maximum independence in their homes and communities.

7. The War on Poverty is the name given to a series of social programs first introduced by President Johnson during his State of the Union Address on January 8, 1964. The speech led the U.S. Congress to pass the Economic Opportunity Act, which in turn created the Office of Economic Opportunity (OEO) in order to administer to administer the local application of all federal funds which targeted poverty. These programs included Head Start, VISTA, Job Corps, Legal Services, and the Community Action Program. President Johnson saw this legislation as a continuation of President Franklin D. Roosevelt's New Deal.

8. "Rep. Roybal Charges Unequal Division of Anti-poverty Funds," *Belvedere Citizen*, September 9, 1965.

9. "Discrimination Charged By Mexican-American Leaders," *Eastside Sun*, October 7, 1965.

10. The Immigration and Nationality Act of 1965 abolished the national-origin quotas which had been in place since the Immigration Act of 1924 and which favored European immigrants to the United States. The 1965 law established 170,000 visas per year from the Eastern Hemisphere with no more than 20,000 per country. By 1968, the annual limitation was 120,000 visas per year for the Western Hemisphere.

11. "Immigration Bill Signed Into Law By President Johnson," *Eastside Sun*, October 14, 1965.

12. "Immigration Bill Signed Into Law By President Johnson," *Eastside Sun*, October 14, 1965.

13. "Mexicans Here Get U.S. Funds," *Los Angeles Herald-Examiner*, October 27, 1965.

14. Robert F. Kennedy was assassinated at the Ambassador Hotel in New York in 1968.

15. "Robert Kennedy to Make L.A. Appearance in Two Years," *Eastside Sun*, October 7, 1965.

16. "OK Grant for Job Training Program Here," *Belvedere Citizen*, January 27, 1966.

17. "Ed Roybal Awarded Franklin Peace Medal," *Wilshire Press*, February 9, 1967.

18. "Roybal Wins Important Appointment on House Foreign Affairs Committee," *Wilshire Press*, January 21, 1965.

19. "Success Story: U.S. Rep. Roybal." *ELA Tribune*, December 14, 1968.

20. Salvador B. Castro was born October 25, 1933 in Los Angeles, California. His father had been forcefully repatriated to Mexico during the Great Depression. He served in the U.S. Army during the Korean War (although he saw no hostilities). He organized the Chicano Youth Conference in 1963, as a forum for the plight of Chicano students and the lack of college opportunities. In the wake of the 1968 walkouts, Sal Castro and 12 others were arrested and charged with 15 counts of disturbing the peace and 15 counts of conspiracy to disrupt the public schools. Los Trece (The 13) became one of the most important legal cases of the Chicano Movement. In the interim, he lost his teaching position. However, in 1972, the charges were dropped for all 13 defendants, and Castro returned to the classroom. He continued to work to reform the educational system. He passed away April 15, 2013.

21. *Rough Rider*, March 12, 1968.

22. *Civic Center News Source*, January 13, 1992.

23. *Civic Center News Source*, January 13, 1992.

24. *ELA Tribune*, December 14, 1968.

25. *ELA Tribune*, December 14, 1968.

26. *ELA Tribune*, December 14, 1968.

27. Edward Roybal Jr., author interview, July 15, 2001.

28. Edward Roybal Jr., author interview, July 15, 2001.

29. Joseph C. Tardiff and L. Mypho Mahunda. *Dictionary of Hispanic Biography*. (Detroit, Michigan: Gale Research, 1996), 783–784.

30. *ELA Tribune*, December 14, 1968.

31. *Los Angeles Times*, July 1, 1992.

32. Rodolfo F. Acuña, *Occupied America: A History of Chicanos,* 3rd ed. (New York: Harper & Row), 318..

33. Rufus P. Browning, Dale Rogers Marshall, and David H. Tabb, eds. *Racial Politics in American Cities, 2nd Ed.* (New York: Longman, 1997), 281–283.

34. Browning et al, *Racial Politics in American Cities*, 44.

35. Katherine Underwood, "Process and Politics: Multiracial Electoral Coalition Building and Representation in Los Angeles' 9th District, 1949–1962" (Ph.D. dissertation, University of California, San Diego, 1992), 251.

36. Kenneth Hahn Sr. was born in Los Angeles, California, in 1920. After his long service in the Los Angeles County Board of Supervisors, he died in 1997. He was the father of Kenneth Hahn Jr., who was elected as Los Angeles mayor in 2001.

37. Gordon Hahn was born in Kindersley, Saskatchewan, Canada, in 1910. His family moved to a small house on Flower Street in downtown Los Angeles in 1920. He served in the U.S. Naval Reserve and then earned a B.A. from Pepperdine College (now Pepperdine University) in 1950. After leaving the Los Angeles City Council he explored unsuccessfully higher office and subsequently turned to real estate business. He died of respiratory failure from pneumonia in 2001.

38. Underwood, "Process and Politics," p. 253.

39. *Los Angeles Times*, August 10, 1963.

40. Jaime Regalado, author interview, January 10, 2000.

Chapter 9

1. James Diego Vigil, *From Indians to Chicanos: The Dynamics of Mexican-American Culture* (Prospect Heights, IL: Wavelength Press, 1998), 1–2.

2. José Angel Gutiérrez, *The Making of a Chicano Militant: Lessons from Cristal*, (Madison: University of Wisconsin Press, 1998), 13.

3. Luis Valdez, "Introduction: La Plebe." In *Aztlan: An Anthology of Mexican American Literature*, Luis Valdez and Stan Steiner, eds. (New York: Vintage Books, 1972), xxxii–xxxiii.

4. Carlos Munoz Jr., *Youth, Identity, Power: The Chicano Movement* (New York: Verso, 1989), 12.

5. Rodolfo F. Acuña, *Occupied America: A History of Chicanos, 3rd edition*. (New York: Harper & Row), 324.

6. Mario T. Garcia, *Mexican Americans: Leadership, Ideology and Identity, 1930–60* (New Haven, CT: Yale University Press, 1990), 300.

7. Munoz, *Youth, Identity, Power*, 15–16.

8. Gutierrez, *Making of a Chicano Militant*, 11.

9. Acuña, *Occupied America*, p. 308.

10. Edward R. Roybal (United States Representative, 30th District of California 1963–1975 and 25th District of California 1975–1993), author interview, August 11, 1999.

11. Irma Núñez, author interview, December 10, 1999.

12. George Mowry and Blaine A. Brownell. *The Urban Nation 1920–1980*, Rev. ed. (New York: Hill and Wang, 1981), 221–222.

13. Acuña, *Occupied America*, 331.

14. *Cisneros v. Corpus Christi v. Independent School District* (1970) was the first case to extend the U.S. Supreme Court decision in *Brown v. Board of Education* (1954) to Mexican Americans. The case involved

school segregation, and it established Mexican Americans as "an identifiable minority" that had frequently been the victim of discrimination.

15. Jaime Regalado, author interview, January 10, 2000.

16. Industrialization in Mexico made it more vulnerable to United States economic control. Multinational corporations came to dominate the marketing of Mexican agricultural products. In 1967, Del Monte was the world's largest canning corporation. By 1964, Mexico had shipped 334 million pounds of vegetables north; and by 1980, 1,108 million pounds (60%) of U.S. fresh vegetables. The Anderson Clayton food processing company lent more credit to Mexican farmers than the El Banco Nacional Ejidal, leading to an increase in food production for export and basically eradicating subsistence and small farmers. This happened at the expense of the production of staple crops of corn and beans. Unites States investment into the Mexican economy totaled $1.1 billion in the 1960s, while total U.S. profits of $1.8 billion in payments (interests, patents, royalties) abroad drained the Mexican economy. It further indebted Mexico to the International Monetary Fund and the World Bank.

17. Edward R. Roybal, author interview, August 4, 1999.

18. By the 1980s, Chávez was a revered Mexican American leader and national figure. He was awarded the Aguila Azteca by Mexico's president and, in 1993, posthumously received the Medal of Freedom awarded by President Bill Clinton. Chávez's image is seen in a postal service commemorative stamp issued in 2003.

19. Matt S. Meier and Margo Gutierrez. *Encyclopedia of the Mexican American Civil Rights Movement* (Westport, CT: Greenwood Press, 2000), p. 40.

20. Edward R. Roybal, author interview, August 11, 1999.

21. Lillian Roybal Rose, author interview, April 29, 2005.

22. Richard Santillan, author interview, July 17, 2001.

23. Richard Santillan, author interview, July 17, 2001.

24. Lucille Roybal-Allard (United States Representative, 40th District of California), author interview, April 29, 2005.

25. Ed Roybal Jr., author interview, April 29, 2005.

26. Lillian Roybal Rose, author interview, April 29, 2005.

27. In the 1970s, suffering government harassment, more arrests, and dogged by litigation, Tijerina's efforts were hampered to the point of having diminishing influence except among a few stalwarts. Tijerina succeeded in bringing to light long-ignored land alienation issues. The failure of government to respond on these issues had a corrosive social effect that necessitated these new kinds of redress. Tijerina's influence stemmed from his visceral appeal to people. His nondenominational congregations were deeply conscious of their political powerlessness.

28. Meier and Gutierrez, *Encyclopedia of the Mexican American Civil Rights Movement*, 235.

29. Edward R. Roybal, author interview, August 11, 1999.

30. Lillian Roybal Rose, author interview, April 29, 2005.

31. Ed Roybal Jr., author interview, April 29, 2005.

32. From an early age Gonzalez boxed, becoming a Golden Gloves champion. He turned pro and was a featherweight contender from 1947 to 1955. In 1957, he became the first Chicano district captain of the Democratic Party. He was part of the Viva Kennedy Clubs but was disillusioned with the Democratic Party and its exclusion of Mexican American concerns from the party. A charismatic and fiery speaker, he later became a bail bondsman to make a living, and in 1963, founded Los Voluntarios, a group organized in reaction to police brutality. In 1966, he founded the Crusade for Justice, a community organization and a key entity throughout the Southwest between 1968 to 1978. His epic poem, "I Am Joaquin," was one of the most important pieces of Mexican American literature that sparked the imagination of Chicano youth and arguably one of the movement's most powerful recruitment tools.

33. Meier and Gutierrez, *Encyclopedia of the Mexican American Civil Rights Movement*, 95.

34. Edward R. Roybal, author interview, August 11, 1999.

35. After teaching in two Oregon colleges, Gutierrez returned to Texas and civil rights work as the head of the Greater Dallas Legal and Community Foundation. In 1988, he became an administrative law judge in Dallas. After a failed run for the U.S. Senate, he continued his civil rights work with a legal aid center. He is the only major leader of the Chicano Movement to have written a book about his experiences. His book, entitled *The Making of a Chicano Militant: Lessons from Cristal*, was published in 1998.

36. Richard Santillan, author interview, July 17, 2001. Santillan was born in East Los Angles in 1947 to a family of union members who were actively involved both in Mexico and in the United States. He began teaching Chicano Studies at CSULA in 1972 and taught thereafter at Cal Poly Pomona. He has authored numerous articles on the Chicano experience and a book entitled *La Raza Unida: Chicano Politics*.

37. Richard Santillan, author interview, July 17, 2001.

38. Richard Santillan, author interview, July 17, 2001.

39. Edward R. Roybal, author interview, August 11, 1999.

40. Ed Roybal Jr., author interview, April 29, 2005.

41. Edward R. Roybal, author interview, August 11, 1999.

42. Irma Núñez, author interview, December 10, 2005.

43. Edward R. Roybal Jr., author interview, July 15, 2001.

44. Irma Núñez, author interview, December 10, 1999.

45. Richard Santillan, author interview, July 17, 2001.

46. Paul Johnson, *A History of the American People* (New York: Harper Perennial, 1998), 887.

47. Edward R. Roybal, author interview, August 11, 1999.

48. Edward R. Roybal, author interview, August 11, 1999.

49. Edward R. Roybal, author interview, August 11, 1999.

50. Edward R. Roybal, author interview, August 11, 1999.

51. Edward R. Roybal, author interview, August 11, 1999.

52. Edward R. Roybal, author interview, August 11, 1999.

53. Letter from Senator Alan Cranston to Congressman Edward R. Roybal. January 16, 1969.

54. Letter from Congressman Edward R. Roybal to Mrs. S. C. Crane. January 14, 1969.

55. Letter from Congressman Edward R. Roybal to Miss Linda Carrier. February 10, 1969.

56. Ruben Salazar, "Bradley Seeking Racial Coalition in Mayor Race," *Los Angeles Times*, January 27, 1969.

57. "La Raza Por Bradley Para Mayor," political advertisement, *Eastside Sun*, March 27, 1969.

58. "Roybal Asks Permanent Status for Mexican-American Affairs Unit," *Eastside Journal*, March 13, 1969.

59. Ed Roybal papers.

60. Ed Roybal papers.

61. Johnson, *A History of the American People*, 889.

62. Edward R. Roybal, author interview, August 11, 1999.

63. "Roybal Bill Proposed $2 Minimum Wage Level," *Los Angeles Citizen*, August 29, 1969.

64. "Roybal Demands Removal of San Jose Judge," *Belvedere Citizen*, October 16, 1969; "Judge's Inappropriate Outburst against Mexicans Investigated," *Eastside Sun*, October 9, 1969.

65. Marlene Cimons, "Clara Ignatius: Head Gal in Congressman Roybal's Office," *Los Angeles Times*, September 8, 1968.

66. Mowry and Brownell, *The Urban Nation 1920–1980*, 311.

67. Stuart Loory, "President OKs Cabinet Group to Assist Latins," *Los Angeles Times*, January 1, 1970.

68. "Congress Oks bill to aid Spanish-speaking citizens," *Eastside Journal*, December 25, 1969.

69. Jean McDowell, "Mexican American Unity Congress Convention Report," *Eastside Journal*, February 19, 1970.

70. "Bradley Gives Roybal Support In Campaign," *Wilshire Press*, May 21, 1970.

71. Letter from Congressman Edward R. Roybal to Carlos V. Delgado. February 19, 1970.

72. "Calif. Congressmen Oppose Bussing," *Los Angeles Times*, March 15, 1970.

73. Bill Boyarsky, "Chicanos Angered Over Legislature's Redistricting Plan," *Los Angeles Times*, February 13, 1971.

74. "White Memorial Receives Funds to Build Rehabilitation Center," *Eastside Journal*, February 11, 1971.

75. Richard M. Nixon, *Memoirs*, 454.

76. Letter from Congressman Edward R. Roybal to Mr. Robert Barricklow, May 6, 1970.

77. Letter From Councilman Thomas Bradley to Congressmen Edward R. Roybal, April 28, 1970.

78. Letter from Congressman Edward R. Roybal to the Elgin Company, July 24, 1970.

79. Letter from Congresman Edward R. Roybal to Los Angeles City Council, July 27, 1970.

80. Erwin Baker, "Plan to Expand City Council to 17 Members Loses by One Vote," *Los Angeles Times*, July 28, 1970.

81. "Police Face Charges in Deaths of Two Mexicans," *Eastside Journal*, July 23, 1970.

82. Acuña, *Occupied America*, p. 346. Too often the young men, lacking specialized skills, served in infantry units and in the Vietnam conflict suffered a disproportionately high number of casualties. Although the Mexican American population was only 10–12% of the Southwest population, Mexican-descent soldiers made up 19.4% of those killed in Vietnam from January 1961 to February 1967. Mexican Americans made up 19% of all Vietnam casualties of soldiers from the Southwest from December 1967 to March 1969. Texas Mexican Americans were 25.2% of the total casualties from that state.

83. Thomas Foley, "Police-Chicano Relations in L.A. to be Studied by House Group," *Los Angeles Times*, February 14, 1971.

84. "Congressional Endorsements," *Los Angeles Times*, October 27, 1970.

Chapter 10

1. The CETA program provided job training for underemployed and long-term unemployed individuals and summer jobs for low-income high school students.

2. George Mowry and Blaine A. Brownell. *The Urban Nation 1920–1980, Revised Edition* (New York: Hill and Wang, 1981), 311.

3. *Belvedere Citizen*, September 14, 1972.

4. *Industrial Post*, September 2, 1972.

5. *Grass Roots Democrat*, September 1972.

6. Dan Bus, "For Demo Headquarters: California Solon Cuts Ribbon Here," Del Rio (Texas) *News-Herald*, November 10, 1972.

7. Edward R. Roybal (United States Representative, 30th District of California 1963–1975 and 25th District of California 1975–1993), author interview, August 13, 1999.

8. Thomas J. Foley, "Police-Chicano Relations in L.A. to be studied by House Group," *Los Angeles Times*, February 14, 1971.

9. "Chicano walkouts expose EYOA irregularities," *Eastside Sun*, October 14, 1971.

10. Ignacio M. Garcia, *Chicanismo: The Forging of a Militant Ethos Among Mexican Americans* (Tucson: University of Arizona Press, 1997).

11. George Schroeder, "Chicano Letters Answered: Congressman Roybal Discusses EMPLEO School Project," *The San Quentin News*, September 8, 1972.

12. "Report Asked On Spending By 'Plumbers,'" June 14, 1974.

13. Romana Acosta Bañuelos was born in 1925 in Miami, Arizona, to a poor Mexican family. An entrepreneur, she founded the successful Romana's Mexican Food Products, Inc., based in East Los Angeles. She established a scholarship for low-income Mexican American

students. In 1963, she co-founded with Ed Roybal and others the Pan-American National Bank of East Los Angeles and was appointed chairperson of the bank's board of directors.

14. Two other important Latino appointees were Henry Ramirez and Fernando C. de Baca.

15. *Del Rio* (Texas) *News-Herald*, November 10, 1972.

16. Rodolfo F. Acuña, *Occupied America: A History of Chicanos*, 3rd ed. (New York: Harper & Row), 379.

17. After Allende's election, commercial banks, including Chemical, First National City, Chase Manhattan, Morgan Guaranty, and Manufacturers Hanover, canceled credits to Chile. In addition, the U.S. government also established an economic boycott.

18. Frank Del Olmo, "Latin Leaders Report few Gains since Riot," *Los Angeles Times*, August 30, 1971.

19. Manuel Luján, born May 12, 1922, was a Republican politician from the state of New Mexico. He served as the U.S. secretary of the interior from 1989 to 1993 under President George Herbert Walker Bush. Previously he had served in the U.S. House of Representatives for New Mexico from 1969 to 1989. He was the first Republican to join the Congressional Hispanic Caucus in 1978.

20. *Eastside Journal*, September 30, 1971.

21. "Roybal asks recount of Spanish-speaking," *Eastside Sun*, December 23, 1971.

22. Edward R. Roybal, author interview, August 11, 1999.

23. Box C1972, Edward R. Roybal Collection, Third and Federly Public Library.

24. Antonia Hernandez, author interview, January 11, 2000.

25. Antonia Hernandez, author interview, January 11, 2000.

26. Gerald Rudolph Ford Jr. (July 14, 1913–Decemebr 26, 2006) was born Leslie Lynch King Jr. in Omaha, Nebraska. He attended the University of Michigan for undergraduate and law school. During World War II, he served in the Pacific theatre in the U.S. Navy.

He served as a Republican congressman for Michigan from 1949 to 1973.

27. Edward R. Roybal, author interview, August 11, 1999.

28. Paul Johnson, *A History of the American People* (New York: HarperCollins, 1999), 906.

29. Johnson, *A History of the American People*, 906.

30. Edward R. Roybal, author interview, August 11, 1999.

31. The War Powers Act requires presidents to inform Congress within forty-eight hours after they send troops overseas or want to reinforce troops already sent. If the Congress does not approve within sixty days, the president has to bring the troops home. The president could ask for thirty more days if that time is required to bring them home. During 1973–1974, the Jackson-Vanik and Stevenson Amendments imposed further limits on the use of troops. By late 1975, the Arms Export Control Act took away the president's discretion to supply arms to other nations. Congress further controlled the number of presidential agreements with foreign powers.

32. Johnson, *A History of the American People*.

33. Officials elected at large are elected by an entire government unit, rather than a subdivision. For example, a candidate or incumbent would not represent a specific part of the community, but the entire district or a larger group of constituents.

34. Bill Boyarsky, "Support Rises for Latin Rights Move," *Los Angeles Times*, March 26, 1975.

35. *News from Congressman Roybal*, June 1976.

36. Congressional Hispanic Caucus, *AVANCE*, February–March 1979.

37. James Earl "Jimmy" Carter Jr. was born October 1, 1924 in Plains, Georgia. He was educated at Georgia Tech and graduated from the United States Naval Academy at Annapolis in 1943. During World War II, he served in the Atlantic and Pacific fleets in both surface ships and submarines. After his service ended in 1953, he returned to his hometown and took on the family business, becoming successful in peanut

farming. In the 1960s, he served two terms in the Georgia Senate. He served as the governor of Georgia from 1971 to 1975. In 1976, he entered national politics for the first time and was elected U.S. president.

38. *News from Congressman Roybal*, March 9, 1977.

39. Edward R. Roybal, author interview, August 13, 1999.

40. Matt S. Meier and Margo Gutierrez, *Encyclopedia of the Mexican American Civil RightsMovement* (Westport, CT: Greenwood Press, 2000), 161.

41. Latino voter turnout at the national level was 2.1 million in 1976, 5.9 million in 2000, and 7.6 million in 2004 and increased to 11.2 million in 2012.

42. Antonia Hernandez, author interview, January 11, 2000.

43. Acuña, *Occupied America*, p. 440.

44. "Defeat the Rodino Bill," *Mexican-American Sun-Eastside Sun*, February 16, 1976.

45. Robert Pear, "Immigration Bill Is Cleared for House Debate," *New York Times*, December 9, 1982.

46. Pear, "Immigration Bill Is Cleared for House Debate."

47. "Roybal introduces measure to reform immigration laws," *Commerce Tribune*, April 6, 1983.

48. "The Roybal Bill," *Miami Herald*, February 8, 1984.

49. Ellen Hume, "Immigration Bill Passed by Senate," *Los Angeles Times*, May 14, 1983.

50. *The Southside Journal Wave*, March 28, 1984.

51. *La Prensa de San Diego*, May 10, 1985.

52. Robert L. Jackson, "Results Meager as Korea Scandal Splutters to an End," *Los Angeles Times*, July 14, 1978.

53. George Ramos, "Wasn't Bribed, Roybal Claims," *Los Angeles Times*, July 28, 1978.

54. Statement of Edward R. Roybal, September 13, 1978.

55. Thomas H. Henderson Jr., letter, United States Department of Justice, November 29, 1978.

56. Robert L. Jackson, "Groups Try to Soften Roybal Censure," *Los Angeles Times*, October 13, 1978.

57. *News from Congressman Roybal*, October 14, 1978.

58. Statement of Edward Roybal, October 13, 1978.

59. Three members of the California congressional delegation did not vote for the amendment: Representative Leon E. Panetta of Carmel Valley voted against; Representatives George E. Brown Jr. of Colton and John L. Burton of San Francisco abstained.

60. Lillian Roybal Ross, letter to Congressman Leon Panetta, December 6, 1978.

61. *News from Congressman Roybal*, March 1, 1978.

62. *News from Congressman Roybal*, April 12, 1973.

63. Claude Denson Pepper (September 8, 1900–May 30, 1989) was a liberal Democratic leader and spokesman for the elderly. He represented Florida in the U.S. Senate from 1936 to 1951 and the U.S. Congress from 1963 to 1989.

64. Spark Masayuki Matsunaga (October 8, 1916–April 15, 1990) was a Democrat representing Hawaii in the U.S. Congress from 1962 to 1977 and the U.S. Senate from 1977 to 1990.

65. The U.S. Permanent Select Committee came to an end on October 9, 1992, at the end of the 102nd Congress. The committee was not renewed during the 103rd Congress because significant pressure was brought to bear on the House to streamline the legislative process and also cut internal costs.

66. Jorge Lambrinos, author interview, July 20, 2001.

67. Jorge Lambrinos, author interview, July 20, 2001.

68. Legislative Report, August 1977.

69. *Eastside Journal*, August 15, 1979.

70. Henry Lozano was born in Texas and came to California after his discharge from the Marine Corps in 1957. He then worked at organizing auto and aerospace workers and was active in the American GI Forum in Pico Rivera. He also ran political campaigns.

71. Henry Lozano, author interview, June 2000.
72. Henry Lozano, author interview, June 2000.
73. Jorge Lambrinos was born in Panama. He obtained his B.A. in education and political science at the University of Michigan and his M.A. in Latin American studies at Georgetown University. He had first worked with the Federal Commission on Aging.
74. Jorge Lambrinos, author interview, July 20, 2001.
75. Jorge Lambrinos, author interview, July 20, 2001.
76. The Meals on Wheels program delivers hot and ready-to-eat meals to seniors who are unable to serve themselves. Evidence reveals that hunger is a serious challenge facing many seniors.
77. Jimmy Carter's books include *Why Not the Best?* (1975); *Keeping Faith: Memoirs of a President* (1982); *Negotiation: The Alternative to Hostility* (1984); *The Blood of Abraham* (1985); *Everything to Gain: Making the Most of the Rest of Your Life*, written with his wife, Rosalyn Carter (1987); *An Outdoor Journal* (1988); *Turning Point: A Candidate, a State, and a Nation Come of Age* (1992); *Talking Peace: A Vision for the Next Generation* (2003); and *Always a Reckoning* (2004).
78. Edward R. Roybal, author interview, August 11, 1999.
79. Jorge Lambrinos, author interview, July 20, 2001.
80. Jorge Lambrinos, author interview, July 20, 2001.

Chapter 11

1. Ronald Wilson Reagan (February 6, 1911–June 5, 2004) was born in Tampico, Illinois, and moved to California in the 1930s. He worked as a sports broadcaster and debuted as an actor in 1937. He gained a measure of stardom with the film *King's Row* in 1941, but he was often overshadowed by more charismatic film stars at his home studio Warner Bros. He spent World War II making training films. In the late 1940s, he was an informer for the FBI in the Hollywood communist witch hunt and was a "friendly witness" for the House Un-American Activities Committee (HUAC). When his

film career declined in the early 1950s, he turned to television. He served as the president of the Screen Actors Guild; his leadership was judged by its members as insignificant. Reagan served as the governor of California (1967–1975) and ran unsuccessfully for president in 1976. He was married to Academy Award–winning actress Jane Wyman and, later, to the lesser-known Nancy Davis. He died of Alzheimer's disease.

2. The idea of supply side economics was first championed by Jack Kemp. The argument went that the social welfare system had no incentives for people to rise above poverty. Therefore, eliminating social welfare funding while cutting taxes (meanwhile increasing defense spending), would lead to more jobs, which would be the mechanism by which people would pull themselves out of the welfare system. Senator Daniel Patrick Moynihan exposed it as a reckless policy. All the while, budget deficits increased. During the 1984 presidential campaign, George H. W. Bush, one of Reagan's rivals for the Republican nomination, had termed Reagan's approach "voodoo economics."

3. Policies termed "neoconservative" in the United States are, confusingly perhaps, referred to as "neoliberal" abroad.

4. Edward R. Roybal (United States Representative, 30ᵗʰ District of California 1963–1975 and 25ᵗʰ District of California 1975–1993), author interview, August 13, 1999.

5. Jorge Lambrinos, author interview, July 20, 2004.

6. *Eastside Journal*, November 10, 1982.

7. *Santa Fe Springs News*, April 27, 1983.

8. *Los Angeles Herald-Examiner*, November 20, 1982. Ben Fernandez had run for the Republican nomination for president twice against Ronald Reagan. He had been a Nixon fundraiser and had later been caught up in the Watergate Sandal.

9. The Equal Rights Amendment (ERA) has been a proposed amendment to the U.S. Constitution to guarantee equal rights for women

under federal, state, and local laws. It was first introduced by its creator, Alice Paul, and has been introduced in every U.S. Congress since 1923 but has failed to get ratification.

10. *Highland Park-Herald & Journal*, May 4, 1983.

11. *Los Angeles Times*, June 16, 1983.

12. *Valley News & Green Sheet*, June 17, 1983.

13. *Los Angeles Times*, March 10, 1984.

14. *San Diego County Evening News Tribune*, March 1, 1985.

15. Alzheimer's disease (AD), also called Senile Dementia of the Alzheimer Type, is the most common form of dementia. This incurable, degenerative, and terminal disease was first noted by German psychiatrist and neuropathologist Alois Alzheimer in 1906 and is named in his honor. It is generally believed to afflict those over 65 years of age, although there can be an early onset of the disease. In 2006, it is estimated that some 26.6 million people suffered from in it worldwide.

16. "Death Alone Ends the Suffering from Alzheimer's, Panel Is Told," *San Diego County Evening Tribune*, May 22, 1985.

17. In a June 2000 interview with the author, Jorge Lambrinos recalled about Roybal, "He got an award from the Westside for his work on Alzheimer's and again nobody wanted to talk about it, everybody wanted to keep it secret, more so in the Latino community…I remember we would be speaking about national defense or any subject unrelated to health and he would always mention Alzheimer's disease. People always wondered what he is talking about. What's this guy going to do with this one? But he was just trying to plant the seed in people's minds, the fact that this issue needed to be addressed."

18. "Drug Flow Across U.S. Border Decried," *Los Angeles Times*, May 26, 1985.

19. *Eastside Journal*, September 3, 1983.

20. Philip Burton (June 1, 1925–April 10, 1983) was an attorney and served in the California State Assembly. He was elected to the U.S. House

of Representatives though a special election. He served in Congress from February 18, 1964, until his death on April 10, 1983.

21. John Lowell Burton (b. December 15, 1932) began his career as an attorney and deputy attorney general for the state of California. He followed his brother Philip Burton in being elected to the California State Assembly in 1964 and then served in the U.S. House of Representatives 1974–1983. He returned to private life but then was re-elected to the California State Assembly and then to the state senate in 1996–1994, where he was elected president pro tempore.

22. Jorge Lambrinos, author interview, July 20, 2001.

23. Jorge Lambrinos, author interview, July 20, 2001.

24. Jorge Lambrinos, author interview, July 20, 2001.

25. Paul Johnson, *A History of the American People* (New York: Harper Perennial, 1998), 924.

26. Edward R. Roybal, author interview, August 18, 1999.

27. Jorge Lambrinos, author interview, July 20, 2001.

28. In June 27, 1986, the International Court of Justice ruled in favor of Nicaragua in a case entitled *Military and Paramilitary Activities in and Against Nicaragua*. The United States refused to pay, claiming that the court was not competent. The United Nations General Assembly passed a resolution to press for payment. Only El Salvador and Israel sided with the United States. The United States never paid the fine. Both North and Poindexter were indicted on charges of conspiracy to defraud the United States. Poindexter was convicted on a series of felony counts, including obstruction of justice, lying to Congress, and destroying documents related to the investigation. The 1988 report of the Senate Subcomittee on Narcotics, Terrorism, and International Operations concluded that several individuals involved with the Contras were involved in drug trafficking. It also stated that "there are some serious questions as to whether or not U.S. officials involved in Central America failed to address the drug issue for fear of jeopardizing the war effort against Nicaragua."

29. Consequently, Nicaragua underwent an incredible level of suffering and misery. Hostilities resulted in at least 40,000 Nicaraguan dead in the decade beginning in 1980. In 1989, the presidents of Central American nations supervised the disarming of the Contras, and Nicaragua began its reconstruction. Regarding El Salvador, Reagan allotted an additional $25 million for military assistance and U.S. advisors to the military government (that is, the government that had denied the Christian Democratic Party its electoral victory in 1977). Military and paramilitary death squads routinely kidnapped, tortured, and murdered suspects (including four United States nuns), and even women and children, in the war against the Faramundo Marti National Liberation Front (FMLN). As a member of the Foreign Relations Committee, Congressman Roybal was a vocal critic of Reagan's one-track policy in Central America.

30. Oscar Arnulfo Romero y Galdamez (August 15, 1917–March 24, 1980) was a Roman Catholic bishop in the country of El Salvador. As the nation fell into a violent civil war, he called for social justice and an end to government repression. He was assassinated while conducting mass by what is widely believed to be right-wing death squads.

31. Jorge Lambrinos, author interview, July 20, 2001.

32. For more on Central America during the 1970s and 1980s see: John A. Booth, *The Nicaraguan Revolution* (Boulder, CO: Westview, 1982); Harry Sims and Edward F. Leboucq, *Sandinista Nicaragua: Pragmatism in a Political Economy in Formation with Repression* (Philadelphia: Institute for the Study of Human Issues, 1982); Robert Kagan, *A Twilight Struggle: American Power and Nicaragua, 1977–1990* (New York: The Free Press, 1996); Enrique Baloya, *El Salvador in Transition* (Chapel Hill: University of North Carolina Press, 1982); Tommie Sue Montgomery, *Revolution in El Salvador: Origins and Evolution* (Boulder, CO: Westview, 1982); Thomas M. Leonard, *Central America and United States Policies, 1820s–1980s* (Claremont, CA: Regina Books, 1985).

33. *Washington Post*, March 11, 1999.

Chapter 12

1. George Herbert Walker Bush was born June 12, 1924, in Milton, Massachusetts. During World War II, he served in the U.S. Navy where he distinguished himself as the youngest fighter pilot and earned several medals, including the Distinguished Flying Cross. After the war, he returned to finish his degree in economics at Yale University. Thereafter, he joined the family oil business. He served two terms in the U.S. House of Representatives as a Republican from Texas, from 1966 to 1970. He was appointed as U.N. ambassador by President Nixon. He served as director of the CIA from 1976 to 1977. He served as Ronald Reagan's vice president for two terms, 1981–1989, and was elected to the presidency in 1989. He married Barbara Pierce. They had two daughters and four sons, including George Walker Bush, who would be elected president and serve from 2001 until 2009.

2. Thomas V. DiBacco, Lorna C. Mason, and Christian G. Appy. *History of the United States* (Boston, MA: Houghton Co., 1992), 276.

3. The U.S. invasion of Panama, according to the U.S. State Department, resulted in 516 Panamanians' deaths. However, the National Human Rights Commission of Panama and the Commission for the Defense of Human Rights in Central America estimated that at least 2,000 Panamanians were killed. The Catholic and Episcopal Churches estimated the actual total at 3,000 dead. Despite evidence to the contrary, President Bush claimed that the invasion had been a "surgical operation." Noriega was subsequently hunted down, apprehended, and taken to Florida, where he was tried and convicted on charges of drug trafficking. He was sentenced to forty years in prison. As the Panamanian invasion receded into memory, Panama meanwhile became a prolific center for money laundering and drug running, a quagmire of political corruption and grinding poverty. Democracy, contrary to President Bush's intentions, was neither restored nor born.

4. Edward R. Roybal (United States Representative, 30th District of California 1963–1975 and 25th District of California 1975–1993), author interview, August 18, 1999. When asked about President George Bush and his two sons, George Walker Bush (United States president after Clinton) and Jeb Bush (future governor of Florida), Congressman Roybal commented, "Well, I thought he was a pretty well-adjusted individual but one who took the opportunity to be doing something that was on his side...Well, they're astute politicians, there's no doubt about it. The one that's from Florida, he learned Spanish. He married a Mexican girl and used it to his advantage. Each of the sons used his advantage whatever was best for them coming from their respective states."

5. Edward R. Roybal, author interview, August 18, 1999.

6. Edward R. Roybal, author interview, August 18, 1999.

7. Jorge Lambrinos, serving at the time of Roybal's retirement as his chief of staff, recalled during a June 20, 2001, interview how strenuous the work was: "He came just about every weekend to the district. He diligently, Thursday evenings, would fly out and then come back on Monday and then be in the office on Tuesday morning and—the Congressional schedule is pretty much laid out that way but they actually don't start business until Tuesday—and then Tuesday, Wednesday, and Thursday and then everybody goes home to their districts. The reason for Monday is because to allow a lot of the members from the West Coast to get back and especially the ones from Hawaii...He did this diligently every weekend, he would go to senior centers, he would go to the Boys Club, he would go to the schools, Monday morning before he flew out, so this was a way that he, in a sense, got his message out and kept contact with the constituents. Some members would never get back to the district and they would just print a lot of flyers and get themselves elected. Mr. Roybal never did that; he primarily worked face to face with people."

8. "I was friendly to Congressmen of both parties, both Republican and Democrat—provided, of course, they were interested in the fields of health and education…Well, I was impressed with Senator Dennis Chavez of New Mexico and [Joseph] Montoya later, I think those were the two that I was most impressed with."

9. During an interview on July 15, 2001, when asked whether he had ever considered running for public office, Edward Roybal Jr. commented, "I didn't run for office or follow in my father's footsteps. I think it was just one of those things that I've known since I was young that I didn't want to do that. I think it has something to do with having some sense of a normal home life compared to the way I grew up and I didn't want the political limelight. I was never discouraged. I think it's gone as far as my father sort of letting me know that if I were to want to run that I could have a career there. I could run on my father's name. No, I never went as far as seriously considering to run. I'm glad it wasn't me. I was very proud of her [Lucille Roybal-Allard]. She had not set out with ambitions to follow my father, and so it was really a product of circumstances. I think my father was really pleased that one of his children was finally following in his footsteps. I think in a lot [of] ways my sister used her role in politics like my father. For one thing, she is totally hardworking; she is not in for the glory. She also…invests in earning the respect of her colleagues and in working with people."

10. William Jefferson "Bill" Clinton (William Jefferson Blythe III) was born on August 19, 1946, in Hope, Arkansas, in abject poverty. When his father died in a car accident, his mother married Roger Clinton, and they both assumed the new surname. He attended Georgetown University and thereafter earned a Rhodes scholarship to study at Oxford University, in England. On his return, he earned a law degree at Yale Law School, where he met his future wife, Hillary Rodham. He was elected Arkansas Attorney General in 1976 and was elected Arkansas governor, serving from 1979 to 1981. He served as president

of the United States from 1993 to 2001. He and his wife have one daughter, Chelsea Clinton.

11. George Ramos, "Roybal's Daughter Expected to Sweep In," *Los Angeles Times*, May 27, 1992. Lucille Roybal-Allard ran a grass-roots campaign opposing the proposed state prison near Boyle Heights and other unwanted projects. Her opposition, and that of Los Angeles County Supervisor Gloria Molina, stopped the building of an incinerator and a toxic waste recycling plant, both of which had been proposed for Vernon. She told the *Los Angeles Times* (May 27, 1992), "Latino communities really have to empower themselves... There can be friendly arrangements with companies coming to provide jobs and at the same time meet the concerns of the communities."

12. Edward R. Roybal, author interview, June 2000.

13. Edward R. Roybal, author interview, August 18, 1999.

14. Edward R. Roybal, author interview, August 18, 1999.

15. Roybal's boyhood friend Anthony Quinn passed away on June 3, 2001.

Epilogue

1. Edward Roybal Jr., author interview, July 15, 2001.

2. Edward Roybal Jr., author interview, July 15, 2001. Today, Edward Roybal Jr. is a full-time faculty member at New College of California School of Law and heads the Roybal Foundation.

3. Henry Lozano, author interview, June 2000.

4. Antonia Hernández, author interview, January 11, 2000.

5. Jaime Regalado, author interview, January 10, 2000.

6. Antonio Olivo, "Grandfather of Latino Politics Faults New Leaders," *Los Angeles Times*, July 27, 1999.

7. Ignacio M. Garcia, *Viva Kennedy: Mexican Americans In Search of Camelot.* (College Station: Texas A & M University Press, 2000), 70.

About the Author

FRANK JAVIER GARCIA BERUMEN GREW UP IN BOYLE HEIGHTS (ROYBAL'S city council district) and Lincoln Heights in East Los Angeles. He attended CSULA and later Harvard University, where he earned a master's degree and doctoral degree in education. In addition to his work as an educator, he has published several books on Latino film images: *The Chicano/ Hispanic Image in American Film, Ramon Novarro: The Life and Films of the First Latino Hollywood Superstar, Brown Celluloid: Latino/A Film Icons and Images in the Hollywood Film Industry,* and *Latino Image Makers in Hollywood: Performers, Filmmakers and Films Since the 1960s.* He has also published poetry and short stories. He lives in Southern California.

CPSIA information can be obtained at www.ICGtesting.com
Printed in the USA
BVOW11s0931020615

402807BV00003B/3/P

9 780866 240109